Marketing Research in Action

Marketing research is a valuable tool for any organisation, but if it is not properly targeted, the time and money spent may well be wasted. It is important to diagnose thoroughly the situation or marketing problems facing an organisation before research can be designed that will provide timely and accurate information, that can in turn be used for planning and implementing marketing programmes.

Raymond Kent explains how market researchers assess their clients' needs and apply their skills to find the best solutions to marketing problems, to keep track of events in the marketplace, or to assess how well marketing strategies achieved their objectives. Based on extensive empirical evidence, the author shows how market measurement, usage and attitude studies, advertising tracking and pre-testing, media audience measurement, product testing, and volume and brand share predictions are used to maximum effect. Any research project is a unique combination of data capture instruments, data collection methods, data analysis procedures and these special applications. Instead of presenting the reader with a catalogue of standard types of research, Raymond Kent focuses on assembling the tools of research to address real questions like, 'How big is my market?', 'Will my new product sell?' and 'What people buy my products?'

Marketing Research in Action provides an invaluable guide to the UK market research industry as well as a stimulating analysis of the latest techniques and developments. As such it is both an important text for students of marketing and business as well as an informative guide to users of marketing research.

Raymond Kent is Senior Lecturer in the Department of Marketing at the University of Stirling. He is author of *Continuous Consumer Market Measurement.*

Marketing Research in Action

Raymond A. Kent

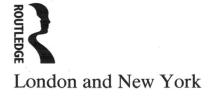

London and New York

First published 1993
by Routledge
11 New Fetter Lane
London EC4P 4EE

Simultaneously published in the USA and Canada
by Routledge
29 West 35th Street, New York, NY 10001

© 1993 Raymond Kent

Typeset in 10/12 Times by Leaper & Gard Ltd, Bristol
Printed and bound in Great Britain by
Biddles Ltd, Guildford and King's Lynn

British Library Cataloguing in Publication Data

*A catalogue reference for this book is available from the
British Library.*

ISBN 0-415-06759-6
       0-415-06760-X

*Library of Congress Cataloging in Publication Data has been
applied for.*

ISBN 0-415-06759-6
       0-415-06760-X

Contents

List of figures

List of tables

Preface

So, why another book on marketing research? How does this one differ from the others? The author began teaching methods of social research in 1967, and those of marketing research in 1982. The problem, he felt, was that in both sociology and marketing, research tended to be treated as something apart from the core discipline – but *doing* sociology or *doing* marketing (as opposed to studying them) means doing research. Ideally, research should be part of every topic within the discipline. What this book offers is a step towards the integration of marketing principles with marketing research. Furthermore, there is a need to link how marketing research is actually carried out with concepts that relate to the nature of research and scientific discovery. Conceptual and practical issues need to be married. At the end of the day, when it comes to taking action that is both efficient and effective, there is nothing so practical as a good theory.

Like any bag of tools, the tools of research are of little value unless they are used to address a real problem; it is not possible to design useful research except in the context of a proper diagnosis of the situation faced by an organisation, and a clarification of the decisions that need to be taken and which hinge on inputs from marketing research. It is one thing to know what the tools are and what they do; it is quite another to design research that addresses problems or issues effectively. Most textbooks are fine on the former; but tend to be woefully inadequate on the latter. This book shows how research actually is designed by market research executives, and relates this to the theory and principles of marketing research.

The book is unique in being part textbook and part research monograph. It takes what the author feels are the 'best' aspects of theory and principle and relates these to the results of empirical enquiry. Since 1986 the author has contacted, and in many cases visited, a large number of market research agencies in the UK, talking in detail to the 'doers' of marketing research at the sharp end. These conversations were all tape recorded and used as the basis for an analysis of real practice. The results of this investigation are infused in all the chapters, relating this sharp end to guiding principle. The chapter on research techniques and applications is based almost entirely on this empirical work.

There are other ways, too, in which this book differs from what is currently available. First, it focuses on the *elements* that go into the design of research. These elements in practice are combined in many different ways and marketing research cannot be compartmentalised into the discrete categories of research that have become written in tablets of stone in chapters of standard texts. Second, research design is considered in detail at the end of the book, not, as is more usual, in a quick 'once over' in an introductory chapter. This is to enable the reader to see how, at the end of the day, the elements may be put together to address specific issues. Third, whenever techniques are explained, they are illustrated – and they are related to what market research companies in the UK actually do. In short, the focus is on marketing research in action. In commenting on this action, the author has taken what he considers to be examples of some of the 'best' practice in the UK. It is not a comprehensive handbook on the services offered by the market research industry. There are many market research companies and organisations that offer excellent services which do not receive a mention; I hope they will not feel aggrieved.

Those who are familiar with marketing research textbooks will spot other differences. The standard styles of research to which most texts devote separate chapters are encompassed within one, albeit substantial, chapter on data collection methods. These methods are distinguished from the instruments of data capture and from the techniques and applications in which they, and a range of data analysis procedures, are used. It is these instruments, methods, procedures, techniques and applications that are combined together to make each research project unique. The applications themselves are not the usual ones – industrial marketing research, research for overseas markets, research for services or small business, advertising research and so on. Such topics are well covered in the standard texts. What manufacturers and other kinds of organisation are more concerned about, however, is how market research companies can help them to diagnose the markets they are currently addressing, the attitudes consumers have of their brands, the effectiveness of their advertising, and the nature of the audiences who use the various media in which they currently advertise. They also want to be able to predict which products are likely to be successes or failures, whether advertising is likely to achieve its objectives, and what the volumes of sales of new or modified products are likely to be. The techniques used for all these applications are detailed in Chapter 7.

The book will be of value to students, undergraduate or postgraduate, who are pursuing courses in marketing research as part of a marketing qualification, or for the Diploma of the Market Research Society. The businessman and the marketing manager will also be able to find much of interest and value if he or she wishes to find out more about what marketing research has to offer. The book, in short, should be of value both to those who need to design research and those who wish to use research to achieve marketing objectives.

The author has tried very hard to make the book 'user-friendly'. At the end of each chapter are detailed summaries of the key points, and there are exercises and points for further discussion to assist students to review their understanding and to help course tutors in course planning. There is a glossary of terms at the end of the book. These terms are put in bold the first time they are used (or are a heading or subheading). Where the author feels that readers may need to refresh their memories in later chapters, the terms that appear in the glossary are again put in bold. There are frequent cross-references both backwards and forwards to other parts of the text so that the reader who wishes to dip into later chapters rather than reading the book from cover to cover can locate key terms in the glossary and check explanations of concepts elsewhere in the book. There are, in addition, a number of boxed sections that elaborate or illustrate points made briefly in the text.

Raymond A. Kent
University of Stirling

Acknowledgements

I owe a huge debt of gratitude to many individuals in market research companies who have given me considerable amounts of their time to explain in detail the procedures they use and the services they offer; in most cases they have also checked through the parts of this book that refer to their company. Any omissions or errors, of which there are bound to be some, will, of course, be mine and not theirs. I would, in particular, like to acknowledge the help of the following individuals:

Geoff Allan, Millward Brown,
John Archer, BJM,
Tim Baker, Nielsen Consumer Research,
Bill Blyth, AGB,
Simon Chadwick, Research International,
Rachel Craig, BMRB,
Geoffrey Elton, Novaction,
Anita Emery, Taylor Nelson,
Paul Harris, NOP,
Michael Roe, Research International,
Nigel Roth-Witty, Burke Marketing Research,
Trevor Sharot, AGB Television,
Richard Silman, BMRB,
Sharon Sims, Nielsen Marketing Research,
Nigel Spackman, AGB Surveys,
Caroline Walker, Taylor Nelson.

Chapter 1

Perspectives on marketing research

THE SCOPE OF MARKETING RESEARCH

It is often said that marketing is an approach to business that is based on the idea that the most important person to the company is the customer. The company adopting the marketing concept is, according to marketing wisdom, customer-oriented; it must make what it knows it can sell, not try to sell what it can make. If this were true, then marketing research would be all about collecting data on customer requirements and anticipating their future needs.

As always, reality is not quite so simple. Companies offering goods and services in commercial transactions are constrained to be customer-oriented with what they have: with their existing plant, machinery, work-force, location, company reputation, and with their own particular strengths and capabilities and their own shortcomings and weaknesses. Furthermore, they must operate in an immediate, 'micro' environment not only of customers, but of competitors, suppliers, distributors, trade unions, shareholders, financial institutions, government departments and so on. In the less immediate 'macro' environment will be general economic, techno-logical, social, political and legal factors that, to varying degrees, all need to be taken into account. Successful **marketing**, in short, is about matching organisational characteristics with the environment in which the organis-ation exists, and doing so in ways that will achieve its planned objectives. For profit-making organisations, these objectives may be concerned with short-term or long-term profits, with company growth, company stability, image or survival, or with becoming market leaders in chosen market segments. Objectives may be very different for non-profit-making organis-ations.

In this situation, marketing research is as much about diagnosing company or organisational problems as it is with researching its target market. Increasingly, it is as involved in the analysis, interpretation, use and application of data in solving problems and reducing the risks of marketing decisions as it is with collecting the data in the first place.

In its early days, marketing research was seen simply as a data collection service on markets. Clients stated what data they wanted, market researchers collected them, and the client took away the tables of results. When a company is the only one – or one of a few – using systematic marketing techniques, *any* data on customers might enable it to exploit market opportunities. When all or nearly all the companies have access to such data, being simply customer-oriented is no longer adequate. It must not only do its marketing, but do it better than its competitors. This means:

- diagnosing the current situation or problem based on detailed information,
- clearly identifying company strengths and weaknesses,
- constantly analysing what is happening in the marketplace,
- planning to match company strengths with market opportunities by outlining objectives for product and market development, and devising strategies and tactics to achieve them,
- watching out continuously for threats to the achievement of these plans,
- monitoring the progress of strategy implementation.

Marketing research can help with all these areas. It is concerned with the collection, analysis, interpretation and use of data both on the company and on its environment so that information can be provided that is relevant to the diagnosis, planning and control of marketing strategies. This can serve as a definition of marketing research which will be adequate for the purpose of this book.

Consider for a moment the following case:

John Ambrose and Co. Ltd

John Ambrose is a medium-sized, family-owned, flour-milling business which has been in existence for over 100 years. It supplies a complete range of flours to the bakery trade to cover every specialised need. Its customers are mostly small to medium-sized family bakers who have been customers for decades. It does not supply anything to the general public; it has no advertising and only limited sales representation.

Sales have been falling steadily in the last few years to a point where the company will need to take corrective action to stay in business. Among the alternatives being considered are:

- Move into the convenience foods market with flour-based products such as stir-fry or boil-in-the-bag curries, Chinese dishes and other pasta-based meals. These would be packaged and would be similar to the lines already on the market produced by large food manufacturers.
- Supply the general public the same highly specialised flours currently supplied to the trade. These would be more expensive than standard flours.

- Co-operate with family bakers to produce a range of packaged cakes that will retail at a price above any other established brands. The cakes are to be of exceptional quality.

How can marketing research help John Ambrose and Co. to choose between these options?

Marketing research can help in a number of ways. First of all it can help to clarify and diagnose the problem. The problem presented is the steady decline in sales in the last few years. This is probably only a symptom of an underlying cause: for example, are family bakers going out of business (perhaps because of competition from the in-store bakeries in the large supermarkets), or is there a general decline in the demand for bread? Market research can help by finding out which of these explanations holds. More data are required on the seriousness of the problem – for example, what exactly has been the decline in sales over, say, the last five years and how has this compared with other flour-milling businesses? Is the decline getting faster or is it bottoming out? What other factors may be affecting the demand for John Ambrose's flour, and what are the company's overall strengths and weaknesses? It appears to have had a lot of experience in the flour-milling business, but how are its flours regarded by its customers? Is this really a strength?

Marketing research can next help by clarifying the decisions that need to be taken: for the first option, which particular flour-based products are likely to sell well, and how should they be priced in relation to the competition? Some product-testing research and perhaps some pricing research may be required here. There is, in fact, a whole range of subdecisions that will need to be taken in respect of each option before any of them can be pursued. For each of these decisions, particular kinds of information will be required, for example, on the kinds of flour that housewives normally stock if the second option is to be pursued. Research will then need to be designed that not only collects this information in the most cost-effective way, but which can then be used in such a way that specified hypotheses (for example, about the causes of the sales decline) can be tested, and a final decision taken about the likely 'best' course of action. If, for example, family bakers are going out of business, then the third alternative being considered by John Ambrose is no solution!

The key message that should come across from this case is that marketing research can be designed only in the context of specific marketing decisions that need to be taken, or specific marketing issues that need to be resolved, otherwise the research may well be a waste of time.

MARKETING RESEARCH, MARKET RESEARCH AND MARKET ANALYSIS

Marketing research, as we have seen, is concerned with the whole enterprise from diagnosing the problem for which the research is required, through project design and data collection, to a concern for the implementation of the results once the research has been carried out. In the process, data may need to be be collected on:

- companies, for example, their current strategies for products and markets,
- the immediate competitive environment of the marketplace that includes customers, potential customers, competitors, suppliers, distributors and retailers,
- the wider environment of social, political, legal and cultural parameters within which the firm operates or hopes to operate locally, nationally and perhaps internationally.

Researching markets – the second of the above areas of activity – is often referred to specifically as 'market research' as opposed to 'marketing research', which is wider and includes researching all areas of marketing activity. However, since researching markets has, historically, been a major activity of companies supplying research services, the term 'market research' is often used synonymously with 'marketing research', or taken to be its colloquial equivalent. Most, but not all, textbooks on the subject, both in the UK and in the USA, use the word 'marketing' in their titles, but between the covers, many lapse into the more colloquial use of the term in such phrases as 'market research activity', 'market researchers' or the 'market research industry'. To avoid confusion, and to avoid the punctiliousness of carefully changing all phrases like the ones just mentioned to 'marketing researchers' or the 'marketing research industry', this book will use the term **market analysis** to refer to the process of researching markets. 'Marketing research' will be used to describe the whole enterprise which is the subject of this book, and **market research** to refer to the activities of those people involved in the market research industry who buy and sell data or research services.

It is a peculiarity of most textbooks on marketing research that, having defined it as going beyond simply researching markets, they proceed to ignore precisely what researching markets (market analysis) involves. Market analysis is, however, a key component of marketing research, and comprises the activities of measuring the size and structure of a market, analysing purchasing behaviour, product usage and attitudes, segmenting markets, market tracking, volume and brand share prediction, and forecasting trends. These topics are taken up in detail in Chapter 7.

TYPES OF MARKETING RESEARCH

The answers that you get to the question 'What types of marketing research are there?' will vary according to a number of different dimensions, and will depend in the first instance on whether you consult textbooks on marketing research, market research companies, or academics and researchers in universities and colleges.

Textbook categories

Many textbooks distinguish different types of marketing research according to two different dimensions: the objectives that the research is designed to achieve on the one hand and the source of data on the other.

Research objectives tend to be classified into three main kinds:

- exploratory,
- descriptive,
- causal (or experimental).

Exploratory research according to the majority of the textbooks, is research aimed at generating insights, ideas and hypotheses rather than measuring them or testing them. According to Chisnall (1992: 23), exploratory research designs attempt to identify the real nature of research problems and, in some cases, to formulate hypotheses or generate explanations for testing in later research. Crimp (1990: 16) argues that the research planner undertakes exploratory research in order to generate an adequate basis for designing research, and she includes searching for data that are already available both within the company and from external sources, consulting experts, conducting observational studies, consulting people in the marketplace, and buying into an omnibus survey.

However, exploratory research does not necessarily imply the use of specific methods of data collection (or, indeed, that such methods are limited to exploratory purposes); rather it implies that whatever style of research is seen by the researcher to be a preliminary phase before the main research is set in motion may be regarded as 'exploratory'. In this way, a formal, quantitative survey could be regarded as exploratory if it were seen as a preliminary to a larger or more detailed study later on. On the other hand, consulting a few experts informally may be seen as adequate for the purpose of the decision that needs to be taken, and this becomes the basis of the 'final' results.

Descriptive research is characterised in the textbooks as typically concerned with measuring and estimating the frequencies with which things occur, or the degree of correlation or association between variables. Market research reports are often descriptive; for example, they measure market size, market structure, and the behaviour and attitudes of consumers in the marketplace. They might describe the characteristics of certain groups, they may try to estimate the proportion of people who behave in a particular way, or they may make specific predictions. Churchill (1987: 82) emphasises that descriptive research is not just a fact-gathering exercise. It presupposes prior knowledge about the issues being studied, and may rest on one or more hypotheses, or be designed to secure specific kinds of information. The variables being measured and the mode of their analysis will be spelled out in advance. Churchill then proceeds to include practically all types of marketing research except experimental research as types of descriptive study, as if such research were necessarily limited to being descriptive and could not be used for either exploratory or explanatory purposes.

Causal research is typically seen as being concerned with establishing cause-and-effect relationships in an attempt to explain why things happen. Such research is usually equated with experimental procedures since, it is argued, only when some form of experimental control is established can causality be demonstrated. The implication here is that experimental research can be used only for causal analysis and that survey research, for example, cannot be used for such purposes at all. As is explained later in Chapter 6, many different types of research can, with varying degrees of success, attempt to establish the extent to which one or more factors or variables exercise some degree of influence over others. At the same time, any style of research, including experimental research, may be used for descriptive or, indeed, exploratory purposes.

The difficulty with the textbook distinctions between these three types of research design is that most research in practice will be some combination of exploration, description and explanation. Most research projects will have an exploratory phase, will produce descriptive data in the main research stage, and will go on to analyse the nature of relationships between variables. It is not a distinction that enables us to classify different types or styles of research; nor would it help us in any discussion with a marketing research executive on the kind of design needed for a particular problem. The precise point at which descriptive analysis becomes causal analysis is, in any case, difficult to define. Is the measurement of the degree of association between two variables just description or is it the first stage of a causal analysis?

The other dimension along which textbooks tend to distinguish different types of marketing research is according to the two main sources of data:

- secondary,
- primary.

Secondary research is based largely on data that have been previously collected for purposes other than the research at hand. Such data might include:

- published articles in journals, books, newspapers or magazines,
- data that have been published in various statistical sources, for example, government statistics or trade association statistics,
- data that may be available for purchase from a business publishing house, a market research company or an advertising agency,
- data that the company already possesses as a result of its everyday operations.

The term 'secondary' refers to the idea that the data are being used for a secondary purpose. The original material may well have been collected and used for other ends. Such data are commonly looked at while sitting at a desk, and such activities are often referred to as 'desk' research. These sources are considered in more detail in Chapter 5. Secondary research may involve **secondary analysis**, which is a process in which secondary data are used as inputs to further statistical analysis rather than just being gathered together and re-presented in more or less their original or condensed form.

Primary research entails the collection of data specifically for the problem or project at hand. Most of this book is about different ways of collecting primary data. It is often forgotten, however, that secondary data were originally collected using the same primary methods. The corollary is that researchers using data for secondary purposes need to bear in mind how they were collected in the first place and their associated strengths and limitations. Many government statistics, for example, were collected using questionnaire surveys, sometimes for whole populations of people or organisations, but sometimes only for samples, in which case the figures produced are only estimates.

As with making distinctions between types of marketing research based on research objectives, so distinctions based on data source and calling it 'secondary research' or 'primary research' are of limited value since in practice, once again, these sources are usually combined. Secondary data collection is more likely to be just a stage in a research project, probably exploratory, but possibly descriptive or even explanatory.

Market research company distinctions

Nearly all research undertaken by market research companies is commissioned, although a number of individuals working in such organisations do sometimes contribute to academic, scholarly seminars, conferences or journals. The dimensions that such companies use to categorise different types or styles of research may often be deduced from the way they are structured. Different departments, teams, or even separate subsidiary companies may specialise in a particular type of research. Five common dimensions may be distinguished:

- the kind of data collected,
- the duration of the research,
- the customisation or syndication of services,
- the amount of value added,
- the type of customer.

Some market research companies categorise their activities according to the kind of data collected: qualitative or quantitative. **Qualitative research** is geared primarily to the collection of qualitative data, which arise as words or pictures; the main features of such data are outlined in the next chapter. Some companies specialise in this type of research, which consists mainly of 'depth' interviewing or group discussions. These are explained in Chapter 5. The larger organisations may well have a department, or a whole subsidiary company, devoted to qualitative research.

Quantitative research is geared primarily to the collection of quantitative data, which arise as numbers. It consists of research that involves formal questionnaire techniques at some stage, whether for face-to-face interviews, telephone research, postal research, or various forms of experimental or quasi-experimental research. Again, these are described in Chapter 5.

Other market research companies will make a distinction in terms of the duration of the research: whether it is ad hoc or continuous. **Ad hoc research** is a 'one-off' piece of research that has a beginning point, and ends with a final report of the results. It will go through a number of stages from an initial brief or analysis of the problems to be investigated, to data collection, data analysis, and presentation of the findings. Qualitative research and experimental research (which are explained in Chapter 5) are usually ad hoc since they are not suited to monitoring change on a regular basis.

Continuous research, by contrast, takes measurements on a regular basis in order to monitor changes that are occurring in the marketplace. Such research, which includes consumer panel and retail panel operations (see Chapter 5), goes through cycles of data production which, in many respects, resemble a production line that has to meet given deadlines by scheduling its activities, and has to achieve agreed standards of quality control. There is no envisaged 'end' to the research process. The data are normally fed into some kind of management or marketing information system where they are added to a database and used as a core asset for a variety of analyses.

Overlapping with the distinction between ad hoc and continuous research is the slightly different distinction between customised and syndicated research. **Customised research** is tailor-made for a particular client to meet the needs of that client. **Syndicated research** means that either the research process or the research data are shared between a number of clients. The word 'syndicated' arose when manufacturers got together as a syndicate to supply data that they all required. This function has now largely been taken over by the market research companies, who use the term 'syndicated' to mean either that the data are sold to a number of clients, or that several clients share a survey. Such research may be thought of as 'off-the-peg' research which is not customised for any one particular client.

There is a tendency for ad hoc research to be customised and for continuous research to be syndicated, particularly since continuous research requires a lot of investment and other resources, and is usually too expensive for one client to afford. However, some ad hoc research may nevertheless be syndicated, while some continuous research is commissioned by one client and may be thought of as ad hoc. Some research, such as advertising tracking studies, may take place over a period of time, so is continuous, but over a limited period. Some agencies use the term 'ad hoc' to denote a survey carried out for a single client.

Another basis on which some market research companies structure their activities is by the amount of value that is added. In some cases the client requires only **contract research** – the market research company is contracted only to collect data or to collect and analyse them according to specification; it has no remit, for example, for making recommendations. At the other extreme, the market research company may be involved not only in data collection and analysis, but in a considerable degree of consultancy work before data collection even begins. Such **consultancy research** may:

- assist in the diagnosis of the problem or problems facing a client organisation,
- help to draft a research brief,
- make recommendations for action that needs to be taken,
- monitor their implementation.

Consultancy research is, clearly, going to cost the client a lot more, but a recent trend is towards greater involvement of the market research company in the business of its clients, sometimes to the point where it becomes part of the client's marketing team. Some companies have set up special teams or offer a special service when such involvement is wanted.

There is a growing trend for market research companies to separate out different kinds of research according to the kind of customer. Some may distinguish broadly between consumer research and business research. **Consumer research** takes the end-user – private individuals or households – as the point of data collection. **Business research** takes other organisations who use the client's products or services in the provision of a further product or service as the point of data collection. Again, there may be a separate division or company that specialises in each type of research.

Some go further and divide up the markets in a little more detail: for example, they may have teams devoted to food and drink, home and personal care, finance, leisure and tourism, medical products and agriculture.

Academic perspectives

Academics involved in researching markets and organisations may approach these activities from two very different perspectives depending on whether the research is:

- commissioned,
- scholarly.

Some academics undertake **commissioned research** on behalf of clients on a fee basis. Clients will determine the problems or issues which the research is to address, but there is likely to be a substantial consultancy element. From this perspective, the academic is a kind of 'doctor' who sees the client as his or her 'patient'. There is a diagnosis of the symptoms, a search for causes and remedies, and the prescription of a treatment. The aim is to make the patient 'well' again, which usually means improving the client's performance in the marketplace. While commissioned research is objective in the sense that it is uncoloured by the emotions and feelings of the researcher, it is not neutral. It is interventionist and partisan, acting on behalf of the client in the same way that a doctor acts in the interests of the patient. From this perspective, the world of business is seen as an *arena* in which competition in the struggle for competitive advantage – even survival – takes place, using various strategies and tactics. The quality of commissioned research is judged by its efficacy, not on the scientific rigour of the procedures used. The timescale for its completion is usually agreed and strictly limited, while the end-product is normally a report that is not published, since the results are confidential to the client.

Scholarly research, on the other hand, tries to be not only objective but neutral; it is non-interventionist and non-partisan. Its aim is to add to a growing body of knowledge and understanding rather than to meet the needs of a specific client. The subject matter is decided by the researcher, following his or her own interests. The timescale of the research is relatively flexible, and the results are publicly available – usually either in journals or as reports, for example, from the Economic and Social Research Council, one of a number of funding bodies for scholarly research.

Scholarly research carried out by academics (which we could call 'research in marketing' as opposed to 'marketing research') may itself, however, be approached from two rather different perspectives:

- positivist,
- interpretive.

The **positivist perspective** is based on the methods used in the natural sciences, which are rigorous, quantitative, and seek to test hypotheses set up in advance of data collection and according to criteria that are also determined before the study begins. The researcher is a kind of business 'scientist' who sees the business world as a **system** of interrelated parts that has a structure that can be studied. The system can be observed, measured and eventually predicted from discovered patterns, regularities or laws. Human action itself is seen to be a result of external stimuli that can be analysed into cause-and-effect relationships.

The **interpretive perspective**, which itself comes in a number of sub-varieties that may be called 'qualitative', 'ethnographic' or 'semiotic' approaches, is based on methods that have become dominant in some of the social sciences, particularly sociology. They are still rigorous, neutral and non-interventionist, but take into account the subjective dimension of human activity – the internal logic and interpretive processes by which action is created. The aim is to understand how businessmen and consumers make sense of their worlds, and how they create, negotiate and communicate the meanings they give to what they do. Whatever participants in a market see as the 'reality' of a situation, that perception will guide their behaviour. The entrepreneur who feels under threat will adopt defensive or offensive strategies to cope with the perceived situation. The business world is seen as an immense *gallery* of specimens of transactional behaviour that can be understood only by carefully documenting the world of subjective meanings. The approach is more like that of the botanist building up a picture of reality from the ground up, than that of the doctor/physician or the natural scientist.

THE USES OF MARKETING RESEARCH

While academic research for marketing may be used to gain qualifications or to further careers, marketing research can be used by business and other types of non-profit organisations in one or more of a number of ways:

* to help tackle or resolve 'one-off' problems or issues,
* to assist in making plans and setting objectives for the future,
* to monitor changes in the marketplace as they occur,
* to build up a database or marketing information system that can become a resource for a growing range of analyses and database marketing techniques,
* to use as a common 'currency' with which the company can base its negotiations with media owners, advertising agencies, distributors or suppliers.

A typical one-off problem may be how to react to the threat of a new product or new technology being introduced by competitors, or to a sudden decline in sales or in market share. Alternatively, the problem may, like the situation for John Ambrose and Co., be one in which the 'best' course of action needs to be determined. A more proactive, marketing-oriented company will, however, be more concerned with making plans for the future. Marketing planning entails diagnosing the current situation, setting objectives, generating potential alternative strategies for achieving them, selecting the best strategies, and undertaking implementation.

An ad hoc piece of marketing research can help with all these. If a competitor introduces a new product, marketing research may be called upon to examine consumer perceptions of the advantages and any limitations of the new product, and how it compares with existing products. Explaining the decline in sales may mean undertaking desk research to collect information on recent trends in the industry to show whether the company is unique in its problems or whether competitors are experiencing similar setbacks. Various hypotheses about why the decline is taking place can then be tested. Marketing research may be called upon to provide information for deciding on the 'best' course of action to follow; it can help with all stages of planning, not only diagnosing the current situation, but providing background data for determining what are reasonable or feasible quantitative targets, for example, for market penetration, market development or product development.

Monitoring changes in the marketplace clearly requires continuous research, but such research can be used in two different contexts: first, to generate 'advance notice' of changes so that they can be reacted to immediately, before they become a major problem; second, to keep track of the progress of a strategy that has already been implemented. Thus advertising tracking studies – which are explained in Chapter 7 – may be used to measure the 'success' of a company in raising awareness or recall of an advertisement.

While ad hoc research results can be added to a database, it is usual to make regular updates from continuous research. Such a database could be used to show, for example, that although sales of a brand have been fairly steady over the year, there have been considerable changes in the kinds of people purchasing, the quantities they buy, and the frequency with which they buy.

Finally, if a company wishes to persuade a retailer to give shelf-space to its brands, it may need data from retail panels to show that a given increase in such space will generate a particular quantity of extra sales. An advertising agency may need data on television-viewing patterns and audience ratings before deciding which slots will be most cost-effective.

Marketing research, then, can be used for an enormous range of purposes, only some of which are hinted at above. However, the conduct or commissioning of marketing research does not, by itself, guarantee success or that the problem will be solved. There are many examples of companies ending up in trouble after extensive research has been carried out; some highly successful companies have never undertaken marketing research of any kind. There are many other factors besides marketing research which determine the success or failure of a company. Furthermore, a number of reasons can be advanced as to why marketing research can sometimes be a waste of time:

- The research undertaken may be designed without reference to decisions that depend on, or at least will be strongly influenced by, the results of the research.
- The research results are ignored, misused, misunderstood or misinterpreted.
- The research is poorly designed or carried out.
- The results of the research are inconclusive, giving rise to different opinions about the implications of the research.

To put this another way, to be of any value, the research must relate to key issues or decisions within a company, it must be properly executed, and the results must be fully understood and used.

It needs to be clear at the outset, furthermore, that marketing research is no substitute for decision-taking. Like any tool, well used it helps managers to do a better job. It helps to reduce the risks in business decisions, but will not make the decision. Even if action standards are defined before the research begins (for example, 'We'll launch the product provided at least 40 per cent of respondents give it a rating of six out of ten or more'), it is the manager, not the researcher, who defines these standards. Good marketing requires flair and creativity along with sound judgement and experience. Marketing research is no substitute for these either; but good information can help reduce the area in which hunch, gut feeling or simply good luck have to operate.

THE UK MARKET RESEARCH INDUSTRY

The market research industry in the UK may be considered as consisting of three main groups of 'players':

- the research suppliers,
- the research buyers,
- the market research profession.

The research suppliers

The UK is widely regarded as a, if not *the*, world leader in the development and practice of marketing research. Why such talent should be associated with an economy whose performance since 1945 has, in many respects, been disappointing is an open question. Perhaps the market research industry's main shortcoming is its inability to market itself. Certainly, the industry enjoyed a sustained boom during the 1980s, with turnover more than doubling in that period. Only during 1990 were there signs that the steady annual expansion in market research turnover was beginning to falter.

Client companies in the past have tended to commission research when they were optimistic and expansion-minded, and to chop it from their budgets as an easy cost saving when profits were threatened. More recently, however, many manufacturing and service organisations have established research as a vital component of their marketing plans, and as a supplier of data, information and analyses on which to make investment decisions in bad times as well as in good. This bodes well for the health of the market research industry even in times of relative recession.

The largest market research agencies in the UK have formed themselves into a trade association – the Association of Market Survey Organisations (AMSO). This was established in 1964 and initially it focused as a support group for those running its member companies. It collected reliable statistics about the industry and sought to clarify and improve the status of market research interviewers. It set out a code of standards outlining responsibilities of members towards both clients and the public. During the 1980s, membership doubled and it currently stands at 25 companies, including most of the largest UK organisations. AMSO has, with growing membership, become more outward-looking and now represents the industry on a range of bodies such as the Confederation of British Industry, the Advertising Association and the Data Protection Tribunal. To qualify for membership, market research companies must be equipped to undertake full-scale national surveys and be committed to the highest standards of quality and professionalism in their work.

In 1991 AMSO members had a turnover of £265.6 million, which represents about 70 per cent of the estimated total industry turnover. Together they employ over 4,000 permanent salaried staff in their UK companies. Members varied from the largest companies, with turnovers in excess of £30 million, down to those with less than £1 million and employing fewer than 20 people. Some of the companies are multinational public limited companies or are owned by such companies, and do not like to think of themselves any more as 'agencies'. Table 1.1 shows the top ten AMSO companies. The three largest – AGB, Nielsen and MAI – together account for over 40 per cent of AMSO member turnover. During the 1980s, AMSO turnover increased by an average of 10 per cent per annum in real terms. However, by 1991 the recession had begun to bite and the increase over 1990 was only 1.7 per cent – in real terms a decline of just under 4 per cent.

During 1991, AMSO members carried out 13.5 million interviews,

Table 1.1 The top ten AMSO companies by UK turnover, 1989–91 (£ million)

		1989	1990	1991
1	Audits of Great Britain (AGB)	44.9	48.1	38.8
2	Nielsen	30.6	35.3	38.3
3	MAI (UK) Market Research	30.0	33.8	31.3
4	Millward Brown International	16.7	20.3	23.3
5	Research International	16.1	19.1	21.2
6	British Market Research Bureau			
	(MRB Group)	15.7	17.4	17.8
7	Taylor Nelson	17.0	18.8	16.8
8	Research Services Ltd	7.6	9.2	10.1
9	The Research Business Group	8.4	9.4	9.4
10	MORI	8.5	8.7	9.0
Total AMSO turnover		238.6	265.5	265.6

Source: AMSO

excluding retail panels and consumer panels. Personal interviews continue to dominate UK data collection, accounting for about 55 per cent of field-work turnover. Telephone interviews seem to have levelled off at about 15 per cent after a steady rise. Group discussions and hall tests account for about 10 per cent each. While domestic research has since 1990 shown negative growth, the amount of international research carried out by UK companies has continued to be buoyant. The UK is the world leader in multi-country research, and some medium-sized London market research companies have built up a considerable reputation for international surveys.

These industry statistics hide considerable variations from company to company. Thus, during 1991 a couple of companies saw turnover fall by 20 per cent while others increased their turnover by a similar amount. The market leader in the UK (and in Europe) has, since the 1960s, been Audits of Great Britain (AGB), a UK company that established itself as the leading operator of consumer panels, and has held the contract for tele-vision audience measurement since 1981. However, AGB's dominance has been overshadowed by poor performance in 1991, so that Nielsen, the number two company in the UK for many years, has all but caught up. Nielsen is a subsidiary of A.C. Nielsen, the world's biggest market research company based in the United States. In the UK it established primacy for retail panel operations. MAI (Mills and Allen International) claims to be the market leader for ad hoc research in the UK; Millward Brown is regarded as the leader in the field of advertising assessment and advertising tracking; Research International claims to be the world's largest custom research network, operating in over 100 countries.

Besides the big agencies, there are hundreds of smaller organisations in the UK. The Market Research Society Yearbook for 1992 lists 451 companies, but over 80 per cent of these are businesses employing 12 or fewer professional staff (Bryson *et al.* 1990). Only 6 per cent of agencies employ more than 30. The market research industry is thus in many ways a classic, small-business industry. This is an industry in which anybody can start up on their own, and the number of agencies doubled in the 1980s. Together, small firms have about 20 per cent of the total industry turnover (Bryson *et al.* 1990). As with other industries comprising a high proportion of small new companies, there is a rapid turnover of small firms. One half of all market research firms existing in 1980 had disappeared by 1990 (Bryson *et al.* 1990). Both large and small companies are predominantly located in London and the South East of England. Nearly 50 per cent of MRS listed companies are in inner London, while nearly 90 per cent are somewhere in the South East.

The main trends in the market research industry can be listed as follows:

- restructuring through acquisitions and mergers to create larger conglomerates of companies,
- every group of companies now offers a complete range of services,
- a growth in the development of proprietary research techniques,
- continuing segmentation into consultants and data handlers.

Through acquisitions and mergers, power is now concentrated into the hands of a few large groups for whom research is only part of a greater information and communications industry. Thus AGB was owned by Robert Maxwell until 1992, when, after the collapse of the Maxwell empire, it was bought out by Taylor Nelson, the seventh largest market research company in the UK. The two companies are currently restructuring, but are likely to keep the Taylor Nelson and AGB names. Nielsen is a subsidiary of the US company, A.C. Nielsen, who in turn are owned by Dunn and Bradstreet. Millward Brown, Research International and the MRB Group have all been acquired by Martin Sorrell's WPP advertising agency. The companies are run separately, but the viability of WPP itself is now looking a little uncertain. The industry, at the moment, is thus dominated by four groups: the WPP group with a combined turnover of £60.3 million, Taylor Nelson/AGB with a combined turnover of £55.6 million, Nielsen and MAI. Together these account for over 70 per cent of AMSO member turnover.

During the 1980s the large market research companies tended to specialise in different segments of the market. Thus AGB concentrated on consumer panels, Nielsen on retail panels, Millward Brown on advertising research and so on. However, competition in the late 1980s grew fierce. AGB bought up the National Market Research Association (NMRA), a retail panel operator and Nielsen's main rival in that area. At the same time, Nielsen set up its own consumer panel, Homescan, in direct competition with AGB's Superpanel. Both are illustrations of the trend towards full-service suppliers who can offer the complete range of research to all clients.

The market research industry has, in 25 years, moved from a cottage to a high-tech, computer-dominated industry in which companies have now packaged their services so that clients can buy 'off-the-peg' services with standardised, proprietary techniques, each claiming to offer 'unique' advantages over the competition. Some of these services are described in Chapter 7.

Another trend is towards segmentation of the industry into those who provide high value-added consultancy and complete customer care, and those who handle enormous databanks, all captured electronically. The existing trend towards globalisation of markets and the needs of trans-national consumers will also mean that multi-country research will be the flavour of the next few years.

Finally, there has been a trend for the market research companies themselves to segment their business more by type of market and type of customer than by type of research. This is part of the trend towards increased value-added research in which the market research company is expected to become part of the client company marketing team so research executives need to become expert in particular markets.

The research buyers

Traditionally, market research companies received most of their business from consumer goods manufacturers, but in the last five years or so there has been a shift towards buyers in organisations of other kinds. By value, some 60 per cent of commissioned research is now sought by non-consumer goods companies. The biggest buyers are the media owners, public services, advertising agencies, pharmaceuticals and financial services. The main consumer goods companies include food and drinks companies, manufacturers of health and beauty aids, and the producers of alcoholic drinks. The sources of revenue for AMSO members are outlined in Table 1.2. From this table it can be seen that, not unexpectedly in the climate of recession, makers of consumer durables, vehicle manufacturers, pharmaceuticals, industrial companies, advertising agencies, retailers, and travel and tourism have all reduced their expenditure on marketing research. The biggest increases were in government and public services, alcoholic drinks, health and beauty aids, and household products.

The market research profession

The UK is well served with professional associations. It has a professional body based on individual membership – the Market Research Society –

Table 1.2 Source of revenue for AMSO companies (£ million)

	1990	1991
Non-consumer companies		
Media	23.9	24.3
Public services and utilities	20.8	21.6
Financial services	14.2	14.3
Vehicle manufacturers	15.7	13.9
Government	11.0	13.2
Pharmaceuticals	13.3	12.4
Industrial	12.1	11.4
Advertising agencies	10.7	9.8
Retailers	8.8	7.7
Travel and tourism	7.4	6.8
Oil	2.8	3.8
Consumer companies		
Food and soft drinks	50.3	51.7
Alcoholic drinks	19.0	21.0
Health and beauty aids	17.5	19.0
Household products	4.4	7.7
Tobacco	3.3	3.5
Consumer durables	6.8	2.9

Source: AMSO

which is the largest body of its kind in the world. It was founded in 1947, and now has about 6,500 members, about half of whom are women. The Market Research Society seeks to ensure the maintenance of professional standards in the practice of marketing research of all kinds, to provide its members with an educational, information and social forum, and to represent the interests of the UK market research profession in the world at large. It offers one of the few UK academic qualifications solely covering market research – the Diploma of the Market Research Society. Members of the Society subscribe to a code of conduct that puts a premium on confidentiality, so that the anonymity of respondents is carefully protected.

Code of Conduct

This was introduced in 1954 as a self-regulatory code and has been amended several times since. The code is agreed by the Market Research Society and the Industrial Market Research Association and is designed to support all those engaged in marketing or social research in maintaining professional standards, and to ensure that research is conducted in an ethical manner. It also currently has to ensure that research is conducted in accordance with the principles (and spirit) of the Data Protection Act.

In terms of responsibilities to respondents, a selection and summary of some of the key rules follows:

- Any assurances given to secure co-operation must be honoured.
- Confidentiality must be guaranteed. Thus no information that could be used to identify individuals or companies should be revealed to anybody, except those who need to check the validity of the data or who are engaged in processing them. Such people, in turn, must not make any other use of the information or pass it on to anybody else.
- Adverse effects must be avoided. Thus respondents should not be adversely affected or embarrassed as a result of any interview.
- Each interviewer must carry means of identification that specifies his or her name and organisation, and should include a photograph.
- The respondent's right to withdraw or to refuse to co-operate must be respected.
- Special care must be taken in interviewing children. Permission from a parent or guardian must be sought, and a detailed description of the content and questions must be given.

Responsibilities to the general public and the business community include:

- No activity should be misrepresented as research, for example, the compilation of lists for non-research purposes.
- Conclusions from research that are not warranted by the data will not knowingly be communicated.

Responsibilities to clients include:

- No contract should include provisions that infringe the code.
- Research specifications are confidential to the client.
- Any subcontracting of work must be revealed to the client before any commitments are made.
- The identity of the client must not be revealed to respondents unless authorised to do so.
- All information relating to the client must be held in strict confidence unless it is information in the public domain.
- All reasonable precautions should be taken to ensure that interviewers do not combine two or more surveys in one interview without the explicit permission from the agency who, in turn, must make the intention to give such permission clear to the client before contract.

Other rules relate to the details of a survey that clients may reasonably expect, the retention of the original questionnaires, and the circulation of the results.

Practitioners in the non-consumer field may belong to the Industrial Marketing Research Association (IMRA), whose members also subscribe to the same code of conduct binding upon MRS members. The trade association AMSO has already been mentioned, but there is also the Association of British Market Research Companies (the ABMRC). This was founded in 1982 and consists of the smaller research companies and consultancies. In 1981 the Association of Qualitative Research Prac- titioners (the AQRP) was formed and now comprises over 500 individual members who work variously in research companies, advertising and major client organisations. It provides a forum for all those interested in the conduct and development of qualitative research.

Most of the large market research companies are members of the Interviewer Quality Control Scheme (IQCS). This is an offshoot of the original Market Research Society Interviewer Identity Card Scheme. To be a member of the IQCS, a company has to meet specified market research fieldwork standards that cover recruitment, training, supervision and back-checking. Members are audited every year and a report goes to the full Council of the IQCS.

Besides those individuals in companies buying or selling research, there are academics and researchers in universities and colleges, mostly in departments of marketing, business or management, who undertake commissioned market research, consultancy or scholarly research. In addition, there are those employed in large organisations that have their own in-house market research departments or capabilities. Some of these individuals may be responsible for actually conducting research; others may oversee the commissioning of research or of certain parts or stages of the project, like data processing, from agencies, some of whom may specialise in that kind of activity. Not a lot is known about the nature and value of the research conducted in-house, since reports remain confidential, and the value of the labour and resources involved may be difficult to estimate. In-house research, while not 'commissioned' in the sense of being a result of a client–agency transaction, is very similar to commissioned research in terms of the characteristics described above.

SUMMARY

Marketing research is nowadays no longer just the collection of data on markets and consumers. Increasingly, it is part of the marketing function within an organisation and has extended itself forwards to providing data for the diagnosis of organisational problems, and backwards to the generation, selection, implementation and monitoring of solutions to these problems. It is, furthermore, no longer restricted to the provision of data, but includes the analysis and interpretation of the results. In short, marketing research is concerned with the collection, analysis and interpretation of data that may be used for the diagnosis, planning and control of organisational marketing objectives and strategies.

Although market analysis is still an important, if not crucial ingredient in marketing research, and a great deal of research that is commissioned from market research companies is limited to researching markets, such activities will be a waste of time unless they are designed and executed in the context of marketing decisions that need to be taken or specific issues that need to be resolved. Marketing research, whether commissioned or carried out in-house, can help with all stages of the marketing planning process.

Textbook categorisations of types of marketing research have their limitations; market research company distinctions are perhaps a better guide to the differing approaches to marketing research. It must also not be forgotten that, apart from research whose purpose is to further the objectives of a particular organisation, there is also research carried out for academic purposes.

The UK market research industry is a world leader with research suppliers who have an international reputation, ably supported by a range of professional and trade associations. The fact that UK organisations have not always seen fit to make full use of the services offered by market research companies is perhaps testimony to a reluctance, until recently, of those companies to apply their expertise to their own backyard and market themselves.

QUESTIONS FOR FURTHER DISCUSSION

■   What are the main components of marketing decision-making to which marketing research can contribute?

■   Consider how the different types of marketing research, as indicated in the textbooks and as indicated by market research companies, are suited to the various uses to which marketing research can be put.

■   What are the key groups of people who can be involved in or affected by ethical issues in marketing research?

■   What do you think *are* the key ethical issues in the conduct of marketing research?

■   Imagine two academic researchers, one a positivist and the other a keen advocate of the interpretive perspective. Compare how each would approach a study into how manufacturers of soft drinks decide on the size of their product ranges.

■   Do you think the major trends in the market research industry are ones that will make it easier or more difficult for the inexperienced research buyer?

Chapter 2

Marketing research data

In Chapter 1 it was explained that marketing research is concerned with the collection, analysis and interpretation of data that are useful in the diagnosis, planning and control of marketing strategies. However, before considering how data are collected and analysed, it is essential to understand what 'data' are in the first place, and what types of data emerge from research activity. This chapter will consider the nature and types of data that market researchers collect, showing in particular how quantitative data result from the process of measurement.

WHAT ARE 'DATA'?

Data are a product of systematic record-keeping. The different kinds of records or instruments used for capturing data are the focus of the next chapter. For the moment, let us focus on what kinds of things count as 'data'. If a marketing manager presents you with a table of sales figures for the last 12 months for each product that the company manufactures, you will probably accept that you are being presented with 'data'. If it were just one figure for one product for last month, you might be inclined to say, 'Tell me more' on being told, 'Here are the data'. A single piece of information – a datum – is not of much value on its own – we need at least two pieces of information to make comparisons.

At the same time, the historian likes to think of parish registers, diaries of famous people, or transcripts of what was said in the House of Commons as 'data'. A sociologist with a tape recorder studying 'street corner society' or some unusual, remote tribe of people, considers that he or she is collecting 'data'. The archaeologist uses physical traces or remains as evidence or data on past events, conditions or social behaviour. Provided some systematic record is kept of what people say or of physical artefacts, then it is possible to talk of possessing 'data'.

TYPES OF DATA

It is possible to discern from the discussion in the previous section that there are two broad categories of data:

- qualitative data,
- quantitative data.

Qualitative data

Qualitative data arise as words, statements, commentary or narrative and may be spoken or they may be written or printed text. The spoken words may have been recorded in writing or captured electronically. Printed text merely needs to be accessible, which may mean taking a photocopy or making notes from the text. Pictures of various kinds may also be seen as qualitative data; they may be one-off snapshots captured by drawing, painting or taking photographs, or they may be monitored over a period of time using film or video.

Market researchers often collect qualitative data. These may arise as some kind of narrative or text, for example, a story, account or description of what happened or what 'normally' happens in particular circumstances. Alternatively, they may be isolated statements made by respondents or participants and could be in response to a series of open-ended questions. Such statements will reflect their knowledge, beliefs, attitudes, opinions or aspirations, very often in respect of products or services that they buy, or in respect of their reactions to attempts made by business organisations to communicate with customers or potential customers through advertising, publicity, sponsorship, personal selling or sales promotions.

Most qualitative data in marketing arise from informal or 'depth' inter-views or from group discussions. Such research is usually called 'qualitative research' and this is considered in detail in Chapter 5 along with the pro-cedures used for the analysis of the narrative or text that arise from that form of research. However, qualitative data may also emerge in the course of formal, quantitative research, such as in surveys or experiments when respondents are asked to give some of their answers in their own words in response to open-ended questions. Such data may also arise from unstruc-tured observation carried out by researchers. The analysis of this kind of qualitative data involves procedures that are a little different from the analysis or narrative and text, and these are considered in detail in Chapter 6 on data analysis.

Quantitative data and the measurement process

Quantitative data arise as numbers, and they are a result of the process of measurement. When we measure something, we make a systematic record of a value that some case (an object, person, group or people, organisation or situation) possesses. Thus we may ask a person their age. Accepting their answer as a correct measure of the number of years elapsed since they were born, we may record a value of, say, '39'. This value will be from a defined set of values that refer to a specified dimension or characteristic, in this case, age, where the defined set is likely to be in the range 16–99, if we are interested only in adults. At a minimum, when we take measurements, there must be at least two values to select from: one for cases that possess a characteristic, and one for cases that do not, for example, watched/did not watch a particular television programme, or made a profit/did not make a profit last year. Such sets of values where there are only two categories are often referred to as **dichotomies**.

Sometimes there are three or more categories or values. The set of values (or **scale**) may be in no particular order like 'multiple', 'co-operative' and 'independent', to define different types of shop. Such scales, often referred to as **nominal scales**, may list the categories in any order without changing the sense of the data being presented. To be useful for the purposes of measurement, however, (and hence for the capture of data that have a quantitative element), it is necessary that sets of categories are:

- exhaustive of all the possibilities,
- mutually exclusive, that is, non-overlapping,
- referring to a single dimension.

To make a set of categories exhaustive, it is sometimes necessary to have a 'catch-all' category for observations that do not fit into any of the scale values specified. For example, the answers to the question, 'For which of the following purposes do you mostly use cooking fat?' may be categorised into:

Deep frying   [   ]
Shallow frying   [   ]
Roasting   [   ]
Pastry making   [   ]
Other uses   [   ]
(please specify) ....

By adding the 'other' category, the set of values is now exhaustive of all the possibilities and there is no answer that cannot be put into a category.

If the set of categories is overlapping, then the value of measurements taken is severely limited. Consider the following set of categories for Region of Head Office:

England
Wales
Scotland

Northern Ireland
London and the South East

An office in or around London will get counted twice, making analyses of head office location statistics dubious, to say the least.

Sometimes, sets of categories have more than one dimension implicit in them. To say that the categories 'baby', 'telephone', 'railway ticket' and '*Twin Peaks*' do not refer to a single dimension is fairly obvious. However, many marketing people make a distinction between different types of consumer goods into:

- convenience goods,
- shopping goods,
- speciality goods.

Quite apart from the fact that these categories may be overlapping for many products, there are two very different dimensions implicit here. One refers to the degree of search behaviour involved in selecting a brand (convenience goods versus shopping goods), while the third category, speciality goods, has more to do with brand loyalty. That more than one dimension is being referred to is not always obvious.

Sets of scale values, in short, do not automatically achieve the status of being even a nominal scale unless certain criteria are met. Unless the sets of categories are exhaustive, unique and unidimensional, then their value for generating quantitative data is limited. Remember that sets of three or more categories can always be transposed into sets of dichotomies, for example, convenience goods/non-convenience goods; shopping goods/non-shopping goods; speciality goods/non-speciality goods. Such a procedure may be followed either to reduce the number of categories being considered in any one table to only two because the sample size is very small, or to take advantage of statistical operations that are possible on dichotomies, but not on nominal scales with three or more categories.

Some sets of scale values may be categories, but there is an implied order as in 'heavy', 'medium', 'light' and 'non-user' of a product. There is a sense in which such sets of categories could be written 'out of order'. Sets of scale values ordered in this way may be referred to as **ordinal scales**. The standard social class groupings used by market researchers (see Table 2.1) form such an ordinal scale that goes from high to low. Notice that the scale values for dichotomies, nominal and ordinal scales appear as words or phrases. We could give them numbers, but such numbers would act only as labels, like hotel room numbers. There would be no point in adding up such numbers.

All scales that are just sets of categories, whether ordered or not, do not give any measure of the 'distance' between one category and the next. There is no measure or metric with which to calibrate such distances. We

Table 2.1 Social grade definitions

Social grade	Social status	Head of household's occupation
A	Upper middle class	Higher managerial, administrative or professional
B	Middle class	Intermediate managerial, administrative or professional
C1	Lower middle class	Supervisory or clerical, and junior administrative or professional
C2	Skilled working class	Skilled manual workers
D	Working class	Semi and unskilled workers
E	Those at lowest level of subsistence	State pensioners or widows (no other earner), casual or lowest-grade workers

Source: JICNARS *National Readership Survey*, 1986

cannot, for example, compare the 'distance' between social class B and social class C1 with the 'distance' between classes C2 and D. All such scales may be referred to jointly as 'non-metric' or 'categorical' scales.

In the earlier example where a person's age was '39', the scale value itself *is* a number. This is because for a characteristic like age there is a calibrated measure or metric, in this case units of time, that can be applied to say to what extent that characteristic is possessed. Using a rules to measure length, a pair of scales to measure weight, or units of time or money, will result, if we take a lot of measurements, in a very large number of scale values, each one arising as a number. For such **continuous metric scales**, it does usually make sense to add up the scale values to arrive at a grand total, for example, of amounts of money.

There is, however, another way of arriving at a numeric scale: we sometimes count up how many times an event occurs as a measure of size, magnitude or extent. Thus, we could count up the number of people in a group as a measure of group size, the number of employees in an organisation as a measure of organisational size, or the number of checkouts in a supermarket as a measure of shop size. In this situation we must necessarily arrive at a whole number – we cannot have a fraction of a person or of a checkout. The implication of this is that the number of scale values is finite, whereas in the case of calibrated measures it is potentially infinite and depends only on the accuracy or precision of the measuring instrument. Where the scale values are a result of counting whole occurrences, then we have a **discrete metric scale**.

The distinction between continuous and discrete metric scales is, however, sometimes a little difficult to draw. For example, in the case of money, it is not possible to have a fraction of the smallest unit of currency, but the number of scale values can, nevertheless, be very large. Only when the number of scale values is very limited – as with measures of household size (one-person, two-person, three-person household and so on) does it have any statistical consequences, for example, for the 'smoothing' of a graph, which should really be done only for continuous metric variables.

The main types of scale

- Sets of categories that are exhaustive, mutually exclusive and refer to a single dimension but are in no particular order (nominal scales).
- Sets of categories in which there is an implied order from high to low or big to small (ordinal scales).
- A result of calibrations, made with some degree of precision, that give us a measure of the distance between one measurement and the next, and in principle possessing an infinite number of scale values (continuous metric).
- Counting up the number of times an event occurs as a measure of size (discrete metric).

Table 2.2 gives examples of variables used by market researchers that may be put into each kind of scale. One type of scale that straddles both categorical and metric scales is a scale created by ranking a series of cases according to a characteristic, but where there are as many ranks as cases to be ranked. Thus, seven brands of a product may be ranked 1–7 by a customer in terms of 'preference' or 'value-for-money'. Thirty children in a classroom may be ranked 1–30 in terms of ability and so on. While there is still no notion of 'distance' between ranks, the fact that we can, for example, compute an 'average' ranking, or compare rankings of a set of cases on two or more variables to measure the degree of correlation, means that such ranking scales take on some of the characteristics of metric scales. Some of the statistical operations that may be performed on ranking scales are explained in Chapter 6.

The distinction between nominal, ordinal and metric scales becomes, as we shall see, crucial for deciding what kinds of statistical operation it is possible or sensible to perform on the data. Many more and more sophisticated statistics can be calculated where data are metric, but, as is clear from Table 2.2, there are many variables that market researchers use that are not metric. In some circumstances, market researchers try to 'upgrade' scales in order to take advantage of these more sophisticated procedures. There are two main ways in which this may be accomplished. The researcher may allocate numerical scores to ordinal categories, and then treat the scores as if they referred to metric qualities. Thus the level of interest in a television programme may be recorded on a five-point scale:

Table 2.2 Examples of market research variables

Scale type	Values
Nominal scales	
For an individual:	
Sex	Male, female
Employment status	Employed full-time, part-time, unemployed
Marital status	Single, married, widowed, divorced, separated
For an organisation:	
Location of head office	England, Wales, Scotland, Northern Ireland
Ownership	Private, public, co-operative
Type of business	Manufacturing, agriculture, construction, services
Ordinal scales	
For an individual:	
Interest in gardening	Very interested, fairly interested, not interested
Social grade	A, B, C1, C2, D, E
Product usage	Heavy, medium, light
For an organisation:	
Size	Small, medium, large
Centralisation	Centralised, decentralised
Ethical stance	Explicit code of ethics, general statement of principles, no code
Discrete metric scale	
For an individual:	
Number of brothers and sisters	
Number of purchases of brand X	
Number of pairs of shoes owned	
For an organisation:	
Number of employees	
Number of product lines	
Number of factories	
Continuous metric scales	
For an individual:	
Age in years	
Height in centimetres	
Time spent viewing television	
For an organisation:	
Turnover in £ sterling	
Square footage of the factories	
Exports in tons	

	Allocate score
Extremely interesting	5
Very interesting	4
Fairly interesting	3
Not very interesting	2
Not at all interesting	1

A score is allocated to each individual response and the total for all respondents can be added up and divided by the number of respondents to give an average score. A number of assumptions are being made in this process, the main one that the 'distances' between each point on the scale are equal so that, for example, the distance between 'very interesting' and 'fairly interesting' is the same as the distance between 'fairly interesting' and 'not very interesting'. Such an assumption may well be unwarranted, and it would certainly be unwise to treat total scores in any absolute sense. However, for measuring change, for example from one week to the next, changes in the average scores are likely to reflect real changes in people's level of interest. Error, provided it is constant, does not affect measures of change.

The other way to create metric scales is to define categories of an ordinal scale in numerical terms. Thus a distinction between 'small', 'medium' and 'large' organisations is only an ordinal distinction. However, if the researcher defined 'small' organisations as having fewer than 50 employees, 'medium' as having between 50 and 200 employees, and 'large' as having over 200 employees, then a discrete metric scale has been created, the 'metric' in this case being size measured by the number of employees. With a larger number of categories, more precisely defined, with upper and lower limits, it becomes possible to calculate an average size. This procedure is fine provided there is accurate information, for example in the situation above, on the number of employees in each organisation of interest.

The components of measurement

Any *single* measurement that we take can be said to have four key components:

- a case,
- a variable,
- a scale,
- a value.

When we measure, we always measure a characteristic of some object. A **case** is the type of object, person, group of people, organisation, situation or event whose characteristics are being measured and recorded in the process of data capture. The cases may be objects, people, groups and so on of a particular kind, for example, 'motorists', 'mothers with babies', or even 'motorists with a driving conviction who have held a licence for over 15 years'. In any one particular piece of research there may be more than one type of case, for example, a study may measure characteristics of both organisations and the individuals within them.

A **variable** is a characteristic, feature or property of the case which is being measured or classified. Variables vary, at a minimum, between two values (like 'male' and 'female'), although for continuous scales there may be many values. Some variables are relatively unchanging conditions or circumstances and are usually referred to as **demographics**, like the sex of a person or the size of a household. Other variables may be the characteristics the researcher is trying to predict or explain and will be changing all the time, for example, sales by volume over a four-week period. Such variables are normally called **dependent variables**, while **independent variables** are the ones being investigated as causes or influences on the situation. Some of these causes may be demographic, or treated as a demographic, in a particular piece of research, for example, using a person's age or sex to explain differences in product-purchasing behaviour. Other independent variables may be more changeable, like price awareness. Some variables may get used either as a dependent or as an independent variable by different researchers. Thus one researcher may take price awareness as an independent variable used to explain or help to explain buying behaviour. Another may use it as a dependent variable that he or she is trying to explain by invoking other independent variables, like purchase frequency or price labelling system (pack or shelf).

Variables are what we use to indicate the behavioural dimensions, facets or properties of the more abstract ideas that we use to think about and to order or classify our experience of the world. These abstract ideas are **concepts**. We tend to think in terms of concepts, but take measurements of variables. Some concepts like social class may be translated into a variable in many different ways, for example, based on personal or family incomes, on the occupation of the head of household, or on perceived or self-defined social class. Concepts like sex and age translate into variables very easily; others, like brand loyalty, may be very difficult to measure. Thus we cannot directly measure a person's 'loyalty' to a brand – it is not something we can actually observe. All we can do is take an indirect measure, using some indicator like brand-purchasing behaviour over a period of time, or stated preferences for a brand. In other words, we infer the characteristic from the indicator. Very often, particularly in the measurement of attitudes, several indicators may be needed and added together in some way. Any description of a concept in terms of how it is to be measured is called an **operational definition**.

A **scale**, as we have seen, is a set of values that meets certain criteria and may be one of the four main kinds outlined above.

A **value** is what we actually record in the process of record-keeping. For metric scales these values may, as explained above, be recorded as numbers that represent calibrated measures, or may arise from the process of counting. For categorical scales they may be recorded as words, letters or numbers used as labels. Table 2.3 gives examples of these key components for a selection of single measurements.

Any measurement we take needs, as far as possible, to be both valid and reliable. A measurement is said to possess **validity** if there is evidence that the instruments, techniques or processes used to measure the concept do indeed give a true reflection of the intended concept. This entails that the indicators selected do properly reflect the entire domain of the concept or variable being measured, and that diferences between measurements taken do correspond with true differences among the cases of interest. Thus, measuring brand loyalty for brand X by asking, 'How many other brands have you personally purchased in the last four weeks?' does not reflect that aspect of brand loyalty that has to do with the length of time somebody has been purchasing brand X. Furthermore, the difference between a respondent who purchased one other brand and those who purchased two or three may not reflect greater brand loyalty at all.

Validity is often associated with lack of **bias**. Bias is systematic error that occurs in a consistent manner each time something is measured. The problem, of course, is that we know the extent of such bias only if we also know the 'true' value. Since we often do not, all we can do is to infer validity either from the success of the measure in predicting other measures or in predicting behaviour (sometimes called predictive validity) or, if there are two or more independent measures of a variable, from the internal consistency of these measures (sometimes called convergent validity).

Reliability refers to the extent to which repeat measures produce similar or consistent results. It is often associated with the degree of random or variable error, and has more to do with the precision of the measuring instrument. Sometimes it will overestimate and sometimes underestimate.

Table 2.3 Examples of components of single measurements

Case	Variable	Scale	Value
The shop	Stock level	Discrete metric	36 packets
The product	Price	Continuous metric	65p
The household	Type of accommodation	Nominal	Private rented
The customer	Product usage	Ordinal	Heavy

Reliability is usually checked either by comparing two or more repeat measures (sometimes referred to as test–retest reliability), or comparing two or more different, but equivalent, measures taken at the same time (sometimes called alternative form reliability).

Reliability is no proof of validity since a measure may be consistently wrong. Some researchers argue that a valid measure, on the other hand, must be reliable because there is no error, systematic or random. If validity is, however, limited to the notion of bias, then a valid measure is not necessarily reliable since there may still be random error. At the end of the day it is probably easier to think of a valid measure as being, by definition, reliable.

Frequencies

In a lot of marketing research, the researcher is interested in more than just one case, so for any one variable there will be a separate value for each case. For nominal and ordinal scales, it is not possible to add up any of the scale values in the same way that we can add up, say, units of currency. All we can do is state how many times each scale value occurs, that is, report its **frequency**. The results will often be laid out as a **table**, the scale values forming the rows, and the frequencies (and perhaps relative frequencies) forming the columns. Tabular analysis is considered in detail in Chapter 6.

Where scales are continuous then, in principle if not in practice, each scale value may be unique, each having a frequency of one and perhaps measured to several decimal places. The measurements may be rounded off, in which case frequencies greater than one may arise, for example, 16 people aged 39. Discrete data will be whole numbers anyway, but the frequencies may be low where there is a large number of scale values (or where the number of cases is fairly limited). Simply tabulating the results in this way may not be particularly useful.

If scale values are grouped together, then the frequency of each grouping may be reported. Thus the individual ages of respondents to a survey may be grouped into categories of 15–19, 20–24, 25–29, and so on. The number of shops selling brand X at various prices may be grouped into under 40p, 41–45p, and over 50p. For discrete variables, where the number of scale values is very limited, then it may be sensible to report the frequency of each one (for example, the number of individuals with one brother or sister, the number of individuals with two brothers or sisters, and so on).

A characteristic of all metric scales, however, is that it is possible to add up the scale values. For some variables, it may make sense just to report the grand total (for example, of money from various sources). For others (for example, ages) it makes little sense to report the total sum of the values, but if divided by the total number of cases to give an average, it may provide a useful figure.

Datasets

Any particular piece of research will normally collect data on a large number of variables, perhaps for a large number of cases. Some of these data will be qualitative, some will be quantitative. Some of the quantitative data will be metric, some non-metric. A dataset consists of all the values for all the variables for all the cases in a piece of **ad hoc research** or data collection phase or period in **continuous research**. Thus an enquiry that has 200 respondents to a questionnaire survey with 100 questions with an average of three response categories will produce a dataset that contains $200 \times 100 \times 3$, or 60,000, pieces of information.

A dataset may be stored in many different formats, but the most useful is as a **data matrix**, since this interlaces each case with each variable to produce a 'cell' containing the appropriate value, as illustrated in Figure 2.1. The cases form the rows and the variables form the columns. The size of the matrix is, therefore, a product of the number of cases and the number of variables. Data matrices will have different shapes depending on the nature of the research (see Figure 2.2). Usually, they are rectangular in which all the rows and all the columns are of the same length. However, intensive research will have relatively few cases but many variables; extensive research will have many cases and few variables. An opinion poll is a good example of the latter where a large sample (of 1,000 or so) are asked a few questions about voting intentions and party support. Where there are many cases and many variables, such as in a large-scale survey, the dataset will be very large. Occasionally they may be ragged, where some cases have more variables recorded against them than others (for example, because not all variables are applicable to all cases). Approaches to the analysis of entire datasets and the creation of data matrices are considered in Chapter 6.

A **database** is created from the accumulation of several or many datasets into a combined system of data storage and retrieval. It will normally be updated periodically from inputs from continuous research, and will be used as a resource for a number of purposes. Thus a database may be explored by looking at backdata from several surveys to analyse trends. Database marketing is the use of a database on customers to target marketing propositions in a very specific manner.

SUMMARY

Provided it is approached systematically, any record of narrative, text, physical objects, behaviour, observations or responses to a question will constitute data. Qualitative data are non-numerical, whereas quantitative data result from a process of measurement to produce frequencies of categories, metric assessment of quantities, or frequencies of groups of

Variables C1 ... Cm

	Col. 1	Col. 2	Col. 3	Col. 4	... Col. m
Row 1	Cell R1C1 Value = 'Male' = 1	Cell R1C2 Value = 34	Cell R1C3 Value = C1 = 3		
Row 2	'Female' = 2	23	C2 = 4		
Row 3	2	19	B = 2		
Row 4	1	56	D = 5		
⋮ Row n					

Cases R1 .... Rn

Figure 2.1 A 'case by variable' data matrix

Notes: 1 Column 1 may be labelled to identify variable, e.g. 'Sex'; col. 2 = 'Age'; col. 3 = 'Social class', etc.
      2 Each cell will normally contain only the numeric value which either identifies a category or indicates a metric value, e.g. case 4 is male, aged 56 and social class D.

metric quantities. Sets of categories may be ordered or non-ordered; metric assessment may be discrete or continuous.

A single measurement consists of a record of a value from a scale of values for a case in respect of a given variable. Where there is a set of cases, then the potential for recording frequencies arises. Where there are not only many cases but also many variables, then a dataset is produced. This may be laid out in the form of a data matrix. Several datasets may be combined together to create a database that would normally be regularly updated.

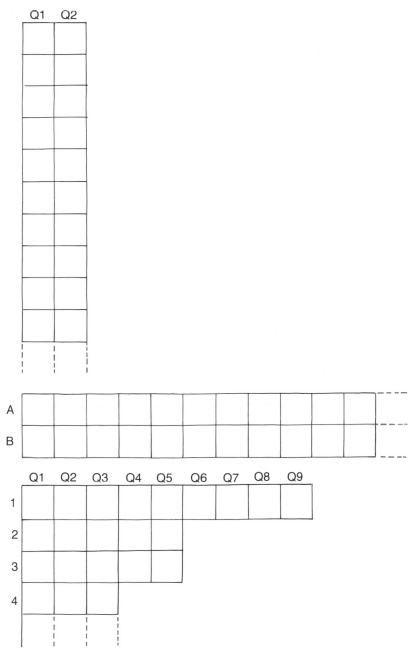

Figure 2.2 Different data matrix shapes. *Top*: Many rows, few columns, e.g. opinion poll with two questions. *Middle*: Few rows, many columns, e.g. comparison of two organisations, A and B. *Bottom*: Non-rectangular or 'ragged', e.g. Q6–Q9 not appropriate to (or answered by) cases 2, 3, 4.

EXERCISES AND POINTS FOR FURTHER DISCUSSION

■ Suggest some examples of the different types of scale that may be used by market researchers other than those given in Table 2.2.

■ Continue Table 2.3 with more examples.

■ To what extent, or in what circumstances, is ascribing numbers to ordinal categories and adding up the results for a set of cases a legitimate operation?

■ How would you define in operational terms the concept of 'news-paper reading'?

Chapter 3

Sampling cases

Chapter 2 has explained that data arise from the process of keeping systematic records on one or more cases – the individuals, households, families, products, events or organisations that are the focus of the researcher's interest. This chapter turns to issues concerning when it is necessary to take samples of cases, how samples are taken, and what are the consequences of doing so.

WHEN SAMPLES ARE TAKEN

In some kinds of research it is not necessary to take or to consider taking a sample. If a company asks a market research agency or a management consultant to investigate a particular problem which is totally internal to the company, then there is only one case – the company – whose characteristics are being measured.

Sometimes, the set of cases that are the focus of the researcher's attention, the **population**, is sufficiently limited in number for him or her to study them all, that is, to take a **census**. This often happens when it is necessary to study organisations in a particular industry or sector of the market. There may only *be* a total of 20 or 30 firms that manufacture a particular product, and the researcher will almost certainly try to contact each one. In other situations, the electronic recording of data enables data to be captured for the total set of a large number of cases. Thus where retail outlets all have laser-scanning equipment, then it is possible to measure the sales of every product, brand and brand variant in every store without having to take a sample of stores, and to use the sample to make estimates of sales for all stores.

It makes sense to take a census of all cases in which the researcher is interested whenever possible. However, the population of cases may be very large, consisting of many thousands, perhaps millions. Thus a study of all households in the UK will involve some 20 million such cases. To study them all would take a very long time, and would be very expensive (although it *is* done every 10 years in the official Census carried out by the

Office of Population Censuses and Surveys). Market researchers, however, have limited funds and results are usually required quickly. In such circumstances, it is necessary to take a **sample** – a subset of cases selected by the researcher for the purpose of being able to draw conclusions about the entire population of cases. Such a procedure may be deemed preferable even where contacting or observing every case would be feasible but nevertheless difficult. Attempts to contact every case may not be totally successful, and the researcher may end up with an incomplete census. This may be less representative than a carefully drawn sample. Researching a small sample carefully may, in fact, result in greater accuracy than either a very large sample or a complete census, since the problems associated with handling a large number of interviewers and a large number of questionnaires may create errors of a greater magnitude than those arising from the sampling process.

BASES FOR SAMPLE SELECTION

The selection of a subset of cases to study may be made on two very different bases:

- purposive,
- representative.

Purposive samples are generated when the selection of cases is made by the researcher using his or her own judgement. The selection may be made on the basis of contacting those cases that are easiest to access, or those that are deemed to be the most important, or those that reflect a variety or extremes, or those that are typical. A researcher may, for example, select those organisations in which he or she already has contacts, or those that are within travelling distance. If the study is of retailers and electronic data are not available, then a sample of retailers may need to be taken; but some have much higher turnovers than others. So the researcher may deliberately choose all the major multiples, and then make a purposive selection of the remainder based on turnover, type of shop and location. The researcher may choose cases on the basis that each one is an example of every type of situation that the researcher wishes to cover. Sometimes the researcher may pick extreme cases, for example, all the most marketing-oriented companies may be selected in order to look at the extent to which, or the manner in which, they use marketing planning procedures. Finally, cases may be chosen because they are 'typical'. Thus particular towns, cities or areas may be chosen because they have typical or average population, industrial, institutional and social structures.

Purposive samples are used, quite legitimately, for exploratory research, for qualitative research, and for a lot of experimental research where the focus is on understanding situations, generating ideas, or evaluating products, ideas for products, advertising or ideas for advertising. These research methods are described in detail in Chapter 5. Purposive sampling is also sometimes used in quantitative research. Thus Nielsen's selection of shops for its Retail Index system includes purposive elements (see Chapter 7).

Representative samples, by contrast, are chosen in such a way that they reproduce the structure and features of the population of cases from which the sample was drawn; in short, that they are a microcosm of the entire set of cases. They are used primarily for quantitative analysis, either to make estimates of the size or frequency of population characteristics, or to measure and test the extent to which the characteristics of cases are related together in the population. Ideally, the results obtained from the sample should be broadly the same as those that would have been obtained had the whole population of cases been studied. The selection of cases is made either using some technique for ensuring that it is done independently of human judgement, or by getting interviewers to make selections, following certain rules that limit the potential for bias.

Provided the selection of cases is undertaken carefully, it is possible to make quite accurate estimates of population characteristics from a very small fraction of them. Thus opinion polling is normally carried out on samples of between 1,000 and 2,000 adults, and these are used to make estimates of the standing of the political parties in the country as a whole with 40 million potential voters. Measures of the size of television audiences for particular channels and programmes are based on the viewing of a representative panel of just 4,700 homes. How this is done is explained in Chapter 7. Clearly, if we take a sample and make estimates from it, there will be errors of various kinds. Some of these sources of error it is possible to minimise or control to some extent; otherwise it may be necessary to rely on a measurement of the likelihood that error will be no greater than a given magnitude. A lot depends on the techniques used for drawing samples, the impact of error from a variety of sources, the sample design, and attempts made by the researcher to control error.

TECHNIQUES FOR DRAWING REPRESENTATIVE SAMPLES

Three main techniques are used for drawing representative samples:

- randomised,
- systematic,
- interviewer selection.

Randomised selection is the selection by chance from a complete list of the population of cases which is to be sampled (the **sampling frame**), using some form of lottery, like taking names out of a hat, tables of random numbers to select numbered units, or computerised random procedures.

Systematic selection creates a rule that determines the selection of the units, thereby removing, or largely removing, human judgement. This may mean taking every nth name from a list at N/n intervals where N is the population size and n is the sample size, or taking every nth house along a street and following some rule about the selection of streets.

Interviewer selection clearly involves human judgement, but this judgement will, normally, be limited in a number of ways, often in combination, by:

- restricting the numbers of types of people to be chosen, that is, interviewers are given quotas, for example, of so many men and women, so many of different age groups,
- restricting the time of day at which interviews may take place, for example, allowing no interviews of males before 5 p.m. to get a cross-section of men in employment, or observing customers in pubs and bars at specific times of the day,
- restricting the area in which the interviewer may make his or her selection, for example, to particular streets or other locations.

Where a complete list has been used, and randomised or systematic selections are made from it, then, so it is argued, human judgement is removed from the selection process and the result is deemed to be a **random sample**. Typically, this means in practice that interviewers are given lists of names and addresses, and they have to make concerted efforts to obtain interviews with the individuals listed, and to take no substitutes. Where the interviewers make the selection, even if that selection is constrained in various ways, then the resulting sample is regarded as a **non-random sample**. Even systematic selections made by the interviewers – for example, by calling at every nth house – are regarded as non-random, since the potential for bias is considerable. Thus the sample will be a sample of the 'at-home-and-available' population, missing out or under-representing those who are normally at work or just often out or away.

The distinction between random and non-random samples often, however, becomes clouded because some or all of these procedures will be mixed and combined in various ways. Thus interviewers may be given lists of names and addresses selected at random, but asked to meet specific quotas from them. Systematic selections may be made from random lists or random selections from systematically drawn lists. Samples are often drawn in several stages, each stage using different combinations of technique.

SOURCES OF ERROR

In reviewing the accuracy of samples, it is helpful to bear in mind that not all errors in a piece of marketing research are necessarily a result of the sampling process. Accordingly, it is helpful to distinguish between:

- non-sampling errors that are unconnected with the procedures used for selecting cases,
- sampling errors.

Non-sampling errors

These errors may arise even if a complete census is taken; they may be put into four main groups:

- response errors,
- interviewer errors,
- non-response errors,
- processing errors.

Where research is based on asking people questions, then response errors may arise where, for one reason or another, respondents give 'wrong' answers. This may be through dishonesty, forgetfulness, faulty memory, unwillingness, or misunderstanding of the questions being asked. Many of these errors arise as a result of poor or inadequate questionnaire design. Putting it the other way round, the potential for such errors to arise can be minimised by careful design of question wording, question formulation and questionnaire layout. This topic is considered in detail in Chapter 4.

In interview surveys, whether face to face or by telephone, interviewers may themselves misunderstand questions or the instructions for filling them in; they may be dishonest, inaccurate, make mistakes or ask questions in a non-standard fashion. Interviewer training, along with field supervision and control, can considerably help to remove the likelihood of such errors, but they will never be entirely eliminated, and there is always the potential for systematic differences between the results obtained by different interviewers. The process of interviewing is considered in more detail in Chapter 5.

In nearly all research there will be missing cases, but in survey research there will always be a degree of non-response because some people will refuse to be interviewed or to complete a questionnaire, some will be ineligible because they turn out not to be part of the survey population, some will terminate the interview or refuse to answer some of the questions, and some will be non-contactable (for example, because they have moved away, died, or are on holiday at the time of the survey). Even where a census is attempted, it will often remain incomplete. The extent of non-response will vary considerably according to the type of research, the topic of the research and, where based on face-to-face interviews, on the experience and training of the interviewers. Calculating the amount of non-response can be confusing since some researchers will, for example, take the proportion of refusals in the sample drawn, others will take refusals and non-contacts as a proportion of those found eligible, and so on.

Processing errors can arise back at the office, particularly at the stage of entering answers to questions onto a computerised database via a keyboard and screen. Agencies sometimes validate these entries by, in effect, entering them twice, and the computer checks to see if the two entries are identical. Alternatively, some agencies check samples of the entries. It is possible, in addition, to apply range checks and logical checks. The various procedures for checking and editing questionnaires are explained in Chapter 8.

There are, then, a number of sources of non-sampling error, and it is important to bear these in mind when interpreting survey results, whether based on a sample or not. The crucial point is that such errors can arise even if a complete census is taken.

Sampling errors

These errors arise from the sampling procedure itself and may be defined as the difference between a sample result and the result that would have been achieved by undertaking a complete census. Such errors arise because of the under- or over-representation of particular types of cases in the sample compared with the population as a whole. If, for example, the cases are individual consumers, then the under- or over-representation of the sexes, ages or social classes will affect the measurements (and, more importantly, the estimates made from them) of a large number of variables. Lack of representation in the appropriate quantities may be a product of two factors:

- systematic error (or bias),
- random error.

Systematic error

Bias arises when the sampling procedures used bring about over- or under-representation of types of cases in the sample which is always in the same direction. This may happen because:

- the selection procedures are not random,
- the selection is made from a list that does not cover the population, or uses a procedure that excludes certain groups,
- non-respondents are not a cross-section of the population.

If the selection procedures are not random, then it means that human judgement has entered into the selection process. For example, interviewers may be asked to choose respondents at some geographical location or to select households in specified streets. The result is likely to be that certain kinds of people or households or organisations are excluded from the sample. Thus choosing respondents in a shopping centre will miss out people who seldom or never go shopping; the selection of households by an interviewer may result in the omission of flats at the tops of stairs.

If the Electoral Register is used to select adults aged 16 or over, then 16 and 17 year olds and many of the 18 year olds will be missing from the list and will be under-represented in the final sample. The use of telephone directories will under-represent certain social groups less likely to be in the telephone book (or those who are ex-directory). Duplication in lists, for example in the *Yellow Pages*, may result in some over-representation. If we try to estimate sales of soap from a sample of private households, then all users in institutions of various kinds will be excluded.

Non-response is a problem for both censuses and samples. For censuses, it means that the enumeration will be incomplete. If large numbers were missing, it would be inappropriate to treat those successfully contacted as a representative 'sample'. For samples, it means that estimates made from the sample will be biased if non-respondents are not themselves representative of the population. If they are representative, then non-response is not so much of a problem; but it may still mean that analyses are made on the basis of too small a sample.

Whatever the reason for the systematic error, the effect will be that all samples that could be drawn from a population will tend to result in the same direction of over- or under-representation of particular values or types of case. The average of all these samples will then not be the same as the real population average or proportion. Thus if we took lots of samples using a procedure that tended to omit working mothers with young children, then all the samples will manifest such under-representation rather than some over-representing them and some under-representing them so that the average of all samples was very close to the real population proportion.

Non-sampling errors cannot be reduced simply by increasing the sample size. If certain kinds of people are not being selected, cannot be contacted, or are not responding, it will not be 'solved' by taking a bigger sample. Indeed, some kinds of errors will increase with more interviewers, more questionnaires and greater data processing requirements. All the researcher can do is minimise the likelihood of bias by using appropriate sample designs. Biases for some variables can be checked, for example against Census data or data from other sources. Sometimes attempts are made to discover the characteristics of non-responders: for example, by sending out interviewers to non-respondents to a postal survey, taking 'late' responders as typical of non-responders, or gaining demographic data from the results of another survey that the non-responders *have* taken part in.

Random error

If we take a number of random, unbiased samples from the same population, there will almost certainly be a degree of fluctuation from one sample to another. Over a large number of samples, such errors will tend to cancel out, so that the average of such samples will be close to the real population value. However, we usually take only one sample, and even a sample that has used unbiased selection procedures will seldom be exactly representative of the population from which it was drawn. Each sample will, in short, exhibit a degree of error. Such error is often called 'sampling error', but it would be clearer to think of it as 'random sampling error' to distinguish it from bias (which some statisticians and some textbooks, confusingly, categorise as 'non-sampling' error).

Unlike bias, which affects the general sample composition and relates to each variable being measured in unknown ways, random sampling error will differ from variable to variable. The reason for this is that the extent of such error will depend on two factors:

- the size of the sample – the bigger the sample, the less the random sampling error (but by a declining amount),
- the variability in the population for that particular variable – a sample used to estimate a variable that varies widely in the population will show more random sampling error than for a variable that does not.

These two factors are used as a basis for calculating the likely degree of variability in a sample of a given size for a particular variable. This, in turn, is used as an input for establishing with a specified probability the range of accuracy of sample estimates, or that sample findings are only random sampling fluctuations from a population of cases in which the findings are untrue. These calculations are explained in Chapter 6.

Total survey error

Any research that is based on addressing questions to people and recording their answers risks error resulting from the respondents themselves and from interviewers, where these are used, in addition to those kinds of error that arise in any research from data-handling, and from inadequacies of sampling. Total survey error is the addition of all these sources of error, both sampling and non-sampling. It is difficult to estimate what the total survey error is in any one survey, and it will tend to vary from question to question. What is certainly true is that the error that results from random sampling fluctuations accounts for only a very small proportion of the total survey error. Assael and Keon (1982), for example, estimate that it is perhaps only about 5 per cent. For a full discussion, see Kish (1965, Chapter 13, 'Biases and nonsampling errors') or Churchill (1987, Chapter 11).

Errors of various kinds can always be reduced by spending more money, for example, on more interviewer training and supervision, on random sampling techniques, on pilot testing, or on getting a higher response rate. However, the reduction in error has to be traded off against the extra cost involved. Furthermore, errors are often interrelated, so that attempts to reduce one kind of error may actually increase another, for example, minimising the non-response errors by persuading more reluctant respondents may well increase response error. Non-sampling errors tend to be pervasive, not well-behaved, and do not decrease (indeed may increase) with the size of the sample. It is sometimes even difficult to see whether they cause under- or over-estimation of population characteristics. There is, in addition, the paradox that the more efficient the sample design is in controlling random sampling fluctuations, the more important in proportion become bias and non-sampling errors.

SAMPLE DESIGN

Sample design needs to take account not only of sampling and non-sampling errors, but also of very practical considerations like cost, speed, feasibility and credibility to clients. Textbooks that cover sampling tend to distinguish between random and non-random samples, the former allowing a calculation to be made of a non-zero probability that any one unit will be selected. They then, typically, give a list of different types of each. Thus random samples will usually include simple random samples, stratified samples, cluster samples, and multi-stage samples. Quota samples are the main example of non-random sample, but random route, random location and purposive samples are also usually included in this category. The problem with this 'shopping-list' type of approach is that most samples are, in practice, a mixture of different elements, and it is seldom possible to classify any particular sample into one of the categories. Furthermore, there are varying degrees of 'independence' from human judgement, so the distinction is not always as clearcut as the theory suggests. Moreover, neither practitioners nor theorists agree amongst themselves as to which particular sample selection procedures count as 'random'.

What statisticians do tend to agree, if not insist, upon is that the 'theory' of statistical inference (which is explained in Chapter 6) is based on the assumption that the kind of sample drawn is a **simple random sample**. Such samples use either randomised or systematic selection techniques (and some purists would argue that systematic procedures are not strictly 'random') from a complete list of the population of cases, giving all cases to be sampled an *equal* chance of being selected. Thus if we select a sample of 300 names from a list of 3,000 students at a university, then each student has a one in ten chance of being selected.

However, in practice, simple random samples are seldom used. Three key reasons may be advanced:

- They require a sampling frame for the total population of cases to be sampled – this could mean taking random selections from lists containing maybe 40 million people, perhaps on a regular basis.
- If face-to-face interviewing is to be carried out (or even questionnaires or diaries left personally for respondent completion), the interviews would be scattered throughout the length and breadth of the geographical area to be sampled, and interviewers would have a considerable amount of travelling to do.
- The resulting samples still may not accurately reflect the structure of the population of cases in respect of a number of variables whose incidence or size is already known – in other words, simple random samples do not utilise data that are already available on the population structure.

Departures from simple random sampling are a result of the application of one or more of three main procedures:

- stratification,
- imposing quotas,
- clustering.

Stratification is a procedure that utilises information already contained in sampling frames in order to construct a sample that is guaranteed to be representative in respect of that information. Thus if a list of individuals contains information on the sex of each person, then the proportion of males to females is known. Suppose it is a list of members of a golf club, and 60 per cent are male. We can then ensure that 60 per cent of our sample is male. Thus if we wanted a sample of 100 members, we could select 60 men at random and 40 women at random (using either randomised or systematic techniques). If the list also contained data on age, and we knew that 30 per cent of members were aged 16–30, we could select 30 individuals from this age group (again at random) and the appropriate numbers from other age groups. If we stratified by sex *and* age together, then our 30 individuals aged 16–30 could be selected on the basis of 60 per cent (that is 18) men and 40 per cent (12) women. Provided the proportions in the sample are the same as the proportions in the population (usually called 'proportional stratification'), then the resulting sample is likely to be *more* accurate and representative than the simple random sample because some of the sources of variation have been eliminated. However, it does require an accurate sampling frame and one that contains information on the factors we want to use for stratification.

Sometimes the stratification is disproportionate. Suppose our golf club contained only 10 per cent women and we wanted to be able to compare the views of the women with those of the men on the facilities provided to members. A proportionately stratified sample of 100 would give only 10 women – not enough on which to base an analysis of responses to a questionnaire, so we might select 50 women and 50 men, that is, deliberately oversample the women. This would enable us to make our comparisons. But if we wanted to estimate the extent of certain views or characteristics overall, then the answers of the men would have to be upweighted and the answers of the women downweighted to their original proportions. This type of weighting is described in some detail in Chapter 6.

While stratification is normally combined with random methods of selection from a list, when there is no such list, then **quotas** are usually applied. Quotas are predetermined proportions of respondents to be sampled from different subgroups. They are normally applied to each interviewer, who has to find and interview respondents who meet specified requirements, for example, a male, aged 20–29 in social class C2. As with stratification, the use of quotas *imposes* a structure on the sample. Usually that structure will be proportionate to known population structures. However, since there is no list, these proportions must be determined from other sources which will typically include data from the Census (which is, of course, a complete list of the residents of a country), or from other surveys that are well respected and which use random, not quota, selection procedures.

Where interviewing is to be face to face, it makes sense for each interviewer's respondents or potential respondents to be geographically concentrated in order to minimise travel time. Accordingly, it is normal to **cluster** interviewing in limited geographical areas. Market research agencies do this by selecting (usually at random) a fixed number of **sampling points** and allocating one interviewer to each. These will usually be parliamentary constituencies, electoral wards, polling districts or postcode districts/sectors. The sampling points are usually carefully chosen to be a representative cross-section of types of area. Normally the selection will be stratified by a number of variables. This is possible because although there may be no lists of individual respondents that contain data on variables that can be used for stratification, there will be lists of polling districts or whatever area is to be used as a sampling point, and there will usually be plenty of information about each.

The key stratification factor used by most market research agencies is region. Thus if the selection of sampling points is 'stratified by region', then the selection done within each region is such that the number of sampling points in each reflects its population size. This keeps the sample in line with the regional distribution of the population. Further stratification may be by degree of 'rurality' so that appropriate proportions of urban, rural and mixed sampling points are selected.

Because equal numbers of interviews are given to each interviewer at each sampling point, the selection of the points within the region will usually be made with 'probability proportionate to size'. This means that sampling points with more people in them are given a higher probability of selection, thereby offsetting the lower probability of households or individuals in the larger sampling points being selected.

The selection of sampling points will often be carried out in two or more stages. Thus the first stage may be to sample parliamentary constituencies from the population of 635 constituencies (there are a further 17 in Northern Ireland). The selection will probably be stratified by type of constituency – typically the proportion of Conservative or Labour vote in order to get a balance of political complexion. Those selected may constitute a 'master sample' of first-stage units that are used for all future survey work. Thus an agency's fieldwork may be concentrated in 200 constituencies and all samples are drawn from these as required.

In the second stage, within the constituencies selected, polling districts may be subsampled, usually with probability proportionate to size and stratified by region, so that the number of polling districts reflects the regional population size. The polling districts may then be used as sampling points and the interviewer is given a list of names and addresses in that district if it is a random sample, or may be given quotas to fill if it is a quota sample.

While, as explained earlier, the effect of stratification is to reduce the random sampling error, the effect of clustering is to increase it. How great the increase depends on how 'tight' the clustering is. For small-area clusters, the error will be greater than for larger areas. In practice, the reduction in error due to stratification is very limited since it is only the selection of sampling points that is stratified, not the selection of individuals or households within them. Accordingly, the departure from simple random sampling brought about by the stratified selection of clusters has the effect, overall, of increasing the sampling error. This may be taken into account in the calculation of estimates and tests against the null hypotheses by applying a design factor. These factors are explained in Chapter 6.

Random and quota sampling

Random samples

The main advantage of random sampling is its accuracy. Compared with sampling techniques that are not strictly random, random samples:

- minimise bias in the selection procedure,
- minimise the variability between samples,
- will, with a measurable degree of error, reproduce *all* the character-

istics of the population from which the sample was drawn, not just
those selected as quota controls,

- will, where samples are drawn at regular intervals, reflect any changes
  that are taking place in the population,
- allow probability theory to be applied to calculate the chances that the
  sample result was not a random sampling fluctuation.

There are, however, disadvantages to random samples:

- They are slower and more expensive than non-random techniques.
- They need a sampling frame.
- The sample achieved will almost certainly be smaller than the sample
  drawn.

Surveys using quota samples can often complete fieldwork in two to
three days: for random samples, it is likely to be two to three weeks. This
can be important when quick result are needed. Random samples are,
furthermore, an expensive process in terms of administration and interviewer costs. The sample drawing procedures can be quite complex, while
interviewers may be instructed to make at least three callbacks in the even-
ings or at weekends before recording a 'non-contact'. This all adds to the
cost. Random samples can easily be twice the cost of quota samples of the
same size. However, some statisticians argue that, because such samples are
more accurate, it is more cost-effective (in terms of accuracy per £1 spent
on fieldwork) to design a smaller, high-quality random sample than a larger
quota sample (Wolfe 1982: 5).

Random samples need a sampling frame, that is, a complete list of the
population that is to be sampled (normally within selected sampling
points). Ideally, such lists should:

- be adequate, that is, cover exactly the population which is to be
  surveyed,
- be complete, that is, have no cases missing,
- not duplicate any entries,
- be up to date.

Sometimes such lists do exist, for example, a list of all branches of a
major multiple retailer from which a sample is to be drawn. To obtain
names and addresses of consumers within sampling points, there are two
main sources in the UK:

- the Registers of Electors,
- the Post Office Postcode Address File.

The Registers of Electors have been the standard sampling frame for
decades, but there are problems associated with them. They are completed
every October and published the following February, so they are already

four months out of date. They contain the names and addresses of all British subjects aged 18 and over who are entitled to vote and are registered. No information about age and sex of the person is available (other than first names). Many of the market research agencies take 'adults' to mean 16 and over, so 16–18 year olds will be missing from the frame. Special procedures are often used to obtain a sample of that age group. Also, many of the 18 year olds will be missing from the lists; so too will people who are not entitled to vote (e.g. non-British subjects), or who are not registered. While the Registers are readily accessible, their validity is constantly affected by deaths and removals. Up to 12 per cent of electors are no longer at their registered address by the time the Registers come up for renewal. Non registrations are almost certainly higher since the Poll Tax was introduced.

The Postcode Address File covers some 22 million addresses in 1.5 million postcodes within 8,900 sectors within 2,700 districts within 120 postcode areas. The file tends to be more complete and more up to date than the Registers of Electors, and is good for sampling households in a multi-stage process. However, for sampling individuals, it is necessary to have some procedure for selecting individuals within a household.

Other kinds of sampling frame include:

- membership lists of clubs, associations, societies or other kinds of organisation,
- registers of various kinds, for example, the *Kompass Directory*,
- frames that have been constructed from market intelligence or from surveys that have been carried out on a regular basis.

One 'solution' to an inadequate sampling frame is to redefine the population of cases being studied. Thus it is known that certain kinds of people are missing from the Registers of Electors. If the problem is ignored, then the survey population is being redefined as only those addresses appearing in the Registers. A sample that uses the telephone directories can define its population as all telephone subscribers. It is common for market research agencies to exclude outlying areas and sparsely populated parts of the country, for example, in the North of Scotland. Again, the survey population is being redefined.

Perhaps the most serious drawback of random samples, however, arises from the fact that there is always a degree of non-response. There will always be non-response, whatever method of selection is used, and at least the response rate is known for random samples. However, it does mean that the sample which is drawn (the target sample) is seldom the sample which is achieved. For ad hoc surveys, the response rate will typically be 60–70 per cent of the sample drawn. Provided those not responding are not significantly different in key respects from those who do, the size of the achieved sample may simply have to be lived with, and the response rate reported as part of the results.

For continuous market measurement purposes, however, this procedure may not be adequate because results are to be used for making estimates of purchases, sales and so on, not only for the population as a whole, but for a wide range of subgroups within it. Consequently, all these subgroups must be represented in appropriate numbers so that estimates can be made for that subgroup. Furthermore, response rates where people are asked to join a panel will tend to be considerably lower than for independent surveys.

The problem may be approached in one of two main ways:

- *Oversample* so that the achieved sample size is the one originally desired. A variation on this is to continue drawing samples and obtaining interviews until the required sample size is reached. This is fine as long as those not responding are not significantly different from those who are, because this procedure will emphasise their significance.
- *Apply quotas* Interviewers may be given lists of names and addresses drawn at random, but be asked to fill quotas by sex, age and social class. While this does mean that, in respect of the quotas, the sample is of the desired composition (and overall size), if interviewers are given long lists from which to select a few respondents, and particularly if no callbacks are made, then this procedure is no better than some of the quota sampling techniques described below.

Quota samples

Quota sampling is generally regarded by statisticians and the textbooks on market research as 'non-probability' or 'non-random' sampling. This is mainly because the final selection of respondents is made by the interviewer, so human judgement enters into the selection process. The interviewer, instead of being issued with a pre-selected list of names and addresses, is given an assignment in the form of a quota. This might, for example, require the interviewer to find, usually at a fixed sampling point, 20 adults aged 16 and over:

- 10 of them female,
- 10 aged 45 or over and 10 aged 16–45,
- 8 in social class ABC1,
- 12 in social class C2DE.

In this case, sex, age and social class would be described as the 'quota controls'. These controls may be interlaced (or 'interlocked') as in Figure 3.1. While this ensures that, for example, not all ten under-45s are in social class ABC1, the interlacing can get quite complicated, and independent quotas are often applied. The selection of which variables to use as quota

		Social class		
		ABC1	C2DE	**Total**
Age	Under 45	3	7	10
	45+	5	5	10
	Total	8	12	20

Figure 3.1 Interlaced quota controls of age and social class

controls depends on which variables the researcher thinks are most strongly associated with the variables being estimated or tested. The usual quotas are on sex, age and social class, because these are associated with many other characteristics, behaviours and attitudes. However, for some products like double-glazing, type of property or tenancy may be more relevant.

The advantages of quota samples are that:

- they are quicker, cheaper and relatively more simple to administer than random samples,
- they do not require a sampling frame,
- the sample size and sample composition in terms of the quota controls are always achieved.

The speed of quota sampling is derived from two sources. First, for in-home quotas, no callbacks are required, and for street quotas, there is no travelling time between interviews. Second, the procedures for drawing the samples are very simple and there is no need to give interviewers lists of names and addresses. In terms of cost per interview, quota samples therefore work out a lot cheaper. Furthermore, no sampling frame is required – however, data on the structure of the population being sampled are needed in order to be able to set the size of the quotas. Since each interviewer continues until his or her quotas of sexes, ages and social classes are filled, the exact size and basic structure of the sample can be determined in advance.

There are, however, a number of disadvantages:

- There is considerable potential for bias.
- There is more variability between samples.
- The application of probability theory to such samples is questionable.
- They impose a structure on the sample.

Bias arises from two main sources: the interviewer and the high (and generally unrecorded) level of non-response. It is normally left to the inter-viewer how he or she goes about finding respondents who meet quota requirements in the sampling point. This leaves open the possibility of the interviewer avoiding certain types of locations or types of people, and for there to be systematic differences between one interviewer and another. Thus one interviewer may consciously or unconsciously avoid approaching people in groups, while another may avoid people who look like they are in a hurry.

It is, furthermore, often forgotten that there is considerable non-response when either street or in-home quotas are used. On the surface, there is no problem of non-response since all quotas are filled, or mostly filled. However, this is only because the non-response is undeclared and, effectively, substitution is being allowed. People who cannot be contacted or who refuse at the first attempt are excluded. The effective response rate in quota sampling is unknown, but certainly huge. The average random sample survey achieves a response rate of only about 25 per cent at first calls. This is boosted by subsequent callbacks to 60–80 per cent. So quota samples, at best, probably have an effective response rate of 25–30 per cent.

Work on actual surveys suggests that even high-quality quota samples produce at least twice as much variability from one sample to another than do random samples. The implication, according to some researchers, is that calculations made of the extent of variability based on simple random samples need to be multiplied by a factor (called a **design factor**) of not less than 2.5. Others will argue that, because quota sampling is non-random, the application of probability theory to such samples is not legitimate, since the probability of inclusion in the sample for any one case is unknown. In practice, agencies do not usually produce any calculation of sampling variability unless clients specifically ask for them – and clients seldom do.

The structure imposed on the sample by the quotas will have been derived from data that reflect the population of cases as a whole. This, in turn, means that these quotas will not reflect the different composition of the sampling points, nor any changes that have taken place since the original data were collected. Thus social classes A and B may be over-represented in a sampling point in a depressed mining village, and under-represented in expensive, fashionable areas. It can even be difficult to fill some quotas in some of the sampling points.

Some agencies have attempted to get around these limitations of quota samples without the considerable additional expense of probability random sampling by using **random location sampling**, or **random route sampling**. In both cases, quotas on social class (and sometimes additionally on age) are dropped, although quotas on sex and working status are retained since the latter reflect the probability of selection rather than the survey variables.

Thus, women and individuals not in paid employment are more likely to be at home (or in a shopping centre). In place of quotas on social class, the interviewer's discretion over who to interview is restricted in one of two ways. In the case of random location sampling, a sub-selection of streets chosen at random within the sampling point and with probability proportionate to size is made, and the interviewer is confined to locating respondents in those streets. In the case of random route sampling, the interviewer is given a random starting point and then told in which direction to turn at road junctions, but taking every nth house.

The aim of both of these forms of sampling is that the sample chosen is representative of the particular sampling point selected rather than in accordance with quota controls that may not reflect the area.

Where telephone interviewing is to take place, there is no need to cluster into sampling points because all parts of the country can be reached from a central location. Furthermore, it is easy to make a random selection from the telephone directories. However, since not everybody has a telephone, it may be necessary to redefine the population; alternatively, some agencies impose quotas to derive samples that match the demographic characteristics of the total population. The assumption here, however, is that those people with given demographic characteristics that are included in the directories do not differ in terms of the market measurement variables from those not included. Only for some variables may this be a valid assumption.

SAMPLE SIZE

Determining the size of sample that is needed for a particular piece of research is a complex issue that needs to take account of a large number of factors. Textbooks tend to ignore these factors, taking instead a statistical approach which calculates the size of sample required in order to achieve a specified degree of sampling error and a minimum level of accuracy. The problem with such calculations is that they are based on the notion of simple random samples. These, as we have seen, are in fact seldom taken, although adjustments can be made for stratified random sampling. Perhaps more importantly, however, such calculations fail to take account of more practical issues, for example:

- Larger samples tend to cost more and to take more time, and there may be a limit to the size of sample that can be afforded.
- How big a sample is needed depends on the variability of population characteristics and on the purpose of the research.

If the population characteristics being measured vary very little, then small samples will suffice for making quite accurate statements about the population. Where such characteristics vary widely, then larger samples are required. Unfortunately, of course, it is often unknown beforehand what the variability is. If the purpose of the research is to generate ideas for new products from a sample of product category users, then a sample of 30 or so may well be adequate. For any kind of quantitative analysis, a minimum of 100 is needed even to be able to calculate straightforward percentages on each variable. If, as is often the case, analyses need to be performed on subgroups, then the smallest subgroup must contain sufficient cases for reliable estimates to be achieved. If the variables are to be **crosstabulated** (see Chapter 6), then much larger samples are required, say 300 or so at a minimum. Most market research companies, however, doing a series of numerical breakdowns of variables for clients, tend to take about 1,000 as a minimum sample size. Few samples for **ad hoc research** will be much above 3,000. Where research is continuous and based on different individuals each time, it may be possible, however over the course of a year, to accumulate samples of 30,000 or more.

CONTROLLING ERROR

In practice, market research agencies make all reasonable attempts (within the limits imposed by cost and time constraints) to minimise, measure the impact, or make some estimate of non-sampling errors and of bias in the sampling procedure. Thus, as far as response errors are concerned, agencies may:

- pilot-test questionnaires in order to check for misunderstandings of questions,
- analyse tendencies to overclaim or underclaim for certain kinds of consumer behaviour – for example, the tendency to underclaim the consumption of alcohol, or to overclaim television watching,
- use 'aided-recall' techniques (prompted lists) to help respondents remember products that they may have purchased and forgotten about, or radio programmes that they forgot they had listened to,
- use questioning techniques that minimise the effort respondents need to make.

These techniques are considered in more detail when we look at questionnaire design in the next chapter.

To minimise interviewer error, agencies will often:

- set rigorous training standards for interviewers,
- monitor the process of interviewing by doing 'backchecks' – calling or telephoning respondents who have already been interviewed to check that the interview was carried out properly, or sending supervisors to accompany interviewers on a regular sample basis,
- make computer analyses of questionnaire errors to identify interviewers who may need retraining or reminding of particular points.

To minimise errors resulting from non-response, agencies do one or more of several things:

- For interview surveys, interviewers may be asked to make a specified number of callbacks if the respondent was not at home on the first call. Three or four such callbacks may be made, ideally at different times and days of the week.
- Interviewers may make an appointment by telephone with the respondent.
- Self-completed questionnaires may be left where no contact has been made.
- Monetary incentives or gifts may sometimes help to improve the response rate.
- Interviewers may get a 'foot-in-the-door' by having respondents comply with some small request before presenting them with the larger survey.
- Non-respondents to a postal survey may be sent interviewers to persuade them to complete the questionnaire, or they may be sent further reminders.

Processing errors will be minimised by careful editing and checking of the questionnaires in addition to the use of data entry validation procedures.

Market research agencies will try to minimise bias with carefully constructed sample designs that use random procedures wherever possible, or by imposing restrictions on interviewer choices where random procedures cannot be used. These sample designs were described earlier. Biases will still remain, however, and sometimes these are known. Thus, it may be known that there are too many women in the sample, or too few men aged 20–24, compared with known population proportions. Many agencies will make corrections to the data to adjust for these biases by 'weighting' them (see Chapter 6).

SUMMARY

Where it is not feasible, economic or practical to study every case for the purpose of undertaking any particular piece of research, a selection of cases will have to be made. This may be done on a purposive or on a representative basis. Purposive samples are selections made by the researcher and are used mainly for exploratory or for qualitative research. Representative samples are chosen by randomised or systematic techniques, or by an interviewer following certain rules, and are used for quantitative research where the objective is either to estimate the size or frequency of characteristics, or the relationships between them, in the population of cases from which the sample was drawn.

The errors that arise when taking samples are a combination of those errors that might happen irrespective of the procedures used for selecting cases and will occur even when census studies are carried out, and those errors that arise from the over- or under-representation of types of case when sample selections are made. Sampling errors include both bias and variance. Statistical measures based on probability theory that are used to estimate 'sampling error' in fact refer only to variance, and, strictly speaking, only to those samples where random selection of the final cases is made. Variance, furthermore, accounts for only a very small proportion of total survey error.

In designing samples, the researcher will almost certainly want to make use of procedures for stratification, imposing quotas or clustering. Clustering is needed only where face-to-face interviews are to be conducted. The selection of clusters to use as sampling points is nearly always on a random basis, but is usually combined with stratification. The final selection of cases may be random or quota, and both procedures have their strengths and limitations. For telephone and postal surveys, no clustering is required and there is no need to use interviewer selection of respondents. However, where the sampling frame used to get telephone numbers or postal addresses is felt to be inadequate, quotas may be imposed, even if the selection from the list was random. Whether this procedure counts as a 'random' sample is an issue that will either be hotly debated – or send people to sleep!

In the final analysis, market research agencies go to considerable lengths to minimise and control both non-sampling and sampling errors. The attention paid by statisticians and textbooks to measuring the incidence of sampling variance is probably misplaced.

EXERCISES AND POINTS FOR FURTHER DISCUSSION

■   Identify the relevant population for the following projects. Decide whether sampling is necessary and if so suggest an appropriate sample design:

   (a) A manufacturer of domestic lawnmowers in Scotland wants to know the proportion of households that own various types of lawnmower.

   (b) A hospital administrator wants to find out if the single parents working in the hospital have a higher rate of absenteeism than parents who are not single.

   (c) A company is about to launch a new product which is a vibrating massage cushion for use by motorists. The manufacturer wants to know what kinds of motorists are likely to consider purchasing the product.

■   Use the table of random numbers (Table 3.1) to select a sample of n = 15 without replacement from a population of N = 73.

■   ABC Products has 200 workers whose output in units per week is measured and recorded on a card (Table 3.2). The cards are numbered 001 to 200. Use Table 3.1 to draw 10 numbers at random between 001 and 200. Use the outputs of these employees to calculate the average output of that sample. Compare this with the results of a sample drawn systematically (i.e. every N/n = 200/10 = 20th name after a random start between 1 and 20).

■   Quota sampling is universally condemned by statisticians, but extensively used by practitioners of marketing research. Why is this?

■   Develop a logical argument explaining why random sampling error will be *less* for proportionate stratified sampling than for simple random sampling.

Table 3.1 Random numbers

85967	73152	14511	85285	36009	95892	36962	67835	63314	50162
07483	51453	11649	86348	76431	81594	95848	36738	25014	15460
96283	01898	61414	83525	04231	13604	75339	11730	85423	60698
49174	12074	98551	37895	93547	24769	09404	76548	05393	96770
97366	39941	21225	93629	19574	71565	33413	56087	40875	13351
90474	41469	16812	81542	81652	45554	27931	93994	22375	00953
28599	64109	09497	76235	41383	31555	12639	00619	22909	29563
25254	16210	89717	65997	82667	74624	36348	44018	64732	93589
28785	02760	24359	99410	77319	73408	58993	61098	04393	48245
84725	86576	86944	93296	10081	82454	76810	52975	10324	15457
41059	66456	47679	66810	15941	84602	14493	65515	19251	41642
67434	41045	82830	47617	36932	46728	71183	36345	41404	81110
72766	68816	37643	19959	57550	49620	98480	25640	67257	18671
92079	46784	66125	94932	64451	29275	57669	66658	30818	58353
29187	40350	62533	73603	34075	16451	42885	03448	37390	96328
74220	17612	65522	80607	19184	64164	66962	82310	18163	63495
03786	02407	06098	92917	40434	60602	82175	04470	78754	90775
75085	55558	15520	27038	25471	76107	90832	10819	56797	33751
09161	33015	19155	11715	00551	24909	31894	37774	37953	78837
75707	48992	64998	87080	39333	00767	45637	12538	67439	94914
21333	48660	31288	00086	79889	75532	28704	62844	92337	99695
65626	50061	42539	14812	48895	11196	34335	60492	70650	51108
84380	07389	87891	76255	89604	41372	10837	66992	93183	56920
46479	32072	80083	63868	70930	89654	05359	47196	12452	38234
59847	97197	55147	76639	76971	55928	36441	95141	42333	67483

Table 3.1 continued

31416	11231	27904	57383	31852	69137	96667	14315	01007	31929
82066	83436	67914	21465	99605	83114	97885	74440	99622	87912
01850	42782	39202	18582	46214	99228	79541	78298	75404	63648
32315	89276	89582	87138	16165	15984	21466	63830	30475	74729
59388	42703	55198	80380	67067	97155	34160	85019	03527	78140
58089	27632	50987	91373	07736	20436	96130	73483	85332	24384
61705	57285	30392	23660	75841	21931	04295	00875	09114	32101
18914	98982	60199	99275	41967	35208	30357	76772	92656	62318
11965	94089	34803	48941	69709	16784	44642	89761	66864	62803
85251	48111	80936	81781	93248	67877	16498	31924	51315	79921
66121	96986	84844	93873	46352	92183	51152	85878	30490	15974
53972	96642	24199	58080	35450	03482	66953	49521	63719	57615
14509	16594	78883	43222	23093	58645	60257	89250	63266	90858
37700	07688	65533	72126	23611	93993	01848	03910	38552	17472
85466	59392	72722	15473	73295	49759	56157	60477	83284	56367
52969	55863	42312	67842	05673	91878	82738	36563	79540	61935
42744	68315	17514	02878	97291	74851	42725	57894	81434	62041
26140	13336	67726	61876	29971	99294	96664	52817	90039	53211
95589	56319	14563	24071	06916	59555	18195	32280	79357	04224
39113	13217	59999	49952	83021	47709	53105	19295	88318	41626
41392	17622	18994	98283	07249	52289	24209	91139	30715	06604
54684	53645	79246	70183	87731	19185	08541	33519	07223	97413
89442	61001	36658	57444	95388	36682	38052	46719	09428	94012
36751	16778	54888	15357	68003	43564	90976	58904	40512	07725

Table 3.2 Employee output for ABC Products

Employee	Output	Employee	Output	Employee	Output	Employee	Output	Employee	Output
001.	30	041.	59	081.	65	121.	47	161.	62
002.	38	042.	56	082.	42	122.	64	162.	29
003.	33	043.	65	083.	73	123.	55	163.	37
004.	49	044.	50	084.	44	124.	50	164.	27
005.	33	045.	54	085.	54	125.	65	165.	36
006.	43	046.	61	086.	67	126.	53	166.	43
007.	60	047.	57	087.	49	127.	32	167.	30
008.	31	048.	55	088.	38	128.	44	168.	41
009.	34	049.	26	089.	59	129.	38	169.	59
010.	61	050.	41	090.	42	130.	37	170.	63
011.	49	051.	64	091.	46	131.	53	171.	55
012.	64	052.	25	092.	30	132.	44	172.	32
013.	62	053.	28	093.	64	133.	27	173.	32
014.	37	054.	49	094.	28	134.	40	174.	31
015.	25	055.	53	095.	64	135.	43	175.	35
016.	38	056.	25	096.	46	136.	45	176.	33
017.	65	057.	33	097.	59	137.	33	177.	58
018.	56	058.	28	098.	60	138.	60	178.	31
019.	55	059.	25	099.	46	139.	62	179.	38
020.	43	060.	60	100.	27	140.	30	180.	29
021.	58	061.	34	101.	59	141.	51	181.	43
022.	38	062.	25	102.	43	142.	49	182.	56
023.	71	063.	61	103.	50	143.	31	183.	53
024.	47	064.	42	104.	51	144.	29	184.	64
025.	65	065.	48	105.	39	145.	36	185.	38
026.	54	066.	57	106.	59	146.	50	186.	36
027.	74	067.	26	107.	33	147.	54	187.	59
028.	36	068.	55	108.	60	148.	38	188.	68
029.	62	069.	36	109.	26	149.	60	189.	26
030.	31	070.	33	110.	72	150.	65	190.	72
031.	48	071.	63	111.	25	151.	36	191.	29
032.	35	072.	48	112.	44	152.	25	192.	32
033.	26	073.	37	113.	58	153.	28	193.	73
034.	62	074.	49	114.	49	154.	56	194.	63
035.	51	075.	46	115.	31	155.	51	195.	69
036.	67	076.	31	116.	56	156.	53	196.	57
037.	30	077.	26	117.	37	157.	40	197.	38
038.	57	078.	28	118.	66	158.	33	198.	50
039.	50	079.	63	119.	55	159.	26	199.	60
040.	62	080.	37	120.	66	160.	42	200.	28

Chapter 4

The instruments of data capture

In Chapter 2 it was suggested that data arise from any form of systematic record keeping. This chapter will explore the different ways in which various data capture instruments may be used by market researchers to create such records. The focus is on the instruments themselves, not on the social or organisational context in which the data capture takes place – that is data collection. Data collection techniques are considered in detail in Chapter 5. Most marketing research uses questionnaires at some stage, and the questionnaire as a data capture instrument is the focus of the first major section. Other sections consider diaries and devices, both manual and electronic, for recording observations, events and discussions.

QUESTIONNAIRES

Asking people questions and systematically noting their responses has been a method of conducting social research in Britain since the 1790s (see Kent 1981, for a historical account of social research in Britain). Questionnaires in marketing, certainly in the textbook literature, tend to be associated exclusively with survey research, but in fact may be used in a number of different data collection contexts, as we shall see in the next chapter. Some market researchers, indeed, refer rather loosely to all documents from the field as 'questionnaires', although we will be distinguishing questionnaires from diaries, manual recording sheets, and interview guides, which are also used 'in the field'.

A **questionnaire** is a document used as a data capture instrument and which does two things: it lists all the questions a researcher wishes to address to each respondent, and it provides space or some mechanism for recording the responses. Lists of questions (and the responses to them) that are held in electronic form are treated separately later in this chapter under electronic recording devices. Where documents are *not* used for recording purposes, but are simply lists of questions, then they, too, are considered separately as 'interview guides' used in in-depth interviews. These are discussed in Chapter 5.

Types of questionnaire

Questionnaires can take many forms, but a key dimension along which they vary is the extent to which they are structured. At one extreme, an **unstructured questionnaire** may be just a checklist of open-ended questions with spaces for writing in the replies in the respondent's own words, producing **qualitative data**. At the other extreme are fully **structured questionnaires** which:

- list *all* the questions to be asked,
- put them in a logical sequence,
- specify the precise wording that is to be used,
- provide predefined categories for recording the replies.

The idea of such questionnaires is that all the questions are standardised and asked in the same way so that responses from different individuals can be counted up and compared. In practice, questionnaires are often a mixture of structured, semi-structured and unstructured elements, so that only a few of the questions give rise to qualitative data. Semi-structured questions arise where respondents are asked to write in specific pieces of information which then need to be classified and coded back in the office after the interviews have taken place.

Questionnaires, whatever the degree of structuring, are of two main kinds:

- those that are completed by the respondent (self-completed questionnaires),
- those that are completed by the interviewer on behalf of the respondent (interviewer-completed questionnaires).

Self-completed questionnaires are usually sent and (hopefully) returned through the post, so are often referred to as postal or mailed questionnaires. However, they may be personally delivered by an interviewer, either to be returned by post or to be collected at the next visit.

Interviewer-completed questionnaires, sometimes called 'interview schedules', are generally used in face-to-face interviews, either at the respondent's home or place of work, or in a public place such as a shopping precinct or airport lounge where potential respondents may be approached and asked if they would help with a survey by answering a few questions. However, the use of the telephone for marketing research is increasing, and questions may be addressed using that medium. Answers may be recorded on a questionnaire or may be entered directly into a computer.

The distinction between self-completed and interviewer-completed questionnaires has implications for questionnaire design, which are considered later. However, in some situations the two kinds of questionnaire may be mixed: for example, in formal interviews, respondents may be given sheets or items to complete for themselves, or, in a postal survey, interviewers may be sent to non-respondents.

Types of question

All questionnaires, whether self-completed or interview schedule, will comprise one of, or some mixture of, two main types of question:

- open-ended (or unstructured),
- set-choice (or structured).

Open-ended questions leave respondents free to formulate replies in their own words. The interviewer (or the respondent in a self-completed questionnaire) writes in the answer, usually word for word. Normally there will be one or more blank lines for this purpose. Open-ended questions tend to be used where:

- the researcher is unsure about what the responses could be,
- the researcher wants to introduce a topic by getting the respondent to formulate his or her own thoughts and words before more detailed questioning takes place (this avoids pre-judging responses with fixed alternatives),
- the possible responses are too many to list.

Open-ended questions can be used for factual responses, for example, 'What is the name of the shop where you last purchased toothpaste?' Alternatively, they may be used for recording attitudes, opinions, images or beliefs in the respondent's own words, for example, 'How do you feel about the safety of microwave ovens?', or 'What influenced you to choose brand X?'

Most questionnaires, even highly structured ones, will contain some open-ended questions. These often help to relieve some of the tedium involved in responding to batteries of set-choice questions by giving the respondent the opportunity to express his or her views. If such 'open-enders' are put at the beginning of new topics they may, furthermore, help to focus the respondent's attention on the subject; if put at the end they may act as a 'safety-net' to mop up views not elicited in the structured questions. Responses may even allow the researcher to enliven his or her report with suitable or apposite quotes, for example, 'As one respondent put it . . .'.

However, except for those eliciting a factual response, open-ended questions are difficult and time-consuming to analyse. They produce qualitative data that need to be interpreted, evaluated or content-analysed. (Chapter 6 will review the analysis of qualitative data.) In consequence, the number of open-ended questions is normally kept to a minimum. Even factual open-ended questions require that the responses be classified and numbered later, usually back in the office (a process called 'post-coding'), so that the frequency of types of response can be counted up.

Set-choice questions give respondents a list of possible answers from which to choose. These are usually numbered beforehand or **pre-coded** so that the numbers can be entered directly into a computer program. Set-choice questions are of two main kinds:

- single-answer,
- multi-answer.

Single-answer questions allow the respondent to pick only one response from a list. The simplest of these results in a dichotomous variable, for example, a yes/no answer to a question like, 'Do you own or rent a freezer?' However, since many yes/no questions also require a 'don't know' or 'no response' category, they are not dichotomous in this sense, but result in a **nominal scale**. Attitude questions may ask respondents to select from a list one statement that most closely corresponds with their view. If these statements are in some kind of order, for example, of liking or disliking, then an **ordinal scale** is produced.

Multi-answer questions allow respondents to pick more than one category, for example, 'Which of the following places have you been to on holiday in the last five years?' Here, of course, the total number of responses will probably be greater than the total number of respondents. This means that it is possible either to report the proportion of respondents who tick a particular response, or the proportion of total responses accounted for by each category. Such questions may pose problems at the analysis stage because some computer programs cannot handle multi-answer questions, so each response has to be treated as a separate yes/no question.

One of the mistakes frequently made in questionnaire design is not to make it clear to the respondent whether the question allows for more than one response category. It is usually a good idea to add an appropriate instruction like, 'Tick one box only' or 'Tick as many responses as apply in your case'. Set-choice questions, whether single- or multi-answer, are relatively easy to analyse since all that is required is a simple frequency count of each answer category. However, they do tend to force respondents into answering in ways that may not correspond with their true feelings. They may be tempted to pick responses without a great deal of (or any!) thought.

Both open-ended and set-choice questions may be used to cover any of three main areas of question content, namely:

- classification,
- behaviour,
- attitudes.

Classification questions

These are usually factual and refer to demographic characteristics; indeed, some agencies refer to them as 'demographics'. The classification variables most widely used by market researchers are listed in Table 4.1. In addition, many researchers increasingly use various life-cycle, lifestyle (sometimes called 'psychographic') or geodemographic variables for classificatory purposes. These are explained in more detail in the next section.

The information from classification questions may be used in two rather different ways:

- structurally,
- analytically.

Structurally, demographics provide the framework for any marketing research by defining the population – for example, in terms of geographical areas, sex and age composition – by serving as a basis for sample design, and acting as controls or weights to ensure that the results represent the population correctly. With quota sampling, the demographic questions may be used for quota controls. With random samples, such questions are used to check that the achieved sample is representative of the population in terms of known characteristics, for example, age structure.

Analytically, the role of demographics is to shed as much light as possible on how far economic and social factors 'explain' the survey findings. This may be done by making comparisons between demographic subgroups in the population in terms of the variables being analysed (for example, to determine whether women are more brand loyal than men). Alternatively, demographics may be used for testing discovered relationships and statistical associations against such subgroups (for example, whether the relationship between price awareness and brand loyalty holds for men as well as for women).

Demographics used for structural purposes need, above all, to be reliable and consistent between surveys and source materials. For analytic

Table 4.1 The most widely used classification variables

Sex
Household status (head of household, housewife, other adult)
Marital status
Social class
Occupation
Income
Education or terminal education age
Size and composition of household
Accommodation
Area (e.g. ITV reception areas, Standard Regions)

purposes, it is more important that the demographics correspond with fundamental economic and social factors that are important to the objectives of the survey. Thus the variable 'sex' may be both reliable and robust for structural purposes, but for analysing purchasing behaviour, the role of 'housewife' (who may be male) may be more important.

Demographic questions are usually asked at the end of any questionnaire as 'rounding-off' questions – they may be a little too personal to begin with. However, any demographics that are used for quota controls need to be asked at the outset. An example of a demographic section of a questionnaire is illustrated in Figure 4.1. Notice that the information required in the right-hand column is for identification rather than classification purposes, that is, it identifies one particular interview. It will be completed by the interviewer once the interview is finished. The information is required in case any checkback is needed, either to ensure that the interview took place, or if questions are missed out or completed incorrectly. The respondent may need to be reassured that his or her name and address are required only in case queries arise concerning any of the answers.

A committee of the Market Research Society attempted in 1971 and again in 1984 to generate a set of standard questions (reported by Wolfe 1984). However, many market research companies have continued to approach the design of classification sections in accordance with their own inclinations or 'house styles'.

Of particular difficulty has been the measurement of social class. This has always been one of the most dubious areas of market research, but at the same time the concept of social class is widely used by market researchers. Along with age, it is commonly used as a control in the selection of quota samples, and therefore has to be assessed before the interview begins. This requires an easy and simple system for the interviewer to apply in the field with a reasonable degree of reliability and validity. Most measurements are based on the system developed for the National Readership Survey. The categories (see Figure 2.1) are determined by the occupation of the head of household. Unfortunately, a considerable amount of probing on the part of the interviewer is sometimes necessary in order to establish the class into which the occupation falls. These probes vary according to type of job and whether the respondent is self-employed or not, and it is often difficult to elicit the necessary information without using half a page of questionnaire space. Usually the interviewer actually makes the classification, but details of the occupation of the head of household on which it is based are normally required for checking purposes. Details of the *National Readership Survey* system are given in a manual to interviewers that runs to 19 pages. Not all market research companies, however, adhere to the system and, in consequence, measures of social class by different companies may not be strictly comparable.

A SEX OF RESPONDENT
       MALE   1
       FEMALE   2

B In which of these age categories
   are you?
   SHOW CARD 12
       15–24   1
       25–34   2
       35–44   3
       45–54   4
       55–64   5
       65+   6

C How many adults (aged 16 or
   more) live here including yourself?

   WRITE IN NUMBER

D How many children aged 15 or
   less live here?

   WRITE IN NUMBER

E What is the occupation of the
   head of household or chief wage
   earner?

   JOB TITLE
   WHAT HE/SHE DOES

   TYPE OF BUSINESS ACTIVITY

   INDICATE SOCIAL CLASS
       A   1
       B   2
       C1   3
       C2   4
       D   5
       E   6

F SAMPLING POINT NUMBER

   [   ][   ][   ][   ]

G INFORMANT'S NAME
   USE BLOCK CAPITALS

   SURNAME _____
   FIRST NAME(S) _____
   ADDRESS _____
   _____
   POSTCODE _____

H DATE OF INTERVIEW

   Day   Month
   [   ][   ] [   ][   ]   1992

I LENGTH OF INTERVIEW

   UP TO 15 MINS   1
   15–29   2
   30–45   3
   OVER 45 MINS   4

J I certify that this interview has
   been personally carried out by me
   with the respondent at his/her
   address. He/she is not a friend or
   relative and I have not interviewed at
   this address in any survey in the last
   six months.

   SIGNATURE _____
   DATE _____
   NAME (BLOCK CAPITALS)
   _____
   _____

K INTERVIEWER NUMBER

   [   ][   ][   ][   ]

Figure 4.1 Example of a demographic page of a questionnaire

There have been many criticisms of the NRS classification system. It was developed at a time when lifestyle, income and status were all reflected in occupation, and when there were few working wives. Nowadays, these conditions no longer hold. The classification ignores the impact of multiple household incomes, and it fails to reflect changes both in attitudes and behaviour that have affected the consumption of many products and changes arising from the creation of new jobs, particularly in new technologies. Furthermore, social class classifications may be pointless in some countries like Denmark and Australia that are allegedly classless. However, in spite of attempts to find a system of measuring social class that is manifestly better, none, so far, has been generated.

In 1981 a working party representing the advertisers, the advertising agencies, the television companies and the Market Research Society published a report which concluded that:

- Social grade provided satisfactory discriminatory power (that is, individuals or households in the six social grades showed different patterns of consumer behaviour across a wide range of variables from product purchasing to going on holidays, and varying patterns of possessions, disposable income, lifestyle and so on).
- No alternative standard classification variables were found to provide consistently better discriminatory power.
- There was no evidence to show a decline in the discriminatory power of social grades over the previous decade.

However, more recent evidence (such as that presented by Rothman 1989) suggests that while social class *is* a good discriminator, gradings made by interviewers in the field or based on details collected by such interviewers may be unreliable, which certainly makes social grade problematic when used for structural as opposed to analytic purposes.

Household status is another classification variable that has caused some problems. The usual categorisation is into head of household, housewife, and other adult. The head of household is the chief wage-earner or the person responsible for the accommodation. Where there are two equal candidates, the male is taken to be the head of household, and the older of two people if both are of the same sex. A housewife is usually the person most directly concerned with shopping and cooking in the household. Problems arise, however, if we ask, 'Can such a person be male?' and 'Can a household have no housewife, or more than one?' Usually the housewife is assumed to be female, but some market research companies do allow for male housewives. The National Readership Survey in July 1992 changed its definition of housewife from the person 'mainly responsible for, or shares the household duties such as shopping or cooking' to 'main shopper', in turn defined as that person (male or female) who does *most* of the shopping. Under the old definition, there were 4.6 million male housewives;

under the new definition there will be about 7.4 million male main shoppers. This produces a more realistic marketing definition.

These difficulties with the traditional demographic variables have prompted some market research agencies to use life-cycle, lifestyle or geodemographic variables instead of social class and household status.

Life-cycles are usually defined into a number of stages that families typically undergo. Thus respondents may be classified according to whether they are:

• dependants,
• single, but independent,
• married, but no children,
• married with young children,
• married with older children,
• retired.

People tend to have different aspirations, opinions and needs as they go through the various stages, exhibiting changing patterns of consumer behaviour in the process. Different market research companies will have their own particular classifications and may combine these stages with other demographic characteristics. Thus Research Services Limited in 1981 developed a system it called SAGACITY, which generated 12 groups combining life-cycle (dependent, pre-family, family and late) with income (better off, worse off), and occupation (ABC1 and C2DE). This, claims Cornish (1981), provides better discrimination than any single dimension on its own. Life-cycle stages may be used either to classify individuals, as above, or to classify households. In both cases, questions will need to be asked about marital status, presence (and perhaps ages) of children, plus some measure of individual and/or household income.

Lifestyle analyses tend to include any variables that are not demographics and may relate to the activities, interests, attitudes and opinions of respondents. Activities may include hobbies, entertainment, club membership and sports. Interests may concern the home and family, the community, fashions or the media, while opinions may be about themselves, social issues, politics, education and so on.

Statistical analysis like factor analysis and cluster analysis (explained in Chapter 6) are then used to identify groups or categories of people who tend to have similar characteristics. The typologies generated, however, tend to be specific to particular classes of product. Attempts to develop more generalised classifications have not been widely accepted. Thus Baker and Fletcher (1989) generated six clusters using data from British Market Research Bureau's Target Group Index, which includes nearly 200 lifestyle statements on a regular basis. The system, which the authors called 'Outlook', defines the groups as:

- *trendies*, people 'into' current fads, demographically up-market, affluent and concentrated in the 25–44 age group,
- *pleasure-seekers*, people who want things now. They are against long-term planning and have a low sense of responsibility,
- *the indifferent*, who do not react in any particular way,
- *working-class puritans*, who are 'anti-fun', parochial and traditional,
- *social spenders*, who like to go out and enjoy themselves, be lavish and sociable,
- *moralists*, who are against everything that is enjoyable.

This system, the authors claim, maintains its validity across sub-samples and over time, is a powerful discriminator, and is independent of the social class components of attitude and behaviour patterns. Ward (1987) argues, however, that such systems are unidimensional and cannot compete with interlaced demographics for discrimination and predictive ability. Product-, or, rather, market-specific studies are usually more helpful than generalised systems. Furthermore, attitude-based systems are difficult to apply in the field and are thus not easy to utilise for structural purposes, for example, to apply quota controls. Finally, they provide too simple a view of humanity – people may change category depending on their mood or on the social context; they may be 'trendy' about some things and 'moralist' about others.

Geodemographics are based on the demographic composition or structure of a small local area – a neighbourhood. All households and all individuals in a neighbourhood are given the 'average' characteristics for that area, characteristics that may be used as a basis for market segmentation, targeting, drawing samples, the planning of store locations, or, more recently, for database marketing.

CACI Ltd, an international firm of management consultants, was the first agency to develop a classification of residential neighbourhoods in a system it called ACORN (A Classification of Residential Neighbourhoods). Other competing systems of neighbourhood classification have been subsequently generated, and the use of such procedures has become known as 'geodemographics'. The various systems of classification are based on the principle that knowing where people live enables them to be defined as living in a certain type of area, and hence as likely to have certain social characteristics, lifestyles or buying habits that are of interest to marketers.

ACORN is based on a classification of 38 neighbourhood types derived from a multivariate analysis of Census data. Each Census enumeration district is classified into one of the types, for example, 'cheap modern private housing' or 'recent council estates'. Each district is then matched against postcodes, so that any list of customer addresses (with postcodes) can be readily analysed by ACORN criteria. Working this the other way round, it is possible to pull out all the postcodes that cover neighbourhoods with specified characteristics.

Other companies such as Pinpoint Analysis Ltd, CCN Systems, and Credit and Data Marketing Services Ltd, have produced refinements to this technique, as has CACI itself. Most of these refinements entail adding more information to the classification system, for example, on lifestyles, household composition and likely ages of respondents (which, using a system CACI calls MONICA, is derived from the first names of people on the Electoral Registers). Some systems use more than 38 types, for example, CDMS offers Super Profiles, which has 150 neighbourhood types based on details from Census data.

O'Brien and Ford (1989) report from a study commissioned by Granada Television in 1987 that both social class and lifestyle remained powerful discriminators. While lifestyle was better for some variables, it could not be used for quota control since it depended on administering a large number of attitude statements. The use of postcodes to identify geodemographic characteristics remains the most powerful potential alternative to social class. It has considerable discriminatory power and can be applied robustly for structural purposes. More research is needed, however, on which geodemographic systems work best in a range of different circumstances.

Behaviour questions

Behaviour questions are essentially factual and relate to what people actually did in the recent past. The research problem, therefore, is one of obtaining complete and accurate recall. Specific questions are usually better than more general ones. Thus, 'Have you bought any shampoo in the last seven days?' is better than 'About how often do you normally buy shampoo?' If the response to the first question is 'Yes', then it is possible to follow up with further specific questions concerning which brand or brands were purchased, prices paid, size of pack, where bought, and so on. Respondents may be given recall aids, for example, a complete list of brands to jog memories of purchases. Items that are used or consumed very quickly may require more elaborate techniques, for example, keeping a diary (see next section). Typical measures of behaviour taken in the analysis of consumer markets relate to the purchase and use of products and brands: for example, purchase/non-purchase of a product or brand over a specific time-period; brand variant purchased; quantity/size of pack; price paid; source of purchase; other brands bought; nature of purchase; and use/consumption of the product. These measures may, in turn, be used to generate calculations of brand loyalty, brand-switching behaviour and frequency of purchase. If it is a product test or product concept test, consumers may be asked about likelihood of trial of a new product and their likely frequency of purchase.

Attitude questions

Attitudes are relatively enduring likes or dislikes, preferences or other positive or negative evaluations of objects, persons, organisations, events or situations. Their measurement is central to many marketing decisions, for example, in market segmentation, evaluating the effectiveness of advertising campaigns, or making predictions of product purchases. They play a key role as explanatory variables in most of the major models describing consumer behaviour. While attitudes do not always correspond directly with behaviour, they are, by definition, 'predispositions' to act in particular ways, and hence strongly influence behaviour. This means that when attitudes of a large number of people are measured or estimated, then predictions about future behaviour, particularly purchase decisions, can usually be made with some degree of accuracy.

Opinions are somewhat different from attitudes. They do not necessarily have a directional quality and may express feelings or views about what other people should or should not do in the world. Beliefs refer to what people think they know about situations, products or communications, but which cannot usually be underscored by factual evidence, while knowledge refers to awareness or memory of such factual knowledge. Perceptions or images are somewhat vaguer than beliefs, being representations in the mind of the character or attributes of a person, object or organisation.

The term 'attitude' is sometimes used in a very general sense to refer to all these non-factual or non-behavioural phenomena, but it saves confusion to restrict the term to the narrower sense defined above. Measuring attitudes in the sense of positive or negative evaluations is not easy, and may be attempted in a number of different ways. Basically, there are two main approaches:

- direct,
- indirect.

Direct approaches ask respondents to give their evaluations through self-reply. Thus respondents may be asked to:

- agree or disagree, or indicate their degree of agreement or disagreement with statements about the object being evaluated (see Figure 4.2),
- pick a statement from a group of statements which most closely corresponds with their attitude (see Figure 4.3),
- give some rating from positive to negative, that indicates the direction and strength of their attitude (see Figure 4.4).

Notice that all of these measures will result in ordinal data since the categories are themselves in some kind of order.

Some researchers believe that ratings with even numbers of points elicit

---

The new biscuit is too sweet

PLEASE TICK ONE BOX: STRONGLY AGREE   [   ]
                        AGREE   [   ]
                        NEITHER AGREE
                            NOR DISAGREE   [   ]
                        DISAGREE   [   ]
                        STRONGLY DISAGREE   [   ]

This question format is similar to those used in Likert scaling techniques (see Figure 4.5), but is not a Likert scale as such. Some people, however, do (erroneously) refer to questions of this type as 'Likert scales', so they are referred to here as 'Likert-type attitude statements'.

Figure 4.2 Likert-type attitude statements

Which of the following statements do you agree with *most*?

TICK ONE OF THE BOXES:
        IT'S WORTH THE EFFORT OF COOKING YOUR
            OWN PUDDING   [   ]
        READY-MADE PUDDINGS ARE ALMOST AS GOOD
            AS ONES YOU MAKE YOURSELF   [   ]
        READY-MADE PUDDINGS ARE BETTER THAN
            I CAN USUALLY MAKE   [   ]

Figure 4.3 Attitude statement choices

better discrimination than those with odd numbers, usually 3, 5 or 7, which allow a 'no opinion' or 'no preference' in the middle. However, some people genuinely have no particular view towards the attitude object and may resent being forced to express one. It has, furthermore, been argued that some people exhibit what is sometimes referred to as 'acquiescent response sets', in which they tend just to agree with all statements, including contradictory ones. It is also a good idea to bear in mind that attitude attributes will be of varying significance to different individuals. Thus a respondent may feel that a bank's interest rates on loans are high, but that this is not very important to him.

People's opinions are more likely to be elicited by using forced choice questions, so instead of getting them to agree or disagree with a statement outlining a particular policy, they are asked to choose between two alternatives, for example, 'Should the government keep the principle of the

Non-verbal rating scales

How much do you like the new biscuit?

TICK THE BOX THAT APPLIES TO YOU:

[   ]

[   ]

[   ]

OR

PUT A CROSS ON THE LINE WHICH SHOWS HOW YOU FEEL:

+   0   −

OR

CROSS THE NUMBER THAT GIVES YOUR SCORE OUT OF TEN FOR THE NEW BISCUIT:

10   9   8   7   6   5   4   3   2   1

Non-verbal rating scales are useful:

- for children or people who cannot read or read well,
- for multi-country studies where translation to another language might affect the meaning of a verbal scale.

For interview schedules, the question and the instructions can be read out by the interviewer, and the responses shown to the respondent on the card.

Verbal rating scales

How much do you like the new biscuit?

TICK ONE BOX:

LIKE A LOT   [   ]
LIKE A LITTLE   [   ]
NOT SURE   [   ]
DISLIKE A LITTLE   [   ]
DISLIKE A LOT   [   ]

This would be called a 'five-point verbal rating scale'. It could be used either in a self-completed questionnaire or in an interview schedule, provided the interviewer either reads out the responses, or shows them on a separate card.

Figure 4.4 Rating scales

Community Charge in which everybody pays something for local services, or should local finance depend on some kind of property tax?' It is often not possible or sufficiently reliable to measure a person's attitude by asking one single question. Attitudes are multidimensional with many different facets. Several questions, each relating to a slightly different aspect of the attitude object, may be asked and the responses added up to give a total score. Such scoring systems are generally referred to as **attitude-scaling** techniques. There are a number of such techniques, but most popular amongst market researchers are **Likert scales** (see Figure 4.5).

Likert scales, sometimes called 'summated rating scales', are generated by following a number of steps:

- A list of attitude statements, both positive and negative, about the topic under investigation is generated, usually from qualitative research.
- The list is tested on a screening sample of respondents using Likert-type attitude statements.
- Statements are scored 5–1 (or 1–5 depending on whether agreement or disagreement with the statement expresses a positive view) and the total added up for each respondent.
- Statements that do not discriminate or that do not correlate with the overall total are discarded, a procedure usually called 'item analysis'. This procedure avoids cluttering up the final scale with items that are either irrelevant or are inconsistent with the other items.
- The remaining statements, such as the ones below, are then administered to the main sample of respondents, usually as part of a wider questionnaire survey. Totals are then derived for each respondent.

BELOW IS A SERIES OF STATEMENTS THAT PEOPLE HAVE MADE ABOUT THE NEW SKY YOGHURT. PLEASE INDICATE HOW MUCH YOU AGREE OR DISAGREE WITH EACH STATEMENT BY PUTTING A CIRCLE AROUND THE APPROPRIATE NUMBER:

SKY IS:	Strongly agree	Agree	Neither	Disagree	Strongly disagree
RICH IN TASTE	5	4	3	2	1
LIGHT AND FLUFFY	5	4	3	2	1
REAL FRUIT FLAVOUR	5	4	3	2	1
SOFT IN TEXTURE	5	4	3	2	1
EXPENSIVE	1	2	3	4	5

If Likert scaling is to be used as part of an interview schedule, then the response will normally be printed on a card and the statements read out in turn by the interviewer.

Figure 4.5 Likert scaling

The problem with Likert scales is that the totals for each respondent may be derived from very different combinations of response. Consequently, it is often a good idea also to analyse the patterns of each response on an item-by-item basis. It must also be remembered that the derived total scores are not absolute, so that somebody scoring 20 is not 'twice' as favourable as somebody scoring 10. At most, the scores may be used to generate ordinal data. Some researchers, however, have argued that not much error arises if we treat such ordinal scales as if they were metric. For example, some researchers will calculate an average score for groups of respondents or for particular items. It must also be said that the screening sample and subsequent item analysis is often omitted by market researchers who just generate the statements, probably derived from or based on previous tests, and go straight to the main sample. This is in many ways a pity, since leaving out scale refinements and purification will result in more ambiguous, less valid and less reliable instruments. In fact, whether such a collection of Likert-type items represents 'Likert scaling' is an open question.

Semantic differential scales are slightly different in the sense that the items are not added up, but a profile is described that can be used to compare different products or organisations in terms of their overall image (see Figure 4.6).

Semantic differential scales present dimensions as a series of opposites, which may be either bipolar, like 'sweet ... sour' or monopolar, like 'sweet ... not sweet'. Thus respondents may be asked to indicate, usually on a seven-point scale, where (between two extremes) their views about brand A beer lie, for example:

PLEASE PUT AN X IN ONE OF THE BOXES THAT MOST CLOSELY CORRESPONDS WITH YOUR VIEW ABOUT BRAND A BEER:

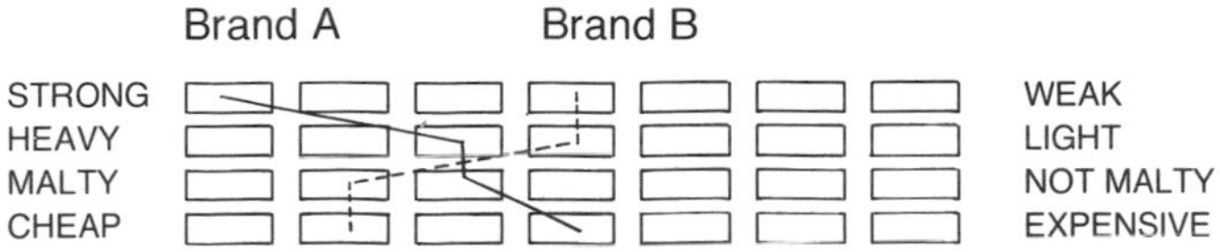

Brand A   Brand B

STRONG   WEAK
HEAVY   LIGHT
MALTY   NOT MALTY
CHEAP   EXPENSIVE

The boxes may be scored 1–7 and an average score calculated for each item. A brand profile is then constructed which can be compared with another brand, for example brand B, the brand leader. Ideally, item analysis, as with the Likert scales, should be performed in order to purify the scale and remove items that do not discriminate or that do not correlate with the overall total. In practice, this is rarely done.

Figure 4.6 Semantic differentials

Attitudes and opinions may be measured using a variety of more indirect techniques, which include the observation of overt behaviour, disguised questioning (or 'projective') techniques, and measuring physiological reactions. What is common to all these methods is that respondent behaviour or reaction has to be interpreted by the researcher so that attitudes may be inferred or deduced. This is what makes them 'indirect'. These methods are considered in detail in Chapter 5.

Questionnaire wording and layout

Designing an effective series of questions is never easy. Three conditions need to be satisfied to maximise the possibility of obtaining valid responses:

- Respondents must understand the questions, and understand them in the same way as other respondents.
- Respondents must be able to provide the answers.
- Respondents must be willing to provide the information.

For respondents to understand the question, attention needs to be paid above all to the wording. This means avoiding:

- long words that people may not be familiar with,
- leading questions,
- complex sentences,
- ambiguous questions,
- vague questions.

Using words like 'unilateral', 'devolution', 'proximity', or jargon like 'marital status' or 'retail outlets', will cause misunderstanding of questions. Never present the respondent with just one of the answer categories – that amounts to a leading question, for example, 'Do you agree that dogs should be banned from public parks?' Always present both or all the alternative responses equally, so instead of 'Do you like brand X?', ask 'Do you like or dislike brand X?' or 'Do you agree or disagree that ... ?'

Complex sentences often arise because the researcher wishes to qualify statements or define terms. Where such qualifications or definitions *are* necessary, then it is better that they are part of a separate sentence, for example, 'Do you have full central heating in this house? By "full" I mean outlets in living rooms and most bedrooms.' Beware of the double question like 'Do you know or are you known personally by the shop assistants?'

Avoiding ambiguity is notoriously difficult. A question like 'How many children are there in your family?' may refer to brothers and sisters for somebody who is unmarried, and to offspring for those married with their own children. 'Where did you buy this packet of soap?' may mean 'In what shop?' or 'In what geographical location?' Words like 'frequent', 'good' or 'recently' may be interpreted in various ways. Vagueness and ambiguity tend to go together, but, as a general rule, be as specific as possible, for example, by defining timings and frequencies of purchases. Thus, 'Have you personally bought shampoo in the last seven days?' is better than 'Have you personally bought shampoo recently?'

Hypothetical questions, for example, 'What would you do if ... ?', or questions that relate to future behaviour, need to be avoided as far as possible. However, they sometimes are required to establish purchase intentions, for example, 'Would you buy this product for your personal use?'

Successful questions, in short, are brief, specific, clear, unambiguous and concern a single issue. Bear in mind that people, on the whole, like to be helpful and co-operative. This often means that they will try to give you the answers they think you want. Most questionnaires, it has been discovered, generate more 'yes' answers than 'no' answers.

Eliciting motivations or reasons for doing or not doing things can be particularly difficult. This may be approached by asking the respondents what they do and then asking 'Why do you do that?' It is tempting for the researcher to try to list most of the possible responses in advance and then get the interviewer to tick the appropriate categories. This can only be done, however, if there has been considerable pre-testing or exploratory research in advance. If this has not been done, then it is probably better to leave the question open-ended and to classify answers at the analysis stage. If the questionnaire is self-completed, the respondent will be able to see whatever is listed and this will prejudice the kind of answers that are likely to be received.

In 1951 Payne published a book that was devoted entirely to the wording of questions in formal questionnaires. In it he emphasises that responses people give are extremely sensitive to the words or phrases used, and that experiments with questions where perhaps a single word was changed, for example from 'ought' to 'might', show very different results. He gives a 'rogues' gallery' of problem words like 'all' and 'you', and concludes with a checklist of 100 'considerations' that need to be kept in mind when phrasing questions. While there are more recent works on survey questions, such as by Sudman and Bradburn (1982), Converse and Presser (1986) and Belson (1986), Payne's book stands as a 'classic' of its kind and is still worth a careful reading today.

For respondents to be able to provide information, it is essential that they are asked only those questions that they are likely to be able to answer with some accuracy. This may mean establishing that the respondents have some experience of the situation or products that they are to be asked about, and not asking them to perform unreasonable feats of memory about past events. Filter questions may be used to establish that the respondent is a user of a product or, for example, actually does the shopping before asking about shopping behaviour. It is, furthermore, advisable to ask people only about very recent purchases, particularly of products that may be relatively unimportant to them.

In short, it is as well to realise that questionnaires are addressed to a variety of individuals who are very differently qualified to answer. For respondents to be willing to provide information, once they have agreed to an interview or begun to complete a self-completed questionnaire, attention must be paid to:

- the sequence of questions,
- the total number of questions.

As a general rule, the questionnaire should begin with simple questions that relate clearly to the topic the respondent has been led to believe the survey is about. Topics need to flow logically, rather than jump about, although this may be difficult in an omnibus survey where respondents can be asked about anything from dog food to airline travel in the same questionnaire. If this happens, it is useful to indicate that a change of topic is taking place, for example, 'I would now like to turn to the topic of holidays', or 'May I now ask you a few questions about motoring?' It is usually better to put general questions before more specific ones. This may mean, for example, introducing the topic of leisure activities, then clothing used, then type of footwear, and finally the use of a particular brand of trackshoe. This procedure is often referred to as 'funnelling'.

It is usually necessary to use 'filter' questions which sort respondents into categories so that follow-up questions can be asked only where appropriate. If the respondent does not fit into that category (e.g. does not smoke), then the next few questions, relating to people who do, need to be skipped. This is usually described as **routing** the respondent through the questionnaire. Very often there is a special 'Skip to' column which includes what is the next relevant question for each response category, or just indicates those responses for which the next question is *not* the relevant one to follow.

When drafting questionnaires there is always a tendency to put in all questions that might seem relevant or just interesting. This often happens when the objectives of the research have not been clearly defined and questions are added 'just in case'. The result can be very long questionnaires which may have an impact on the respondent's willingness to finish. Interviews carried out in the street need to be very short, perhaps taking no more than 10 minutes or so. Some researchers argue that self-completed questionnaires also need to be very short, although there are examples of successful questionnaires that take an hour or more to complete. However, to keep the questionnaire within reasonable limits:

- Make sure every question is actually needed to fulfil the objectives of the research.

- Restrict the amount of classificatory questions to what is needed for sample validation and analysis. A page of classification questions can take 10 minutes to fill in, perhaps more when detailed occupational data are required.
- Use checklists or grids wherever possible to condense the material, for example, Question 5 in Figure 4.7.

Willingness is, of course, also affected by respondents' interest in the subject matter, the method of questionnaire administration (personal interview, telephone or post), the amount of work involved in producing an answer, respondents' ability to articulate an answer and the sensitivity of the issue.

Where questionnaires are self-completed, then willingness to finish all questions will, in addition, depend on:

- questionnaire layout,
- overall presentation.

The basic requirement for questionnaire layout is that it must be clear to the person filling in the questionnaire how replies are to be indicated and where the answer is to be put. This means allowing sufficient space for people to write in replies to open-ended questions, and giving an instruction about how responses to set-choice questions are to be indicated. This will usually mean ticking boxes, putting circles around appropriate code numbers, or deleting responses, as appropriate. Since all responses will need to be numbered anyway for computing purposes, having the responses **pre-coded** is nearly always the best policy.

Instructions for completing the questionnaire need to be distinguishable from the questions themselves and from the pre-coded answers. The convention – by no means universally followed – is to use capitals underlined for instructions, capitals for the responses, and lower case for the questions themselves.

Responses are usually best listed one underneath the other and the codes put in an answer code column. This means that:

- the respondent can be given a general instruction at the beginning of the questionnaire for completing all questions, rather than separate instructions for each,
- the questionnaire analyst can glance down the answer code column for data entry purposes (rather than search all over the page for the answers).

Figure 4.7 illustrates some of these general principles of layout. Types and styles of questions need to be as varied as possible, so that various forms of set choice questions are interspersed with open-ended ones. However, never mix up the mode of indicating answers – stick to ticking boxes or circling numbers.

SHOPPING AND TRAVEL

Please indicate your answer by putting a circle around the number that corresponds with your reply in the 'Answer code' column. The 'skip to' column tells you which is the NEXT relevant question for you to answer if it is not the next question.

		Answer code	Skip to
1 About how often do you buy groceries for regular major shopping?	EVERY DAY 4–5 DAYS A WEEK 2–3 DAYS A WEEK ONCE A WEEK LESS OFTEN NEVER	1 2 3 4 5 6	 Q5
2 Are there any particular days you buy most of your regular major shopping?	YES NO	1 2	 Q4
IF YOU HAVE ANSWERED 'YES' TO Q2 3 Which days are they? PLEASE SELECT NO MORE THAN TWO DAYS	 MONDAY TUESDAY WEDNESDAY THURSDAY FRIDAY SATURDAY SUNDAY	 1 2 3 4 5 6 7	
4 When you make your regular major grocery purchases, what form of transport do you usually use?	CAR BUS TRAIN BICYCLE/ MOPED/ MOTORCYCLE WALK	1 2 3 4 5	

5 During a normal week, how many hours would you spend travelling, using each form of transport, for whatever purpose, not just shopping?

PLEASE REMEMBER TO INCLUDE WEEKEND AS WELL AS WEEKDAY TRAVEL. PLEASE CIRCLE THE APPROPRIATE CODE IN EACH COLUMN.

HOURS PER WEEK	CAR	BUS	TRAVEL BY TRAIN	BICYCLE, ETC.	WALK
NONE	1	1	1	1	1
LESS THAN 1 HOUR	2	2	2	2	2
1–2 HOURS	3	3	3	3	3
3–4 HOURS	4	4	4	4	4
5–8 HOURS	5	5	5	5	5
9 HOURS OR MORE	6	6	6	6	6

Figure 4.7 Questionnaire layout

Overall presentation is very important for a good response rate for self-completed questionnaires. Getting them printed properly is an advantage if the expense can be met, otherwise word-processing packages, desk-top publishing, and some survey analysis packages can be used to produce presentable questionnaires.

For interview schedules, layout and presentation may not be so vital, but, particularly where many part-time interviewers are to be employed, clear layout is still required. A key feature of the layout of interview schedules arises from the fact that respondents cannot see the question-naire. While, on the one hand, this makes it possible to use the funnelling technique because the respondents cannot see questions yet to come, on the other, it means that if the researcher is looking for choices from pre-set categories then, because the respondent cannot see the responses, it is necessary to do one of three things:

- Incorporate all the possible responses into the question, for example, 'Do you personally eat baked beans less than once a week, between one and three times a week, or four times or more?'
- Get the interviewer to read out the categories to the respondent.
- List the categories on a separate card that can be shown to the respondent.

The interviewer will need an instruction as to whether he or she is to read out the responses or show a card, as illustrated in Figure 4.8. Where a large number of cards are needed, they should ideally be clipped or bound together in the order of use to help the interviewer. Incorporating responses into the question is, clearly, only possible when there are no more than three or four categories.

Testing questionnaires

Designing questionnaires is always difficult. It is a skill that cannot be learned from books, but has to be acquired through experience (although reading guides to questionnaire design like the one above can, to some degree, make these experiences more productive). The first draft of a questionnaire is invariably a far cry from what is needed. In consequence, these drafts need to be tried out on colleagues and on a 'pilot' group of respondents similar to those who will be used in the main study. The questionnaire is likely to go through several major redraftings before reaching its final form. There will inevitably be questions that:

- do not mean what the researcher intended,
- have been missed out completely,
- people do not understand or find too difficult,
- everybody gives the same answer to, that is, do not discriminate,

Q12 How much would you say you knew about computer languages *before* you watched last night's programme?

READ OUT

A LOT	[ ]	1
A LITTLE	[ ]	2
NOT VERY MUCH	[ ]	3
NOTHING AT ALL	[ ]	4

Q12 Which of the following phrases on this card best describes how you feel about trying this product?

SHOW CARD C

I CERTAINLY WOULD LIKE TO TRY THIS PRODUCT	[ ] 1
I MIGHT LIKE TO TRY IT	[ ] 2
I AM NOT SURE WHETHER I WOULD LIKE TO TRY IT	[ ] 3
I DON'T THINK I WOULD LIKE TO TRY IT	[ ] 4
I CERTAINLY WOULD NOT LIKE TO TRY IT	[ ] 5

CARD C

I CERTAINLY WOULD LIKE TO TRY THIS PRODUCT	[ ] 1
I MIGHT LIKE TO TRY IT	[ ] 2
I AM NOT SURE WHETHER I WOULD LIKE TO TRY IT	[ ] 3
I DON'T THINK I WOULD LIKE TO TRY IT	[ ] 4
I CERTAINLY WOULD NOT LIKE TO TRY IT	[ ] 5

Figure 4.8 Examples of instructions to interviewer

- give response categories that do not allow some respondents to answer in ways that are relevant to them,
- do not provide sets of categories that are exhaustive, mutually exclusive, and refer to a single dimension (key requirements for **nominal scales**),
- have routings that leave the respondent 'stranded' in the middle of the questionnaire or lead them into inappropriate sections of the questionnaire.

The piloting of questionnaires is frequently short-changed by market researchers and by students undertaking research in marketing. It is, however, critical for successful research. Once the questionnaire has been taken forward into the main data collection phase, it is too late to make any changes. There are three main kinds of pilot study:

- qualitative research amongst the target population to check language and the range of likely opinions,
- pre-testing the questionnaire to see how it works,
- a small-scale pilot survey to obtain approximate results.

Pre-testing is essential for a successful survey – it is surprising how many errors of design are uncovered at this stage, particularly if it has not been preceded by qualitative research or based on questionnaires that have already been tried. Small-scale pilot surveys are often regarded as a luxury except for large projects.

DIARIES

While questionnaire design is a topic which is treated at great length in all texts on marketing research and on social research generally, diary design is rarely mentioned. It is possible to treat diaries as just another form of questionnaire, and, indeed, all the issues and problems of design normally associated with questionnaires apply equally in the construction of diaries. However, they are sufficiently distinct to require separate treatment. Diaries are distinguished by the fact that they refer to consumer behaviour on or between specific dates, perhaps even at specified time periods during the day. Furthermore, they require the respondent to complete an entry every time that behaviour occurs over the time period to which the diary refers – often a week, but may be two weeks or longer. Diaries thus record behaviour which is normally repeated at fairly frequent intervals, and which it would be difficult for a respondent to recall at one time in a question-naire. Normally, attitudes are not measured in a diary, since such an activity may well influence the consumer behaviour being recorded. Thus if a respondent indicates certain negative views concerning a brand, then he or she may well be tempted to swap brands at the next purchase in order to be more 'consistent'.

Diaries are often used in continuous research either for panels or in regular interval surveys (see Chapter 5), but may also be employed in ad hoc survey research, experimental research of various kinds, and perhaps even to record observations made by the researcher. Normally, however, diaries will be self-completed; some may be placed personally by the inter-viewer, or sent by post, and may be collected personally or returned by post. Diaries may relate to individual consumers or to household activity.

In the latter case, one person (usually the housewife) is made responsible for diary completion for the whole family.

There are two rather distinct kinds of diary:

- product diaries,
- media-use diaries.

Product diaries record consumer purchasing and in some cases product use behaviour. They normally arrange entries on a product-by-product basis, usually covering a whole week's purchases. An example of a page from such a diary is illustrated in Figure 4.9. Such an arrangement makes it easier to obtain the specific details required for different brands, for example, to determine the flavour of yoghurt, or the kind of toothpaste dispenser. A diary also acts as a 'reminder' to the respondents, and this improves the completeness of reporting. Depending on the size of the product field, the level of detail required, and the frequency of purchasing, the diary format may be either structured (that is, all the answers are pre-coded) or semi-structured (where respondents write in the brand, brand variant, shop, price, type of offer and so on). Many are a mixture of the two. Pre-coded diaries are better from the data entry and data analysis point of view but may require very long code lists, and may need to be changed frequently as new brands are added or existing ones withdrawn. Semi-structured diaries, on the other hand, require less space but need to be supported by sophisticated data entry systems that can allocate the appropriate codes at the data entry stage.

Some product diaries are more time-based. Thus Taylor Nelson's Family Food Panel diary is organised on a daily basis by 'meal occasion' – breakfast, lunch, evening meal, and snacks between meals. For each occasion, 'who ate what' is recorded for 70 product fields covering foods and 13 measuring drinks. Brands are recorded where appropriate, but not product variants. For some foods, like raw meat, the method of preparation is also noted.

Diaries recording the use of broadcast media tend to arrange entries by time segment on a daily basis. Usually, there are 15-minute or 30-minute periods down the left-hand side of the page, and particular stations, programmes or commercial breaks across the top, as illustrated in Figure 4.10. The respondent may be asked to tick every box against any station listened to or watched for each time segment, or to draw vertical lines through all the time segments where listening or watching took place.

In continuous research, a new diary may be issued to members of a panel every week or every two weeks. However, in the case of the Taylor Nelson's Family Food Panel, it is every six months to cover a two-week period. Thus panellists have a 'rest' between periods of diary-filling.

Coffee	Brand name	Type (please tick one)					(please tick)		Weight or size on pack	No. of packs bought	Price paid per pack	Shop name	Offer on pack
		Instant		Ground			Decaffeinated				£ | p		
		Powder	Freeze	Fine	Med		Yes	No					
Ground instant, freeze-driec													
Tea													

Figure 4.9 Sample page from a product diary

Monday	Station listened to							
	BBC Radio 1	BBC Radio 2	BBC Radio 3	BBC Radio 4	Local BBC Radio	Radio Clyde	Any other station	
6.00–6.15								
6.15–6.30								
6.30–6.45								
6.45–7.00								
7.00–7.15								

Figure 4.10 Sample page from a media-use diary – radio listening

Diary design

A key problem with the design of all diaries is the need to keep them up to date. Thus for structured product diaries, new brands or brand variants may need to be added and others deleted where a manufacturer has dropped them from its range. Even semi-structured product diaries need to take into account the introduction of new product categories. For media diaries, the stations that radio listeners or television watchers can receive need to be continually updated, while programme diaries are notoriously difficult since last-minute changes may be made to the published programmes. Furthermore, there may need to be several versions of such diaries to take account of the different ranges of programme that may be received in different parts of the country.

In considering the overall layout and design of diaries it is necessary to bear in mind the potential sources of error in diary-keeping:

* The diary-keeper forgets to enter purchases, listening or viewing in the diary. This will often be because instead of making entries as they go along, many respondents will try to remember after a couple of days or even at the end of the week before sending the diary off.
* The record-keeper makes an entry, but makes a mistake on the details through faulty memory or erroneous recording.
* The diary is deliberately falsified either by omission of purchases or of media-use behaviour, or by the inclusion of imaginary purchases or media use.
* The diary-keeper is unaware of purchases made by other members of the household, or of their listening or viewing of broadcasts.

All of these sources of error may be affected by a number of factors, for example:

* the type of product or programme,
* the frequency of the activity,
* the position of the page in the diary,
* the position and prominence of the entry on the page,
* the complexity of the entry,
* the overall length and workload involved,
* the method of contact between researcher and respondent.

Thus, grocery items are more likely to be remembered by housewives than personal care products, which are more often purchased by other household members. The more frequent the activity, the more likely it is to be remembered. Items at the beginning of the diary and on the tops of pages are more likely to be remembered than those in the middle and at the end of the diary, and those lower down the page. Deliberate falsification is likely to increase with the complexity of the entry and with the overall length and workload involved.

In designing the layout of a diary, those products which are most likely to be forgotten should be put at the beginning or at the tops of pages. The effects of small diary changes can be measured by introducing changes in only a subsample of the total and noting differences in response. From the results of experiments in the USA, Sudman and Ferber (1979: 74) report that adding or deleting a check box or changing the wording does not measurably affect the level of recording, but changing product headings, moving the position of a product listing in the diary, and putting in special reminders may alter, temporarily or more permanently, the level of product recording. In short, diaries are probably more sensitive than questionnaires to overall presentation and layout, but less sensitive to wording.

While it has been reported (for example by Sudman and Ferber, 1979: 77) that for consumer purchasing there is some evidence to suggest that survey recall data from questionnaires tend to overstate purchases compared with diaries and that the difference is greatest for well-known brands and for perishables, for media use it has been found that *diaries* produce more listening or watching than questionnaire recall methods. Menneer (1989) reports that the diary technique used for the Joint Industrial Council for Radio Audience Research (JICRAR) regularly produces twice as much radio listening as the BBC's 24-hour recall Daily Survey (18 hours per head per week, compared with nine hours). Twyman (1989) has suggested that recall techniques tend to pick up mostly motivated listening, while diarists were asked to record *all* listening, including incidental listening. However, there was also some evidence of memory failure using the BBC's questionnaire recall technique.

In short, there needs to be more research on the effect of diaries versus questionnaires on the levels of recording of the activities involved. On present evidence, questionnaires appear to produce more activity in the case of purchasing behaviour, and less in the case of media use. The difference, however, may be explicable largely in terms of the particular circumstances in which the evidence so far was collected. Thus questionnaires may produce overestimates for product purchase, but only for brandleaders and well-known brands, while for media usage, questionnaires suffer from tendencies to forget periods of viewing or listening, and a tendency to fill in 'normal' behaviour instead of what was actually watched or listened to over the diary period.

RECORDING DEVICES

Questionnaires and diaries are mechanisms for capturing data that have been elicited by addressing listed questions to individuals. However, where a researcher observes products on a shelf or how consumers behave, where some event is taking place (like the purchase of a product or the watching of a television programme) or where a discussion without listed questions is being pursued, then some form of device, manual or electronic, needs to be employed to capture such data.

Manual recording devices are legion in business. Invoices, credit notes, stock lists, delivery notes, receipts, ledgers and accounts are often filled in by hand. The market researcher may, for example, use invoices to check the number of customers, what they purchased, how frequently, what they paid, and where they came from. Delivery notes may be used for retail panel operations as an input to making an estimate of sales once changes in stock levels have been checked.

When engaging in primary data collection, the researcher may use manual record-sheets of various kinds to record observations. Thus inter-viewers from a market research company conducting a shop audit may use a manual audit form for writing in quantities of branded products observed on the shelves, on the counter and in the stockroom, and for recording the deliveries made after inspecting delivery notes. Structured observation may involve the researcher as observer, noting on a record-sheet the number of times a particular piece of behaviour occurs, and the amount of time taken to do or perform it. The difference between a manual record-sheet and an unstructured questionnaire is that the latter depends on addressing ques-tions to people and writing in their answers, while record-sheets are used mainly to record observations made personally.

Electronic recording devices are becoming increasingly popular, particu-larly among the large market research organisations, who can afford the cost of the capital equipment involved. Electronic data capture may be put into four main groupings of technology:

- electronic point-of-sale data capture using scanning technology,
- electronic questionnaires and diaries,
- television set-meters and 'people' meters,
- audio and video recording devices.

One innovation that, more than any other, is changing the focus of instruments of data capture away from paper questionnaires and paper diaries is the introduction of bar-coding on products and the utilisation of laser-scanners at the point of sale (sometimes called 'electronic point of sale' or EPOS technology) to capture the details of each purchase made. Bar-codes give unique identification of products down to country of origin, manufacturer, brand, size, flavour and offer. In Europe a 13-digit code is used. The first two identify the country of origin; the next five are allocated by the Article Numbering Association to identify the manufacturer; the next five are allocated by the manufacturer to identify products; and the last is a check digit allocated by a computer. When a laser is run over the bar-code, the price and other details are looked up from a central file held on a computer in the store, and are then printed out at the checkout cash-desk.

Retailers have used such technology to improve the efficiency of stock control and the speed of checkout operations. Each time a sale is made, the stock inventory is automatically amended, while details of products at the checkout are entered much faster. The customer also receives a detailed receipt giving a printout of each item, right down to the flavour of a brand of cat-food.

.Customer-based information can now be linked with each purchase by using 'smart' cards. These are similar to credit cards, and are presented at the checkout. Details of household demographics derived from the card application form and perhaps from the geodemographic characteristics of the postcode address are linked through the identification number to the purchases made on any shopping trip. However, not only do such systems require co-operation from the customer but also, in order that manufacturers benefit from such information, the retailer has to pass it on, either directly or to a market research agency. It also requires that a substantial number of retailers have scanning equipment. Purchase data from such electronic recording devices can be linked with in-store customer behaviour and in-store pricing, layout and ranges of products to test the effectiveness of 'below-the-line' activity.

Scanning technology is now also being used in the home. The two largest market research organisations in the UK – AGB and Nielsen – have set up consumer panels equipped with electronic scanners able to read bar-codes. This means that details of purchases can be recorded by the panellist simply by running the scanner over every item as the shopping is unpacked. Computer terminals may be used to enable panellists to key in prices and the names of the shops where the goods were bought. All this information is then transferred to a central computer, enabling rapid analyses of purchasing patterns to be produced.

Electronic questionnaires are increasingly used in two main contexts:

- computer-assisted telephone interviewing (CATI),
- computer-assisted personal interviewing (CAPI).

With CATI, the questionnaire is programmed into a central computer before interviewing begins. It is then displayed, question by question, on a number of visual display units in a central location. An interviewer sits in front of each screen and telephones the selected number. The replies are immediately entered via the keyboard. The advantages of this system are as follows:

- No paper questionnaires are required.
- Last-minute changes can be made to the questionnaire.
- Routing is automatic, with the interviewer being passed straight to the next relevant question.

- Results can be assessed at any time during the survey.
- Tables can be run as soon as interviewing is completed.
- Range checks and logical checks can be automatically applied.

With CAPI, the interviewer has a market research terminal (or MRT, also sometimes called a 'portable data entry terminal, or PDET) which is, in effect, a small portable computer with a screen that displays the questions, as for CATI. Either the interviewer can key in the answers, or, in some cases, the respondent is given the MRT to key in his or her own. The data can then be sent down the telephone at the press of a button (using portable telephone technology). Using CAPI has slashed the time it takes to produce comprehensive research results, but, of course, it is very much more expensive.

MRTs are also used for the purpose of retail auditing. Thus details of products on the shelves in shops can be entered directly into the MRT. Electronic diaries have been tried (for example by AGB), but have been overtaken by scanner technology, which makes the data on products much quicker and simpler to enter. Paper diaries, on the other hand, do still retain the great advantage of cheapness!

Meters have been used for measuring the use of television since the 1940s in the USA. Early meters simply recorded the total time the television was turned on, and were used as a check against gross error in diary completion amongst a representative sample of panel households. More recent 'set-meters' recorded the channel to which the set was tuned on a continuous basis, but were still used in conjunction with diaries to record who was watching. Diaries could be abandoned only with the introduction in 1984 of AGB's 'peoplemeter'. This uses a remote-control hand-set associated with each television belonging to the household. Each member of the household indicates his or her presence in the room where a television is switched on by pressing a button with a personally allocated number. They press the number again when they leave the room. Such 'push-button' or 'active' meter systems have had to become more sophisticated to cope with the use of VCRs to time-shift viewing, viewing on pre-recorded video tapes, viewing and recording at the same time, multi-set households, the use of television for teletext, home computers and the introduction of cable and satellite television. At present, the peoplemeter system can cope with guest viewing by allocating button numbers to additional guests, but viewing by household members outside the home is still a problem.

Every television set owned or rented by panel households (of which there are currently about 4,800 in the UK) is equipped with a 'slave' meter or remote detector unit. It sits on top of the television and has its own display screen for giving messages to, or seeking responses from, the people in the room. Each feeds to a master meter via the domestic wiring system. The master meter is, in turn, linked to the domestic telephone line, and the day's electronic data are passed every night to a central computer which dials up each household to retrieve the viewing data. The figures are processed the following morning. The record is on a second-by-second basis, although viewing is aggregated to the nearest minute or some multiple of that.

An emerging technology is that of 'passive' meters that detect automatically the presence of people in the room and even who is watching or facing the screen by using an infra-red camera which takes a picture every second. Such technology may well, however, be in advance of the willingness of panellists to accept such intrusion and surveillance of their activities. The process of measuring television audiences is explained in more detail in Chapter 7.

Audio and video recording devices may be used for marketing research in a number of different ways. Traditionally, the tape recorder has been employed for qualitative research, particularly for depth interviews, but increasingly group discussions are tape recorded. The tape recorder has the advantage of cheapness and portability. It also captures everything the respondent says and so cannot be accused of selectivity. Normally, the respondent's answers are transcribed before being used for analysis. Since the interviewer's questions are also recorded, the tape can be used to check that the interview was conducted in a proper manner. Tape recorders can, of course, also be used by the researcher for recording in words what he or she is observing, plus any thoughts that come to mind.

Video recorders, by comparison, are relatively recent, but the development of the 'camcorder' has facilitated the recording of consumer behaviour on a continuous basis and in most lighting conditions. Video recording may be in an organised data collection context (for example, for group discussions) or it may be in place of personal observation (for example, using the video to record the movement of people in and out of shops).

A key factor in all means of electronic data capture is that a complete census is normally taken of all transactions or behaviour – there is no need to sample and then make estimates. Furthermore, the records will be accurate and the data will be available almost immediately. However, such equipment tends to be expensive (except for tape recorders), and there may well be problems about who owns the data once they have been captured.

Further developments may well take the form of linking some of the various technologies together. Thus it is technically possible to link the purchases made by homes that have scanning equipment or 'smart' cards with those that have television meters installed. This means that television viewing may be directly linked with purchasing behaviour and with below-the-line activity in the shop. The direct effect of television advertising can thus be monitored on a continuous basis. As yet in the UK, television audience measurement panels are not linked up in this way, but the technology is there to make it possible.

While the introduction of such systems may be somewhat futuristic, their development would create a major leap in the quantities of data captured. Whether our ability to analyse them will be outstripped could turn out to be a major issue.

SUMMARY

Data may be captured using one or more of three key instruments: questionnaires, diaries, or recording devices, which may be manual or electronic. Questionnaires may be structured to varying degrees and may be self-completed or interviewer-completed. Formal, structured questionnaires tend to have a predominance of set-choice, pre-coded questions which may be used to collect demographic, behavioural or attitudinal data. Questionnaire wording needs to ensure, as far as possible, that respondents understand the questions, have the information to be able to provide answers, and are willing to provide the answers. Questionnaire layout and presentation are particularly important for self-completed questionnaires, but must not be overlooked where part-time, paid interviewers are being used. Layout needs to bear in mind not only the respondent's convenience, but also the needs of the interviewer and the data analyst. Questionnaires that are not pre-tested in some way are unlikely to meet the needs of the researcher and his or her client.

Diaries may be distinguished from questionnaires on the basis that they are time-based, and refer exclusively to repeated behaviour rather than to attitudes or possessions. Product diaries tend to be laid out on a product-by-product basis while media diaries utilise time segments. Diary design needs to bear in mind the potential sources of error in diary-keeping and the various factors that affect them. The issue of whether diaries or questionnaire recall methods result in the recording of higher or lower levels of activity is one on which the evidence so far is, at best, inconclusive.

Recording devices may be manual or electronic, but it is the latter which have seen the major development in recent times. These devices include point-of-sale scanning equipment, electronic questionnaires and diaries, television meters, and audio and video recording equipment. Further developments in technology are likely to see these devices being used in conjunction with one another to provide quantities of data which, on present data analysis expertise and facilities, may be difficult to handle. While the use of electronic equipment often obviates the need for sampling and making estimates, they tend to be expensive and consequently, in their more sophisticated versions, the preserve of the larger market research organisations.

EXERCISES AND POINTS FOR FURTHER DISCUSSION

■   A manufacturer of hair-dryers wants to find out:
(a) what proportion of households in the UK owns no/one/two/or more hair-dryers;
(b) what proportions and types of individual in households with a hair-dryer use it on every occasion after hair-washing;
(c) the major product features respondents are looking for.
Design a questionnaire for use in face-to-face interviewing that will obtain this information from a sample of households.

■   Specify what changes will be needed if the questionnaire in the previous exercise is to be used as a postal questionnaire.

■   Design a Likert scale to measure attitudes towards a new flavour of yoghurt.

■   Design a semantic differential scale to measure the image of a new local supermarket in a small village in England.

■   British Telecom wants to discover the age profile and telephone use behaviour of the different age groups. Discuss the strengths and limitations of using a diary or a questionnaire to capture such data.

Chapter 5

Data collection methods

The instruments of data capture – questionnaires, diaries and recording devices – may be used in several different social and organisational contexts. Thus questionnaires are used not just in survey research, but in some forms of qualitative research, in continuous research, and in a range of different experimental and quasi-experimental situations. Similarly, diaries and recording devices may be used in different data collection contexts. Socially, the relationship between researcher and researched may be direct or indirect. Thus face-to-face interviews and telephone contacts are direct and interactive – the researcher is responding and reacting on the spot to respondent answers. Postal questionnaires and diaries, by contrast, are indirect. The relationship is non-interactive, and the researcher waits for the respondent to complete the set of tasks assigned to him or to her before looking at the results.

Organisationally, the context of data capture may be one in which respondents are approached in a pre-formatted or in an open-ended fashion. Thus in a questionnaire survey, respondents may be asked to choose between pre-selected responses. By contrast, in qualitative research, respondents are encouraged to respond in their own words or in their own way. Putting these two dimensions together gives a loose categorisation of the sections that follow in the remainder of this chapter, as illustrated in Table 5.1.

DESK RESEARCH

Desk research entails the proactive seeking-out of data, qualitative or quantitative, that already exist and which may be useful in the analysis, planning or control of marketing activity. It often generates data different in kind from those that primary research is designed to collect. Typically, desk research is used in an exploratory phase of research, but, on occasion, it may be discovered that sufficient data are available to avoid the need to collect data specially for the research at hand. Activities that may be included in desk research are making library searches, searching in-house

Table 5.1 Data collection methods

| Organisational context | Social context | |
	Direct methods	Indirect methods
Unstructured	Informal and depth interviews, group discussions, unstructured observation	Desk research
Structured	Formal and telephone interviews, laboratory experiments, structured observation	Postal surveys, field experiments, continuous research

company records and information systems, making on-line database searches, and buying data and reports from commercial sources.

Data to which a desk researcher may have access will have been collected for purposes other than those currently being pursued, and accordingly these data may not be in an ideal form. Nevertheless, it is often unwise to begin a project before seeking out what has already been written or data that have already been collected on the topic. For academic, scholarly research this is an essential part of any dissertation, thesis, article for publication in an academic journal, or research monograph. For text-books such as this one, however, it would probably be distracting to have a review of the entire literature on every topic or subject mentioned, so only those sources that might be of interest to the reader are referred to.

In commissioned research, there is frequently no desk research phase. In many studies, particularly of the consumer market, desk research may be less relevant since secondary data are, by definition, largely historical, whereas what is required are the most recent data on consumer behaviour or consumer attitudes. Clients, furthermore, would not be interested in reading literature reviews, for example, on the origin and design of tracking studies, before getting to the results of the tracking of their own products. However, the use of accumulated databases that go back several years for the analysis of trends or for the purpose of parametising market models may be thought of as desk research which is used as inputs to **secondary analysis**, that is, the reanalysis of existing data. There are, however, a lot of data on organisational, business and industrial markets, and market research on these (often referred to as 'business-to-business' research) is more likely to have a specific desk research phase.

Sources for desk research

A lot of data that may be usable for marketing purposes are often already available within the organisation that is the focus of the research. Three main sources may be distinguished:

- operating data and company accounts,
- previous research,
- data contained in information systems.

Operating data might include information on the performance of individual products that the firm makes: for example, on sales, profits and costs; on the various sections, divisions, factory sites or subsidiaries of the company; on the functions it performs – manufacturing, distribution, marketing, purchasing, or research and development. Company accounts will supply information on the overall performance of the organisation – turnover, costs, revenue, profits, a balance sheet and profit and loss statement. Invoices or records of purchases may be able to supply information on customer addresses, types of purchases, dates and frequencies of purchase, discounts, credits, deliveries and so on.

Previous research may have been carried out both on the company and on the market to which it sells. Reading the reports of such activities may enable researchers to familiarise themselves with the background of the current situation, and perhaps use them as a guide or input to the design of the research to be undertaken. It may even be possible to utilise such research as a benchmark for measuring change from an earlier period. It makes sense to classify and store such reports in a library and in such a way that they may be easily retrieved on future occasions. Unfortunately, it is still common practice for copies of reports to be kept on the shelves of the managers who commissioned them.

Management and marketing information systems combine various data inputs, store them on a computerised database, and produce integrated reports on a regular basis using an agreed system. They may operate at various levels of sophistication. At a basic level, they are simply data storage and retrieval systems that make existing data more readily accessible and presentable. Standard database packages do this very well and they provide the mechanisms for abstracting and indexing information and retrieving it in particular formats. More sophisticated are systems for monitoring and control that check progress and alert management to variations, departures or variances from plans, criteria or budgets. Analytical information systems are the most sophisticated and use statistical models to answer 'Why?' questions, to make forecasts or recommendations, or to answer 'What if ... ?' questions using simulation techniques. While such systems can thus produce large amounts of data and endless reports, the ability of management to absorb and react to such information may be limited.

Data from sources external to the organisation may be derived from:

- environmental scanning,
- official and unofficial published statistics,
- buying data or reports from business publishing houses, market research companies or advertising agencies.

Environmental scanning refers to the process of compiling and evaluating qualitative and quantitative information on what is happening generally in the marketplace, particularly the activities of competitors, and in the wider social, political, economic and technological environment. The result is usually referred to as 'market intelligence', which is a collection of pieces of information, often incomplete and subjective, but which allows the researcher to keep abreast of events as they unfold. These sources include:

- reading business and financial newspapers like the *Financial Times* or the *Wall Street Journal*, general business magazines like *Business Week* or *The Economist*, trade and technical journals like *Computer Weekly*, and academic periodicals like the *Harvard Business Review* or the *Journal of Management Studies*,
- personal contacts in other organisations,
- feedback from the salesforce,
- watching competitors,
- going to conferences, exhibitions, courses or meetings.

In many market research organisations, executives are assigned to particular groups of clients and are expected to familiarise themselves with their markets. Most environmental scanning, however, is probably undertaken in-house by company managers. The process of environmental scanning may be very informal with no specific purpose in mind, it may be conditioned to a particular type of information, it may be a proactive but unsystematic search, or there may be formal procedures for finding, storing and retrieving the information. Whatever form the scanning takes, the resulting market intelligence should enable the firm to adapt more easily to a changing environment; it may act as a source of inspiration for innovation or it may alert management to opportunities or threats. (See Piercy and Evans 1983, Chapter 4, for a detailed exposition of marketing intelligence.)

A problem with market intelligence data lies in the procedures used for their collection. Unless these are systematic, the data will be unrepresentative and may be misleading. Managers and salespeople need a straightforward reporting system organised in a way that minimises the work involved. Perhaps more importantly, however, there needs to be a feeling that such reports are of real value to the organisation and that they do actually feed into the decision-making process.

Official statistics may be subdivided into governmental and non-governmental sources. In the government, the Business Statistics Office is responsible for producing *Business Monitors*, a very potent source of data on trends in the industry on a sector-by-sector basis. The Office of Population Censuses and Surveys produces a number of continuous, multi-purpose datasets, including the *Family Expenditure Survey*, the *General Household Survey*, the *National Food Survey*, in addition to a range of ad hoc studies and, of course, the Census itself. The Central Statistical Office organises a range of multi-source publications including the *Annual Abstract of Statistics*, the *Monthly Digest of Statistics*, *Economic Trends*, *Social Trends* and *Population Trends*.

Other official statistics will include those published by various kinds of official or quasi-official bodies like the BBC Audience Research Unit, by the European Community, the United Nations, and local government.

Non-official sources might include:

- trade associations,
- trade unions,
- banks,
- television networks,
- market research agencies,
- Chambers of Commerce,
- professional institutes.

All these organisations produce and make available data to their members or to clients or may even publish their own journals.

A lot of data already exist, then, in published form, and they may be adequate for the purpose of the decision that needs to be taken. Published data are in the public domain and are either free or available at very little cost. More expensive are data that have been collected by market research companies or gathered by business publishing houses who sell the data to as many clients as possible. Purchasing such data will, however, normally be cheaper than conducting primary research. Thus data specially designed for market segmentation research can be purchased from British Market Research Bureau's Target Group Index (outlined later in this chapter). Reports on particular industries or markets may be obtained from Key Note Publications, from *Market Research GB*, published by Euromonitor, from *Retail Business*, published by the Economist Intelligence Unit, and from Mintel. These all tend to be a mixture of data gathered from other sources, like *Business Monitors*, and from their own primary research. The British Overseas Trade Board produces an annual publication, *Market-Search*, which gives a guide to what is available both in the UK and overseas.

Financial analysis reports, business news services or computer access to on-line databases may be purchased from some agencies. Subscribing to continuous market measurement services such as consumer panels (like those offered by Audits of Great Britain) or retail panels (such as offered by Nielsen) is another possibility (again, these are described later in the chapter). A year's subscription will pay for 12 four-weekly reports on the products or brands you choose, detailing sales by volume and by value on a brand-by-brand basis, broken down by a whole series of geographical, demographic and behavioural characteristics.

There are a number of guides to sources of secondary data. Key Note Publications produces its *The Source Book*; Euromonitor offers a *Compendium of Marketing Information Sources*; Industrial Aids Ltd has *Published Data of European Markets.* There is also the government's own *Guide to Official Statistics* (HMSO). Apart from such guides there is a range of indexing services, for example, the British Humanities Index, the Social Sciences Citation Index, the Research Index and the Financial Times Index. There are a number of compendiums giving all sorts of useful marketing data, for example, the *Marketing Pocket Book*, published by the Advertising Association.

The uses of desk research

There are two key uses of desk research:

- providing background materials for primary research,
- providing an alternative to doing primary research.

In the former application, desk research is one of a number of stages in the conduct of a marketing research project. Usually, it will be an early stage and may need to be completed before the primary research can be designed; or it may be necessary to check that a similar study has not already been carried out; or that the data required are not already available. However, desk research may also continue while the primary research is in progress, deepening the understanding of the market research executive, keeping him or her abreast of current developments in the marketplace. The results of desk research may be used in the final report to provide an overview of the general economic environment, the size and structure of and trends in the market, and the main competitors before looking at the performance of the client's brand derived from the primary research.

In the second application, desk research may reveal that no further research is required, for example, because it has shown that the potential market is just not large enough to support a new product under consideration. Many an annual marketing plan is preceded by a desk research review of the market with no further research input. Sometimes the re-analysis of existing data provides a sufficient basis for making a marketing decision or pursuing some marketing activity.

Strategies and tactics of desk research

Desk research is never fully structured. It is more like a treasure hunt or piece of detection work; what will emerge is often unknown beforehand. It requires skills of methodicalness, persistence and ingenuity. It means knowing where best to begin and how to proceed thereafter. For the research executive in a market research company, the first step will be to determine from the client what data are accessible in the company itself. There will certainly be accounting and operating data, but there may also be a customer database, and the client may well be subscribing to one or more syndicated sources that provide data on products, brand by brand, and on markets and consumers on a continuous basis. The client may have a library containing past reports or a management information system that can be accessed. The executive may next check what statistical series are kept by the agency itself. These are likely to include *Business Monitors, Market Research GB, Retail Business, Marketing Week, Business Week* and so on. Next, the executive may contact the appropriate trade associations to see what data they hold (usually generated from their own members).

To obtain information on companies, the most accessible source is usually one or more of the excellent company directories. One of the best on the UK industry is *Kompass.* It lists over 30,000 companies, grouped by county and town, together with their addresses, directors, number of employees, main activities and brief financial data. Comparable information may be found in *Kelly's Directory, Manufacturers and Merchants* volume, and in two directories published by Dunn and Bradstreet, *The National Business Directory* and *The Key British Enterprises.* Some agencies, like Extel Statistical Services, gather this information together and will provide company profiles.

Increasing quantities of data are now available on electronic databases and going 'on-line' can save considerable time. Most are available commercially and the client can subscribe to a particular supplier. Some skill, however, is required for using such databases and the infrequent user may consider it better to buy in searches on databases from organisations providing this kind of service. Key word searches are particularly beneficial – it can take just a few minutes to find every mention of a word, phrase or product in the database being used. Thus Finsbury Data Services offers its Profile database, which gives full text retrieval of media articles in British newspapers, magazines and selected commercial outputs, for example, from Euromonitor and Mintel. Reuters' Textline offers an international database of media sources; ABI Inform covers academic periodicals in the business area.

Limitations of secondary sources

Because secondary data normally appear in printed or even published form, it is often forgotten that they were originally collected as primary data, albeit for some other purpose, using the data capture instruments described in the previous chapter and the primary data collection methods explained in the remainder of this chapter. Very often the data are estimates based on samples, so it is necessary to bear in mind also all the potential sources of error outlined in Chapter 3.

Not all secondary data are of the same quality in terms of validity and reliability, and it may be necessary to ask a number of questions about them, for example:

- Who produced the data?
- Why were the data collected in the first place?
- How were they collected?
- When were they collected?
- What definitions were used?

It is a good idea to bear in mind the agents who were responsible for the original collection, analysis and presentation of the data. Irvine *et al.* (1979) argue that statistical practice is not a purely technical matter of utilising the 'correct' sampling techniques, statistical analyses, probability theory and so on. Data are social products that have been created by individuals, groups or governments with their own economic and social agendas. Data are never totally neutral; they are a selection of the data that could have been collected. There may well be a convenient lack of information on sensitive topics like the real levels of poverty or unemployment, and the data that would have been useful to the researcher are not collected. So, in asking who produced the data, it is as well to recognise that, for example, trade associations exist to further the interests of their members and may well hesitate to publish data that are inimical to those interests.

Answering the question concerning why the data were collected in the first place may well give insights into the value of that information. Thus the original purpose of the Family Expenditure Survey, begun in 1957, was to provide information on spending patterns for the Retail Prices Index, not to measure the levels of poverty.

Some secondary data may originally have been collected by using methods that are prone to error or bias, for example, using quota samples to select respondents, or random samples with a poor response rate. Some published data may well have been collected some time before their publication. This is particularly true of government statistics.

Finally, definitions of the original case – whether 'household', 'housewife', 'establishment' – or of the original variables and the scales of values used, may not be the ones the researcher would have chosen. The result is that the data are published in a format that is not particularly useful to him or to her, or that, because of changes in definitions, the analysis of trends becomes dubious.

PERSONAL OBSERVATION

Personal observation can be used whenever it is possible to collect data without actually speaking to people. It may, in fact, be the only option available if there are no mechanical or electronic means of observation and if asking people might result in misleading information. Provided it is carried out in a systematic manner, it has several uses in marketing research. The two main contexts in which personal observation is used include:

* watching the behaviour of consumers in the process of purchasing goods or services,
* observing the availability, quantity and prices of branded goods on shelves in shops or in the home.

Consumer behaviour can be watched either in its natural or in an artificial setting; furthermore, it may be structured or unstructured. In a natural setting, an observer may, for example, note the length of queues at checkouts in a supermarket at specified intervals during the day; the length of time motorists spend in a filling station; or whether or not they are wearing seat-belts. In pubs and bars, at least one market research company positions observers to watch how people go about ordering drinks. Observation in a natural context is often disguised, that is, the people being observed are unaware of the fact. This is perfectly acceptable if the behaviour is in a public place where it can be watched by anybody. Disguised observation has the added advantage that the behaviour being recorded cannot be affected by the process of observation. If people are aware of being observed, they may try to act more 'rationally' than they would normally do.

In an artificial context, the process of group discussion may be observed in a systematic manner, or consumers may be invited to purchase goods in an artificial 'store' where their choice behaviour is watched. A number of market research companies, particularly those that offer retail panel services, send observers into selected shops to record systematically, for a specified range of branded goods, whether these products are available on the shelves, in display areas or in the stockroom. The length of facings occupied by a brand may be measured, its price noted, and perhaps quantities counted. In a full retail audit, such data may be used in combination with records of deliveries to calculate sales. Some agencies restrict themselves to 'distribution checks' or offer 'shelf-observation' services. It is also possible, of course, to observe what products and what brands people have on the shelves, in cupboards, or in the fridge at home. Some consumer panels use such a 'home audit' procedure as a data-gathering technique (see Kent 1989). In shops, the shop owners are usually aware or made aware that an observer from an agency is checking the availability and prices of goods on the shelves.

Except where observation is being used for exploratory research in order to get the 'feel' for some situation, it is usually structured. This means that observations are recorded into predetermined categories so that the frequency of behavioural occurrences, or duration of time, or length of shelf can be noted. The result is quantitative data that may be **nominal**, **ordinal**, **continuous** or **discrete metric**.

The key advantage of observation over asking people questions is that no reliance is placed on people's memories, guesses or honesty. There is little point in asking people if they always wear a seat-belt when driving; they will always say 'yes'. It is better to observe how many in fact do.

Observation, clearly, has its limitations and drawbacks. Often it is just not possible or feasible. It is also labour-intensive – one person can observe the occurrence of only a limited number of phenomena. Observation can be only of behaviour – it is not possible to observe attitudes, opinion, or what people think. Observation is probably underutilised as a data capture technique in market research; it is usually best used not on its own, but in combination with other techniques.

QUALITATIVE RESEARCH

Qualitative research in marketing is characterised by two main features:

- it is based on open-ended interview methods,
- it collects data that are largely qualitative and in the form of narrative rather than isolated statements.

Not all qualitative research is based on interview methods: in sociology, for example, participant observation is a key method. However, participating in and observing social groupings or communities in their own natural environment is not so appropriate in marketing. The open-ended nature of the interviews used in marketing means that the process of questioning is flexible and responsive to what individuals or groups of individuals say – it is not predetermined as in a formal survey. This maximises the opportunities to obtain from the respondents what they, uniquely, have to offer by way of information, experiences, feelings, images, attitudes, ideas and so on.

The narrative offered by respondents will usually be captured using either a tape recorder or video camera. The problems and features peculiar to analysing and interpreting such data are considered later, once we have looked at the main types of qualitative research and their applications.

Other features common to qualitative research, but which are not defining characteristics, include:

- the use of small samples of respondents who are not necessarily representative of a larger population,
- the direct involvement of the research executive in a number of stages of the research, including the planning and design of the research, conducting the interviews, analysing the results, and presenting them to clients,
- it is concerned with understanding consumer perceptions and consumer behaviour rather than measuring the extent of their occurrence.

Until the 1970s, qualitative research was very much the Cinderella of market research, often dismissed as not serious, lacking in scientific rigour, non-replicable, non-generalisable and subjective. However, in the last decade, the amount of qualitative research undertaken has undergone an explosive growth. By 1990 the value of qualitative market research undertaken by members of AMSO was just over £26 million, some 10 per cent of all commissioned research. This undoubtedly underestimates the proportion of qualitative market research carried out by non-AMSO agencies or conducted in-house. In 1981 the Association of Qualitative Research Practitioners (AQRP) was established, and it now has over 500 members who variously work in research agencies, advertising and in major client organisations. The *Association Directory*, first published in 1992, lists over 100 agencies offering qualitative research. Of the 451 agencies listed in the *Market Research Society Handbook* for 1992, 397 or 88 per cent claimed to offer qualitative market research amongst their data collection methods. Many agencies were established to specialise in such activity; the larger ones set up separate divisions to handle qualitative research or bought out a subsidiary company to whom such work could be passed on.

The main reasons for this growth include:

- a greater understanding and appreciation of the role of qualitative market research,
- its relative cheapness and speed,
- its proven effectiveness in a growing range of applications.

The main types of qualitative research

In the market research industry, practitioners talk about 'groups' and 'depths' in the context of qualitative research. The terms distinguish the two main types of qualitative research in marketing: group discussions (called 'focus groups' in the USA), and depth interviews. It is tempting to suggest that the key difference between them is that depth interviews are on a one-to-one basis between researcher and respondent, and that groups involve several respondents together with the researcher in the same room at the same time. However, some depth interviews may take place with married couples, families, or even two or three friends together; some group discussions may be in groups as small as five or six respondents. A more crucial difference is that in depth interviews, the main lines of communication are between interviewer and respondent; in group discussions, it is the verbal interactions between respondents that assume a major role.

Group discussions

Most of the qualitative research conducted in the UK is by way of group discussions; so much so that qualitative research is regarded by some buyers and clients as synonymous with such methods. Clients, furthermore, often see group discussions as being little more than a convenient (and relatively cheap) way of gathering the views of more than one person at a time. However, as indicated above, it is the interactions between respondents that are important. Groups take on a life of their own, varying from group to group, and are influenced by a large number of factors including the size of the group, its composition, the personalities of those present, the tasks they are asked to perform, the physical conditions of the meeting place, and the 'chemistry' between interviewer and respondents. The group itself has an influence back on the individual, and what is said relates to the total experience of being in the group. The results achieved by group discussions are more than, or at least different from, the sum of what would be obtained by interviewing respondents individually.

Clearly, different views may be taken about the optimum size of group, but the norm that has developed in the UK is that 'standard' groups have seven to nine respondents, with eight being the favoured number since it facilitates different combinations in terms of the composition of the groups. A standard group discussion will normally be no longer than an hour and a half. Where it is felt that a longer time is needed, for example, to perform more complex tasks, then such groups will be referred to as 'extended' groups.

When planning group discussions, the main considerations in terms of setting up and running the groups include:

- the type of group,
- group composition,
- the number of groups,
- recruitment,
- topics to be discussed,

- method of running the group,
- the places, venues and timings.

Apart from the standard groups already referred to, the main variations in types of group include those outlined in Table 5.2. Most groups, however, are standard. The variations may be used where standard groups have not produced fresh information or the kind of information required.

Group composition is a difficult decision. There are two main issues here:

- Who does the researcher want to talk to?
- Should the groups be homogeneous or heterogeneous in terms of key characteristics?

The first issue means defining the population to be studied and from which the sample of respondents will be chosen. For branded products, a key choice is in terms of product usage. Should the groups consist of:

- brand users only,
- product class users only,
- users and non-users of the product?

It also needs to be decided whether the usage categories should include both sexes, all ages, all social classes or just some of these.

Table 5.2 Characteristics of the main variations from standard discussion groups

Group types	Characteristics
Mini-groups	For 5–6 people. Used for interviewing children, for sensitive, intimate or personal subjects, when there is a need to explore individual behaviour, or for brief, quick-reaction groups.
Extended groups	Standard size, but last 3–4 hours. Use more complex tasks, a lot of stimulus material, or projective techniques. For more in-depth explorations of psychological issues or for studying complex or fragmented markets.
Reconvened groups	Meet on more than one occasion, for example, two sessions separated by a week. Normally used for trying out a product between meetings or setting up experimental experiences between discussions.
Sensitivity panels	The same respondents are used on a number of occasions, attending weekly or two-weekly sessions. Respondents are trained to respond using a variety of different techniques. Best for exploration, invention and diagnosis, *not* evaluation.
Creativity groups	Use brainstorming or synectics for problem-solving in an innovative manner.

In terms of the second issue, the choices range from making each group homogeneous in terms of key characteristics to deliberately ensuring a cross-section in each group. Key variables will commonly be product usage, sex and age. If, for example, it has been decided to use four groups with product usage and age as the key variables, the creation of a relatively homogeneous group might be as illustrated in Table 5.3.

Table 5.3 Example of homogeneous grouping in qualitative research

Group	Usage	Age
I	Users	20–35
II	Non-users	36–50
III	Non-users	20–35
IV	Users	36–50

This facilitates analysis since, apart from perhaps mini-groups, it is not usually possible to identify which individuals have made which comments. However, if a particular comment comes only from groups I and IV, these are users; if it comes from II and IV, it is the older groups. The drawback is that discussions between users and non-users is eliminated; so is discussion between younger and older people. If the four groups are all mixed, there is maximum potential for divergent opinions, but relating these opinions to product usage or demographic characteristics will be difficult.

Using more categories (for example, four age groups and three usage categories – heavy, medium and light) or more variables (for example, sex and region) makes too many combinations for the number of groups required. One possibility is to use other experimental designs like Latin squares in which not every combination is applied (see 'Experimental design', pp. 140–3).

Qualitative research is small-scale research, and it would not be normal to run more than about 12 groups. Diminishing marginal returns rapidly set in thereafter and interviewers will find themselves anticipating most responses and learning little new from additional groups. In the 1980s a common design was to have four groups, two North, two South, two ABC1 and two C2DE. Further multiples of four facilitate other permutations. Goodyear (1990) suggests that for strategic projects or for exploratory research, more groups – perhaps up to 30 – may be required; tactical projects on the other hand may require only 2–8 groups. Gordon and Langmaid (1988), however, suggest that unless the research is working in a highly segmented market, for example, financial services, it becomes unwieldy to conduct a large number of group discussions.

There are two aspects of recruitment: sampling and persuading those selected to attend the group discussion. Sampling is usually **quota**

sampling. Part-time recruiters, who either work for the agency conducting the research or who operate freelance and who live in the area selected for one or more groups, are asked to recruit the required number of people who meet the quota requirements. Recruiters will receive both telephone and written instructions on the project.

Usually there will be a short recruitment questionnaire that screens out those not part of the population to be studied. For those remaining, the recruiter will ascertain the information required for quota controls and, where appropriate, for allocation to a particular group. The quotas will normally be in terms of sex, age, social class and product usage, but not necessarily proportionate to their numbers in the population. Thus the recruiter may be asked to obtain eight users and eight non-users of brand A, even though, say, only 10 per cent of the defined population uses brand A. More recently, life-cycle, lifestyle and attitudes may be used as quotas, but this complicates considerably the recruitment questionnaire.

How individuals who meet the quota requirements are located is usually up to the individual recruiter. Normally it will be by door-to-door interviewing, but if, for example, the recruiter is asked to obtain mothers with young children, she may stand outside a number of school gates or health clinics. This may be a supplement to or instead of the normal approach. Care is usually taken to avoid recruiting friends or relatives to the same groups, and to avoid people who have frequently or recently been interviewed for market research purposes.

Some difficult-to-find respondents may be obtained through social networks using snowball sampling – that is, using contacts to suggest others who may be in the same category, then using these contacts to suggest further contacts, and so on.

Qualitative research agencies each have their own way of operating. Some may use field managers or supervisors; others may employ direct researcher-to-recruiter contact. There is often a problem of over-researched areas where recruiters happen to live. There has also been talk of 'professional groupies' – those who seem to make a habit of appearing in group discussions.

Unlike other areas of market research, respondents in group discussions are usually paid an 'incentive' to cover travel expenses, time and inconvenience. Few people, however, attend just for the money. Curiosity is a powerful motivator, but it is usually the skill of the recruiter in establishing rapport on the doorstep that is the deciding factor. Good recruiters plan where and how to recruit, setting daily targets, and try to find the most difficult categories of people first. Sometimes, former respondents are recontacted after a statutory 'fallow' period, or members of the respondent's family are co-opted by telephone.

The topics to be discussed in the groups will be those agreed between the client and the agency at the briefing meeting, and may even be formalised in a written research proposal. The interviewers will normally be given guidelines on how the topics are to be introduced and in what order, but it will be up to the interviewer to decide when to move on to the next topic. This may be because time is pressing, because the interviewer has decided that the topic has been sufficiently aired or senses that respondents are beginning to dry up or tire of the topic.

It is in the method of running groups that there is probably most variation. The three key dimensions here are the role of the group interviewer, the use of stimulus material, and the use of projective techniques. The group interviewer is usually referred to as a 'moderator' who will usually be a research executive from an agency that specialises in qualitative market research. He or she will have been involved in the initial discussions and briefing with clients, and will write up the results and possibly present them. Where the number of groups is small, the same person will probably do them all, otherwise a small team may be required. Sometimes agencies will subcontract to professional moderators operating on a freelance basis.

The main tasks of the moderator are to:

- ensure that the conditions of the discussion are correctly set up,
- get the discussion going,
- introduce new topics as appropriate,
- wind up the discussion in a satisfactory manner.

If the venue is a private house, then the moderator will need to check out the seating arrangements. As far as possible, this should be in a circle with all the chairs the same height. This is often difficult with a mixture of sofas, armchairs, stools and dining chairs. Normally, the discussion will be tape recorded, so it is necessary to check that this is correctly placed and in working order. If stimulus materials are to be used, they, too, will need to be checked.

There is no agreed pattern or routine for getting the discussion going. Sometimes respondents are shown into the room where the moderator is present as they arrive. The moderator will need to engage them in small talk until all are present, but it does mean that some rapport is set up in advance. Sometimes the respondents gather elsewhere in the house and are shown into the room together. When beginning, the moderator will introduce himself or herself, say on behalf of which agency the research is being conducted, and indicate the topics that are to be covered. Usually there will be reassurances that all responses are confidential, that it is not a 'test', so there are no 'correct' answers, that the tape recorder is only to help make a note of what people say. Some moderators believe in warm-up or ice-breaking strategies, for example, getting respondents to introduce themselves and say what they do. There is a danger here of establishing a 'turn-taking' routine with each communication being directed to the moderator. The moderator needs to encourage the respondents to interact and to communicate with each other.

Once a discussion begins, the moderator can follow one of three main roles: take a 'back seat' and just observe what is happening with little intervention (although the 'fly-on-the-wall' model is no longer accepted); become one of the group; continue to be the focus of attention. Each of these has its strengths and drawbacks. In the end it is probably best for the moderator to play the role that he or she feels most comfortable with or feels is appropriate for that particular group.

There are few general rules or guides as to how the moderator should proceed as he or she introduces the appropriate topics. The sequencing of topics and tasks will have been agreed with the client before the discussions begin: for example, should respondents be shown the new packaging for the product before they discuss the existing brand, or afterwards? The moderator will have a topic guide or perhaps even a full interview guide which explains how respondents are to be asked to take part in all stages of the interview. The moderator will need to understand the processes of group dynamics to ensure a successful outcome. Thus it has been suggested (for example by Tuckman 1965) that all groups go through four key stages: forming, storming, norming and performing. In the forming stage there is a lot of superficial chat. The moderator needs to give respondents easy tasks to do and encourage them to develop a group spirit. As participants begin to size each other up, competitiveness creeps in, and there may be rivalries for attention and control. This is the storming stage, and the moderator will need to help the group to get to the next stage, norming, before it can work together effectively. Acceptable ways of doing things become established and people settle down to the task at hand. In the last stage, performing, the group should be ready to tackle more demanding tasks.

Winding up the discussion in a satisfactory manner is all too frequently neglected. A group that has been operating well together needs a few moments to wind down. Signals that the discussion is nearly over need to be given, for example: 'The last thing I'd like you to do is ...' If the moderator brings the discussion to an abrupt end, people my feel that they have been used and then just dropped, and a sense of dissatisfaction may develop.

In running groups, not only does the moderator have to be aware of group dynamics, he or she needs to use non-verbal communication – body language such as posture, tone of voice, eye contact, facial expression – to keep the social interaction proceeding smoothly. At the end of the day it is the moderator's responsibility to:

- direct the flow of the discussion over areas that are important to the research,
- recognise important points and encourage groups to explore them and elaborate on them,

- observe all the non-verbal communication between respondents and between respondents and moderator,
- create an atmosphere that allows respondents to relax and lower some of their defences,
- synthesise the understanding gained with the problems and objectives of the research,
- test out hypotheses generated by the information gained as the discussion proceeds.

All this requires training and it takes practice. Gordon and Langmaid (1988: 51) suggest that, in their experience, two years is an absolute minimum from setting out as a novice to attaining a thorough grounding in both group and individual interviewing skills.

The role of the moderator, then, is crucial for how group discussions are run. There are, however, two other key factors that come into play: the use of stimulus materials and the use of projective techniques. Stimulus materials may be shown to respondents to communicate the idea of a new product, pack or advertising, and may be realistic or rough. Real materials include actual products, advertising or promotional materials. Wherever possible, real materials are to be preferred. If the topic for discussion is a particular existing brand of snack or drink, then it can become part of the discussion. However, if the products are not yet fully developed, the rough materials might include:

- concept boards,
- storyboards,
- animatics,
- narrative tapes,
- physical mock-ups.

Concept boards are single posters in which the product, pack or advertising for the product is described in words or expressed as drawings. It would be usual to use a set of concept boards for comparative purposes rather than one on its own.

Storyboards illustrate key frames from a commercial, drawn consecutively like a comic strip. They may be accompanied by a script written below or by a tape recorder with sound effects. Sometimes the frames are revealed one by one, using flip-over boards to stop respondents reading ahead.

Animatics are a bit like crude cartoons with a sequence of frames videoed to represent live action and accompanied by a sound track. Variations are photomatics, using photographs to show the story more realistically, or admatics, which use computer-generated images to improve on animatics.

Narrative tapes are audio tapes on which the product, the dialogue, the scene and characters are explained. The tapes may be accompanied by key visuals.

Physical mock-ups may be of the product itself or of the packaging. The idea is to make the product as 'real' as possible.

The problem with such rough materials is that they are usually seen as 'real' by respondents, who do not 'see' the concept board but a real advertisement. In consequence, many researchers use more indirect means where the stimulus materials are ambiguous. Such **projective techniques**, as they are called, have their roots in psychoanalysis and are based on theories that suggest that as children develop, they deal with those aspects of their behaviour and personality that are unwanted by projecting them out onto the environment, or by repressing them, that is, denying their existence. As a consequence, there are aspects of adult personality, feelings and emotions that people are not aware of at a cognitive level. Projective techniques tap these repressed or projected elements by asking individuals to respond to ambiguous stimuli. The result, so advocates of these techniques argue, is that respondents reveal layers of their personality, emotions and feelings that would otherwise remain hidden.

Practitioners tend to have their own preferred techniques, but the most common are procedures for:

- association,
- completion,
- transformation,
- construction.

Association procedures include word association (e.g. 'What do you associate with the word ... ?'), collage building (from a wide variety of materials cut out from magazines), or psychodrawing. Completion procedures include sentence completion, story completion or bubble cartoons (asking respondents to fill in thought bubbles of people drawn in simple cartoon style). Transformation procedures involve inviting respondents to imagine transforming brands into people (e.g. 'If this brand came to life as a person, what would he or she be like?') or into animals, or to transform themselves into a brand. Construction procedures ask respondents to construct a role (e.g. acting out a buying situation) or to construct an obituary for a brand, saying what it would be remembered for and so on.

Interpreting responses to these procedures, clearly, requires skill and imagination. It also requires sensitivity to judge when is the most appropriate moment to introduce them. There is also the danger of using such techniques casually and only as a form of substitute stimulus material.

The remaining issues concerning the setting-up and running of group discussions concern the place, the venue and the timing. It is unreasonable to expect respondents to travel long distances to attend group discussions. In consequence, in the UK, there has been a tendency for groups to be held in the home of the recruiter to which both the moderator from the agency and the respondents come. Respondents are more likely to feel comfortable in a private house, particularly if the discussion is held in the evening. However, there are problems. People's living rooms will vary in many ways and are not always suitable in terms of seating arrangements or space to display a large concept board.

In the USA and on the Continent it is more usual to have specially equipped consumer laboratories or viewing rooms to which respondents are invited. Clients may view one or more of the discussions from behind a one-way mirror to get a feel for how they are conducted and the kinds of things that get said about their products. Viewing facilities in London are now becoming more commonplace, but in the regions they are rare. If a client wishes to see groups in operation, he or she will need to join the group in person. However, if clients wish groups to be videoed, then recruiters' sitting rooms may not be suitable. It is frequently argued, however, that central viewing facilities tend to inhibit relaxed discussion and are more likely to induce groups to perform their tasks like committees.

Depth interviews

It has already been suggested that the crucial difference between depth interviews and group discussions is that in the former the main lines of communication are between interviewer and respondent (or respondents), rather than between respondents themselves. To distinguish depth interviews from the kind of standard, questionnaire-based, face-to-face interviews, it is helpful to remember that qualitative research is based on open-ended interview methods. This means that the interviewer is not constrained by pre-coded questions or even by a fixed sequence of questions. It is more along the lines of a conversation on an agreed topic, and the data are captured in the form of narrative rather than isolated statements.

When planning depth interviews, the main design considerations are:

- who to talk to,
- the type of interview,
- the degree of 'depth' required,
- the degree of structuring,
- the use of stimulus material,
- the location and method of data capture.

There are three key sub-issues relating to the first design consideration of who to talk to. First, what kind of person; second, how many people; and third, how they are to be selected. 'Executive' interviews will be with managers in organisations whether business or non-profit-making, and will concern the role, actions or perceptions of that individual in the organisation; alternatively, these interviews will focus on the way in which the organisation (or parts of it) does things. Consumer interviews will be outside the organisational or work context and will treat individuals as private consumers. Since depth interviews are usually one to one, they take a considerable amount of time, but 10–15 interviews may be all that is needed to get a feel for the kinds of views being expressed. The selection of potential respondents to approach will, for executive interviews, be based on the position of the individual in the company. The selection of companies or organisations themselves will often be based on business directories or directories of other types of organisation. The selection and recruitment of consumers will usually be on the same basis as for group discussions, that is, they are 'pre-recruited'. This means that they have already agreed to the interview at the recruitment stage.

Who to talk to overlaps with the consideration of the type of interview because, for example, executive and consumer interviews are different types of interview based on the kind of person. Interview type may also be based on the role the interviewee is expected to play, and on the number of people involved in the same interview. Interviewees may act as either (or both) informants or respondents. As informants, they give information which is not about themselves, but about the organisation in which they work or are members. Many executive interviews are of this kind, where the manager is being asked by the researcher for information about the organisation and the way it operates. However, consumer interviews may be about information on other members of the family – for example, how much television they watch. As respondents, people give personal information – either their role in an organisation or their role as consumers. The researcher may, of course, ask the interviewee to act in both these roles.

Not all depth interviews are one to one. Some are paired, triangular or family interviews. Executive interviewing will sometimes be with more than one executive simultaneously, for example, the marketing manager and the public relations officer. Consumer interviews may be with married couples or the whole family at home. Young children can often be more successfully interviewed in a family context than in a peer group environment. Willis (1990: 256) suggests that triangular interviews, consisting of three participants who often know one another, are very useful among teenagers, particularly in sensitive product areas. Such interviews encourage interaction and can even be set up to encourage debate, for example, by deliberately recruiting a user, a non-user and a lapsed user to discuss a product. At this point the depth interview is barely distinguishable from a mini-group discussion, except perhaps in terms of the number of participants. Family interviews may be necessary where it is important to understand the influences of individual family members on the purchase of shared products.

The term 'depth' interview can be a bit of a misnomer for some of the interviews that are included in this category. Depth is a matter of degree, and some may be quite superficial. Some interviews may be journalistic in nature. They accept what people say at face value, they are descriptive, and they seek basic information from respondents. Genuine depth interviews go beyond the face value, looking for patterns and frameworks, and interpreting the meanings and implications of what was said. Projective **techniques** may be used to tap 'hidden' emotions. 'Mini-depth' interviews may be conducted over a short 15–30 minute period (for example, to test a specific piece of communication such as a pack design, or to explore specific research objectives). A 'standard' consumer depth interview will last 45 minutes to an hour. 'Extended' depths may last for up to two and a half hours and will be used in circumstances similar to extended group discussions.

The degree of structuring may be anything from completely open-ended to a semi-structured interview in which there is a detailed interview guide to the topics to be covered. This is linked to the use of stimulus material. The various kinds of stimulus material and the use of projective techniques have already been explained in the context of group discussions. However, the choice and design of the stimuli must be appropriate to the one-to-one nature of most interviews. It can be more complex than for group discussions since the respondent is not distracted by the interaction of the group environment.

The location of depth interviews is, in the UK, normally in respondents' own homes, but may be in the recruiters' homes, in a central location with a viewing room, or in a hotel. Factors affecting the decision will include the sensitivity of the topic matter; the status, availability and location of the interviewees; the nature and amount of stimulus material to be used; and the need for the interview to be observed by others. Executive interviews will usually be in the office of the executive or occasionally in one of the company meeting rooms.

Normally the interview will be tape recorded. In a central location viewing room, there will usually be facilities for videoing the interview as well as for observing it while remaining unseen. This, however, may be unsettling for the individuals concerned, perhaps more so than for groups, when the feeling of being watched or videoed together may not be so threatening as being individually 'exposed' or 'watched'. A variation here is the 'accompanied' depth interview, where the respondent is accompanied by a qualitative researcher, usually during the purchasing process at a selected purchase outlet. The interview will begin in the respondent's own home with a discussion about his or her state of mind concerning the purchase and the influences that may affect the decision. Both respondent and researcher then go to the shop where the respondent will be encouraged to ignore the researcher and carry on looking, choosing and buying as normal. The researcher will observe and record the respondent's progress.

The last part of the interview will involve a full discussion of what has taken place, how this matched expectations of the visit, and how this differed from recalled behaviour.

The choice of method

Most qualitative research is undertaken using group discussions and it is felt by some writers (e.g. Gordon and Langmaid 1988: 15) that depth interviews are seriously underrated and often misused or misunderstood by buyers of qualitative research. In deciding which of the two methods to use, it is helpful to bear in mind the advantages and limitations of each.

The key advantages of group discussions include the following:

- The group environment with 'everybody in the same boat' can be less intimidating than individual depth interviews.
- What respondents say in a group often sparks experiences or ideas on the part of others.
- Differences between consumers are highlighted, making it possible to understand a range of attitudes in a short space of time.
- It is easier to observe groups.
- Social and cultural influences are highlighted.
- Groups provide a social context that is a 'hot-housed' reflection of the real world.
- Groups tend to be dynamic and often, though not necessarily, more creative.
- Groups are relatively cheaper and faster than depth interviews.

The main disadvantages of groups are as follows:

- Group processes may inhibit some people from making a full contribution and may encourage others to play to the audience.
- Group processes may stall beyond retrieval by the moderator.
- Some groups take on a life of their own, and what is said may have validity only in that context.
- It is not usually possible to identify which group members said what unless it has been videoed.

Turning now to depth interviews, their key strengths are where the group discussion is weak, for example:

- Longitudinal information, for example, on decision-making processes, can be gathered one respondent at a time.
- It is possible to identify exactly who said what.
- Both majority and minority opinions can be captured irrespective of personalities and group processes.
- Intimate and personal material can be more easily discussed.

- Respondents are less likely simply to express socially acceptable attitudes and behaviour.
- Problems of recruitment to a group are avoided.

The main disadvantages of depth interviews are:

- They are time-consuming both to conduct and to analyse; a maximum of three to four a day is often all that is possible and travelling time between interviews can be considerable.
- They are relatively more costly than group interviews.
- There is a temptation to begin treating depth interviews as if they were a questionnaire survey, thinking in terms of 'how many' rather than 'how', 'why' or 'what'.
- There is less opportunity for creativity arising from group dynamics.

Which of these advantages and limitations are important depends, clearly, on the objectives of the research, but also, crucially, on five other key factors:

- the problems of recruitment,
- the geographical scatter of the sample,
- the nature of the product being researched,
- the amount of information required,
- the constraints of budget and time.

With difficult-to-recruit consumers or with busy executives, the only practical solution is to interview individually, irrespective of other advantages and limitations. If the people to be interviewed are widely scattered or very heterogeneous, it may be extremely difficult and costly to bring them together for group discussions. Where the subject matter relates to a personal or intimate topic, like sanitary protection, then, again, depth interviews may be called for, as will be the case where the information required means connecting comments with particular individuals, for example, on the history of the ownership of consumer durables. Perhaps the main reason, however, for the popularity of group discussions relates to time and budget constraints. This is not the best of reasons for choosing group discussions, but the alternative may be no research at all if time and money are limited.

The applications of qualitative research

These may be grouped into four main categories, although they will tend to overlap or be combined in any one particular piece of research:

- exploratory research,
- diagnostic research,
- evaluative research,
- creative development research.

Traditionally, qualitative research has often been seen as a 'preliminary' to a larger-scale, quantitative study and in this sense it is being used for exploratory purposes, usually in uncharted marketing territory. Exploratory research as such is discussed in more detail in Chapter 8 when we look at research design. Qualitative research will tend to be used for exploratory purposes in the following situations:

• The researcher does not know enough about a country or a market or some aspect of consumer behaviour to be able to design a piece of research, submit a worthwhile research proposal, or decide on the priorities and objectives of the research.

• The researcher wants to generate hypotheses or possible explanations before embarking on the main study.

• The researcher needs to design questionnaires in which the consumer perspective on or images of products and brands need to be tested and are not known in advance, or where the words, phrases or categorisations of markets or products need to be checked before proceeding to quantitative research.

Very often companies are aware that they have a marketing problem, but are unsure whether this is a symptom of a deeper-seated problem or the cause of other problems; they may be unclear how it is related to other problems, whether it is urgent or serious, and what factors may be affecting the problem. Qualitative research may be used to diagnose in detail company or organisational circumstances. It may be used for diagnostic purposes for consumers as well; for example, the researcher wants to unravel complex decision-making processes, define consumer perceptions of competitive sets and brand substitutes, or define the dimensions that differentiate brands.

In evaluative research, qualitative methods may be used to assess whether or not a particular marketing proposition or marketing mix will satisfy company objectives. Qualitative research, particularly group discussion, is frequently used to evaluate an advertising or promotional proposition. The procedure can be useful, but only if the criteria for evaluation – the benchmarks of success or failure – are clear. Thus an ad can be tested for understanding, link with the brand, memorability, enjoyability and so on. Some commentators (e.g. Sargent 1989: 118) are sceptical about the use of qualitative research for evaluative purposes. If the objective of the research is, for example, to pick a 'winner' from a range of ideas or executions, it is, argues Sargent, more sensible to rely on quantitative assessment techniques. Such techniques for the pre-testing of advertising are considered in detail in Chapter 7.

One of the major strengths of qualitative research, whether group discussion or depth interview, is its potential for creativity: it is frequently used to generate ideas for new products, ideas for modifying products, to identify gaps in the marketplace, or to generate advertising themes or ideas for promotional activity. Special techniques like **brainstorming**, **synectics** and a range of **projective techniques** are often used to help in this process.

It is important for a research executive in a market research company to recognise what type of application a client is looking for because that will affect the approach to sampling, interviewing, analysis and reporting. Two or more applications may, of course, need to be combined into the same research.

The analysis and interpretation of data from qualitative research

As was explained in Chapter 2, there are two kinds of qualitative data:

- single, isolated statements in words, such as those derived from open-ended questions in a questionnaire survey or from seeking reactions to specific questions in an experimental design,
- narrative text such as is derived from tape recording, videoing or making close notes in depth interviews or group discussions.

The analysis of the first type of qualitative data will be considered in the next chapter on data analysis. This section will look only at approaches to the analysis of narrative text. What, for example, do you do with a set of audio or video tape recordings? There are no standard or 'correct' ways of proceeding, unlike quantitative research, where there are generally accepted routines for the analysis and interpretation of the results. The researcher needs to deliberate on all that was said, to structure it in a meaningful and relevant way, and to identify the key areas of usefulness for the client.

Qualitative researchers each have their own style of analysis, but whatever the style, it may be broken down into three key stages:

- transcription,
- mechanical analysis,
- interpretive analysis.

Most tape recordings are transcribed into written or printed text as a first stage. However, some researchers insist on doing this themselves, or, at least, claim a preference for doing so. The argument is that the person who has to report the results needs to pick up the cues on not just *what* was said, but *how* it was said. If it is a video recording, then other cues are picked up from who said it and the accompanying body language. However, some qualitative researchers do not have the time or the inclination for what, after all, is a tedious activity and will hand the tapes over to secretaries to transcribe. Transcription may, of course, be literal, including all the 'ums', 'ers' and false starts; others may be a paraphrase into grammatically correct English, or may even be just notes and summaries of what was said. For depth interviews, the transcript will be on a respondent-by-respondent basis; for group discussions, on a group-by-group basis.

Mechanical analysis has the aim of sorting and classifying what people said into categories with a view to bringing together comments that are on the same topic. This may mean generating a framework of categories as the analysis proceeds; modifying, developing and refining it as you go along. Several attempts or 'passes' at the transcripts may be needed before a set of categories is satisfactory. As far as possible, the categories should be exhaustive and mutually exclusive, and they should not be too many in number. More than six or so will make the next stage – interpretation – all the more difficult. The search is then on for patterns. Is there a tendency for the replies of users and non-users of the brand to be systematically different on particular topics? Is there a difference between the men and the women; the older and the younger age groups; the ABC1s and the C2DEs?

There are two main approaches to mechanical analysis. First, the 'large-sheet-of-paper' approach, which is basically a crosstabulation of major dependent variables by independent variables, and the cells contain quotes, observations, summaries or interpretations. Essentially, it is a topic-by-topic analysis. Second, there is the 'annotating-the-transcripts' approach. The annotations may highlight differences between sample segments, contradictions, majority and minority viewpoints, or interesting quotes. The process may involve underlining, parenthesising, highlighting, commenting in the margin or cross-referencing, using coloured pens and so on. The process is done transcript by transcript, taking a holistic approach to each one.

Interpretive analysis involves trying to work out the meaning of what was said, and then considering the implications of this for the objectives of the research. It means going beyond what people say; not taking their comments at face value. It means attending to what some writers on qualitative research have referred to as 'the space between the lines', or to the 'Eureka' moments. Those writers who have tried to describe how they do this talk about ideas 'swimming around in the head' or about 'mulling them over'. The brain is a kind of 'black box' that, over time, in an invisible process, sorts things out, comes up with structures, frameworks, patterns, solutions and, hopefully, answers – in short, with 'insight' or a 'way forward', which may involve a 'leap of faith'.

All this sounds very unscientific and unobjective, which worries some clients; but unless it is a process to which the qualitative researcher is prepared to devote time and energy, then the analysis of the data will remain at the journalistic level. Researchers will simply report back to clients what respondents have said. Emphasis will be on the coding of responses and treating the research as if it were a quantitative survey.

Responses will be simply summarised and assumed to be the answer to the problems outlined by the client. For some qualitative research, this may, indeed, be all that the client wants; for others, the client may be getting poor value for his or her money. A proper analysis is slow, labour-intensive and highly energy-absorbing; but to neglect the analysis and interpretation stage may undermine the value of unstructured interviewing – the yield in terms of information, insight and creativity is short-changed, and the analysis and interpretation is more superficial than it should be.

The role of analysis and interpretation does, however, vary according to the type of application. Where the research is for largely exploratory purposes, then the focus may well be on establishing patterns and generating conceptual frameworks. Diagnostic research calls for lateral thinking and insight rather than the mechanical sorting of ideas. For evaluative research, the analysis may be quite straightforward – the responses of consumers are simply compared with intended or desired responses. For creative development, the researcher needs to 'absorb' what the respondents are saying in their own terms and in their own language.

Gordon and Langmaid (1988) have emphasised that analysis is not a stage that takes place after the fieldwork is completed, but that it carries on continuously, right from the initial contact with the client. The client's problem and the research objectives are stored at the back of the researcher's mind as the research proceeds, demanding conscious and unconscious attention, while tentative hypotheses are developed and continually tested.

The presentation of results

Once the analysis has been completed, the researcher involved in the project will usually present the findings to the client in a face-to-face session at the client's own premises, giving managers the opportunity to ask questions about the research. It takes time and skill to convert the findings into a well-structured, oral presentation. When planning what format the presentation should take, the researcher will need to bear in mind:

- the original problems presented in the brief,
- who will be at the presentation,
- what time is available,
- whether visual aids should be used,
- the order of the topics,
- how informal or formal the occasion is likely to be.

Jargon and technical terms need to be kept to a minimum. As far as possible, the presentation should be enjoyable and entertaining, involving all those who are attending. Commentary on the background and methodology should be very brief; busy executives are usually more interested in the results, conclusions and recommendations.

Not all projects require a detailed written report. Creative development work for advertising may need only a quick summary to act as 'evidence' of the findings. In an exploratory study for market entry, a detailed report will probably be very important. There is likely to be too much information to be commented on in a single presentation, while a written report will be required as a 'bible' for decision-making. A typical report will include:

- a title page and contents page,
- an executive summary that says who did what for what purpose, and what the main conclusions and recommendations are,
- an introduction giving a more detailed statement of the background and objectives of the research,
- the methods and sampling used,
- the main findings,
- the conclusions drawn from the findings,
- the recommendations,
- appendices containing tables, charts, copies of stimulus material used, copies of the interview guide and the recruitment questionnaire.

The validity of qualitative research

As is clear from the earlier section on the analysis and interpretation of results, such results are reached not by a scientific, rigorous and objective process, but by a mysterious, subjective and often subconscious 'black box' activity in the brain. This has implications for the validity of the results obtained. There is no single 'truth' buried in the tape recordings that can be excavated and 'discovered' by the researcher. Interpretations depend on the individual and on the broader context of knowledge and data that already exist. No two researchers will come to exactly the same con-clusions; achieving validity through replication is thus not usually possible.

According to Sykes (1990), in qualitative research, 'validity' may refer to:

- the 'goodness' of the data – the kind, accuracy, relevance, richness, colourfulness of the data derived from individual sample units, be they single individuals or groups,
- the 'status' of the qualitative findings – their hardness, generalisability, truth, or the extent to which they are 'scientific'.

Which of these is appropriate depends on the research objectives. If the purpose is to generate ideas for new products, then the number and quality of ideas is important; the question of 'truth' in any absolute sense is certainly not. It is in this sense of validity that qualitative research has a particular advantage over other types of research. Topics and ideas can be pursued from a variety of angles and perspectives; it is the flexible and responsive interaction that sparks ideas and gets respondents to think creatively.

If the purpose of the research is for evaluation, or to pick the 'best' idea for an advertising theme, then the status or truth of the data is crucial, since that determines the confidence with which inferences can be drawn from the data. Some researchers have argued simply that *no* inferences can be drawn – because samples are too small and purposively selected, and because the inductive approach does not allow hypothesis-testing. The smallness of the samples has been shown by some studies not to be a great impediment to the kinds of conclusions arrived at, and that qualitative samples can and do satisfy the theoretical requirements for making generalisations; a point argued by Griggs (1987). It has been argued, furthermore, that quantitative research, too, uses inductive as well as deductive processes and that hypothesis-testing in the sense of relating ideas to data (not tests of statistical significance against the null hypothesis) lies at the very heart of qualitative research.

Inferential validity in qualitative research can be established in a number of ways:

- Face validity is said to exist when the research produces the kind of information wanted or expected.
- Internal validity refers to the internal coherence of the findings and means checking out responses for consistency, and ruling out ambiguity and contradiction.
- Criterion validity is said to exist when the interpretations from qualitative research match the conclusions drawn from alternative procedures.

Face validity, it can be argued, is a necessary but not sufficient condition for establishing validity. Internal validity means examining the text as a whole and seeking support for a particular interpretation from the textual evidence. However, although a high degree of internal validity is usually possible in qualitative research because of the opportunities for responsive cross-checking and amplification of ideas as they emerge from the data, the process is not open to scrutiny and the data may be consistent or be made to look consistent with a number of different interpretations.

Conclusion

Qualitative research provides data rich in ideas, insights, hypotheses, explanations and suggestions. It answers such questions as 'What?', 'Why?' or 'How?', but not 'How many?' The focus is always on understanding consumers or other kinds of respondents from their own perspective; it is

never a key role to measure the extent to which these views, feeli
behaviour are held.

The cost of qualitative research can, at first sight, seem high, but it is
cheaper, on the whole, than ad hoc survey research. Cost is generally based
on the number of interviews rather than on researcher time. Typically, a
group discussion will cost £700–1,000 per group (including analysis and
report). The cost of depth interviews varies enormously. Executive interviews tend to be the most expensive. For the agency, there will be many
variables that affect the cost, and hence profitability, of the research undertaken. These variables include:

- how full and formal a written report is required,
- the number of briefing meetings needed,
- the difficulty of recruiting the sample,
- the size of the groups and how long they are to last,
- the type of venue.

Buyers are often looking only at the cost per group and not at variations in
the levels of service provided by the agency. The Chairman of the AQRP
has argued that costings should be on a professional fee for time plus direct
costs basis. The former would make provision for briefing meetings, setting
up the project, carrying out the fieldwork, analysing and interpreting the
data, presenting the results, and writing the report. Direct costs would vary
according to the number of groups and would include the fees paid to
recruiters, costs of finding and hiring rooms, the financial incentives paid to
respondents, refreshments that may be given during the interviews, and the
travelling and subsistence of the moderator.

SURVEY RESEARCH

A survey is the collection of data based on addressing questions to
respondents in a formal manner and taking a systematic record of their
responses. The record will normally be a questionnaire, but may be a diary
or direct data capture using electronic means. Surveys may be used in
either continuous or ad hoc research. Continuous research is described in a
later section. This section addresses itself to the design and conduct of ad
hoc surveys, which are one-off pieces of research, and are usually custom-
designed for a particular purpose or client. They also tend to be cross-
sectional, that is, they treat the period over which the research is conducted
as one unit of time.

All ad hoc surveys go through a number of stages, which are outlined in
Figure 5.1. The researcher begins by analysing the problem or problems
that the research is to address before designing the most appropriate kind
of survey to conduct. However, before data are collected it may be wise, if
not essential, to undertake some exploratory research, as a consequence of

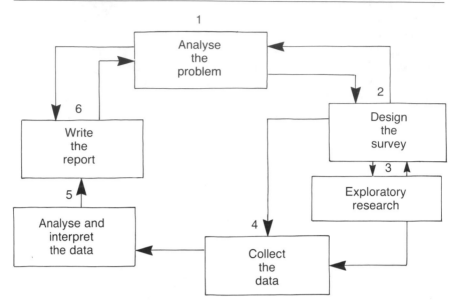

Figure 5.1 The stages of ad hoc survey research

which some redesign of the survey may be necessary – hence the double arrow in Figure 5.1. This time it may be possible to proceed directly to data collection without further exploratory research. Once the data have been collected, they need to be analysed and interpreted, and a report written of the results. The report should, in turn, address the original analysis of the problem to complete the 'loop' in the survey research process. Reflection on this problem may prompt the researcher to revise the report before submission. Between stages 5 and 6 there may be a face-to-face presentation of the preliminary results to the client.

In looking at the various types of ad hoc survey, we can make distinctions along a number of dimensions, for example:

- by topic,
- by type of researcher,
- by method of questionnaire administration.

A basic distinction in terms of topic is between consumer surveys (which study individuals or private households as final consumers of products and services) and business surveys (which address questions to individuals in business organisations concerning those organisations, not their private purchasing behaviour).

Surveys distinguished by type of researcher include:

- in-house surveys, which are carried out by the company itself using its own market research department,

- market research company surveys, which are commissioned by a client organisation. These may be custom-designed for a particular client, or syndicated in some way: for example, companies may share either the organisation of a survey or the data that emerge,
- academic surveys done on a consultancy basis, or for the purposes of scholarly research,
- governmental surveys organised by the Office of Population Censuses and Surveys and carried out by the Government Social Survey Unit.

Methods of questionnaire administration fall into three main categories:

- interview surveys,
- telephone surveys,
- postal surveys.

Interview surveys

Most survey work in the UK is conducted through face-to-face interviews, for the most part by full-time or part-time employees of a market research company or by individuals offering their services on a freelance, self-employed basis. Occasionally they are conducted by research executives or by academic researchers. The prevalence of this method of questionnaire administration is explained largely by the key advantages of this form of social encounter:

- The interviewer can check and ensure respondent eligibility before the interview is started.
- Personally administered questionnaires ensure that all questions are asked in the required order, and that all applicable questions are asked.
- The interviewer can encourage respondents to answer as fully as possible and check, as appropriate, that the question is correctly understood.
- Materials that need to be shown to the respondents can be properly presented.
- Response rates are consistently higher than for other methods of questionnaire administration.
- Where quotas are applied, the interviewer can ensure that the target number of interviews is achieved.
- Interviewers can usually persuade respondents to complete the interview.

These advantages together mean that the quality of the data derived from interview surveys is generally superior to that obtained by other methods.

Interview surveys can be grouped into five styles according to the type of location in which they occur:

- street,
- home,
- hall,
- shop,
- business organisation.

Street surveys are usually conducted in busy town centres, particularly in shopping malls or precincts. In the USA they call them 'mall intercept' interviews. The interviewer tends to stay in one position, approaching potential respondents as soon as a previous interview is completed. This eliminates travel time between interviews and makes recruitment fairly speedy. However, street interviews need to be brief, since respondents are unlikely to stop for more than about 10 minutes, while the use of show materials also needs to be controlled. Furthermore, enclosed shopping malls are considered to be private property and the permission of the centre manager will be required to carry out the interviewing. Some centres have a no-interviewing policy; others may charge for the facility on a pre-booked basis.

In-home interviews are conducted in those surveys where recruitment is door to door. 'Doorstep' interviews, however, may be a more accurate description of the typical location. Interviewers may be given lists of names and addresses; they may be limited to a prescribed number of streets or to an area (a sampling point); in addition, they may have instructions about how to proceed, for example, calling at every fifth house, or missing out a certain number of houses after every successful interview. Whereas street interviews are always 'cold', in-home interviews may be pre-recruited by telephone. Door-to-door recruitment can be time-consuming and it relies on people being at home. Although longer interviews are usually possible, interruptions are always a hazard whether it is from other members of the household (including pets) or from the television or the telephone.

Interviews carried out in a pre-booked location are usually referred to as 'hall tests', even though it may not be in a hall, but in a public room in a hotel, and it may not be a 'test' in the sense of the kind of hall tests conducted and described later as experimental research. Recruitment is usually from a street nearby and respondents are invited to 'answer a few questions' about a particular product or whatever is the topic of the survey. Respondents can be given refreshments while being interviewed and this facilitates completion of more complex tasks. Interviews conducted indoors, furthermore, can use a much greater array of materials, including videos or elaborate displays. A team of interviewers may work from the same hall where they can be supervised and monitored.

In-store surveys may take place in a shop or just outside. The researcher or the market research company will, clearly, need to obtain permission from the store, and in many cases also the co-operation of the store personnel. Recruitment may be on the basis of people entering or leaving the store – the most appropriate approach will be determined by the subject matter or objectives of the research. Thus a study of shopping intentions will require the former approach. As with interviews taking place in halls being called 'hall tests', so interviews taking place either outside or inside the shop are usually called 'store tests', even though they are not, strictly speaking, tests using any form of experimental design.

Business interviews will normally take place in the interviewee's office or in one of the company meeting rooms. Such interviews will have been pre-arranged. There is always the danger, however, that some 'crisis' may occur and the interview will need to be cancelled, postponed or truncated.

How many interviews the interviewer is able to conduct in a day or in a week depends on:

- location,
- recruitment time,
- interviewing time,
- travel time.

It may be possible to conduct 20–30 interviews a day using street quotas; an interviewer will be lucky to do 10 in-home, or perhaps two business interviews.

Wherever the interview is carried out, the interviewer has five key tasks:

- preparation,
- locating the respondents,
- obtaining the agreement to conduct the interview,
- asking the questions and noting down answers,
- completing records of interview assignments and returning completed questionnaires.

Interviewers' jobs begin when their packages of work arrive. The interviewers will need to go through the pack carefully, making sure that all the necessary materials and information needed have been provided. If there are any problems, he or she will have to contact the supervisor or the office. The interviewer may need to prepare a strategy for recruitment, since there may be considerable freedom as to when the interviews are carried out and where recruitment takes place. Strategies may, in fact, be similar to those adopted for recruitment to group discussions. Finally, the interviewer must be thoroughly familiar with the questionnaire. He or she is then ready to face the public.

With random sampling techniques, interviewers are given lists of names and addresses taken either from the Electoral Registers or the Post Office Address File. Having found the address, the interviewer needs to locate the named person drawn as part of the sample. If the person concerned is not at home, there is usually an instruction to make at least three callbacks at different times of the day. No substitutes are allowed. In random location and random route sampling, the interviewer will have instructions about the selection of houses and the streets in which such selections are to be made. With quota sampling, there may be no instruction about how, within a specified sampling point, the interviewer obtains her quotas, but whether the interviews are to take place in-home or in the street is usually specified.

Interviewers are normally trained on the best ways of obtaining the agreement of the named or selected person to participate. The response rate for experienced interviewers is generally consistently higher than for novices. The interviewer will have an identity card which shows that the person named on the card is registered as a bona fide interviewer. This is usually presented while the interviewer explains that he/she is conducting market research on a given topic (usually the agency will be identified, but not the client), and would like to ask a few questions seeking their opinion. Assurances of confidentiality and that personal details will not be used for selling purposes are usually given.

When asking the questions, apart from conversational pleasantries, the interviewer is normally instructed to follow exactly the wording in the questionnaire. Some questions may have 'probe' written against them, indicating that the interviewer has discretion over whether to pursue a more detailed answer than the one the respondent has just offered. When recording the answers to set-choice questions, the interviewer just has to tick boxes or put circles round numbered responses. For open-ended questions, the interviewer may be instructed to write down exactly what the respondent says, or to paraphrase.

An interviewer will normally be given an assignment of perhaps 15–20 interviews to do in a week if in-home, or rather more if based on street interview. A record of all contacts and non-contacts will be kept and this will be returned to the market research company at the end of the week along with the completed questionnaires. In some cases, interviewers have hand-held market research terminals. The terminal will have a screen that displays each question in turn and the responses. The selected response is entered as the respondent gives it. The terminal then prompts with the next relevant question, which may depend on which response has been entered. The data are stored on a disc which is then returned to the agency where the data are read directly into the computer.

Interviewing is a skilled activity. The interview itself is a process of social interaction which is highly artificial and its outcome, including answers to questions, will often depend on the sex, age, social class, dress, accent and personality of both interviewer and respondent. It is quite easy to obtain systematic differences between interviewers that need, as far as possible, to be controlled. The interviewer is, on the one hand, trying to be 'standard' in all his or her approaches to respondents, but, on the other hand, may need to react to individual circumstances for the successful completion of the interview – in short, the interviewer needs to act like a robot but retain the appearance of a human being.

Interviewer bias may present a problem and may occur in one or more of several ways. At the recruitment stage, an interviewer given an assignment with quotas may, consciously or unconsciously, select (or avoid) people of a particular type. The way the interviewer handles the initial approach will affect the response rates and probably differentially by type of respondent; the way she or he asks the questions may affect the responses given, so might the way he or she reacts verbally or non-verbally. Probing or prompting may be approached in different ways. Market research companies recognise these problems and try to minimise their impact in a number of ways. These include:

• training,
• briefing,
• quality control,
• fieldwork management,
• industry guidelines.

All interviewers are put through some kind of training programme, which should have two aspects: teaching the interviewer the skills he or she will need to carry out good interviews, and integrating interviewers into the industry. The skills required include the techniques for approaching respondents, persuading them to take part, and sustaining their level of interest. Interviewers frequently need to be able to classify respondents very quickly into the A, B, C1, C2, D, E social class categories and, for example, to be able to define the head of the household. Being made aware of the potential sources of bias is the first step in their minimisation. Interviewer integration into the industry means that the interviewer needs to be able to understand what marketing and marketing research are about, and that the rules that have to be applied can be understood and appreciated. Training programmes usually involve an in-house session (of, typically, 1–3 days) entailing lectures, exercises and simulations. Normally, there will be a manual for the interviewer to study and for future reference. In-field training will usually be under the supervision of a field supervisor. As each new topic of work is assigned, the interviewer may be accompanied by a senior interviewer or the supervisor.

Before each new assignment, there will be briefing sessions. These may be formal personal briefings where area fieldstaff are gathered together and the researcher explains all the aspects of the survey; supervisors may be briefed first and they, in turn, brief the interviewers; briefings may be over the telephone. There will usually also be detailed written instructions, sometimes standing on their own, sometimes supporting other briefing methods. Any of these methods may be combined together.

The methods used for quality control are various. The accuracy of the data collected and the legitimacy of respondent recruitment may be subjected to 'backchecks'. Supervisors recall on respondents and readminister part of the questionnaire. Some 5–10 per cent of respondents may be recontacted in this way. It may be done over the telephone, by post or by personal visit. Some agencies have a policy of accompanying interviewers in the field on a regular basis. Any bad habits can then be picked up and rectified. Central monitoring may be used to identify interviewers who regularly make mistakes or submit incomplete work; feedback from field supervisors on how well the questionnaire is performing may be used to alert other supervisors to potential difficulties.

The overall management of the fieldforce is an important factor in maintaining standards of interviewing. There will typically be a head office team led by a senior manager. There will be a number of regional supervisors working from home, controlling local teams of interviewers. These people may be salaried or they may work freelance. They all try to ensure a high standard of selection and training in their area; they will try to get each interviewer to work across the entire sample so that any biases will be equally distributed.

In the UK, industry guidelines are given by the Market Research Society, which provides a code of conduct for research, parts of which apply directly to interviewers. This code will feature in any training programme. The MRS and the Association of Market Survey Organisations (AMSO) endorse an Interviewer Quality Control Scheme (IQCS), which is a voluntary programme set up for monitoring data collection procedures, and which ensures that all member companies operate the same minimum standards of fieldwork in terms of interviewer selection, training, supervision and quality control. The MRS has introduced a uniform interviewer identity card, which seeks to reassure the public as to the legitimacy of the interview and to stop the practice of 'sugging' – selling under the guise of doing market research.

The skills of professional interviewers have allowed data collection methodologies to become more complex and sophisticated; but they are costly and time-consuming, particularly where geographically dispersed sampling is required, or where quota requirements make respondents hard to find. While interview surveys are still the dominant mode of data collection, that dominance is being challenged, particularly with the growth in telephone research, to which we now turn.

Telephone surveys

In the 1970s, telephone interviewing became well established in the UK as a method used by industrial or business market researchers to obtain information and opinions from managers and professional people. Business premises were usually on the telephone and managers were accustomed to using them. Only more recently, however, have telephone interviews with the general public become possible. By 1980 some 75 per cent of households in the UK had a telephone, and by 1990 it was approaching 90 per cent. The number of market research companies offering telephone research has grown rapidly in the last decade.

Employing interviewers and supervisors to telephone from their own homes was, however, not practicable and most market research companies offering telephone interviewing services now have central location telephoning. This concentrates interviewing in a small number of closely supervised locations. In addition, most of these centres have taken advantage of computer-assisted telephone interviewing (CATI), which has greatly increased the advantages of central location interviewing. The questionnaire is programmed into the computer prior to the commencement of the interviewing, and is displayed question by question on a visual display unit in front of each interviewer. The reply is immediately input into the computer via the keyboard (see Chapter 4, 'Recording devices').

Telephone interviewing has two main advantages over face-to-face interviewing:

• It is not necessary to cluster the interviewing in sampling points; this has the effect of reducing sampling error.
• It produces faster results.

Sampling for telephone surveys is rather different from that required for interview surveys. In the first place, there is a standard, accessible and comprehensive sampling frame – the telephone directories. Sampling from them can be on a systematic or random basis. Some 10 per cent of numbers, however, are ex-directory in the UK, but by adding one digit to every number selected, the correct proportion of such numbers will be sampled. Telephone ownership, however, is not universal, and non-telephone households are likely to be ones with particular characteristics – the elderly, the poor, students and so on.

Three main approaches to the exclusion of non-owners are possible:

• Redefine the population as all telephone-owning households.
• Impose quotas on the recruitment of respondents so that groups who would otherwise be under-represented are correctly represented.
• Weight the data afterwards to correct for over- and under-representations.

If the research is concerned with luxury consumer durables, then redefining the population may be acceptable and appropriate. For measuring trends, reweighting the data may give accurate results of changes taking place. However, if absolute estimates of market quantities are required, then reweighting may not be adequate since the procedure assumes that the telephone-owning section of the population who are in the under-represented groups are themselves representative of those who do not own telephones. The imposition of quotas faces the same difficulty.

For business research, there are many ready-made lists and directories of companies and organisations. British Telecom offers its Business and Residential UK Telecom User Sampling (BRUTUS) service, which provides samples specifically for market research. The database consists of all BT's business customers' installations, plus a 5 per cent sample of residential users.

In spite of all the advantages of telephone surveys, there are a number of drawbacks:

- They are limited to verbal exchanges – it is not possible to show people lists, cards or other visual materials (unless they are posted in advance).
- There are no observational data; in particular, it is not possible to watch the facial expression and body language of respondents.
- Telephone interviews have to be very short and factual, which does limit their use.
- The rise of telesales – selling over the telephone – has made many people suspicious of calls from strangers.

Postal surveys

While postal research accounts for only about 5 per cent of turnover of commissioned research, some 25 per cent of all interviews are conducted using this method. Postal surveys are, in fact, extremely cost-effective, requiring neither interviewers nor telephone systems. They are perhaps one-third of the cost of telephone surveys and one-eighth of interview surveys. The growth of direct marketing has in recent years, furthermore, given an impetus to postal surveys since recipients of postal questionnaires are likely to be customers of the company and therefore more likely to respond. Other advantages of postal surveys are:

- Central control of the survey is facilitated.
- Unclustered sampling is possible without cost penalties.
- More time can be devoted to the completion of questionnaires by respondents.
- Respondents can fill them in when it is convenient to them.
- Respondents can confer with other members of the household before filling in answers.
- There is no interviewer bias.

It is often argued that the main disadvantage of postal questionnaires is the low response rate. While response rates for some postal questionnaires are, indeed, very low, if they are used in appropriate situations and properly executed with good covering letters, reminders, incentives and so on, the response rates can be equal to that of telephone surveys and may, on occasion, approach that of interview surveys. There are, however, a number of other disadvantages:

- There is no assistance and encouragement from an interviewer.
- Respondents can read all the questionnaire in advance, so 'unfolding' or 'funnelling' techniques cannot be used.
- Responses usually take longer than for telephone or interview surveys.
- The person filling in the questionnaire may not be the one selected in the sample.

Evidence suggests that a good covering letter is crucial to the response rate, other things being equal. The letter must 'sell' the value of the survey to the respondent and encourage him or her to respond. The letter should, at a minimum, explain:

- who is carrying out the research,
- what is the purpose of the research,
- how the respondent was selected,
- that responses will be confidential,
- how to complete and return the questionnaire.

It may, in addition, help to emphasise why it is important for people to participate, how the survey will help others in the future, and that they will receive a mystery gift or token of appreciation if they return the question- naire by a certain date. Enclosing the incentive (for example, a pen) with the original letter is, so it is sometimes argued, more effective. An example of a covering letter is given in Figure 5.2. It is normal to include a stamped, addressed envelope. If it is intended to send reminders after 2–3 weeks, questionnaires will need to be numbered to identify those who have not responded. The letter may need to explain that the number will be used only for this purpose.

Interview, telephone and postal surveys may, of course, be used in combination. For example, pre-recruiting by telephone can avoid a lot of wasted leg-work. After an initial personal interview, a self-completed questionnaire can be left with the respondent to complete in order to collect additional information, perhaps from other members of the house- hold. If the survey requires an interview and follow-up, the call-back may be conducted by telephone, or a postal questionnaire may be sent. Using combinations of techniques in this way can increase the flexibility of research design.

EXPERIMENTAL RESEARCH

Instead of relying on answers to questions addressed to individuals in a survey, in an experiment the market researcher tries out some marketing

Abacus Market Research
Nelson's Column
Trafalgar Square
London WC1

Dear Mr Smith

I am writing to a carefully selected sample of people throughout the country. Your name has been chosen as someone who could answer questions on gardening, and I would appreciate your help. It will only take a few minutes of your time.

The survey, which is organised by Abacus Market Research, is designed to provide information on the way in which gardeners use the products and services that are available from garden centres. The results of the survey will be used to improve the range of products that such centres can offer to gardeners like yourself.

Your reply is very important to us and will be treated as totally confidential. It will be analysed along with other responses and none of your views will be tied to your name. Please take my personal assurance that you will not be pestered by salesmen as a result of helping me.

All you need to do is read through the questions and put a circle around the number that corresponds with your reply. Please remember there are no 'correct' answers; it is YOUR opinion that I am interested in.

When you have finished, please send the questionnaire back to me in the stamped, addressed envelope that I have provided. It would be very helpful if you could do this by the end of the month.

To show my appreciation of your efforts I will send you a mystery gift when I have received your reply.

I look forward to hearing from you.

Yours sincerely

Ray Kent
Marketing Manager
Abacus Market Research

Figure 5.2 An example of a covering letter for a self-completed questionnaire

action on a small scale, carefully observing and measuring the results and controlling, as far as possible, the effects of factors other than the marketing action being taken. Experiments have three main characteristics:

- the manipulation of one or more independent variables that the researcher wishes to test the effects of,
- a comparison of at least two measures of a dependent variable,
- the control of extraneous factors that may affect the results.

Groups or geographical areas to be subjected to a test are usually matched in such a way as to control for selected demographic characteristics that may affect the outcome of the research, for example, sex, age, social class, marital status or neighbourhood type of those participating. In some cases, recruitment to tests may be restricted to certain kinds of people, for example, users of a particular brand. Other factors that are *not* subject to control may, of course, also affect the results of the experiment. These factors may include unanticipated events during the course of the experiment, maturation or fatigue of those taking part, measurement inadequacies or errors, bias in the selection of respondents, or loss of participants during the experiment. The components of an experiment are summarised in Figure 5.3.

The key advantage of experimentation is that the researcher chooses which factors or variables he or she is going to try out. This, in turn, facilitates the drawing of conclusions in respect of causal relationships between

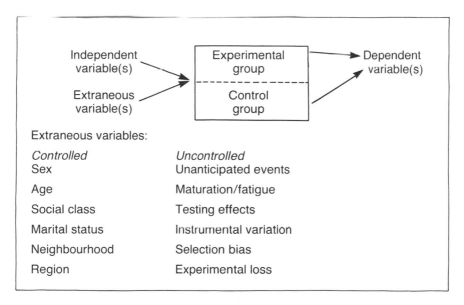

Figure 5.3 The components of an experimental design

variables. Indeed, some textbooks on market research, having made the distinction between exploratory, descriptive and causal research, proceed to equate causal research with experimental procedures. This is not totally justified, since it is possible to draw causal inferences from other types of research, although the analysis is 'ex post facto', that is, after the event. In other words, the investigation of relationships between variables and of the robustness of those relationships when other variables are controlled, is done *after* the data have been collected. Controls are established by performing analyses on sub-groups of the sample instead of assigning categories of people to experimental situations.

Experiments tend to get used where new or revised elements or combinations of marketing mix variables would be difficult or expensive to try out on the entire market; hence the emphasis on 'small-scale' tests in the definition of experimentation. Changing marketing mix variables for the total market is, in any case, not really 'experimentation', but taking the decision itself.

Experimental design

Experiments may be designed in many different ways. There are, however, two main dimensions along which most can be identified:

- whether or not there is an attempt to make observations or take measurements before as well as after the test has taken place,
- whether or not there are control groups of people who are similar in terms of the control variables to the test group, but are not subjected to the test condition.

Table 5.4 combines these two factors in a cross-classification, giving four different types of experimental design.

'After only' designs are not truly experimental, and amount solely to a 'try-it-and-see' approach on a small scale. Thus attitudes towards a product may be measured only after an advertising campaign. The problem is that there may be no measurement of what those attitudes were before the campaign, so the amount of change is unknown. Furthermore, there is no

Table 5.4 Types of experimental design

Control	Measurement	
	After test	*Before-and-after test*
No control	After only	Before and after
Control group	After only with control	Before and after with control

control over extraneous variables that could have affected the results. Such designs cannot justifiably be used to test hypotheses, but can be useful where a 'quick-and-dirty' analysis is adequate for the kinds of decisions to be taken.

'After only with control' designs add a control group to the 'after only' design in order to remove extraneous sources of bias. Participants are normally randomly assigned to the treatment and control groups, and in addition may be matched on a set of demographic variables. The difference between the experimental group and the control group is taken to be a result of the test conditions. However, there is no guarantee that both the control and experimental groups were not affected by extraneous factors and might have changed since before the test was conducted.

'Before and after' designs allow for some calculation to be made of the amount of change in a dependent variable before and after the test. There is, however, the danger that the process of making observations or taking measurements before the test may itself affect the behaviour or attitudes of those participating. In some cases, of course, measurements of, say, sales, already exist before the test and may readily be compared with sales after it.

'Before and after with control' designs add a control group to the 'before and after' design. The difference between the control group and experimental group *before* the test is compared with the difference between them *after* the test has been applied to only one group. The aim is to discount both extraneous variables and the impact of the first measurement on the second.

In practice, control groups may not be used in marketing experiments. More often there will be two or more matched experimental groups, each given a different product formulation, pack design or advertisements to try out or react to. A large number of experimental groups may be set up in different parts of the country to detect any regional differences. This may be done systematically by, in effect, 'stratifying' by region using a **randomised block** design. Suppose there are three product formulations, A, B and C, to test; the market is limited to England, which is divided into three regions, North, Midlands and South. Within each region, the three formulations could be tried separately in each of three branches of a retailer that has agreed to have the experiment staged in some of its branches. The design would look like Table 5.5. The assignment of the product formulations (and the selection of branch) could be by random processes. Analysis of variance (see Chapter 6) may be used to test the statistical significance of differences between product formulations, and to isolate this from regional differences.

Sometimes a factor like region may be only one of two or three crucial factors. To take every combination – for example, every product formulation in every region in every type of outlet – would produce a very large

Table 5.5 A randomised block design

Region	Three branches in each region		
North	A	B	C
Midlands	A	B	C
South	A	B	C

number. A more economical design is the **Latin square**. This could, say, take every product formulation A, B and C and test it in each type of outlet (multiple, co-operative or independent) and in each region, but not in each type of outlet in each region. The design might look like that in Table 5.6. Here, there are two extraneous variables: region and outlet type. These form the rows and the columns of the table. Product formulations A, B and C are then assigned randomly to cells in the table, but subject to the restriction that each appears only once in each row and once in each column. A randomised block design with every combination would have required 3 × 3 × 3 (or 27) test sites. The Latin square reduces this to nine sites, but it is still possible to estimate error due to the two sources of error, again using analysis of variance. There is the assumption, however, that there is no relationship between type of region and type of outlet.

If it *is* necessary to take account of the interaction effects between variables, a **factorial design** may be more appropriate. This design is frequently used for product testing. Suppose a new biscuit can have different levels of salt content (high, medium and low), and different levels of sweetness (high, medium and low). Each combination may then be tested. These combinations are shown in Table 5.7. This would require nine matched groups of testers. This may well be feasible, but if there were, for example, also a crucial decision about making the biscuit with either butter or margarine, then 18 matched groups may be too many. Again, some kind of Latin square may be designed so that the butter and margarine biscuits are tested separately at each level of sugar content and at each level of salt content, but not in each combination.

Table 5.6 A Latin square design

Region	Type of outlet		
	Multiple	*Independent*	*Co-operative*
North	A	B	C
Midlands	C	A	B
South	B	C	A

Table 5.7 A factorial design

Sugar content	Salt content		
	A	B	C
1	1A	1B	1C
2	2A	2B	2C
3	3A	3B	3C

Types of experiment

Experiments in marketing are of two main kinds:

- laboratory experiments,
- field experiments.

Laboratory experiments

These take place in an artificial environment or contrived setting in which the experimenter has direct control over most, if not all, the crucial factors that might affect the experimental outcome. They are often used for product testing, package testing, and in advertising effectiveness studies. Sometimes their purpose is to optimise the marketing mix *before* a product or service is exposed to the open market; such tests may be referred to as 'pre-tests'. However, laboratory experiments may also be used on existing or previously launched products and may be referred to as 'post-tests'. For either type of experiment, a key dilemma is that while elements of the marketing mix such as formulation, packaging, pricing and so on are likely to be the subject of separate experiments to help assess the contribution made by each individually to the overall performance, yet this overall performance, especially consumer perceptions and attitudes, will be influenced by the interaction and impact of all these elements *together*. Ideally, some attempt to assess the interaction effects needs to be included in the design of experiments.

Laboratory-type experiments may be **monadic** or **comparative**. In the former, the respondent experiences only one version of the product; in the latter, the respondents experience two or more versions to compare. While comparison sharpens perception, it is more unrealistic – respondents do not usually directly compare products on the same occasion. Comparisons will normally be 'blind', that is, in plain packaging with no brand name. Very often the brand leader is taken as the standard of comparison, but if the product has been reformulated, then the existing formulation may be taken as the standard. It is normal to rotate the order in which products are presented in case there are general tendencies to prefer products in particular positions. There is some evidence to suggest that preferences are biased in favour of the product tried first.

There are three main research environments in which laboratory-type experiments may be conducted:

- hall tests,
- van tests,
- test centres.

In **hall tests**, people are recruited off the street or shopping precinct in the vicinity of the hall or room that has been hired by the research company. The purpose is to show products, packages or advertisements to people selected by quota sampling in order to measure their reaction. Selection is often restricted to users of the product being tested. Where hall tests are used for product testing, the products are generally new or modified, and the aim is to obtain a measure of acceptance, preference or attitude. The tests are often blind and comparative. Not all products, of course, are suitable for hall tests. Thus toiletries would be more suited to home placements tests (see p. 145). However, hall tests are popular for food and drink. Samples tend to be quite large (maybe 500 or so) and spread over several venues, probably in different parts of the country. They may be subject to various forms of experimental design like randomised block or Latin square.

Van tests are similar to hall tests, but recruitment is to a mobile van that can be taken to many different venues. Van tests have the advantage that all the equipment needed for testing does not have to be set up in every location. However, space may be too restricted for some types of test.

Test centres may be used in preference to vans or halls where the product for testing is too large, expensive or complicated to be taken to the consumer. An example is the car clinic, which is a product test on vehicles held in a test centre. Respondents are invited to evaluate one or more individual aspects of car design such as exterior styling, roominess or interior layout. (For a description of the procedures used in such clinics, see Wimbush 1990.)

What actually takes place in a hall, van or test centre is often really only a survey in which respondents are asked questions and their responses noted. Although they are usually called 'hall tests' or 'van tests', they are experiments only if there are before and after measures and, ideally, if there are control groups. This is frequently not the case.

Field experiments

These are conducted in a realistic research environment in which the products are exposed to the open marketplace and tested in situations where they will be bought, used or consumed in circumstances similar to those where these activities will normally happen. The degree of control exercised by the researcher is considerably less than for a laboratory experiment, but, being less artificial, may be a better guide to future behaviour. Field experiments are used mainly for trying out products or marketing mix variables in the marketplace, be it in the home, factory or selected test area. Inevitably this makes them more expensive than laboratory experiments, since the products need to be made, packaged, priced, possibly even promoted, in their final form. Exposure, furthermore, means that competitors become aware of what the company is about, and may copy the idea and perhaps even launch it first.

Many factors make field experiments more difficult to control than laboratory experiments: for example, uncharacteristic competitor activity during the course of the test. At the same time, however, there are important elements in the marketing mix that do not lend themselves to laboratory tests: for example, experiments relating to distribution, trade incentives or merchandising. Relying on the results of experiments in an artificial laboratory may be an unsound basis on which to make serious estimates of what will happen in a national launch of a new product.

The principles of experimental design explained above apply as much to field experiments as to those in the laboratory, so decisions have to be made about the use of data, the taking of observations before as well as after the test, and whether or not there will be control groups or control areas.

Three main types of field experiment may be distinguished:

- in-home placement tests,
- store tests,
- test marketing.

In-home placement tests give selected consumers the product to try at home and to report back. The consumer may be telephoned or sent a questionnaire after an agreed period of time. Several large manufacturers make regular use of panels of consumers that they have recruited themselves. Demographic and product-use characteristics of panel members are recorded, and experimental and control groups with the required characteristics for the particular tests are then selected. Test products are distributed by hand or through the post to panel members who complete questionnaires on the reactions to the products received. There is the danger, of course, that panel members learn from their testing experience and cease to be typical consumers. However, if the panel is sufficiently large, it is possible to avoid over-exposure of panel members to a particular type of product. On the other hand, if panel members receive products too infrequently, their level of interest tends to drop and the questionnaire response rate drops.

Store tests try out packaging or point-of-sale promotions in selected retail outlets. There will need to be a cross-section of types of outlet, located in different regions of the country. Ideally, there will be control stores matched against those trying the test product, otherwise the design amounts to no more than a 'let's try it in a few shops and see if it sells' strategy.

Obtaining the co-operation of stores to participate in the tests is often a problem. Such co-operation, furthermore, needs to extend to allowing the researchers to control the conduct, layout or positioning of the test product. For most in-store tests, the effect of the test is measured by changes in sales, but for consumer promotions, it may in addition be measured in interviews with matched groups of consumers.

Test marketing is a controlled experiment carried out in one or more limited, but carefully selected, parts of a market area. Test marketing uses a range of experimental designs to predict and explore the consequences of one or more marketing actions for new or modified product introductions, or to estimate the payoffs and costs of changes in the marketing mix for existing products.

The 'consequences' (the dependent variables) that test marketing seeks to predict might include:

- sales by volume and by value,
- market shares,
- profitability and return on investment,
- consumer behaviour, e.g. trial and repeat purchase, and attitudes concerning products,
- the reactions of retailers and distributors to the product,
- the effects of different marketing strategies in different test areas.

The conduct of test marketing includes a number of key stages:

1 Planning

This includes defining clearly the problem or problems to which the test marketing is addressed and the measures that will be used to evaluate the outcome. It also means deciding where the test is to be conducted. In selecting test areas, it will be necessary to pay attention to:

- the demographic structure of the area, which should be representative of the total market,
- the industrial and occupational structure,
- the structure of retailing and distribution,
- the availability and use of media, especially local newspapers that could be used for advertising.

2 Pre-test

Once the test areas have been selected, it is necessary to take measurements of the variables to be used to evaluate outcomes: it is changes in these as a result of the test that will be recorded. Sometimes sufficient base data may be already available; sometimes it may be necessary to conduct primary research. More often, manufacturers will purchase into retail panels so that they can monitor the effects of the test over a period of time. Pre-tests may also be carried out in areas that are to be used as 'controls', that is, not subject to the experimental stimulus.

3 Main test

This might involve the launch of a new or modified product along with associated marketing communications, or the change in the marketing mix itself (for example a new pricing policy). The duration of the test has to be long enough to allow the situation to stabilise after the new experimental conditions have been imposed.

4 Post-test

Measurements are repeated of the key dependent variables and compared with measures derived in the pre-test.

5 Evaluation

Account needs to be taken of the factors that may have influenced the results, and some prediction made of what is likely to happen in a national launch. This is not a simple matter of extrapolation of the results in the test area to the whole country – that would be dangerous. It means taking account of any special circumstances in the test area, including actions of competitors, that may not hold for the country as a whole.

Test marketing has not been so fashionable in recent years, largely because there are a number of problems with it. Thus test marketing may not be the best way of predicting sales or market shares when:

- surprise is vital to the success of the product,
- lead times are too short to protect the advantage of being first into the market,
- competitors can easily sabotage the tests, for example, by running a competitive advertising campaign in the test area,
- competitors are already doing tests that you can capitalise upon,
- the costs and risks of launch are low,

- the product is subject to rapidly changing fashion,
- the product life-cycle is very short.

Quite apart from the circumstances in which test marketing is inappropriate, it can also be very expensive. The direct costs include:

- equipment or plant needed to make the new or modified product,
- the advertising and employment of advertising agencies to support the test product,
- the research data needed for the pre-test and the post-test; this may mean purchasing syndicated data from consumer panels or retail panels,
- sales promotions at the point of sale,
- dealer discounts and incentives for participating in the test.

In addition, there will be indirect costs that include:

- the opportunity cost of what the company could be doing instead of the test market,
- the management time taken up with the tests,
- the diversion of salesforce activity on the new product,
- the impact of the test product on the sales of other products in the range,
- the cost of letting the competition know what you are up to.

Perhaps the key problem of test marketing, however, is that of projecting the results in the test area to the total market. Test results may be unrealistic because:

- there is experimenter effect – for example, salesmen have been trying harder to make the new product a success,
- special inducements may have been used – for example, to get traders to accept the product,
- competitors may deliberately (or unwittingly) confound your results,
- many retail chains will not allow companies to sell products in only part of the country.

Attempts have been made by market research companies to minimise the effects of some of these drawbacks by developing:

- mini-test marketing,
- simulated test market modelling.

Mini-test marketing is designed to simulate test marketing conditions without exposing the products to the open market and without incurring the costs of a full test market. Its purpose is to estimate or predict potential sales volume or market share for new products. Research International ran a Mini-Test Market for over 20 years. This consisted of a panel of 1,000 households who were visited weekly by a mobile grocery van fitted out like a supermarket, but was operated by the company itself. All products in the van were bar-coded, and the panel member had a shopping card with an identification number. The actual purchases made by panel members, including quantity, brand, size, price and any special offers, were recorded electronically at the checkout using EPOS equipment. Panellists were given a magazine that contained high-quality advertisements for selected products, including the one being tested. The procedure enabled measures to be taken of the cumulative market penetration achieved by the new product, the repeat purchases made, and the average purchase quantity.

The key advantages of such simulated test markets are as follows:

- They avoid exposing the test product in the open market until its repeat purchase potential is known.
- They require only small quantities of the test product.
- They need advertising only in embryo form.
- They obtain results more quickly than in the open market because awareness of the test product is rapidly obtained through the magazine.
- New products are tested in a real-life market situation alongside competing products, and may be supported by advertising, promotions and merchandising.
- The agency can control the range of competitive products on sale and the competitive pricing, promotion and so on.
- Different versions of the product can be tried out in different parts of the country.

Research International finally had to abandon its Mini-test Market because of mounting overheads. Furthermore, since it was a real shop on wheels, it had to be run every day, whether or not there was a client, while competition from the superstores meant that people could not be bothered with the van, and it still took 16–20 weeks to complete a study.

Simulated test market modelling uses sophisticated modelling techniques to estimate trial and repeat purchase for new, modified or relaunched products. Trial and repeat purchase is, in turn, used to make predictions of sales volume and brand shares that will be achieved. These models are described in detail in Chapter 7. They are not really field experiments since most are based on some kind of hall test in which a product or product concept test takes place.

Conclusion

The distinction between laboratory and field experiments sometimes gets a little blurred. Thus Research International's Mini-Test Market was really part van test and part test marketing. Furthermore, different procedures may be used in combination. Thus participants in a hall test, say for a new brand of whisky, may be given a bottle to take home and try. They are then subsequently telephoned or sent questionnaires to record their reaction.

It must be remembered that since experiments are, by definition, small scale and based on samples, they are subject to sampling error. This means that, although compared with surveys there are many more controls over extraneous variables, there will be random sampling fluctuations, so that discovered differences between treatments may not, in fact, represent real differences in the population from which the sample was drawn. Alternatively, the failure to discover differences may also be a result of random errors.

CONTINUOUS RESEARCH

In Chapter 1 continuous research was distinguished from ad hoc research. The latter is 'one-off' research, usually geared to specific issues or problems and custom-designed for a particular company. As a 'piece' of research, it has a beginning point and comes to a conclusion, going through a number of stages from an initial brief or analysis of the problem to be investigated to data collection, data analysis and the presentation of a final report. Continuous research, by contrast, takes measurements on a regular basis in order to monitor changes that are taking place, often in the consumer market, but also perhaps in the business market or even within the client organisation itself. There is no envisaged end to the research process, and it is not normally custom-designed on a client-specific basis. Because of the expense of setting up and maintaining a system for the continuous or regular collection and production of data, continuous research is typically syndicated, that is, the research process or the data, or both, are shared between a number of clients. Usually this means that a large market research organisation collects the data and sells them to a number of clients, or that several clients buy into a survey conducted by the market research company.

Some continuous research really *is* continuous, in the sense that interviews are conducted every day of the year, even though aggregation of the results may take place weekly, two-weekly or four-weekly. Other research, which some purists might argue is, strictly speaking, not continuous, is conducted at regular intervals with a gap between periods of data collection. The continuity of data collection, whether periodic or not, may be achieved in only one of two ways:

- obtaining data from the *same* individuals, households or organisations on a continuous or regular basis,
- picking a fresh sample of respondents every day or every measurement period.

Panel research uses the first procedure and regular interval surveys use the second.

Panel research

In panel research, the same data are collected repeatedly from a representative sample of the defined survey population. In marketing research, a panel is a representative sample of individuals, households or organisations that have agreed to record, or permit the recording of, their activities or opinions in respect of an agreed range of products or services on a continuous or regular basis. Panels are used mostly to provide quantified, grossed-up estimates either of market characteristics (market measurement panels) or of the use of the media (media panels). For the most part, they measure behaviour rather than attitudes, since there are problems in asking respondents their attitudes towards products on repeated occasions. However, for the purpose of evaluating television or radio programmes, television opinion panels or listeners' panels are asked their opinions of the programmes they have watched or heard.

Market measurement panels are of two main kinds:

- consumer panels,
- retail panels.

Consumer panels

Consumer panels are representative samples of individuals or households whose purchase and use of a defined group of products is recorded either continuously or at regular intervals, usually over a considerable period of time. The first commercial panel in the UK was launched in 1948. Since then the number of panel services available has grown steadily, and the defined groups of products concerned have extended from panels concerned with groceries and fresh foods to panels recording the acquisition of consumer durables and electrical goods, to motorists' panels, household (non-food) panels, and panels recording the purchase of toiletries and cosmetics, or baby products. The 1992 *Market Research Society Yearbook* lists over 70 market research companies that now offer continuous consumer panel services.

The largest single service (in terms of turnover) in the UK, if not in Europe, was AGB's Television Consumer Audit (the TCA), which ran for over 25 years before being replaced. The TCA estimated the purchases of packaged groceries, frozen foods, meat and poultry for in-home consumption throughout the UK based on a samples of 6,300 households in Britain and a further 400 in Ulster.

Unlike regular interval surveys whose respondents are approached for information only on one occasion (or twice if there is some kind of follow-up), panellists are asked to provide information or to perform data collection tasks on a regular basis, often without any specified time limit. Consequently, besides the problem of making the initial selection of panellists in such a way that they are representative of the population being studied, there is the additional problem of keeping the panel representative on an ongoing basis. Furthermore, panels can provide consistent trend data over time only if, once they have been set up, there are no changes in panel methodology. Consequently, the initial design needs to be as accurate as possible, and capable of being sustained at a consistent quality over time.

The principles of sample design for selecting panellists are similar to those for ad hoc surveys, but recruitment tends to be a little more difficult, since respondents are being asked to do rather more than in a one-off survey. In consequence, some form of quota sampling is normally preferred if panellists are to be directly recruited. Alternatively, recruitment may be on the back of another large-scale survey operation that the market research company or one of its subsidiaries or sister companies is already conducting. Thus recruitment to the panel may be sought from respondents to an omnibus survey (see p. 158) who have the required demographic characteristics and who can be screened for willingness to participate in the panel at the time of the interview. Recruiters may then subsequently approach such respondents to explain the tasks involved, the incentives offered, and to give any training needed.

Once the panel has been recruited, it needs to be maintained at a consistent quality of representativeness; furthermore, its members need to be encouraged to report regularly for as long as is desirable. Each year the panel is, of course, getting a year older and would, if no other changes took place in membership, rapidly become unrepresentative. It is, therefore, necessary to recruit younger members and to retire some of the older ones just to keep the age profile correctly balanced. However, for a variety of reasons, people leave the panel or their circumstances change: for example, they may get married, set up separate households, have children and so on. In consequence, there is the constant need to 'balance' or 'control' the panel by replacing those who leave with respondents whose demographic characteristics are under-represented. It must be remembered, that the population that the panel is meant to represent is itself changing all the time, and panel composition must reflect these changes.

To locate individuals or households required for panel balancing, it is normal to use a database of screened respondents from a regular interval survey that the agency undertakes anyway. To keep panellists reporting, there is usually a system of newsletters, prizes, competitions, mystery gifts or points accumulated for catalogue gifts. It is not normal to pay panellists directly. The newsletter can be important for making the panellist feel a member of a team and to keep him or her informed of developments or reminders to complete certain tasks. If panellists repeatedly fail to report or to perform the agreed tasks, then they may be dropped.

The capture of data from panellists is undertaken using one of the three main instruments, namely, diaries, questionnaires or electronic recording devices. Until recently, diaries have been the most common. Diary design was considered in detail in Chapter 4. See Figure 4.9 for an example of diary layout for a consumer panel. Diaries are designed either for the individual or for the household; in the latter case details will normally be entered by the housewife. The details collected will normally include:

- brand name,
- size of pack,
- flavour, colour, type of dispenser, or other brand variant,
- price paid,
- quantity bought,
- any special offers,
- name of shop,
- type of shop.

Questionnaires have been used to a lesser extent, largely in an interviewer-based, home audit procedure. Interviewers visit panel members on a regular weekly basis, they carry out a visual inspection of stocks of groceries and other household items by checking cupboards, pantries, fridges and so on, and enter on a questionnaire all items purchased since the previous week. Items consumed during the week are recorded from packaging or labels that are retained. The costs of undertaking home audits are, clearly, very high, and the main example of such a procedure in Europe, if not in the world, namely AGB's Television Consumer Audit (TCA), has been replaced by an electronic panel.

New technology has transformed consumer panel data collection techniques, and AGB's new electronic panel, Superpanel, is described in detail in Chapter 7. Essentially, it involves equipping each panel household with computer terminals and laser-scanners for reading the bar-codes on packs following each shopping trip.

Panels provide a wealth of data that, if not translated into succinct information that can be absorbed and acted upon, can readily become indigestible. Most market research companies offer both standard and special analyses. Standard trend analyses are produced usually at monthly or four-weekly intervals, and they show the progress of the market and its major brands since the previous period. Clients usually subscribe on an annual basis to receive these reports over the year. The reports are tables of figures that give results by product field grossed up (see Chapter 6) to the Great Britain population (Ulster is usually treated separately), or to a particular region. Such tables typically show for the current month, the previous month, and the same month in the previous year:

- sales volume for the total market, for each brand and each brand variant,
- consumer expenditure at current retail prices for the total market, for each brand and each brand variant,
- market shares for each brand,
- market penetration,
- special offers,
- average prices.

Summary tables may show for overall brands the last 12 or 52 weeks. Special analyses tend to be fairly standard 'optional extras'. Thus a 'source of purchase' analysis will show volume, value and prices paid by type of outlet, including breakdowns by key accounts like Tesco, Sainsbury, Asda or Gateway. A 'cumulative penetration' analysis will measure the rate of increase in the number of new buyers over time, and can be used to show the effect of promotional support. A 'frequency of purchase' analysis shows the percentage of buyers purchasing each brand at least once, twice, three times and so on. This will show the extent to which a brand is dependent on a small number of regular buyers rather than a larger number of infrequent buyers. There will, in addition, be a variety of demographic analyses, describing the buyer profile of the market and its major brands in terms of age of purchaser, social class, household size, ACORN classification, presence of children, and so on. Because panel data are longitudinal and can track individuals through time, it is possible to look at inter-purchasing between brands, brand loyalty, repeat buying, and gains from and losses to competitors. These, in turn, can be used as inputs to making volume and brand share predictions (see Chapter 7).

Because panels are samples, they are subject to the kinds of sampling and non-sampling errors described in Chapter 3. Although panels are balanced to keep them representative as far as possible, this is not always, if ever, totally achieved. In consequence, the results from panels are weighted (see Chapter 6) to make finer adjustments for over- and under-representation of sub-groups. In addition, they suffer from problems of coverage and pickup. Lack of coverage means that consumer panels may produce lower estimates of total sales than are reflected in either ex-factory shipments or trade estimates. Consumer purchase panels measure only purchases made by private households, not purchases by offices, forces bases, old people's homes, student accommodation, exports, purchase by other organisations, nor items lost, damaged or pilfered in transit. Some market research companies may apply 'field weights' to their data to make adjustments for lack of coverage, so that market estimates eventually reflect actual total market volumes and values.

Pickup errors result from tendencies of panellists to overlook some of their purchases, or not to know about the purchases made by other members of the household. Occasionally, deliberate falsification may be provoked by the complexity of the tasks respondents have to perform, or they may be suffering from lack of motivation and commitment to the panel. The level of pickup tends to vary from product to product, and may be anything from 50 per cent to 200 per cent of independent market estimates. However, provided this level is fairly constant, then 'product field' or 'market size' weights may be applied before estimates are grossed up to the population.

Retail panels

Retail panels are representative samples (or, in some cases, the complete universe) of retail outlets whose acquisition, pricing, stocking and display of a defined group of products are recorded either continuously or at regular intervals. Such panels were first set up by the A.C. Nielsen Company in the USA in the 1930s. Nielsen began retail tracking operations in the UK in 1939. In the 1950s and 1960s, demand for manufactured products tended to exceed their supply; the key problem for any manufacturer to solve was efficient distribution to ensure product availability. In this situation, information on distribution was crucial. Nielsen rapidly expanded its operations and a number of companies set up competing retail panel services. The current Nielsen Retail Index system is described in detail in Chapter 7.

Retail panels are used largely to provide estimates of over-the-counter sales of products, brand-by-brand and brand variant basis. This information is sometimes available directly from the use of electronic data capture techniques using EPOS equipment. It is otherwise necessary to undertake a **retail audit**. This involves physically counting the stocks in the panel shops at the beginning and at the end of the audit period (usually four weeks or a month). By subtracting stocks for each brand and brand variant at the end of the audit period from deliveries and those stocks held at the beginning, sales can be deduced. Even where electronic data are available, it is still often necessary to undertake retail audits in order to determine the prices charged, the shelf-space allocated to brands, the quantities held in the 'reserve' areas, and any in-store promotions. Auditors from the market research company offering panel services visit the panel shops on a regular basis. They may spend two or three days in the shop, counting stocks and entering their observations into a portable data entry terminal. These may then be placed in a modem for transmission of the data to a central computer via the telephone.

Where **universe data** are not available, it is necessary to take a sample of shops from which to make estimates. The key problem with sampling retail outlets is that stores vary enormously in terms of turnover. Over- or under-representing stores of different sizes will seriously affect the estimates made. Consequently, it is necessary to stratify the selection of shops by turnover range as well as by type of shop (e.g. multiple, co-operative or independent) and by region. Unfortunately, in order to do this it is necessary to know:

- how many shops of a given type fall into a particular turnover range in that area,
- the annual turnover of the sampled shops,
- annual turnover of the universe.

Acquiring this information is a major undertaking. For most of the major multiples and for the co-operatives, this information may be provided by the multiple chain, or by the Co-operative Wholesale Society in the case of co-operatives. For independents and smaller multiples, Nielsen, for example, carries out an extensive enumeration followed by a survey of a sample of enumerated shops.

Once shops have been selected and have agreed to co-operate, data collection is likely to be some combination of:

- visual inspection of products on shelves and their location in the store,
- checking delivery notes,
- getting retailers to complete questionnaires or other records specially for the agency,
- obtaining data that have been captured electronically or that have been entered on a computerised database.

All operators of retail panels produce tables that give distribution and price data along with estimates of sales volumes and values on a brand-by-brand and brand variant basis. Since the major multiples normally supply data on deliveries to their outlets and allow access to their bar-coded data only on the understanding that the tables do not identify particular named groups, the tables aggregate data for these groups. It is not possible, for example, to compare what is happening in Tesco with the situation at Sainsbury, Asda or Gateway. The tables and charts produced by Nielsen are described in Chapter 7.

Consumer panels and retail panels compared

Both consumer panels and retail panels generate estimates of sales volumes, values and market shares on a brand-by-brand and brand variant basis every four weeks or every month. Such information helps companies to:

- evaluate company strengths and weaknesses in the marketplace,
- diagnose market opportunities and competitor threats,
- set realistic long-term objectives,

- develop plans to achieve these objectives,
- monitor the impact of trends in the market.

Beyond this, consumer panels and retail panels are suited to different purposes. Consumer panels are able to track consumer behaviour, for example, in terms of purchase frequency and brand loyalty; retail panels can track what happens in the distribution system up to the point where the consumer makes a purchase. The manufacturer can, for example, tell how many shops who usually handle his stock were out of stock in the last period; what competitor brands are set alongside his own brands and in what kinds of shops; what price differentials there are; what levels of stock are held where in the shop; and how these have changed since the last measurement period.

Operators of both types of panel will make claims to the superior accuracy of their service for the data produced in common. Consumer panel operators will point out that by asking consumers about where they purchased their products, *all* the outlets selling the particular brand will be covered. Retail panels cover only those outlets included in the particular sample of shops. Because their data are derived from consumers, consumer panels are able to produce named group data, that is, data broken down by named account. Retail panels are restricted by their agreement with the major multiples *not* to produce such data. Retail panel operators will claim, on the other hand, that retail panels do not rely on the memories of consumers, but systematically record actual sales in the sample shops. Some of the data, furthermore, are not estimates based on samples, but universe data. They will argue, too, that in highly fragmented markets, consumer panels will pick up only small quantities of a particular brand. Retail panels, by contrast, will record all the sales of every brand in the sample shops.

Since the services are, in many ways, complementary, the trend has been for the larger agencies to offer both types of panel. Thus, AGB purchased the National Market Research Association (NMRA) from the Mars Group so that it could do its own retail panel operations. By the same token, Nielsen has set up its own Homescan service to provide consumer panel data. This means that clients can have access to both types of data from the same market research organisation.

Other types of panel

Media panels are used mostly for television audience measurement and for estimating audience appreciation of television and radio programmes. These panels are described in detail in Chapter 7. Some panels are 'single source', that is, they collect data both on product purchasing and on media usage. Thus Taylor Nelson's 'Adlab' is based on a sample of 1,000 housewives in the Central Television area. Panel members complete two separate weekly diaries. One records purchasing of groceries, toiletries and household items; the other is in a daily format to record housewife television viewing, radio listening and her readership of newspapers and magazines. By collecting both types of data from the same source, it is possible to look more directly at the effect of media exposure on purchasing behaviour.

Regular interval surveys

These are surveys of respondents carried out at regular intervals using independent samples for each measurement period. Like panels, they are used for market measurement and for media usage, but, in addition, they are used by the Office of Population Censuses and Surveys (the OPCS) and other government bodies for collecting various forms of government statistics.

Market measurement regular interval surveys include:

- omnibus surveys,
- market tracking surveys.

Omnibus surveys

These are surveys that market research companies undertake to run with a stated frequency and with a predetermined method: clients buy space in the questionnaire by adding and paying for questions of their own according to number and type of question. The agency draws a fresh sample of respondents each time, administers the questionnaire, processes the data, and reports the results. This means that the costs of setting up the survey, administration, collection of demographic data, and analysis are shared between several clients. Over the past decade, omnibus research has become more popular, varied and competitive, giving clients the opportunity to buy inexpensive research as and when required. More than 30 companies in the UK now run such surveys; other companies 'offer' the service on a consultancy basis, buying their fieldwork from those organisations actually running an omnibus. Omnimas, the biggest, is described in detail in Chapter 7. There are, however, different types of omnibus depending on:

- the general or specific nature of the population being sampled,
- the type of sampling method,
- the method of questionnaire administration.

General consumer omnibuses sample a general cross-section of the adult population, while special omnibuses are dedicated to specific groups in the population, for example, motorists, mothers with babies, doctors, businessmen, architects, travel agents or farmers. Random omnibuses use random sampling techniques to select respondents, while quota omnibuses use random location or straight quota samples. Random omnibuses tend to be a little more expensive, but the accuracy of the sampling is, on the whole, superior: they are worthwhile if good estimates are required of population values. Some omnibuses are personal, using face-to-face interviewing, while others use telephone research. The latter are quicker, but may work out a little more expensive; furthermore, no visual material can be shown to respondents. They tend to use a random selection methodology for selecting the telephone numbers, and then to impose quotas on age, sex and social class.

Consumer omnibuses tend to be run on a weekly basis while the more specialised ones may be monthly. Sample sizes vary from 1,000 up to 3,000. Telephone omnibuses are mostly 1,000; face-to-face consumer omnibuses are typically between 1,500 and 2,000.

Most agencies have a master questionnaire with a classification section containing the demographic questions that are asked each time. These are usually completed at the end of the interview. The main part of the questionnaire is often divided into two sections: continuous and ad hoc. The continuous section includes questions that are inserted for clients on every survey. They will usually be in the same order and in the same place every time to avoid any effect that changing the position of the questions might bring to bear on the answers. This will also mean that the question-naire always begins in the same way, which helps the interviewers to begin their interviewing. The ad hoc questions are usually inserted on a first-come-first-serve basis, but the agency will try to put them together in a sensible way. Question sets for competing fields cannot be allowed in the same survey.

Agencies tend to place few restrictions on the topics covered; however, questions on security, for example, 'Do you have a burglar alarm in your home?' may not be allowed. Some agencies place restrictions on the number of questions that may be included from any one client (or on the amount of time they take) plus an overall limitation on the size of the survey. The average number of questions per client is 6–10 – omnibus surveys cease to be cost-effective if too many questions are included.

The questions themselves may be pre-coded or open-ended. Some agencies place restrictions on the number of code positions allowed, or may charge extra. Open-ended questions may cost up to double the cost of pre-coded ones. Sensitive probing of answers is not usually feasible – interviewers already have a tough time handling a questionnaire that is really a series of questionnaires going from topic to topic.

Some clients will submit their questions already worded in the way they want them; others require the help of the market research company in framing them. Such help is normally included in the price of the question.

Most companies will do split runs, that is, testing two or three versions of a question or question-set amongst different respondents. However, these can seriously complicate the organisation of the survey. The use of show cards is fairly common; these might give definitions, lists of products or brands, photographs, copies of advertisements, telepics or pack fronts. Sometimes these may all be made into a specially produced booklet.

All suppliers of omnibus services make a charge per question, currently ranging from £200 per question to over £500. However, it would be misleading to buy into an omnibus on that basis alone. The analyses and services that are included as part of the price vary considerably. Some agencies charge extra for questions with many pre-codes, for prompt cards, show cards or other materials, and for open-ended questions. Some give discounts for more than a certain number of questions, or for inserting them on a regular basis. Some give discounts when only part of the sample is being used. Some charge a joining fee that may vary from £100 to £500 or more. Sometimes this fee is waived when more than a certain amount of business is commissioned. Agencies have different approaches to deciding what counts as one question. A question with four subsections may be treated as one or as four questions.

Basic analyses of the pre-coded questions are usually available within a few days of fieldwork completion. Open-ended questions are usually post-coded (in co-operation with the client) and these will take a little longer. Results may be accumulated over a period of time to produce monthly, quarterly or even annual reports. Most agencies include standard break-downs by key demographic questions within the price of the question. Optional extras include the production of charts, writing mini-reports, market or brand mapping, cluster analysis (see Chapter 6), or analysis by one of the geodemographic systems like ACORN. The tables themselves will normally refer to volumes, frequencies or sterling values that have been grossed up to the population, usually after weighting.

Omnibus surveys may be used for continuous or for ad hoc purposes – or some mixture of the two. The range of uses to which clients put omni-buses includes:

- market measurement, for example, the volume and value of sales, brand shares, frequency of purchase, brand loyalty, brand switching,
- assessing the effectiveness of an advertising campaign, for example, by tracking brand or advertising awareness,
- media measurement, for example, the readership of certain magazines,
- tracking the impact of or forecasting sales of new product launches,
- tracking brand image or corporate image,
- new product concept tests and product tests,
- test market assessment,
- product usage and attitude,

- testing questions using split-run techniques,
- building up samples of minority groups.

The main advantages of omnibus surveys are as follows:

- The questions are custom-designed and the results are confidential to the client.
- They are quick and relatively inexpensive where the information can be gathered with a few questions.
- They are there when needed and can be used at short notice.
- They are, on the whole, well conducted and well respected in the industry.
- They can obtain samples of a reasonable size for minority groups over a period of time.
- They can be used for recruitment purposes for other surveys.

Omnibuses are unsuitable, however, for detailed probing or where lengthy question sets are required. Telephone omnibuses have the additional disadvantage that they cannot be supported by show cards or other visual materials. Sample designs are fixed by the market research organisation and cannot be modified to suit client needs. Clients can, of course, shop around for an omnibus that is more suitable in terms of sample design.

Market tracking surveys

These surveys are carried out at regular intervals, but the market research company designs the whole questionnaire, and the data collected are sold to as many clients as possible. They tend to get used instead of panels where pickup would be a considerable problem. Examples are AGB's Recall survey, which provides market measurement and consumer profiles of slower-moving personal toiletries, cosmetics and fragrances, over-the-counter medicines, and photographic software; Public Attitude Surveys (PAS) operates a drinks market survey; while the British Market Research Bureau (BMRB) offers its Target Group Index as the only single-source, regular interval survey combining product usage with media exposure. The TGI is explained in detail in Chapter 7.

Market tracking surveys use a wide range of sampling techniques, although few go to the expense of random probability sampling. A key advantage of market tracking surveys is that it is possible to base analyses on large numbers of individuals, offering the ability to do lots of breakdowns. Clients can buy from the agency just those data that they require for their purposes. However, the results are not confidential and data are available to groups of competing manufacturers.

Panels and regular interval surveys compared

The main advantage of panels over regular interval surveys are:

- Sampling errors tend to be less since there is statistical association between successive measurements.
- Memory errors will tend to be less because regular interval surveys depend on recall of purchases while panels record purchases in a diary or electronically.
- It is feasible to follow through an individual's purchasing behaviour over time, making it possible to analyse brand switching, brand loyalty and repeat purchasing behaviour.

The main advantages of regular interval surveys over panels are as follows:

- Over a period of time, large numbers of respondents are interviewed, making it possible to build up samples of minority groups.
- It is possible to include attitude questions because there are no fears about respondent conditioning over time.
- They are cheaper to operate, largely because there is no panel maintenance to be undertaken.
- The real response rate tends to be higher because individuals are being asked to do less.
- They will pick up a higher proportion of purchases for products that are bought infrequently or only by minority groups.
- They are more flexible, for example, it is easier to change the questions being asked without upsetting other clients.
- They can be used for questionnaires that take longer to complete.

These advantages and limitations need to be kept in mind when considering what kind of research is appropriate for resolving or analysing the problems faced by a particular company.

SUMMARY

While the instruments of data capture refer to the different mechanisms used to record data, such mechanisms may be used in different social and organisational contexts that define different data collection methods. These include desk research, personal observation, qualitative research, survey research, experimental research and continuous research. Each comes in a number of sub-varieties and each has its own particular strengths and limitations. These need to be kept in mind in designing research to solve particular problems or to use as a basis for making a particular decision. Unless these problems and decisions are clearly analysed, the basis for choosing or justifying one type of research over another remains obscure.

EXERCISES AND POINTS FOR FURTHER DISCUSSION

■   Should primary research be conducted only when desk research does not produce suitable or adequate secondary data?

■   Are secondary data any more 'objective' than primary data?

■   Are data obtained from government sources any more 'objective' than those from other secondary sources?

■   Use the resources of your own library to find out the market shares of major manufacturers of dry cell batteries in the UK.

■   Design a method of sampling and a record-sheet for observing the proportions of car occupants who wear seat-belts.

■   A manufacturer of women's and men's underwear wants to discover the main criteria that purchasers use in selecting the brand and style of underwear. Would you recommend group discussions or depth interviews? Give your reasons.

■   Assuming the manufacturer in the above example has already decided on group discussions, what kind of groups would you recommend and what should the group composition be?

■   A manufacturer of office furniture wants to find out the key market segments for desks and needs information on the characteristics of desk users and on the sizes and uses of desks. He has asked for a survey of medium to large companies in the UK. Would you recommend an interview, telephone or postal survey? Give your reasons.

■   A national multiple supermarket chain has 1,500 retail outlets throughout the country. Management wants to test the relative impact of two different in-store promotional displays for yoghurt and the effect of either compared with having no display. Recommend an appropriate, true experimental design capable of meeting management's information needs.

■   A manufacturer of fresh cream cakes has just developed a new range. The marketing manager wants your advice on whether hall tests or in-home placements tests would be better for evaluating customer reactions to each type of new cake. Give reasons for the advice you would give her.

■   To what extent are retail panels and consumer panels in direct competition for the continuous monitoring of consumer markets?

■   Design 6–10 questions for inclusion in an omnibus survey that would enable a travel company to analyse the relationship between type, destination and duration of holidays in 1992 by UK nationals and a range of demographic characteristics like sex, age, social class and work status.

■   The manager of a large department store in a city wants to estimate the proportion of households in the city that make a purchase in the store at least once a month. He would like to know what are the various methods that could be used to make such an estimate. Advise him on the alternatives and make a recommendation, giving your reasons.

Chapter 6

Data analysis

The different types of qualitative and quantitative data were explained in detail in Chapter 2. The section in Chapter 5 on qualitative research explained the various approaches to handling qualitative data when they manifest themselves as narrative or text. This chapter looks at the analysis of qualitative data that arise as isolated statements or words from open-ended questions in a questionnaire survey or from seeking verbal reactions to specific situations in experimental research. It then turns to what is involved in analysing quantitative data.

Whatever the type of data to be analysed, the process consists of three overlapping activities:

- data reduction,
- data display,
- drawing conclusions.

'Raw' data consist of the original qualitative words, phrases or sentences, or of the original metric or non-metric measurements taken from responses to questionnaires or other means of data capture. In this form, it is usually difficult to grasp the key features of the data, particularly when the researcher is looking at a complete dataset with many variables and many cases. Data reduction summarises the data so that these key features are revealed. Data display illustrates some of these features in a more graphical way so that they may be appreciated and comprehended by an audience. Drawing conclusions entails going beyond the strict confines of the data to make inferences, judgements, interpretations or deductions. These activities overlap; for example, drawing a graph to display quantitative data may also act as a summary and may, indeed, enable certain conclusions to be drawn.

ANALYSING QUALITATIVE DATA

Data reduction for a set of isolated qualitative statements involves one or more of the following activities:

- paraphrasing and summarising what people have said,
- classifying responses into categories,
- using quasi-statistics,
- undertaking content analysis.

If respondents or interviewers have written comments in a questionnaire in response to an open-ended question, or if verbal reactions to new product ideas or advertising copy are recorded, then paraphrasing or summarising may take the form of rephrasing comments in another, clearer, condensed form, or picking out key words, phrases or statements. A more systematic approach is to classify all responses into categories which, ideally, should be exhaustive and mutually exclusive, not too many in number, and should refer to a single dimension that is important to the objectives of the research. Developing such sets of categories may mean making several 'passes' over the data, modifying or refining the categories until all responses can be classified.

Where an attempt is made to summarise further by giving some indication of the numbers or rough proportions of respondents replying in particular ways, using words or phrases like 'a few', 'a large minority', 'most', or 'nearly all', then 'quasi-statistics' are being used. These seek to analyse by in effect converting qualitative data into quasi-quantitative data. Content analysis does actually create quantitative data by systematically counting up the number of times a word, phrase, idea or theme is used in a group or sub-group of respondents. Thus younger respondents may well use different words or phrases in response to a new product concept.

Data display for qualitative data may take the form of:

- quoting extracts from the text,
- producing checklists or tables,
- rearranging or reordering lists.

Where respondents have used words, phrases or sentences that are particularly apposite to the points or arguments arising from data reduction, then a verbatim quote may nicely illustrate, for example, 'As one marketing manager put it ...' This may perform a role somewhat similar to drawing a graph for quantitative data and may, furthermore, liven up the reports of research. However, such quotes should be use sparingly and with caution. There is little point in verbatim reports unless what is said or written down is distinctive or particularly appropriate. Putting in lengthy quotations or sticking extracts of text end to end is pointless. It must be remembered, furthermore, that such extracts are only illustrations; they are highly selective and not necessarily representative of the views or thoughts of other respondents.

Instead of using quasi-statistics to report the preponderance of particular views or statements, it may be helpful to draw up a table or checklist of what individuals or kinds or categories of individual mentioned which particular points, as illustrated in Table 6.1. Such tables enable the researcher to view the data at a glance, to make comparisons, to see where further analysis may be called for, and they may be directly transferred to the report of the findings.

Sometimes reordering or rearranging lists may reveal patterns, or at least make them more accessible. Thus rearranging individuals A–F in Table 6.1 in terms of salary or position in the company may reveal patterns of responses more clearly.

Drawing conclusions from qualitative data, certainly in the sense of testing or validating hypotheses, is a contentious issue. Some writers will argue that qualitative research is supposed only to generate hypotheses, not to test them. Others will argue that ideas are always being matched against the data – and data are data, whether qualitative or quantitative. In the 'interpretive' phase in the analysis of narrative text, it was suggested earlier that 'insight' or the 'Eureka moments' were the result of some mysterious 'black box' activity in the brain. This may be appropriate where the text needs to be treated as a whole – as an entity that may not be accessible to systematic procedures. However, for the analysis and interpretation of isolated statements, it can be argued that conclusions may be derived from:

* noting sequences,
* looking for patterns or relationships,
* looking for explanations.

The order in which people do things, or at least how they perceive the sequences of events, may give some guide to possible causal relationships. Although the fact that one event always follows another does not establish cause, temporal order is a necessary, although not sufficient, condition for causality to exist. Unless there *is* a regular sequence (cause first, effect later), causality can be ruled out. Noting any patterns in the way events, behaviours, characteristics or expressed opinions happen together can also be suggestive of causal connections. Unless there is some pattern, causality can, again, be ruled out. Final proof, of course, is never possible; but

Table 6.1 A checklist for analysing qualitative data

Individual	Safety	Economy	Speed	Reliability
A	✔			
B			✔	
C	✔	✔	✔	
D				✔
E		✔		✔
F	✔			

neither is it for quantitative data. Qualitative data in fact may be better than quantitative where it is possible to ask people for their explanations of events. Where there is a degree of consensus on these explanations, it may be worth the researcher's time pursuing further evidence, perhaps by conducting further research.

Griggs (1987) argues that the process of analysing qualitative data should be a public process, not a private, 'magical' experience. The researchers should be able to demonstrate how conclusions were arrived at, and in such a way that others could, if necessary, dispute them. Sometimes, continues Griggs, it is possible to replicate a study – doing it again to see if the same conclusions are reached. This may not be feasible in market research, but seeing if similar conclusions may be drawn across all groups of individuals in a study may lend weight to those conclusions.

ANALYSING QUANTITATIVE DATA

As was explained in Chapter 2, quantitative data arise as numbers and are a result of the process of measurement. When we measure something, we select a value from a scale of values that corresponds to the observation made of some object or situation, or with a response to a question addressed to an individual. The scales of values may be metric or non-metric; these, in turn, may be subdivided into **continuous** and **discrete**, and into **nominal** and **ordinal** scales.

The need for data analysis arises when measurements are taken of a number of cases – sometimes a very large number; in short, when we have a set of values for a variable. The set of values that we use as a basis for any given calculation or analysis relates to a particular group of cases that we can call the **unit of analysis**. The group of cases is being treated as a complete entity whose characteristics are being summarised, displayed or interpreted. The result is a feature of the unit of analysis, not of any individual case. Thus if we calculate the average age of 20 people, we are treating these 20 as a group – a unit of analysis – and the result (say, 26.5 years) is a feature of that group of people and not of any individual in the set. The unit of analysis is, in short, whatever set of cases forms the basis for any particular calculation, display or interpretation. In any one piece of research, there may be several different units of analysis, either because particular subsets are being analysed at the time or because, for any one calculation or table, there are missing cases, so the base for the calculation may change slightly from table to table.

The analysis of variables may be treated one at a time, two at a time, or more than two at a time. This enables a distinction to be made between:

- univariate analysis,
- bivariate analysis,
- multivariate analysis.

Univariate analysis

If variables are being taken one at a time, then attention will be focused on the processes of data reduction, data display, and, where the measures are based on samples, drawing statistical inferences. Data reduction of quantitative data may be approached in a statistical manner, utilising procedures that are universally recognised. Which particular procedures are appropriate depends in the first instance on whether the measurements are metric or non-metric. If the data are metric, the original or raw data will consist of a series of numbers, like those in Table 6.2. Rearranging the values in ascending or descending order will enable the researcher to 'eyeball' the entire set of values. The **range** – the difference between the highest and lowest figure – can be represented as a single figure (28), as illustrated in Table 6.3, but this may be less useful than saying what the lower and upper values of the range are, namely 16–44. Alternatively, it is possible to encapsulate the total set of values by calculating one 'central' value around which they are arrayed. Such a measure of central tendency or **average** could be the middle or **median value** – the value above which and below which half of the observations lie when arranged in an ascending or descending series. In Table 6.3, this is 28.5 – halfway between the two middle values of 28 and 29. Ten observations are above and ten below this figure. Such a measure, however, ignores which actual values lie above and below the median. For example, the top figure could have been 44,000 instead of 44 – it would have made no difference to the median. An arithmetic **mean**, by contrast, does take into account each value by adding them all up and dividing by the number of values. In Table 6.3, this is calculated as 30.4.

The mean on its own, however, gives no indication of the extent to which the set of values are all close to or are widely scattered about the mean. The mean for 21, 22, 23, 24, 25 is 23; it is also 23 for 11, 17, 23, 29,

Table 6.2 Raw metric data

Age	
27	26
26	25
24	22
20	18
16	28
29	30
31	33
33	35
37	39
40	44

Table 6.3 Data from Table 6.2 rearranged with a calculation of the range, median value, mean and standard deviation

Age	
16	29
18	30
20	31
22	33
24	33
25	35
26	37
26	39
27	40
28	44

Range	Median value	Mean	Standard deviation
$44 - 16$		$\dfrac{\Sigma x}{n}$	$\sqrt{\dfrac{\Sigma(x - \bar{x})^2}{n}}$
$= 28$	$= 28.5$	$= 30.4$	$= 9.1$

35. A measure of dispersion takes the average of the differences between the mean score and all the other values in the set. The generally accepted statistic is the **standard deviation**, which adds up the squared differences, divides by the total number of values in the set, and then takes the square root. For the first set of five numbers above, this involves subtracting 23 (the mean) from each value, squaring the result, and adding up the totals. This gives the sum of the squared deviations of 10 [i.e. $(21-23)^2 + (22-23)^2 + (23-23)^2 + (24-23)^2 + (25-23)^2$]. The standard deviation is then $\sqrt{10/5} = 1.41$. For the second set of five numbers, the standard deviation is 8.5, clearly indicating the wider spread. The standard deviation for the 20 values in Table 6.3 is 9.1. This is the average distance either side of the mean of 30.4.

If the data are non-metric, the raw data may be a set of words, symbols, letters or numbers used as labels. Table 6.4 gives 20 non-metric values, recording the sex of 20 people. For these values it is not possible to re-arrange them in ascending or descending order in order to calculate a range, average or standard deviation. We can, however, report the **frequencies** – the number of times each scale value occurs, for example, that there are 12 males and 8 females; the **proportion**, a relative frequency calculated by dividing the number of cases in a category by the total number of cases, for example, the proportion of men is 0.6; or the **percentage**, which is the proportion multiplied by 100, for example, 60 per cent are men. In this context the **mode** can be a useful statistic – this is the most commonly occurring value, or that category with the highest frequency.

Table 6.4 Raw non-metric data

	Sex	
	M	M
	M	F
	F	M
	F	M
	M	M
	F	F
	M	M
	M	M
	F	F
	M	F

This may not be an insightful statistic for a dichotomy, but in Table 6.5 we could, for example, say that the modal category is the 25–29 age group.

Data display for metric data may take a number of forms that include tables and various types of graph. Arranging the raw data into rows and columns would not be very helpful, but if they are grouped into smaller ranges, then the number of times values fall into those ranges (the frequencies) may be displayed, as in Table 6.5. These ranges may, in turn, be shown as a line graph or as a histogram, as in Figure 6.1.

Non-metric data may be displayed in tables by giving each scale value a separate row, with the frequency or proportion reported for each, as in Table 6.6. Line graphs or histograms cannot be drawn for non-metric data, but pie-charts are feasible (see Figure 6.2).

Drawing conclusions from univariate analysis – going beyond describing strictly what is there – is limited largely to situations where the data are derived from a sample of a population of cases. The sample results may then be used either to make estimates of population quantities or proportions, or to test the probability that statements that refer to only one variable are true for the population of cases from which the sample was drawn. Suppose a sample of 1,000 housewives representative of the UK

Table 6.5 Grouped metric data

Age	Frequency
15–19	2
20–24	3
25–29	6
30–34	4
35–39	3
40–44	2
Total	20

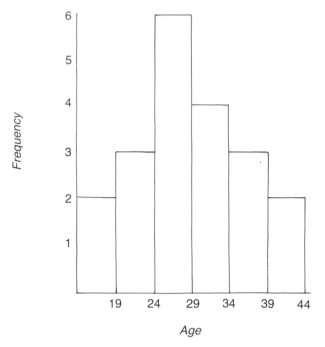

Figure 6.1 Histogram from Table 6.5

population are asked how many tins of Heinz baked beans (of given sizes) they have purchased in the last seven days. The results may be used to estimate UK sales over that period. Textbooks on statistics or on market research will normally focus on the calculation of a range of values (called **confidence intervals**) between which we can be certain with a predetermined probability that the real quantity, average or proportion lies. This is what is usually meant by '**estimation**', and the focus is normally on establishing an estimated population mean value for metric variables and an estimated proportion for non-metric ones. However, market research companies (and their clients) are more concerned with producing a single 'best' estimate of the actual quantities, so instead of wanting to know the average quantity of Heinz baked beans purchased by each housewife over the period of seven days (plus the associated confidence intervals), they will want estimates of exactly how many tins of each size were actually sold. In short, estimation is the process by which sample values are used as a basis for generating a range of statements about population values with a calculable probability of error.

The calculation of confidence intervals begins by making a number of assumptions:

- The sample selected was a simple random sample (the various types of sample design were explained in Chapter 3).

Table 6.6 Respondents by sex

Sex	Frequency
Male	12
Female	8
Total	20

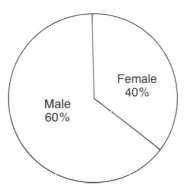

Figure 6.2 A pie-chart from Table 6.6

- There is no bias in the selection procedure.
- The sample is 30 or more in size.
- There is no non-sampling error, for example from non-response.

Once the calculation is made, some of these assumptions can be relaxed so that adjustments can be made when, for example, the sample is not simple random, or where the sample is less than 30. However, given these assumptions, it means that the error remaining is random error, which is likely to fluctuate, but only within certain limits, since the over-representation of certain kinds of cases is just as likely as their under-representation, and many errors will cancel out. How much error there is likely to be will differ from variable to variable, and will depend on two factors:

- the size of the sample,
- the extent to which the variable is widely scattered in the population of cases at large.

The bigger the sample, the less the random sampling error will be, but by a declining amount. Furthermore, a sample used to estimate a variable that varies widely in the population will show more random sampling error than for a variable that does not. This variability is measured by the standard deviation for metric variables, and for non-metric variables by the proportion that possesses a characteristic. Thus a 50/50 split shows the maximum variability.

If we imagine taking a very large number of samples of a given size, say, 5 or 20, from a population and calculating summary measures for a particular variable for each sample, the results may be plotted as a distribution called a **sampling distribution**. This shows the frequency with which values of the summary measures occur, in theory from every conceivable sample that could be drawn from a population. If data are metric, we could, for example, calculate the mean for each sample and plot the means to create a sampling distribution of the mean (see Figure 6.3). Most of the means of the samples will be close to the real population mean, but a few will be 'rogue' samples. In practice, we would not actually take lots of samples, but calculate a theoretical sampling distribution derived from all possible combinations of sample results from that population. Such a distribution takes on a characteristic shape, referred to as a 'normal' distribution, which is bell-shaped, symmetrical, and never quite touches the base, as in Figure 6.4. Such a distribution will arise even if the variable in the population of cases is not normally distributed, provided the sample size is at least 30. This is a proposition derived from what is called the 'central limit theorem'.

The spread of values encompassed by the sampling distribution is measured by its own standard deviation called the **standard error**. The standard error of the sampling distribution of the mean (called the standard error of the mean) may be calculated by taking:

$$\frac{\text{The standard deviation in the population}}{\text{The square root of the sample size}} = \frac{\sigma}{\sqrt{n}}$$

Thus the standard error increases with an increase in the standard deviation for the population of cases, and decreases with an increase in sample size, but as the square root of the sample size. Where the standard deviation for the population of cases is unknown, the standard deviation found for the sample variable is taken as an estimate of the population standard deviation. Because the normal curve has a fixed shape, it is possible to treat the area under the curve as representing total certainty that any observation will be encompassed by it. We can say, furthermore, that 50 per cent of the area is above the mean for that variable, and 50 per cent below. In other words, there is a 50 per cent chance that any observation will be above (or below) the mean. This argument can be taken further so that we can calculate the area under the curve between the mean and one standard deviation. The area is, in fact, 34.1 per cent (see Figure 6.4). Thus just over two-thirds or 68.2 per cent of the area is between plus one standard deviation and minus one standard deviation. Thus if the mean score of a set of cases is 20 with a standard deviation of 6, then just over two-thirds of the area (and, by implication, of the observations) would be within 20 ± 6 or between 14 and 26. Figure 6.4 also shows that all but 4.6 per cent of the

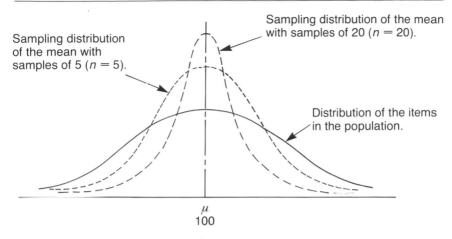

Figure 6.3 Sampling distribution of the mean

area lies between plus and minus two standard deviations. There are, in fact, tables of areas under the normal curve, so that if we wished to know how many standard deviations encompassed 95 per cent of the area, we could look it up and discover that 1.96 standard deviations either side of the mean does so. This, in turn, implies that for 95 per cent of all possible samples of size n that we could draw from the same population of cases, it will be true that the population mean lies within plus and minus 1.96 standard errors of the sample mean. Thus, if the mean score of a sample of 60 cases is 20, and the standard deviation is 6, then we can be 95 per cent certain that the real population mean lies between the achieved sample mean plus or minus 1.96 standard errors, that is, 20 ± 1.96 ($^{6}/_{\sqrt{60}}$), or between 18.5 and 21.5. These are the confidence limits. Different samples may, of course, result in slightly different confidence limits, but these new limits will also hold in 95

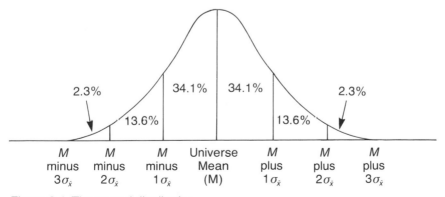

Figure 6.4 The normal distribution

per cent of samples that could be drawn from the population. It is usual, however, to make the slightly less accurate statement that we can be 95 per cent confident that the population mean lies between the confidence limits calculated.

If the variables are non-metric, we cannot, of course, calculate the mean for each sample result. However, we can plot a sampling distribution of a proportion based on the notion of plotting proportions for all possible combinations of a given sample size from a given population. The standard deviation of the sampling distribution of the proportion (the standard error of the proportion) is given by:

$$\sqrt{\frac{p\,(1-p)}{n}}$$

where p is the proportion possessing a characteristic. As for metric data, we use the sample result to estimate the population parameter, in this case the population proportion. Thus if a sample of 300 found that 40 per cent had purchased brand A in the last week, then we can be 95 per cent confident that the real population proportion lies between:

$$0.4 \pm 1.96 \sqrt{\frac{(0.4)(0.6)}{300}}$$

So, the confidence limits are 0.34 and 0.46 (34 per cent and 46 per cent).

For a given sample size, the larger the proportion that reports a given characteristics (up to 50 per cent), the greater will be the sampling error. For example, if only 1 per cent of a random sample of 300 said they had purchased a particular brand, the error will be roughly plus or minus 1 per cent at the 95 per cent level of confidence, i.e.

$$1.96 \sqrt{\frac{(0.01)(0.99)}{300}} = 0.01$$

Thus we can be 95 per cent certain that the true result lies between zero per cent and 2 per cent. If 50 per cent said they had made such a purchase, the error will be plus or minus 5.7 per cent at the 95 per cent level, i.e.

$$1.96 \sqrt{\frac{(0.5)(0.5)}{300}} = 0.057$$

Thus we can be 95 per cent certain that the true result lies between 44.3 per cent and 55.7 per cent. A larger sample would mean that the standard error of both of these results would be lower. A fair estimate of the percentage error can be derived from a chart, as illustrated in Figure 6.5. For example, if in a random sample of 500 adults, 20 per cent said they had been unemployed at some time in the last five years, then by laying a ruler between the 20 per cent sample result on the left and the 500 sample size

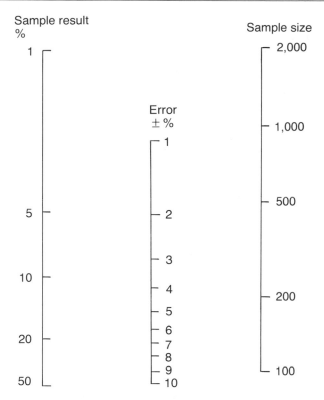

Figure 6.5 Chart for measuring random sampling error (95% probability)

on the right, the error will be approximately 3.5 per cent where the ruler cuts the middle line. Such a chart can be used to determine the minimum size of sample required to achieve various levels of sampling error.

While such calculations do give some idea as to whether estimates are likely to be tight or fairly loose, in practice, calculations of standard errors and confidence intervals are often not made, and many clients would not understand them if produced by the market research company. Providing a single 'best estimate' from a sample entails not calculating standard errors, but utilising the processes of:

- weighting,
- grossing up.

Weighting is an adjustment that is made to the sample result before it is 'expanded' or grossed up to the total set of cases. A weight is a multiplying factor applied to some or all of the responses given in a survey in order to eliminate or reduce the impact of bias caused by types of case that are over- or under-represented in the sample. Thus if there are two few women aged 20–24 in a sample survey compared with the proportions in this age group known to exist in the set of cases, such that only 50 out of a required 60 are in the achieved sample, the number who, for example, purchased brand X in a measurement period of, say, four weeks, will be multiplied by a weighting which is calculated by taking:

$$\frac{\text{target sample number}}{\text{actual sample number}} = \frac{60}{50} = 1.2$$

This means that if, for example, this group are heavy purchasers of brand X, then estimates of sales of brand X will not be underestimated because that group is under-represented in the sample from which the estimate is to be made. A worked example of weighting is given in Table 6.7.

There are, however, many different reasons why the actual sample may

Table 6.7 A worked example of weighting

A random sample of 100 adults produces 40 men and 60 women; but it is known that in the population from which the sample was drawn there are 48 per cent men and 52 per cent women. The weighting for the men would be 48/40 = 1.2, and for the women, 52/60 = 0.87. Table (a) below shows the unweighted results from the sample, who were asked if they had drunk beer in the last four weeks. From this it can be seen that 30/40 or 75 per cent of the men had done so, whereas this was true for only 25/60 or 41.7 per cent of the women. A projection to the population based on the unweighted results will suggest that 55 per cent of the population had drunk beer in the last four weeks. Table (b) shows the weighted results after the responses of the men have been weighted by 1.2 and the responses of the women by 0.87. This shows that the proportion of men to women is now correct at 48 per cent to 52 per cent. The new estimate will be based on the 57.7 per cent having drunk beer in the last four weeks.

(a) Unweighted sample results

	Drank beer	Did not drink beer	Total
Male	30	10	40
Female	25	35	60
Total	55	45	100

(b) Weighted sample results

	Drank beer	Did not drink beer	Total
Male	36.0	12.0	48
Female	21.7	30.3	52
Total	57.7	42.3	100

not reflect the population, and the effect of applying weights differs accordingly. Thus a group may be over- or under-represented because:

- it is part of the sample design,
- there are problems of coverage,
- there are problems of pickup,
- there are problems of unrepresentative non-response,
- there are random sampling fluctuations,
- the selection procedures are not random.

Sometimes minority groups in a population are deliberately over-sampled, otherwise there would be too few on which to base sensible analysis. Thus the BBC's Radio Listening Panel deliberately oversamples Radio 4 and Radio 3 listeners. This ensures that analyses of these programmes are based on adequate numbers. However, when the results from all radio listeners are aggregated, the responses of Radio 4 listeners are downweighted to their correct proportion in the population. Radio 3 listeners are so heavily over-represented that comments made by Radio 3 listeners on the output of other networks are not analysed at all!

Problems of coverage and pickup may be tackled by applying what some agencies call 'field' or 'market size' weights. Thus if it is known that a particular procedure for recording sales in shops misses out certain types of retail outlet that normally account for 25 per cent of total sales of brand X, then future estimates may be multiplied by 4/3 or 1.33. Similarly, where a procedure does not pick up a known proportion of sales or usage, for example, asking people to remember purchase of chocolate bars will fail to pick up all purchases, then weights may be applied. The problem of coverage may be created by an inadequate sampling frame, but if the proportions of specific sub-groups missing from the frame are known, then the responses of those in that sub-group who have responded can be upweighted to their correct proportion.

For random samples, the effect of non-response is to reduce the achieved sample size, usually by different proportions in various sub-groups of cases. The result is bias, and the application of weightings is designed to alleviate the effects of that bias. Correcting for non-response, however, rests on the untested assumption that those people who *did* respond can adequately represent those members in the same sub-group who did not respond in respect of the variable being estimated. This means that sampling error is likely to be greater, and by an amount which is additional to that resulting from the reduction in sample size. The degree to which the effect of bias through non-response is reduced by applying weights depends on the extent to which the variables used for weighting are associated with those being estimated. Thus if we adjust for imbalances in the sex, age and social class composition of the achieved sample, then the effect of doing so will depend on the extent to which these variables are associated with, for example, the purchasing behaviour we are trying to measure. If the behaviour concerned is unaffected by age, for example, then weighting by age will have no impact. Ideally, different sets of weightings should be used for each variable being estimated. In practice, this would be very complex, so most agencies will select sex, age and social class (or employment status – working full-time, part-time, or unemployed) as characteristics that are associated in varying degrees with a large number of variables being estimated.

Even random samples that do not suffer from problems of coverage, pickup or non-response, will show fluctuations in which over- and under-representations are a random phenomenon. Again, those variables used for weighting need to be carefully selected so that adjustments are made where under- or over-representations are greatest, and for variables that are associated with those being estimated. By definition, these over- and under-representations will vary in both extent and direction from sample to sample. Ideally, checks should be made against a large number of such variables – usually demographic, but may include such things as heavy, medium and light usage of a product. Thus individuals giving responses to a television programme may have their answers weighted according to whether the correct proportions of 'heavy', 'medium' and 'light' viewers have been selected in the sample.

Adjusting for random deviations of the sample profile from the known population characteristics is a process sometimes called 'post-stratification' weighting or even 'true' post-stratification to distinguish it from weightings applied in the correction of non-sampling errors or biases. The effect of applying such post-stratification weightings is to reduce sampling error, and hence to increase the efficiency of the sample for the purposes of estimation. By contrast, the use of weightings to correct for sample imbalances where the sampling is non-random is difficult to justify. This is because the weighting does not overcome the basic theoretical weakness of such samples, namely, that the selection method will introduce biases in respect of unanticipated demographic or other independent variables that associate or correlate with those being estimated. The imposition of quotas ensures that the sample is balanced in respect of the quota variables, but not in respect of those not subject to quota control. The degree of non-response in most quota samples is unknown, which makes the assumption that responders can adequately represent non-responders in respect of variables to which weights are being applied even more dubious than for random sampling. Furthermore, the variables used for weighting are often the same as those used for quota controls, so the weightings will be close to unity provided the quotas have been filled.

The use of weightings for *any* kind of sample, random or non-random, to correct for unrepresentativeness is believed by some researchers to be unethical window-dressing of the data. However, Sharot (1986) argues that the correct incorporation of weightings into the overall survey design can improve the cost/accuracy equation beyond what could be achieved by unweighted responses alone. Provided that the details of the weighting process are available and pointed out to users of the data, it is, believes Sharot, difficult to see why this should be unethical.

Weightings are used largely to minimise the impact of sample imbalances and may be seen as a cheaper, and in many respects a cost-effective, alternative to minimising the occurrences of those errors in the first place. Changing research designs so as, for example, to minimise non-response may be a more expensive process than applying weightings after the data have been collected. It also has to be said that attempts to minimise one kind of error, like non-response, may result in increased errors of other kinds: for example, response errors may increase because more potential non-responders have been persuaded to co-operate in a survey.

When all the adjustments have been made to the data, the researcher may want estimation not so much of averages or proportions, but actual quantities, for example, the national and regional amounts spent in pounds sterling on a particular brand in the UK, the actual number of packets sold, or the total number of households that possess a particular characteristic. To do this requires a process of **grossing up** to the population. In principle, this is a fairly simple operation of multiplying the sample quantities by a factor that reflects the proportion of the population constituted by the sample. That is:

$$\frac{\text{population size}}{\text{sample size}} = \frac{N}{n}$$

Thus if a sample of 2,000 households purchased 8,000 tins of baked beans in a four-week period, and the population of households in Great Britain is 24 million, then it can be estimated that,

$$8,000 \ (N/n) = \frac{8,000 \times (24,000,000)}{2,000}$$

or 96 million tins were sold in that period. This is only the same result that would be achieved by multiplying the sample proportion or average by the population figure (i.e. 4×24 million). In practice, as ever, it is not quite so simple. Grossing up is usually done on a cell-by-cell basis, so that if within region X there are 50,000 women aged 20–24 and a sample of 10 showed that they had purchased five packs of brand A, then it can be estimated that (5)50,000/10 or 25,000 packs were purchased by that age-group of women in region X. These results will then be added to the other age group purchase estimates to give a regional figure. The regional estimates may then be aggregated into a Great Britain total. Alternatively, GB estimates for particular age groups can be made. The estimates for brands can be aggregated into product class estimates, and so on. In short, by grossing up on a cell-by-cell basis, estimates can be aggregated in many different ways according to the breakdowns required by the client.

In the real world of the market research, it is unfortunately true that many clients do not understand the basics of sampling and so lack interest in or understanding of standard errors and the processes of weighting and grossing up. In consequence, many clients do not ask for the details of such calculations. At the same time, the market research companies feel that to produce calculations (for example of confidence intervals) for a large number of variables, will only add confusion and perhaps distrust of the data. In consequence, sampling errors are often quietly ignored, and the estimates given are taken to be the 'truth'. Market research executives will instead try to assure their clients that the occurrence and impact of non-sampling errors have been minimised by:

- demonstrating that the procedures for the collection, analysis and reporting of the results are 'respectable', meticulous and thorough,
- showing that the research design features are such as to minimise sources of error within the parameters set by time and cost,
- emphasising the extent of quality control checks that will uncover, correct and minimise the occurrence of 'mistakes',
- making corrections to the resulting data so that known biases are adjusted for.

Beyond these assurances, clients are sometimes given some indication of the extent of random sampling error that remains. However, since sampling is seldom **simple random sampling**, then, strictly speaking, an adjustment needs to be made to the **standard error** to take this into account. This adjustment is in the form of a **design factor**, which is the ratio of the **variance** of the sample actually used to the variance of a correspondingly sized simple random sample. Ideally, this ratio should be specially worked out for each survey; in practice, typical design factors are applied based on experience. Thus, for stratified random samples (which usually include a degree of clustering), the design factor is usually about 1.25, so the standard error is multiplied by this factor. For clustered randomised samples (like random route with several callbacks), the design factor is about 1.5, or 2.0 if there are no callbacks. Heavily stratified, fully interlocking quota samples often have a design factor of at least 2.0, while simple quota samples should be given a factor of not less than 2.5. Unfortunately, these adjustments are not always made and the standard error reported is the one calculated for simple random samples. To make matters worse, whether or not a design factor has been included is not always stated. Charts, like the one in Figure 6.5, or read-off tables, *may* be adjusted to include a design factor. It is, therefore, important to be clear about what adjustments have been made before interpreting the results from sampling.

Estimation is only one aspect of drawing conclusions from univariate analysis. Another is to test statements or predictions made *before* the analysis begins against the results drawn from a sample in order to calculate, with a predetermined probability, whether a sample result was likely or unlikely to have been derived from a population of cases in which the statement or prediction is true. Thus a researcher may have reason to believe – on the basis of a deduction from theory, on the basis of marketing principles, or on the basis of past research or personal experience – that 70 per cent of a population of cases possess a particular characteristic (e.g. that 70 per cent of women in the UK object to advertising of highly personal products on television). If a sample of 100 cases found that 60 possessed this characteristic, could this proportion of responses in the sample easily have been obtained from a population in which the real proportion is in fact 70 per cent? The statement or prediction that is made about the population of cases in advance is usually called the **null hypothesis**. This is a bit of a misnomer, because it is not always negative or null. It is probably better to think of it as the 'test' hypothesis.

Like estimation, a sampling distribution of the test statistic is used. However, unlike estimation, where we use the *sample result* to estimate the mean (or proportion and standard error, in testing the null hypothesis *we assume that the null hypothesis is true* and use the hypothesised mean or the hypothesised proportion to estimate the standard error that would exist if the null hypothesis were true. In the example above, if the null hypothesis is true, then the standard error of the proportion is:

$$p = \sqrt{\frac{p(1-p)}{n}} = \sqrt{\frac{(0.7)(0.3)}{100}} = 0.046$$

This implies that 95 per cent of all samples of size 100 will produce results that vary between:

0.7 ± 1.96 (0.046) or between 61% and 79%

Since the original sample result (60 per cent), lies outside this range it is unlikely to have come from a population in which $p = 0.7$. In other words, random error is an unlikely explanation of the difference between the sample result of 60 per cent and the predicted 70 per cent. Note that we cannot conclude from the sample result that the real proportion is 60 per cent, but only that it probably did not come from a population in which the null hypothesis is true.

Why, it may be asked, did we not simply use the sample result for estimation purposes rather than going to the trouble of setting up a null hypothesis prior to the analysis? The answer is that if we have a theory, a principle, or a wealth of experience that we think allows us to make a prediction, it is this prediction that we want to test. If we wanted, for example, to compare the results of two or more pieces of research, then it is their support or questioning of the theory or principle or experience that we want to compare. Calculating confidence intervals does not test the hypothesis because the results could be consistent with a large number of hypotheses or predictions.

Bivariate analysis

Univariate analysis (or 'hole count', as it is sometimes called – a relic of the days when computer cards were physically punched with holes which were then counted) forms the basis for making precise, quantitative univariate statements about variables one at a time, but takes no account of the relationship between variables. Bivariate analysis looks at these relationships two at a time, and measures the extent to which the values of the two variables tend to exhibit some kind of pattern in the way they vary together. If *any* pattern exists, it becomes possible to predict values of one variable from knowledge of values on the other. Put another way, the extent to which it is possible to predict the values of one variable from values on the other provides a measure of association.

There are a large number of such measures, but they are normally constructed in such a way that perfect prediction gives a measure or 'coefficient' of one, and no association results in a coefficient of zero. Many of these measures are based on the notion of making a prediction or 'best guess' of the values of the variable, which is seen to be the dependent variable for each case in the unit of analysis, first without employing knowledge of values for each case on the other variable, and second comparing this with the predictions made when we do know these values. The extent to which error is reduced by employing knowledge of the second variable gives a measure of association. If all errors in making such predictions are eliminated, there is perfect association; if only the same number of errors or degree of error is made using knowledge of the values of the independent variable as were made without such knowledge, there is no association. In between, we can measure the proportional reduction in error taking place. This we can do by calculating:

> The amount of the reduction in error
> The amount of the original error

Which particular measures of association are used depends, as ever, in the first instance on whether the variables are scaled metrically or not. If *both* variables are metric, then it is possible to calculate the degree of **correlation**, using a statistic called **Pearson's r**. This estimates the direction and strength of any linear relationship that exists. If we have a set of cases like the four cases A–D in Table 6.8, measured on two metric scales, X and Y, and if we take variable Y as the dependent variable, the 'best guess' that we can make for each case A–D (ignoring the values of X) would be to predict the mean value of the set for each. This assumes that we have no knowledge of the individual values of Y for A, B, C or D, but we do know that the mean is $12/4 = 3$. The degree of error using the mean to predict each Y value can be measured by taking the sum of the squared deviations between the value and the prediction for each case and dividing by $n = 4$. This is the same as the standard deviation, but without taking the square root and is usually referred to as the **variance**. The variance is 2.5 for the four values of Y (see Table 6.9).

We now see if we could reduce this error by using knowledge of the values on X to predict the values on Y for each case instead of using the mean of Y as the prediction for each case. If the positions of the four cases are plotted on a graph, a scattergram is obtained, as in Figure 6.6. High values on X appear to be associated with high values on Y and vice versa. If we were to draw a straight line through the points, as illustrated, it would

Table 6.8 Scores for individuals A–D on Test X and Test Y

Individual	Test score	
	X	Y
A	0	1
B	6	2
C	6	4
D	8	5
Total	20	12

Table 6.9 The variance on Y

Variance	Y	$(Y - \bar{Y})$	$(Y - \bar{Y})^2$
A	1	−2	4
B	2	−1	1
C	4	+1	1
D	5	+2	4
			10

$\bar{Y} = 3$, $\sigma^2 = \dfrac{\Sigma(Y - \bar{Y})^2}{N} = 10/4 = 2.5$

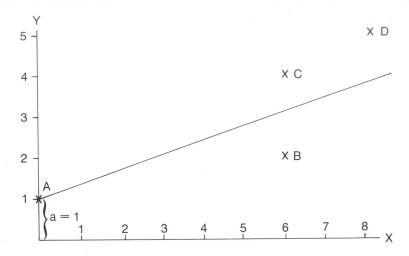

Figure 6.6 A scattergram for cases A–D

be possible to use the formula that describes the line to make a prediction of Y based on the values of X. The general formula for a straight line is Y = a + bX, where a is the value of Y when X is zero, and b is the slope of the line and measures the rate of change in Y per unit increase in X. For a given relationship, a and b are constant. If we know what they are, we can make a prediction of Y from any value of X. The particular line used in correlation is the 'regression' line, which is drawn in such a way that it minimises the vertical distances between each point on the scattergram and the regression line. The method used to determine the line is called the 'least squares' method, and is calculated using the formula:

$$b = \frac{(X - \bar{X})(Y - \bar{Y})}{(X - \bar{X})^2}$$

The formula is derived from differential calculus, so its explanation is beyond the scope of this book and will have to be accepted as a 'black box'. For the four cases above, the constant b is calculated to be 0.4, as illustrated in Table 6.10. Thus for every unit increase in X, Y increases by 0.4. The constant, a, as can be seen from the graph, is 1. When X = 0, Y = 1. This is sometimes called the 'intercept' and denotes where the regression line cuts the Y axis; it can always be deduced by substituting in the formula:

$$a = \bar{Y} - b\bar{X}$$

where $\bar{Y}$ and $\bar{X}$ are the means of Y and X respectively. X and Y can now be related using the formula Y = 1 + 0.4X. Thus when X = 1, Y = 1 + 0.4(1) = 1.4. When X = 2, Y = 1 + 0.8 = 1.8 and so on. Interestingly, when X = 6, the formula predicts that Y = 1 + 2.4 = 3.4. Comparing this

Table 6.10 Calculating the slope

	X	Y	(X − X̃)	(Y − Ỹ)	(X − X̃)(Y − Ỹ)	(X − X)²
A	0	1	−5	−2	+10	25
B	6	2	+1	−1	−1	1
C	6	4	+1	+1	+1	1
D	8	5	+3	+2	+6	9
					16	36

Total

$b = 16/36 = 0.4$

with the actual data, when X = 6 for case B, Y = 2, and when X is 6 for case C, Y = 4, making 3.4 a good average guess!

Comparing the actual values with the guessed values of Y (denoted Y′) using the formula, the variance is 0.74 as shown in Table 6.11. This is the measure of error in predicting Y, knowing X and using the formula. Recall that when predicting Y not knowing X, the variance was 2.5. The coefficient of correlation (sometimes called the coefficient of determination) is r^2 and can now be calculated as:

$$r^2 = \frac{\text{amount of reduction in error}}{\text{amount of original error}} = \frac{2.5 - 0.74}{2.5} = 0.7$$

An r^2 of 0.7 indicates the proportion of the variance in Y which is attributable to the variance in X, as measured by using knowledge of the X values to predict Y values rather than using the mean of Y, and assuming a linear relationship. R^2 indicates the strength of the correlation and shows how close the points are to the regression line. It is always positive, but does not actually enable us to make a prediction. For that, we need to calculate the constants a and b.

Table 6.11 The variance of using X to predict Y

	Y	Y′	(Y − Y′)	(Y − Y′)²
A	1	1	0	0
B	2	3.4	−1.4	1.96
C	4	3.4	+0.6	0.36
D	5	4.2	+0.8	0.64
				2.96

Total

$\sigma^2 = \frac{2.96}{4} = 0.74$

The statistic r measures the rate of change in one variable relative to the other in standardised units. It is positive for a positive correlation and negative for a negative one. Once r is squared, it is always positive; r is always larger than r^2. To compute r it is not necessary to go through all the procedures described above. These were described in order to explain what the statistic does. The calculating formula and its application to the set of four cases in illustrated in Table 6.12.

If the four cases A–D were, in fact, a sample from a population of cases, then the values r, a and b would be only estimates. A sampling distribution for all three coefficients could be drawn, based on the idea of taking lots of samples from the same population and plotting the results. If the sample is large – over 30 or so – then this sampling distribution will be normal in shape, but only provided the two variables are normally distributed in the population. If these assumptions can be reasonably made, the statistical significance of any achieved values of r is dependent entirely on the size of the sample. If the null hypothesis is that the sample is drawn from a population in which there is no correlation between X and Y, then it is possible simply to look up significant values of r at given probabilities in a table. If the achieved value of r is greater than this figure, the null hypothesis may be rejected, and it may be concluded that the sample was *not* drawn from a

Table 6.12 Using the calculating formula

$$r = \frac{\Sigma XY - \frac{(\Sigma X)(\Sigma Y)}{N}}{\sqrt{\left[\Sigma X^2 - \frac{(\Sigma X)^2}{N}\right]\left[\Sigma Y^2 - \frac{(\Sigma Y)^2}{N}\right]}}$$

	X	Y	X^2	Y^2	XY
A	0	1	0	1	0
B	6	2	36	4	12
C	6	4	36	16	24
D	8	5	64	25	40
Totals	20	12	136	46	76

$$r = \frac{76 - \frac{(20)(12)}{4}}{\sqrt{\left[136 - \frac{20^2}{4}\right]\left[46 - \frac{12^2}{4}\right]}}$$

$$= \frac{76 - 60}{\sqrt{(136 - 100)(46 - 36)}}$$

$$= 0.84$$

$$r^2 = 0.7$$

population in which there is no correlation, that is, there is a correlation
with the probability chosen.

Where the bivariate analysis is of two non-metric variables, then it is not
possible, clearly, to calculate Pearson's r. However, we can interlace the
frequencies of the categories of the two variables in a bivariate crosstabulation, as illustrated in Table 6.13. Where the totals at the ends of the
rows or the foot of the columns (the 'marginals') are unequal, direct
comparison of cell frequencies is difficult to make. If, however, we stan-
dardise the frequencies to a common denominator, patterns of association
become more apparent. The best solution is to calculate percentages, either
down the columns or along the rows. Which of these is appropriate
depends on how the researcher wishes to interpret the data.

Suppose we hypothesise that women are more likely than men to recall
prices accurately. Suppose, further, that a sample of 205 people produces
the data in Table 6.13. From this table it looks as though women are,
indeed, more likely to recall accurately than men. However, comparing the
75 accurate recalls for the women with the 40 for the men does not reflect
the fact that there are more men in the sample. What we really want to
know is what proportion of women and men recall accurately.

If we percentage downwards within categories of sex, as illustrated in
Table 6.14, then we can say that 88.2 per cent of the women compared
with 33.3 per cent of the men had accurate price recall. Notice here that we
have percentaged downwards in the direction of the independent variable,
sex. We are interested in the effect sex has on price recall, not the other
way around! It is a convention (not universally followed, but useful nevertheless) that the independent variable forms the columns of the table, and

Table 6.13 Price awareness by sex: frequencies

	Women	Men	Total
Accurate recall	75	40	115
No accurate recall	10	80	90
Total	85	120	205

Table 6.14 Price awareness by sex: column percentages

	Women %	Men %
Accurate recall	88.2	33.3
No accurate recall	11.8	66.7
Total	100	100

the dependent variable the rows. So, as a general rule, put the independent variable at the top and percentage downwards. Notice also that the comparison was made *across* the direction of percentaging – there would be little point in comparing the 88.2 per cent with the 11.8 per cent.

It would, of course, be possible to calculate the percentages in the other direction, as in Table 6.15. This looks at the distribution of sex within categories of price recall: 65.2 per cent of those with accurate price recall compared with 11.1 per cent of those with non-accurate recall were women. The table implies that price awareness has some effect on gender classification! Although this table may be an extreme case of percentaging in the 'wrong' direction, the distinction between dependent and independent variable is not always so clear-cut and the appropriate direction in which to percentage may not be obvious. You will have to watch out for tables that have been percentaged inappropriately.

Comparing percentage differences does not enable us to say how strong is the association between two variables in a crosstabulation, or to compare it with the degree of association in another table. We may wish, for example, to be able to say whether price awareness is more strongly associated with sex than with social class.

Statisticians have developed a bewildering array of different measures of association that give different results on the same data – sometimes very different results. Most have been devised in such a way that a value of unity indicates perfect association, and zero indicates no association. Some of these measures can be applied to crosstabulations of any size; others are restricted to 2 × 2 tables. Some can be used whether or not the categories of the variables are ordered; others depend on the fact that variables contain sets of values that are in order.

There are three rather different bases on which such statistics have been developed. These are:

- pair-by-pair comparisons,
- departure from independence,
- prediction errors.

Table 6.15 Price awareness by sex: row percentages

	Women %	Men %	Total
Accurate recall	65.2	34.8	100
No accurate recall	11.1	88.9	100

Pair-by-pair comparisons

If the values of two variables are associated together, there will be a predominance of instances where this association occurs, and relatively few where it does not. Consider Table 6.16. In this instance, there is a perfect association because in all instances where variable B is present (for example, owns a pet), variable A is also present (has pet food in stock); at the same time, where variable B is absent (no pets), variable A is also absent (no pet food). If we now count up the number of pairs for which there is a perfect association (one of the pair has both pets and pet food, and the other has neither), then there are 10 × 20, or 200, such 'positive' pairs.

In practice, of course, there will often be instances where variable B is present, but variable A is absent (a hungry pet!), or vice versa (bought a can of pet food by mistake). This will create pairs in which there is an inverse association (one of the pair has a pet but no pet food, and the other has food, but no pets). These are 'negative' pairs.

In the 1890s a statistician called Yule developed a measure of the tendency for positive (or negative) pairs to predominate. By taking the difference between the number of positive and the number of negative pairs as a proportion of the total number of positive and negative pairs, he created a statistic that he called 'Q' that varies between zero (there are as many positive as negative pairs) and unity (all pairs are either positive or negative). This measure is now usually called 'Yule's Q', and may be defined as:

$$Q = \frac{ad - bc}{ad + bc}$$

where

a	b
c	d

Table 6.16 Variable A by variable B

		Variable B	
		Present	*Absent*
Variable A	Present	10	–
	Absent	–	20

For Table 6.13, this may be calculated as:

$$Q = \frac{(75 \times 80) - (40 \times 10)}{(75 \times 80) + (40 \times 10)}$$

$$= \frac{6,000 - 400}{6,000 + 400}$$

$$= 0.875$$

This shows a heavy predominance of positive pairs (87.5 per cent of all pairs are positive). There is a strong association between sex and price recall. This result, may, furthermore, be compared with the results of such a statistic calculated for other tables.

The main features of Q are as follows:

- It varies between −1 and +1.
- Zero indicates no association.
- It can be calculated *only* on a 2 × 2 table.
- It has a weakness in that it reverts to unity if *any* cell is empty, as in Table 6.17.

The idea of pair-by-pair comparisons may be extended to larger tables, but to make sense, the sets of categories on *both* variables need to be ordered. The measures that have been developed include Gamma, Goodman and Kruskal's Tau, and Sommers' d. These measures while useful, and while they do appear in some of the survey analysis computer packages (for example, SPSSx), are seldom used by market researchers. If you are particularly interested in following these up, have a look at Blalock (1972) or Bohrnstedt and Knoke (1982).

Departure from independence

Statistical association can be said to be present to the extent that the observed frequencies depart from those we would expect if there were no

Table 6.17 Pet ownership by sex

	Male	Female
Yes	50	0
No	100	70

$$Q = \frac{(50 \times 70) - (100 \times 0)}{(50 \times 70) + (100 \times 0)}$$

$$= 1$$

association. Thus if 120 respondents consisted of 60 males and 60 females responding 'yes' or 'no' to a question, and equal numbers of each said 'yes' and 'no', the marginals would look like Table 6.18. Here 60 out of 120 are male, that is half. Therefore we would expect half of the 60 yesses to be male, that is 30. The expected frequency for any cell can be found by multiplying the row and column marginal for that cell, and dividing by n, in this case:

$$\frac{60 \times 60}{120} = 30$$

The expected frequencies for each cell are illustrated in Table 6.19. This shows that just as many men as women are likely to say 'yes' (or 'no'). Suppose, however, that all the men said 'yes' and all the women said 'no'. The result is shown in Table 6.20. The difference between the observed and expected frequencies for each cell is now either +30 or −30 (the maximum difference that is possible in this table). Simply adding these up will, of course, produce zero. If, however, we square the difference and take that as a proportion of our expectations for each cell, then we take

Table 6.18 Responses by sex: marginal total

	Male	Female	Total
Yes	−	−	60
No	−	−	60
Total	00	60	120

Table 6.19 Responses by sex: expected frequencies

	Male	Female	Total
Yes	30	30	60
No	30	30	60
Total	60	60	120

Table 6.20 Responses by sex: observed frequencies

	Male	Female	Total
Yes	60	−	60
No	−	60	60
Total	60	60	120

account of whether the absolute difference is based on a large or small expectation. We can now add these up for each cell.

If fo = observed frequency and fe = expected frequency, then:

fo	fe	(fo − fe)	$\dfrac{(fo - fe)^2}{fe}$
60	30	+30	30
0	30	−30	30
0	30	−30	30
60	30	+30	30
			120

120 is the maximum value that the sum of the squared differences as a proportion of expected values can take in this table. The result is a statistic called **Chi-square**, usually symbolised as x^2. If we divide this by the number of cases in the table, then we obtain a value of unity, indicating a perfect association. Dividing Chi-square by n gives a statistic called Phi-square, which is another measure of association. If there had been no difference between fo and fe, then, clearly, Chi-square will be zero, and so will Phi-square.

The main features of Phi-square are as follows:

- It varies between zero and +1; it cannot take a negative value like Q.
- Zero indicates no association.
- It can be used on a 2 × 2 table, like Q; but, unlike Q, it can also be used on any table where either rows or columns = 2. On larger tables, the maximum value of Phi-square is greater than unity and is thus difficult to interpret.

Prediction errors

If two variables are associated, then, as explained earlier, it is possible to use knowledge of the value of one variable to predict the value of the other for each case. Thus, if all men say 'yes' and all women say 'no', then for each person, if we know their sex, we can safely predict the answer to the question. In practice, prediction is seldom perfect, so what we can do is measure the extent to which knowledge of the value on one variable reduces the number of errors in predicting the other.

Take the case where nearly all men say 'yes' and most of the women say 'no', as in Table 6.21. To generate our measure of association, we need to calculate how many errors predicting the answer to the question we would make *not* knowing a person's sex. If we know the marginal totals of yesses and noes, but not each individual case, then the 'best' guess we could make for each person is to predict that all answers are 'yes' (since there are more of these), and be wrong for 90 out of the 200 cases.

Table 6.21 Responses by sex

	Men	Women	Total
Yes	90	20	110
No	10	80	90
Total	100	100	200

Suppose, now, that we know a person's sex: then knowing that a person is male and that 90 out of 100 males say 'yes', clearly, it is sensible to predict 'yes' for all males and make only 10 errors. If we predict 'no' for all 100 women, we make 20 errors, that is 10 + 20 = 30 errors in all. This may be compared with the original 90 errors. This is a 66 per cent reduction, or 0.66. Clearly, if we eliminate all errors, we will end up with a measure of unity. If we eliminate none, we will end up with a value of zero.

The measure just described is called **Lambda**, and may be defined as:

$$\frac{\text{number of errors eliminated}}{\text{number of original errors}}$$

In the above example, this is:

$$= \frac{90 - 30}{90} = 0.66$$

This is sometimes referred to as the 'proportional reduction in error' and is clearly using the same basis for calculating association as Pearson's r.

The main features of Lambda are as follows:

- It varies between zero and unity; it cannot be negative.
- It can be used on any size of table. The errors remaining after taking the 'best guess', not knowing, then knowing the value of the other variable, need to be added up.
- It is an asymmetric measure, that is, the prediction is one-way. It makes sense to predict the dependent variable from the independent variable. If the independent variable is at the top, then it is the categories forming the rows that should be predicted.

The three bases for measuring statistical association will give different answers. Thus, while Yule's Q for Table 6.13 worked out at 0.875, Phi-square is 0.3 and Lambda is 0.44. Pair-by-pair comparisons will always give the highest figure, and departure from independence will give the lowest. In one sense this does not matter, provided you use the same statistic for comparing tables. Looking at isolated tables and saying how strong is the degree of association is too susceptible to the choice of statistic. There is no right or 'best' statistic, and the temptation must be to choose the result you want and select the statistic accordingly!

The notion of departure from independence may be used to calculate the probabilities of getting departures of certain magnitudes in order to test the null hypothesis that there is total independence, that is, no association, in the population from which the sample was drawn. The statistic Chi-square, explained in the previous section, can be used to test for:

- goodness of fit of the sample result to some theoretical distribution,
- the departure from independence when the association between two variables is being studied using bivariate crosstabulation.

Suppose a company has two brands of a product and these are measured for preference in a survey of 100 respondents. The results suggest that 60 prefer brand A and 40 brand B. If we wished to test the null hypothesis that there is equal preference for the brands, then, in theory, we would expect 50 to prefer brand A and 50 brand B. The difference between the observed and expected frequencies is 10, so Chi-square is:

$$\chi^2 = \sum \frac{(\mathrm{fo} - \mathrm{fe})^2}{\mathrm{fe}}$$

$$= \frac{10^2}{50} + \frac{10^2}{50}$$

$$= 4$$

If the null hypothesis is true, repeated samples will produce a sampling distribution. However, the χ^2 distribution is not a single probability curve, but a family of curves. These vary according to the number of observations that can be varied without changing the constraints or assumptions associated with a numerical system. Thus if our sample is 100, then any number between 1 and 100 may prefer brand A. Once it is discovered that 60 prefer brand A, then, by definition $(100 - 60)$, 40 prefer brand B. In short, there is only one 'degree of freedom' – only one figure is free to vary. The probability of obtaining Chi-square values of a given magnitude can be looked up in a table of the distribution of Chi-square. A simplified table is illustrated in Table 6.22. This shows, for example, that the value of 3.841 will not be exceeded more

Table 6.22 The distribution of Chi-square

Degrees of freedom (df)	Probability		
	0.05	0.01	0.001
1	3.841	6.635	10.827
2	5.991	9.210	13.815
3	7.815	11.341	16.268

than 5 per cent of the time in a random sample with one degree of freedom. With two degrees of freedom, this value rises to 5.991, and so on. We can conclude that the sample result of Chi square = 4 with one degree of freedom a probability greater than p = 0.05. At this level of probability we reject the null hypothesis and conclude that the difference between the sample result and our expectation was unlikely to have been a result of random sampling fluctuations. However, if we had chosen the 1 per cent level of confidence, then the null hypothesis would have been accepted since the critical value is 6.635.

To see the use of Chi-square as a test of significance, look again at Table 6.13. If 85 out of 205 respondents are women, we would expect 85/205 of the 115 who have accurate recall to be women, i.e. 85/205 (115) = 47.7. In other words, if sex and price recall are independent, then the expected frequency is 47.7. In fact, there are 75 women who have accurate recall. The calculation of Chi-square is set out in Table 6.23. In a 2 × 2 table, once the value of one cell has been determined, the rest are all fixed – it has one degree of freedom. The critical values for one degree of freedom are shown in Table 6.22. Since 60.8 is larger than 3.841, we can reject the null hypothesis that the two variables are independent in the population of cases from which the sample was drawn.

The statistical significance of any size of crosstabulation can be tested using Chi-square. However, as with earlier calculations involving estimates and hypothesis testing, the procedure does assume that random sampling has taken place and ignores the possibility of bias and non-sampling errors.

The procedures for bivariate analysis that have so far been explained relate to situations where both variables are metric or both are non-metric; but what if one is metric and the other non-metric? Basically, there are two main possibilities:

- Treat the metric variable as if it were non-metric.
- Calculate the correlation ratio and test using analysis of variance.

To follow the first procedure, it is necessary to group the metric observations into ranges of values and treat each range as a category. It is then

Table 6.23 The calculation of Chi-square for Table 6.13

Cell	fo	fe	(fo − fe)	$\dfrac{(fo - fe)^2}{fe}$
a	75	47.7	+27.3	15.6
b	40	67.3	−27.3	11.1
c	10	37.3	−27.3	20.0
d	80	52.7	+27.3	14.1
Total				60.8

possible to crosstabulate the two variables, as in Table 6.24, and analyse the degree of association using any of the measures described earlier.

The **correlation ratio** is similar to Pearson's r statistic. Provided the dependent variable is the metric one, then using its mean to make predictions of each value and taking the variance as an index of error in doing so is identical to the Pearson r procedure. However, instead of using the scores on the independent variable to improve predictions by employing a regression line, the correlation ratio compares the original variance to the variance for each category of the non-metric independent variable. If the variables are correlated, the variance within each subgroup will be less than the overall between-group variance. The correlation ratio, eta, is then defined as:

$$n^2 = \frac{\text{between-group variance} - \text{within-group variance}}{\text{between-group variance}}$$

The statistical significance of achieved differences between these variances can be determined by using **analysis of variance**. This calculates the 'F ratio', which is the ratio of between group variance to within group variance, and is defined as:

$$F = \frac{\text{between-group variance}}{\text{within-group variance}}$$

The F ratio follows its own distribution, known as the F distribution, which is the distribution that would result if the null hypothesis is true in the population from which the sample is drawn. The null hypothesis is that the between-group variance is the same as the within-group variance, in which case the F ratio is unity. The achieved values of F can be looked up in a table of significant values of the F distribution. If the ratio is greater than this value, then the result is unlikely to have come from a population in which the null hypothesis is true.

One special type of scale that was introduced in Chapter 2 was the rank-ordered scale, somewhat straddling the line between metric and non-metric. If the two variables to be analysed are both rank ordered, for

Table 6.24 Using grouped metric data to crosstabulate

Sex	Age		Total
	20–39	40–59	
Male	60	40	100
Female	20	50	70
Total	80	90	170

example 1–10, then one particular 'non-parametric' statistic is very good: **Spearman's rho**. This takes the difference in ranking for each case, squares the result and adds for each case. The formula for rho is:

$$rho = 1 - \frac{6 \Sigma d^2}{n(n^2 - 1)}$$

d is the difference in ranking and n the number of cases. The statistic varies between $+1$ and -1: it can take negative values where high rankings on one variable are associated with low rankings on the other. It is sometimes applied to situations where both variables are metric, or where one is metric and the other rank ordered. The metric scales are rank ordered, with the highest number given a rank of 1, the next highest a rank of 2 and so on. Rho may be preferred either where the researcher does not wish to make any assumptions about the variables being normally distributed, or where he or she just wants a quick measure that does not involve the laborious procedures of Pearson's r. Furthermore, it is unaffected by any extreme values in the distribution of either variable.

Multivariate analysis

Bivariate analysis is limited to looking at the relationships between variables two at a time; multivariate analysis techniques allow the analysis of three or more variables simultaneously. It has a number of advantages over univariate and bivariate procedures:

*   It permits conclusions to be drawn about the nature of causal connections between variables.
*   It facilitates the grouping together of variables that are interrelated, or cases that are similar in terms of their characteristics.
*   It provides the ability to predict dependent variables from two or more independent variables, and hence improve on predictions made on the basis of only one variable.

When a high degree of association or correlation is found between two variables in bivariate analysis, it does not follow that one variable is a cause of the other; nor, indeed, that there is any direct influence of one upon the other. This may be for one of three reasons:

*   The association found is a random sampling fluctuation.
*   It is not a sampling fluke, but an accidental association (a correlation has been found between the birth rate and the number of storks in a number of countries!).
*   The association is 'spurious' because both variables are a product of a prior variable, for example, the positive correlation between the amount of damage done in a fire and the number of fire engines that

turn up is not because fire engines cause fires, but because both are a result of the size of the fire.

A further possibility is that there *is* a degree of influence of one variable upon another, but that this influence is reciprocated. Thus expenditure on advertising may increase sales; but an increase in sales may, in turn, encourage further expenditure on advertising.

To establish a causal connection, three things are necessary:

- There must be a degree of association between two variables (and one that, if based on a random sample, is strong enough in relation to sample size to reject the null hypothesis that the sample was drawn from a population of cases in which there is no association).
- The cause (the independent variable) must always precede the effect (the dependent variable) in time.
- The relationship must not be spurious.

Establishing the existence of an association is a necessary but not sufficient condition of causality. Establishing temporal order is not always easy because circumstances may exist over periods of time, making it difficult to say which came first. However, testing for lack of spuriousness is the most troublesome. Relationships between variables can often be 'explained' by prior variables in many different ways. To justify any particular explanation, it is necessary, in principle, to eliminate all other possibilities. In an experimental research design, many of these other variables are controlled, and inferences about causality may be made. In non-experimental research, these eliminations have to take place by seeing what happens to the original relationship when a third, fourth, fifth, ... nth variable is introduced. The introduction of these extra variables may take place one at a time in a series of three-way analyses, or they may be introduced all at one go. The selection of the appropriate variables is a function of the implicit or explicit theories, hypotheses or hunches on which the researcher is working.

Where all the variables are non-metric, it is possible to conduct a series of three-way analyses. Four-way, five-way, up to n-way analyses *are* possible, but they become exceedingly complex and require very large sample sizes as the number of sample splits grows. An example of a three-way crosstabulation is illustrated in Table 6.25. This shows that in the original two-way table, there appears to be a relationship between buying product A and income (63 per cent of those with high income purchased product A compared with 36 per cent of those with low income). However, when age is controlled, then within similar age groups, there is little difference between income and purchase of product A; it is just that older people tend both to have higher incomes and to buy product A.

Where the data are metric, a number of sophisticated multivariate tech-

Table 6.25 A three-way table

All respondents: purchase behaviour by income

Income	High		Low	
	n	%	n	%
Purchased product A	95	63	75	36
No purchase	55	37	135	64
Total	150	100	210	100

Purchase behaviour by income and age

Age	35–50				16–34			
Income	High		Low		High		Low	
	n	%	n	%	n	%	n	%
Purchased product A	85	85	48	80	10	20	27	18
No purchase	15	15	12	20	40	80	123	82
Total	100	100	60	100	50	100	150	100

niques become possible. There are two approaches, however. One is to look at the relationships between variables amongst the set of cases; the other is to take each case in turn and to analyse the pattern of responses, case by case. Three of the most widely used techniques using the first of these two approaches, or 'macro' analysis, include:

- multiple regression,
- factor analysis,
- cluster analysis.

Multiple regression attempts to predict a single dependent variable from two or more independent variables and is an extension of bivariate regression. As we saw earlier, a linear regression line may be used to make predictions of a dependent variable from a single independent variable. The statistic r^2 indicates how 'good' that line is in making such predictions. In reality, not one but several variables are likely to affect the dependent variable. Thus the level of sales is affected not only by price but by, for example, advertising expenditure, interest rates and personal disposable income. The formula describing the regression line was given as:

$$Y = a + bX$$

Multiple regression extends this to:

$$Y = a + b_1 X_1 + b_2 X_2 + b_3 X_3 \ldots + b_n X_n$$

where X_1, X_2, X_3 ... X_n are the independent variables. The values b_1, b_2, b_3, b_n indicate the rates of change in Y consequent upon a unit change in X_1, X_2, X_3 ... X_n. The calculation for each value of b is made with the degree of correlation between Y and the other variables held constant. As with the bivariate procedure, the value for r^2 indicates the percentage of variation in Y associated with the variation in the independent variables.

While multiple regression is one of a number of 'dependence' methods that attempt to explain one or more dependent variables on the basis of two or more independent variables, **factor analysis** is an 'interdependence' method. These methods review the interdependence between variables or between cases in order to generate an understanding of the underlying structure, and to create new variables or new groupings. Factor analysis recognises that when many variables are being measured (usually, but not always, by asking people questions in a survey), some of them may be measuring different aspects of the same phenomenon and hence will be interrelated. It systematically reviews the correlation between each variable forming part of the analysis and all the other variables, and groups together those that are highly inter-correlated with one another, and not correlated with variables in another group. The groups identify 'factors' that are in effect 'higher order' variables. This helps to eliminate redundancy where, for example, two or more variables may be measuring the same construct. The factors themselves are not directly observable, but each variable has a 'factor loading' which is the correlation between the variable and the factor with which it is most closely associated. The effect, and advantage, of factor analysis is to reduce a large number of variables to a more manageable set of factors that themselves are not correlated.

Factor analysis begins by calculating a correlation matrix – a table of the value of Pearson's r for each variable with each other variable. If there are, for example, just five variables, then the correlation matrix might look like that in Table 6.26. From visual inspection, it is clear that variables 4 and 5 are highly correlated and both are negatively correlated with variable 3. Variables 1 and 2 are also correlated, but neither is correlated with variables 4 or 5. A factor analysis might produce a 'solution' like Table 6.27.

Table 6.26 A correlation matrix

Variable	1	2	3	4	5
1	1.00	0.61	0.47	−0.02	−0.10
2		1.00	0.33	0.19	0.32
3			1.00	−0.83	−0.77
4				1.00	0.93
5					1.00

Table 6.27 Factor loading on two factors

	Factor	
Variable	1	2
1	−0.25	0.72
2	0.06	0.87
3	−0.94	0.33
4	0.94	0.21
5	0.95	0.26

Variables 3, 4 and 5 combine to define the first factor and the second factor is most highly correlated with variables 1 and 2.

There are problems associated with factor analysis. First, it is possible to generate several solutions from a set of variables. Second, a subjective decision needs to be made as to how many factors to accept. Third, the grouping has to make intuitive sense. Thus if variables 1–5 above were consumer reactions to a new product, then variables 4 and 5 might be two questions that tap the 'value-for-money' factor, and variables 1–3 are different aspects of 'benefits-derived-from-use'. Factor analysis will always produce a solution; whether it is a good or helpful one is another matter. There may not, in fact, be any factors underlying the variables.

All scientific fields have a need to group or cluster objects. Historians group events; botanists group plants. Marketing managers often need to group customers, for example, on the basis of the benefits they seek from buying a particular product or brand, or on the basis of their lifestyles. Any procedure for deriving such groupings is clearly crucial for market segmentation. **Cluster analysis** is a range of techniques for grouping cases (usually respondents to a survey) who have characteristics in common. Cases are placed into different clusters such that members of any cluster are more similar to one another in some way than they are to members in other clusters.

Two very different approaches are possible, however. One is based on taking individual cases and combining them on the basis of some measure of similarity, such as the degree of correlation between the cases on a number of variables. Each case is correlated with each other case in a correlation matrix. The pair of cases with the highest index of similarity is placed into a cluster. The pair with the next highest is formed into another cluster, and so on. Each cluster is then averaged in terms of the index being used, and combined again on the basis of the average similarities. The process continues until, eventually, all the cases are in one cluster.

The other approach is to begin with the total set of cases and divide them into sub-groups on a basis specified by the researcher. Thus the researcher may want a four-cluster solution of 1,200 respondents on 10 variables. An iterative partitioning computer program might begin by setting up four equal-sized groups at random. The centre of each cluster on the 10 variables is then calculated and the distances between each of the 1,200 respondents and the centres of the four groups is measured. On the basis of these distances, respondents are reassigned to the group with the nearest cluster centre. The new cluster centres are recalculated and the distances again measured, with a further reassignment taking place. This process is repeated until no further reassignments are needed.

Unfortunately, the different methods of cluster analysis can produce quite different solutions. Furthermore, cluster analysis, like factor analysis, *always* produces clusters, even when there are, in fact, no natural groupings in the data. The various techniques work by imposing a cluster structure on the data rather than allowing the structure to emerge from the analysis.

Regression analysis, factor analysis and cluster analysis are all examples of 'macro' analysis. Even cluster analysis, which groups cases, is based on the degree of correlation between cases based on the analysis of variables. The identity of the case is lost as soon as analysis begins. An alternative approach is to analyse the data case by case; in other words, the analysis is based on the patterns of responses given by a particular respondent. Once the analysis has been carried out, the results may then be summarised or aggregated in some way. Currently, there are three main techniques of micro analysis:

- conjoint analysis,
- multi-dimensional scaling,
- micromodelling.

Conjoint analysis (sometimes called 'trade-off' analysis) looks at the ways in which respondents trade off combinations of product characteristics when attempting to maximise their overall satisfaction, and calculates the degree of importance or 'utility' that respondents place on each characteristic. The results are normally input into product design so that customer satisfaction can be maximised.

Suppose a biscuit manufacturer wishes to find the best combination of saltiness, sweetness and butter content for a new kind of biscuit. If there are two levels of saltiness (high and low), three levels of sweetness (high, medium and low), and butter versus vegetable fat, then there are $2 \times 3 \times 2 = 12$ product combinations. In some cases the desired features are fairly clear, but it is a zero-sum operation in which it is not possible to have all the features. Thus everybody wants a car that is fast, cheap, economical, reliable and with high specification. However, it is not possible to combine all these, so to what extent is the customer prepared to trade off petrol economy in order to get more acceleration? Or cheapness to get reliability?

The input data for conjoint analysis are the preferences for each combination of characteristic. Respondents may be asked to rank all combinations, or to take just two at a time. A computer algorithm then produces utilities for each level of each attribute for each individual case. When these are summed for each product combination, the rank order of the total utility scores should match the respondent's rank ordering of preference. The process is an iterative one in which the utilities assigned are continually modified until they can reproduce the rankings for product characteristics that the respondent has given. Each respondent will have his or her own set of utilities and the analysis is conducted one case at a time. An average respondent, however, can be created by averaging the input judgements into 'pooled' utilities.

Conjoint analysis is not without its problems. The task of ranking a large number of product combinations can be quite daunting, and, if treated two at a time, may be unrealistic. However, since the input data are only rankings, conjoint analysis is a technique that can be used for non-metric data, provided they are rank ordered. One particularly ingenious solution to the task of establishing preferences has been developed by Research International for its customer satisfaction research package called SMART (Salient Multi-Attribute Research Technique). The first step is to conduct qualitative research to find out the components of each attribute and to put each on a scale. Thus the attribute 'friendliness' of a banking service may be broken down into:

• they treat me as a friend,
• they treat me as an individual,
• they treat me as just another customer,
• they treat me as a number.

It is important that these scales are expressed in the customer's own language, that they perceive differences between the levels, and that the levels are clearly understood to be progressive.

The next stage is quantitative and gets a sample of respondents to indicate which attributes are most important to them, and at what level the organisation is perceived to be on the salient set of attributes. Next, a trade-off process begins in which respondents are shown the lowest level for each of the attributes – for example, 'They treat me as a number' – and to imagine that a competitor was offering these standards. They are then asked, 'If you could make one improvement to the standard of service described by these levels, which improvement would you make?' The next level is then revealed, and the respondent is asked which attribute should next be improved. This process is continued until there is a profile of priorities for each respondent. As the standards of the mythical bank improve, the respondent is asked to indicate at what point they would switch to the competitor. Conjoint analysis is then performed on the results. Utilities are summed across all respondents to obtain overall indices of importance for all attributes mentioned. These are then subjected to sub-group analysis to see if there are particular market segments.

Multi-dimensional scaling (MDS) is used most often in marketing to identify the relative position of competing brands or shops as perceived by customers, and to uncover key dimensions underlying customers' evaluations. While, like conjoint analysis, it is based on micro analysis, unlike conjoint analysis it is an interdependence technique rather than a dependence one. It seeks to infer underlying dimensions from a series of similarity or preference judgements provided by customers about objects within a given set. In a sense, it does the reverse of cluster analysis: while the latter groups objects according to similarities on prespecified dimensions, MDS infers underlying evaluative dimensions from similarities or preferences indicated by customers. These data can be in the form of ranks (i.e. non-metric, so the technique is sometimes referred to as non-metric MDS), or in the form of numerical ratings.

Suppose a customer is given a set of six multiple chain stores (like Asda, Tesco, Sainsbury) and asked to say how similar each store is to the others. The customer is asked to compare pairs of stores, and then rank the pairs from most similar to least similar. With six stores there are $n(n-1)/2$ or 15 pairs. The ranks given by just one customer might look like those in Table 6.28. MDS, like cluster analysis, is an iterative process that can be carried out using one of several available computer programs. Such a program would generate a geometric configuration of stores so that the distances between pairs of stores are as consistent as possible with customers' similarity rankings, so that the pair of stores ranked 15th are furthest apart, the pair of stores ranked 14th next furthest, while the pair AD is the closest together. The objects are presented usually in two-dimensional space, as in Figure 6.7, which shows a two-dimensional configuration of the six stores in which the interstore distances are consistent with the rankings in Table 6.28.

It is necessary to know, however, what the two dimensions represent. Labelling them is a subjective process and involves inspecting the relative position of the objects along each dimension and inferring what the

Table 6.28 Similarity rankings of six multiples

Multiple	A	B	C	D	E	F
A		12	11	1	7	3
B			5	15	4	10
C				13	6	14
D					9	2
E						8

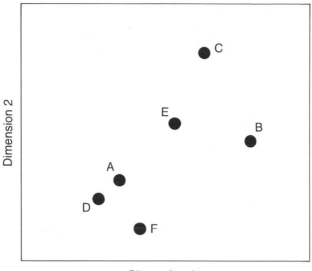

Figure 6.7 A multi-dimensional map based on ranking in Table 6.28

dimension is most likely to represent on the basis of prior knowledge about the objects themselves. Looking at the first dimension, we might notice that the stores D and A offer the lowest prices, and C and B the highest. So dimension 1 could be price. Looking at dimension 2 vertically, we may observe that store C has a large product range and store F a limited product range, with the others in between. So, dimension 2 could be product variety. It is possible, of course, that somebody else looking at the same diagram may see other dimensions. However, it is possible to infer that this customer implicitly used price and product variety as the key criteria for comparing the six stores. Other customers may, of course, have other perceptions, resulting in a totally different multi-dimensional map. Where the maps from customer to customer differ greatly, global inferences may be difficult to make. In such a situation, the researcher may attempt to identify segments of customers with fairly similar multi-dimensional maps, perhaps using appropriate cluster analysis techniques.

Micromodelling so far has had little development. However, Research International's Microtest is based on micromodelling techniques that try to analyse the pattern of responses in a single individual in order to make a prediction, for that individual, of his or her likelihood of trying a new product and subsequent repurchase. The predictions of a sample of individuals are then aggregated so that forecasts can be made of future sales. Research International's Microtest is explained in more detail in Chapter 7. For more details of multivariate techniques, see Alt (1990).

ANALYSING DATASETS

A dataset was defined in Chapter 2 as all the values for all the variables for all the cases in a piece of research. The analysis of complete datasets goes through a number of typical, but not universal, stages, using the range of techniques described earlier in this chapter. These stages may be summarised as:

- creating a data matrix,
- univariate analysis,
- bivariate analysis,
- multivariate analysis.

Creating a data matrix

The process of creating a data matrix from a dataset itself involves three key substages:

- editing,
- coding,
- data entry.

Editing

As was explained earlier in Chapter 3, there are many different kinds of error that can arise in the processes of selecting cases and collecting data on them. A major purpose of research design, which is considered in Chapter 8, is to minimise the sources and impact of such errors. However, the end-point of the data collection process is that questionnaires (either respondent completed or interviewer completed) are returned to the researcher for every respondent successfully contacted; alternatively, the field department in a market research agency passes on data collected from telephone interviewing or from experimental research either in hard (paper) copy or held electronically. Editing is the process of scrutinising completed data collection forms and taking whatever corrective action is required to ensure that the data are of high quality. It is a kind of quality control check on the raw data to ensure that they are complete, accurate and consistent.

A preliminary or field edit is a quick examination of completed data collection forms, usually as they are received at the head office. Its purpose is twofold: to ensure that proper procedures are being followed in selecting respondents, interviewing them and recording their responses, and to remedy fieldwork deficiencies before they turn into a major problem. Speed is crucial and it needs to be done while the fieldwork is still in progress. Typical problems that are discovered in field edits include:

- inappropriate respondents,
- incomplete questionnaires,
- illegible or unclear responses.

When any of these arise, the errors will be traced back to the interviewers concerned who will be advised of the problems and, if necessary, undergo further training.

A second stage of editing, a final or office edit, is undertaken after all the field-edited questionnaires are received. It involves verifying response consistency and accuracy, making necessary corrections, and deciding whether some or all parts of a questionnaire should be discarded. Some of these checks are undertaken by the computer at the data entry stage (see below), but will include:

- logical checks, for example, the 17 year old claiming to have a PhD,
- range checks, for example, a code of '8' is entered when there are only six response categories for that question,
- response set checks, for example, somebody has 'strongly agreed' with all the items on a Likert scale.

Where a question fails a logical check, then the pattern of responses in the rest of the questionnaire may be scrutinised to see what is the most likely explanation for the apparent inconsistency. Range check failures may be referred back to the original respondent. Response set checks may indicate that the respondent is simply being frivolous and the questionnaire may be discarded.

Coding

The tasks involved in transforming edited questionnaires into machine-readable form are generally referred to as coding. Most survey analysis packages will only accept responses or other data that are in numerical form. Metric data already have numerical scale values that can be entered directly, for example, a person's age as '59'. For non-metric data, the scale values may be in words or symbols that the computer cannot accept. Hence all responses or other types of observation need to be classified and numbered. These numbers are the codes, and the process of coding is to ensure that all data that are to be analysed have a code.

Some, if not all, of the non-metric responses will be pre-coded, that is, they are numbered on the questionnaire. If not, they need to be coded afterwards in the office. Qualitative responses to open-ended questions may be classified into categories, and the categories numbered. 'Don't know' responses usually have their own category for each question. A more difficult issue arises when, for a particular question, there is no response at all. It may be that the respondent refused to answer, or that the interviewer forgot to ask it, or forgot to record the answer. These questions for which answers should have been obtained, but, for some reason, were not, are regarded as 'missing values'. These are frequently given a standard code, partly because the computer survey analysis package usually demands an entry to be made for a question that has not been excluded by routing, and partly because, when analysis is taking place, the researcher may wish to exclude or to include such missing values from the analysis.

For some survey analysis packages, it is necessary to keep a separate record of the response categories to which each code refers for each question. Such a record is normally referred to as a 'coding-sheet'. More modern survey analysis packages, however, tend to keep labels (or labels in words can be added) both for the questions and for the responses, so coding-sheets are not needed because the labels are printed out with the results. Dedicated surveys analysis packages, like SPSSx, will tend to accept multi-response questions, that is, questions where the respondent is allowed more than one reply. Where statistical packages like Minitab have been used instead, only one value per question may be entered. In these cases, multi-response questions may need to be recoded so that each response category is treated as a separate question with two possibilities: selected/not selected.

Data entry

When editing and coding is complete, the data are ready to be keyed into an analysis package. Most survey packages will have inbuilt range checks so that invalid responses will not be accepted. However, this does not check that the correct numbers have been keyed in if they are within the range of acceptable values for that question. To overcome this, data may be subjected to double-entry data validation. In effect this means that the data are entered twice, usually by two different people, and any discrepancies in the two entries are flagged up by the computer and can be checked against the original questionnaire. Some market research agencies do this, but only on a sample basis so that, for example, only 10 per cent of the question-naires may be subject to double-entry data validation.

The end-product of data entry is the creation of a data matrix – the record of a numerical score or code for each value for each case for each variable, arranged in rows and columns. This may not, of course, neces-sarily be a physical sheet of paper, but the electronic equivalent. As a spreadsheet or as a Minitab worksheet, the arrangement in rows and columns is visible on a computer screen. In other survey analysis packages, the data matrix will be invisible, but held on an electronic file in the back-ground and used as a basis for creating whatever analyses are being requested by the user.

Univariate analysis of datasets

A first stage in preliminary analysis of a dataset is to obtain a set of 'one-way' tables or hole count of the frequencies of each response, one variable at a time. This may show, for example, that for some variables the responses are very unevenly distributed among the categories, or, indeed, that for some questions nearly everybody has given the same answer. Such variables will be of little use for analysis. Where the response categories are ordinal or grouped metric, it may make sense to regroup the categories by adding some of them together. Suppose respondents are given a satisfaction scale like that in Table 6.29. The frequencies from the hole count on each item are shown in the table. The numbers who indicated 'very satisfied' or 'very dissatisfied' are very low. It would make sense to combine these responses with the 'satisfied' and 'dissatisfied' categories respectively to produce three categories: satisfied; neither satisfied nor dissatisfied; and dissatisfied. Most survey analysis packages will allow the researcher to 'recode' the response categories into a reduced set in this way. Which categories it makes sense to add together can often be determined only from an inspection of the one-way tables.

Where variables are metric, it is possible to summarise them, as we have seen, by calculating ranges, averages and standard deviations. Where the variables are non-metric, it is not possible to calculate these statistics, so it is usual to lay out the results in tables. It is possible also to use tables to present metric data. This sometimes makes it difficult to 'see' what is happening when a range of different types of table are being used. It is, therefore, helpful to understand:

- the different types of table that are normally constructed,
- guidelines on constructing tables for yourself,
- collapsing larger tables into smaller ones.

Table 6.29 Regrouping categories

Please indicate your degree of satisfaction with the following aspects of our service:

	Very satisfied	Satisfied	Neither	Dissatisfied	Very dissatisfied
Opening hours	10	84	90	60	3
Range of goods	3	106	131	6	1
Speed at till	8	98	124	15	2
Parking	4	134	92	12	5
Store layout	1	52	114	72	8

Types of table

People often find reading and interpreting tables very difficult. This is usually because readers have had little help in understanding the various kinds of table that are commonly constructed, and, furthermore, the tables themselves are often poorly presented.

A single number, for example, a sales figure for the year, or the size of a town's population, is often of little interest or use on its own. At least two measures normally need to be compared. To do this the results are usually presented as a table, which is any layout of two or more pieces of information in rows and/or columns. Where there are both rows and columns, the combination of a row and a column is called a **cell**. It is helpful to realise that different kinds of data are put in such cells. We can, in fact, distinguish different kinds of table according to whether the cells contain:

- frequencies,
- metric values,
- correlation coefficients.

Frequency tables contain either the actual number of times each scale value occurs – the 'raw' frequencies – or the percentages in each of two or more categories, ranges of values, or combination of characteristics in each cell. Single-variable frequency tables present the results of a set of measurements for just *one* variable that have been aggregated into more than one category or range of values, as illustrated in Table 6.30.

Multi-variable frequency tables present the results of measurements for two or more variables that are *not* interlaced, for example, the demographic characteristics of purchasers of a brand (Table 6.31).

Crosstabulations present the results of two variables that are interlaced, that is, the frequencies indicate the result of combining two scale values, one for each variable. Thus in Table 6.24 there are 60 individuals who combine the characteristics of being both male and aged 20–39. Notice here that one variable is nominal and the other is grouped metric. Such tables form the basis for calculating the various measures of statistical association described earlier.

Table 6.30 A single-variable frequency table: sex composition of survey respondents

Sex	Frequency
Male	100
Female	70
Total	170

Table 6.31 A multi-variable frequency table: purchasers of brand X (N = 200)

		Frequency	%
Sex	M	104	52
	F	96	48
Social class	AB	30	15
	C1	50	25
	C2	70	35
	DE	50	25
Age	20–29	10	5
	30–39	30	15
	40–49	64	32
	50–59	56	28
	60+	40	20

Multi-variable frequency tables and crosstabulation may occur in the same table, as in Table 6.32. Here, vodka usage is crosstabulated against sex and against age separately, but the results are presented in the same table.

Metric tables contain the values of metric measurements, for example, sales by volume in tons or by value in pounds sterling, or aggregations or summaries of such measurements, for example, average consumption of beer per head in pints per week. Such figures appear in columns, rows or cells of tables.

A variable listing shows individual metric values, one for each of a number of metric variables, that relate to one case or one unit of analysis, as in Table 6.33. Variable breakdowns contain the metric values of a single variable in each of two or more subcategories, or ranges of values. There is

Table 6.32 Combined frequency table and crosstabulation: vodka drinkers

	Heavy users (000s)	Medium users (000s)	Light users (000s)	All users (000s)
Men	795	1,681	2,695	5,170
Women	819	1,818	2,597	5,234
15–24	656	1,341	1,348	3,345
25–34	360	796	1,247	2,583
35–44	267	556	1,027	1,852
45–54	164	330	685	1,170
55–64	94	275	497	865
65+	74	199	307	580

Source: Adapted from the Target Group Index tables

always a minimum of two variables involved: one is a metric scale whose values are recorded in the table, and one or more is a non-metric, discrete metric, or grouped continuous metric scale. The latter break down the original values into subcategories. Thus in Table 6.34 consumer sales and stocks are broken down by brand. Variable breakdowns *must* be distinguished from crosstabulations, which contain frequencies, and for which measures of statistical association may be calculated. It is not meaningful to attempt such calculations on metric tables.

Correlation matrices contain correlation coefficients between every variable and every other variable in a set being analysed. They are used, for example, in cluster analysis. An example of such a table was illustrated in Table 6.26.

Table construction

When presenting the results of fieldwork either face to face or in a written report, dissertation or thesis, it may be necessary to lay out the results in tabular form. The following rules for constructing tables should be helpful:

- Give the table a clear title. This should specify the table number, the set or population of cases to which the table refers, the time and the place or geographical area referred to, and the variables contained in the table, for example:

    Table 10.3 Manufacturers of lawnmowers in Scotland in 1992 by number of employees and annual turnover

Table 6.33 A variable listing

	Profits	Revenue	Employees
Company XYZ	£3.2m	£2.61m	56

Table 6.34 A variable breakdown

	Consumer sales		Retailer stocks (tons)
	(£000s)	(tons)	
Product class Z	4,116	1,714	92
Brand A	1,475	576	28
Brand B	687	269	17

Source: Adapted from Nielsen Marketing Research table

Where each table is presenting the results of the same survey, then it is not necessary to state the set of cases every time, but do specify dependent by independent variable(s), for example:

Table 14.4 Brand preferences by sex and age

Table numbers usually appear at the top of the table and are in two parts. The first identifies the chapter or section in which the table appears, and the second part its place in a sequence of tables. Illustrations such as maps, diagrams or graphs are usually called figures, and are numbered separately, but in the same manner as for tables. Publishers often put the figure number and title at the bottom of the figure.

- Indicate what the values in the table refer to, for example, frequencies, percentages, indexes, metric units like pounds sterling or weight in tonnes, or correlation coefficients.
- Put values that are to be compared close together, for example, if percentages are to be compared, put these in rows or columns next to one another.
- Calculate row and column totals, plus averages where appropriate.
- Rows and columns should, whenever possible, be ordered by size. Thus if we are listing the population sizes of the regions of Great Britain, put them in order of size with the biggest at the top.
- Round large numbers to two or three significant digits.
- Numbers are easier to read downwards than across. Comparing two numbers one underneath the other makes a greater impact than side by side.
- Brief verbal or written summaries help to focus the reader's attention. The reader should not be left to do the analysis.
- Indicate the source of the data.

Further analysis of the dataset at the univariate stage may include a calculation of confidence intervals on the key variables whether these are metric or non-metric, weighting the results and grossing up to the population of cases, and perhaps testing univariate hypotheses.

Collapsing large tables

Large tables with many rows and many columns are difficult to interpret, especially if the tables are crosstabulations and you are interested in the degree of association between the variables. Even for metric tables, it gets increasingly difficult to 'see' what is happening if the table is very large.

Large crosstabulations are a result of using a lot of categories for each variable. Thus two variables crosstabulated, one with six categories and the other with five, will result in a table with 6 × 5, or 30, cells. Unless the total

number of cases on which the table is based is considerable, the frequencies
in the cells will be very small. For example, with 30 cells a sample of 100
respondents will average out at just over three per cell! There are bound to
be many cells that are empty. This not only makes the interpretation very
difficult, it also means that any measures of association we calculate will be
unreliable.

The usual solution is to condense larger tables into smaller ones. Very
often this involves creating two dichotomies and producing a 2 × 2 table
with four cells. Suppose a table is crosstabulating price awareness against
brand loyalty, as in Table 6.35. This table – a '3 × 3' table – has nine cells.
That may still be too many if the sample is small. However, if those who
buy only one brand are contrasted with the rest, and those who recall price
accurately are contrasted with the rest, then we can create a 2 × 2 table, as
in Table 6.36. In effect, both variables are being recoded, and in most
survey analysis packages it will be necessary to carry out this recoding
before the condensed crosstabulation can be produced. From the collapsed
table it is now easier to see that accurate recall is associated with brand
loyalty. Furthermore, it becomes possible to calculate Yule's Q or Phi-
square.

Bivariate analysis of datasets

Once univariate analysis of the dataset is complete, the next stage is either
to look for or to test for relationships between variables. Complete datasets
may, however, be approached in different ways. To explain these
approaches, it is helpful to draw an analogy between the different activities
of dredging, fishing and hunting.

Table 6.35 Price awareness by brand loyalty

	Buys only one brand	Buys two brands	Buys many brands
Accurate price recall	64	9	11
Overestimate	8	24	18
Underestimate	12	13	31

Table 6.36 Price awareness by brand loyalty, reduced to a 2 × 2 table

	One brand only	More than one brand
Accurate recall	64	20
No accurate recall	20	86

Dredging in the normal sense means casting a net or other mechanical device to trawl whatever is on the sea bottom. In the context of data analysis it means trawling the dataset without specific hypotheses to test, or perhaps even without hunches or specific issues to pursue. The data are 'dredged' in every conceivable way to see what patterns emerge. Researchers may, for example, crosstabulate every variable by every other variable in the dataset in order to see which ones produce the strongest associations. It is an inductive process that produces empirical generalisations from the ground up. Data dredging is often seen to be reprehensible: an admission that you do not know what you are looking for. However, some patterns are discovered by chance, and dredging may turn out to be a fruitful way of producing new insights. The researcher should beware, however, of testing sets of tables derived in this manner against the null hypothesis. If 100 tables are produced and tested at the 95 per cent level of confidence, then, by definition, the probability is that five of these will be random sampling accidents. The researcher is, in short, in danger of picking out all the chance results!

At the other extreme to dredging is hunting for a specific quarry. Hypotheses deduced from theory are set up in advance and the hunt is on for data that will put these hypotheses to the test. If the expectations implied by the hypotheses are not fulfilled, then they may be rejected; if such expectations materialise, then the hypotheses stand, at least for the time being, and the theory is substantiated. In between dredging and hunting is the activity of fishing. This is an iterative process of moving backwards and forwards between expectation and reality; of trying out various locations with rather more general empirical aspirations in mind. These aspirations may, in turn, be modified in the light of events. In terms of data analysis, deduction and induction are used in alternation; hypotheses are reworked in the light of empirical findings.

Comparing tables

It is helpful, particularly if there is a clear dependent variable being studied, to compare the degree of association of that variable with a number of independent variables in a series of bivariate crosstabulations. By calculating a measure of statistical association, we can say which independent variables are most strongly associated with the dependent variable. There are, however, as we have seen, a number of different measures of statistical association that we could use, but they will tend to give different answers on the same data. Accordingly, it is necessary to use the same statistic on all crosstabulations that are to be compared. If, for example, all the tables are 2 $\times$ 2 tables, then Yule's Q would be a quick, simple measure. The fact that this statistic gives an inflated indication of association does not matter when the focus of interest is in the comparisons. If, however, some of the tables are larger than 2 × 2, some other statistic will have to be used.

If there are clear distinctions between dependent and independent variables, then Lambda would be a good measure. If the focus is on sampling, then Phi-square is quite useful because its key ingredient – Chi-square – can be used as a test of statistical significance against the null hypothesis. However, all tables must have either rows or columns = 2. It may make sense to collapse the tables that are larger than 2 × m or m × 2 into tables that enable Phi-square to be calculated. It is, however, necessary to watch for tables that will produce rogue results; for example, tables with empty cells will make Yule's Q revert to unity, and tables with uneven marginals will make Lambda revert to zero.

If all the tables to be compared consist of ordinal categories, then it may make sense to use a statistic like Gamma, which makes use of the ordinality in the data. If the variables to be compared are a mixture of metric and non-metric scales, then, when approaching the analysis of a complete dataset, it may be helpful to group metric variables into ranges of values and use them in crosstabulations along with ordinal or nominal variables.

In short, when comparing tables, there are many things to take into consideration. Not all of these, however, have to do with the nature of the variables themselves, but may reflect more practical considerations, like whether the survey analysis package used offers a particular kind of statistic, or whether the client is likely to understand one kind of procedure better than another.

Multivariate analysis of datasets

Bivariate analysis will help to locate those variables that are most closely associated, but it is necessary to proceed to multivariate techniques if the researcher wishes to examine the degree of influence of causality involved, or wants to look at the interdependence between a large number of variables. Where the variables are non-metric, then multi-dimensional scaling and conjoint analysis are possible, depending on what the researcher needs to find out from his or her data. If many variables are metric, then multiple regression, factor analysis and cluster analysis are possibilities. The appropriateness of any particular technique must, of course, relate back to the original objectives of the research.

All these decisions form part of the overall design of the research, which is the topic of Chapter 8.

SUMMARY

Whatever type of data are to be analysed, data reduction, data display and drawing conclusions are all part of the process. Analysing qualitative data can be approached in a systematic manner and in ways that, in many respects, parallel those used for the analysis of quantitative data. Quantitative data tend to be analysed in stages, proceeding from univariate analysis, to bivariate and then to multivariate analysis. Deciding which techniques are appropriate depends in the first instance on whether the variables concerned are scaled metrically or non-metrically.

Researchers are usually faced, however, not with isolated or simple groups of variables, but with a complete dataset that has to be created through editing, coding and data entry. The analysis then proceeds by constructing a complete set of one-way tables followed by an approach to the entire dataset that may resemble the activities of dredging for empirical generalisations, fishing for potential explanations, or hunting for data specifically to test hypotheses.

EXERCISES AND POINTS FOR FURTHER DISCUSSION

■   A bank conducted a survey of 300 of its non-business customers selected at random. One question asked respondents whether they had been experiencing any problems with any aspect of the services in the last three months. One third answered 'Yes', while the remainder answered 'No'. On the basis of respondents' transactions with it, the bank was able to classify respondents into 'high volume' and 'low volume' categories. Of the respondents who said they had experienced problems, ten were 'high volume' customers, while 130 of those not experiencing problems were 'high volume'. The bank wants to explore the question of whether customers experiencing difficulties were likely to do less business with it than those not experiencing problems.
   (a) Construct a bivariate crosstabulation of response versus transaction volume.
   (b) Calculate appropriate percentages.
   (c) Calculate three measures of association – Yule's Q, Lambda and Phi-square.
   (d) Test the statistical significance of your results using the Chi-square test.
   (e) Can you conclude from your calculations that customers experiencing problems *are* likely to do less business with the bank?

■   A random sample of 300 was used to estimate what proportion of households in a particular area owned a microwave oven. Calculate the standard error of the proportion if the number found owning such an oven was:
   (a) 150
   (b) 50
   (c) 10
   Calculate the standard error of the proportion if the sample size had been 30, and the numbers were:
   (a) 15
   (b) 5
   (c) 1

■   A simple random sample of 1,200 individuals recorded that 96 people used product A. Calculate the confidence limits for this result at the 95 per cent and 99 per cent levels. What would the limits be for a result of 24 people from a sample of 300? Compare and explain your results and comment on the assumptions made by your calculations.

If the Product Manager for product A had hypothesised that 10 per cent of people used product A, test this hypothesis at the 95 per cent level.

■   A simple random sample of 81 families in a city had a mean income of £13,000 per annum with a standard deviation of £4,500. Construct the 95 per cent confidence interval. Explain the meaning of the result.

■   *Class exercise.* Using the example of ABC Products from the exercise at the end of Chapter 3, each class member should draw a different sample of 30 employees at random and use this to perform the following tasks:
(a) Calculate the mean output.
(b) Calculate the standard deviation.
(c) Calculate the standard error.
(d) Plot a sampling distribution of the mean outputs.
(e) Calculate the mean of all the mean sample outputs.
(f)   Calculate the mean of all the standard deviations.
(g) Calculate the standard deviation of the sampling distribution using the mean from (e) and each sample result.
(h) Compare your answer in (g) with, first, the standard error of the original sample and, second, the standard error using (g) instead of the original sample standard deviation.

■   From Table 6.8, rank order the four individuals A–D on Test X and Test Y and compute Spearman's rho. Compare your result with Pearson's r.

Chapter 7

Research techniques and applications

Data collection and data analysis are of little value on their own unless they are used to tackle marketing problems or marketing issues. Marketing research needs to be problem-driven, not technique-driven. This chapter explains how market research companies and in-house market researchers combine instruments of data capture, data collection methods and data analysis techniques in particular ways to enable them to diagnose the current circumstances facing an organisation, to make predictions about the likely consequences of their marketing decisions, and to monitor the progress made by or success of past marketing activity. The techniques described below are a selection of some of the more important procedures developed by the larger market research companies, and serve only as an illustration of the possibilities rather than a comprehensive account of all the services available. Since the techniques have been generated and developed in order to apply to specific situations, problems, opportunities or issues, it is often difficult to distinguish a particular research technique from the application in which it is normally used, hence, as is clear from the title of this chapter, they are treated together.

The techniques and applications outlined in this chapter fall loosely into two main groups. First, there are those that are primarily diagnostic: they are used to review, measure or monitor the situation as it currently is or has been up to now. Thus marketing managers may require, or feel they require, a detailed anatomy of the size and structure of the markets they are currently addressing with their product offerings, and of the purchasing behaviour associated with them. They may wish to know how current and potential customers use their own and their competitors' products and what they think about them, or to track the progress of an advertising campaign or some new marketing mix. They may want to know what kinds of media, and which particular media, customers and potential customers watch, listen to or read before they make decisions about marketing communications.

Second, there are those techniques that are intended to be mainly predictive. Marketing managers may want to predict how consumers are likely to respond to a new product idea or to product modifications, or how well a new advertisement is likely to perform in terms of consumers being able to recall the brand and the theme of the advertising. They may require a prediction of likely sales or share of market that will be achieved by a new or modified product before deciding whether or not to launch it on to the market.

Some of the techniques and applications are fairly standard and well known amongst market research executives. Others have been developed by particular market research organisations, often over a number of years, and which in important respects are new or original. These 'proprietary' techniques commonly have a brand name to distinguish them from the procedures used by other agencies. They often have names ending in 'or' like Sensor, Assessor, Conceptor, Locator or ending in 'test' like Microtest, Publitest or Opti-test.

The sections below review the standard approaches to each technique or application. They then illustrate a selection of proprietary tools used by the larger market research organisations. These details should give the reader a better 'feel' for what is actually involved. Many of the branded procedures or systems amount to refinements, developments or combinations of the standard approaches, so these accounts present what are current 'state-of-the-art' applications. Bear in mind that the distinctions between diagnostic and predictive techniques, and between standard and proprietary techniques, are often a little blurred. Diagnosis may constitute a preliminary or input to the process of making a prediction, while proprietary techniques are quite often fairly standard, even though their advocates and supporters in the market research companies may claim otherwise. Some systems offered, furthermore, may be a specific combination of diagnostic and predictive, standardised and proprietary elements.

DIAGNOSTIC TECHNIQUES

Before managers can generate ideas for potential marketing initiatives and then decide which ones are most likely to fulfil the objectives of the organisation, they will usually need to diagnose the current situation so that they can, for example, estimate how serious or urgent are the problems, issues or opportunities facing them, and what factors may be affecting the situation. A lot of data may already be available or at least gatherable by undertaking desk research. If, however, as is often the case, more information is required, then managers may consider undertaking, or commissioning market research companies to carry out on their behalf, one or more of a number of primary research techniques or applications designed to acquire that information. The major diagnostic techniques currently in use may be grouped into four broad categories:

- market measurement,
- usage and attitude studies,
- advertising tracking studies,
- media audience measurement.

As is often the case, these categories do not represent watertight compartments (that is, they do not amount to a mutually exclusive and exhaustive set of categories). There are many overlaps, both in terms of the type of data collected, and in terms of the analyses that are performed on them. What activities agencies will actually include under each heading will also vary. However, for the purpose of exposition, it is convenient to treat them separately.

Market measurement

Marketing managers are always interested in the detailed anatomy of the markets to which they sell or hope to sell, and in the dynamics of their development. In particular, he or she will want to know:

- the size and structure of the market for the company's brands, how that compares with competitor brands, and whether any changes are taking place,
- the purchasing behaviour associated with the company brands, competitor brands, and any trends in that behaviour,
- product usage and attitudes towards the company brands, competitor brands, plus any changes.

Market measurement is the recording or estimation of these market characteristics on a regular or continuous basis using either panel research (consumer or retail) or regular interval surveys (omnibus surveys or market tracking surveys). These forms of continuous research were described earlier in Chapter 5. In this section we will consider in more detail what these market measures are, look at some examples of how some of the larger market research companies actually run market measurement services, and then consider some of the uses to which such data are put.

The size of a market can be measured in a number of different ways, but the four key measures are:

- sales,
- brand share,
- market penetration,
- deliveries.

At first sight it might seem that measuring the level of sales is fairly straightforward. However, sales may be measured either by volume (in weight or in units – packets, boxes, and so on) or by value in currency units (pounds sterling, ECUs or whatever). It may be sales achieved by a complete product category, by a company's own brand or brand variants, or by competitors. Brands often come in different pack sizes, pack types, colours, flavourings, formulations, models, or with a variety of functions, features or associated services. These are generally referred to in the market research industry as 'brand variants', although some manufacturers will call them 'lines', 'models' or even 'products'. The set of brands that constitutes all the competing products of a similar nature or meeting the same consumer need may be referred to as a 'product category', a 'product field', a 'product class' or a 'product type', like shampoos. Similar product categories may be grouped together into 'market sectors', like toiletries and cosmetics, or drinks and beverages.

Sales may be recorded over different periods of time and in relation to different geographical areas. The period of time over which sales are measured may be annual – this may be all that is needed for accounting purposes, but in today's rapidly changing marketing world, sales by the month are rapidly becoming a minimum standard, particularly for fast-moving consumer goods, while weekly sales are produced in some cases. Technically, with the introduction of electronic point-of-sale (EPOS) equipment and the bar-coding of products, daily measurements are quite possible. However, a daily perusal of sales figures for firms that make hundreds of brands, brand variants and types of product, would involve too much data to digest and act upon; in any event it is probably unnecessary for products other than those with a very short shelf life.

Although manufacturers will know what their own ex-factory shipments of products are on a regular or even continuous basis, once their transport and distribution systems have offloaded them to the delivery point, they are unlikely to know the progress of the products thereafter. They will not know the levels of stocks held by distributors and wholesalers; what quantities are being delivered to the shops; what stocks are held in the shops and whether these are on display and accessible to customers; what are the levels of sales in the different retail outlets; and what quantities, brands and with what frequencies consumers buy. Still less will they know any of this information for competitor brands. It is in these circumstances that retail panels, consumer panels or regular interval surveys are needed to make estimates of such quantities on a continuous basis.

Market size, as measured by sales, may, in short, refer to the sales achieved by the client brands or brand variants, or to sales in the product field. Sales may be captured at different points in the distribution system, over different periods of time and over different geographical areas. Sales potential is different again and refers to the levels of sales (in all its varieties) that it is estimated could be achieved if there were 100 per cent penetration of the target market.

Trends in the levels of sales are generally treated by manufacturers both as a benchmark against which company performance is measured, and as a basis for setting goals, targets and objectives for the future. However, the absolute level of sales gives little indication of a brand's performance in relation to that of competing brands. Accordingly, market size is also measured by **brand share**. This is the proportion of total sales in a product category, either by volume or by value (or both) accounted for by a brand over a period of time. Brand share, however, is a measure that has to be treated with caution since in many markets it is not always obvious which other brands fall into the same product category. Furthermore, brand shares may vary from one area of the country to another, and from one market segment to another. Total national brand shares, in short, usually require more detailed analysis.

The main limitation in measuring market size from brand shares is that it is the share of *current* buyers in the product field. Current buyers, however, may be only a small proportion of potential buyers. In consequence, manufacturers often use a measure of market size which is also a measure of market potential, namely **market penetration**. This is the number or proportion of individuals or households in specified categories who are considered to be potential buyers who have actually made a purchase of the brand over a period of time in a geographical area, irrespective of the quantities purchased. Market penetration can itself be broken down by any demographic variable or set of variables: for example, the number or proportion of males in the age category 20–24 who are married and who made a purchase of a particular brand in the last four weeks. A low but rising market penetration indicates considerable potential compared with a situation where market penetration is already very high.

The problem with taking sales, brand shares or market penetration as a measure of market size is that they tend to be known only through the expensive process of subscribing to continuous panel research services, and even then they are usually only estimates. Measuring market size by volume or by value of deliveries to retail outlets may be more direct, particularly where EPOS systems are used. Here, the record will be of total quantities, not just estimates. The difficulty here, of course, is that it is the retailer who captures such information, and it may not be readily available to the manufacturer.

The structure of a market can be described according to a very large number of dimensions. For consumer markets, these may include the **demographic**, **geodemographic** and **lifestyle** characteristics of consumers, and the structure of prices that are paid in the shops for a brand. For business and organisational markets, the structure may be in terms of size of organisation, type of organisation, regional location, profitability and so on.

As with structure, the dimensions used to measure purchasing behaviour depend in the first instance on whether consumer or industrial markets are being considered. For consumer markets, the key dimensions are purchase frequency, quantity purchased, repeat purchase, brand loyalty, inter-purchasing between brands, source of purchase, and nature or occasion of purchase. The purchasing behaviour of retailers will often be recorded in terms of source and quantities of deliveries, ranges stocked, stock levels, shelf-space allocation and merchandising activity.

The uses to which products are put, and the attitudes consumers have of the brands being researched and of competitor brands, tend to be very complex and not amenable to the techniques of consumer and retail panels. Some consumer panels do include items on product use, but seldom on attitudes. Omnibus surveys and market tracking surveys do cover both, but usually not in any great depth. There is, however, a species of survey which is dedicated to the in-depth measurement of product usage and attitude. These are normally referred to as 'usage and attitude' studies, but they are not usually carried out on a continuous or even regular basis, so they are seldom thought of as being part of 'market measurement' research. They are considered in some detail in a later section.

The main sources of data for market measurement are:

- retail panels,
- consumer panels,
- omnibus surveys,
- market tracking surveys.

The general methodology of each of these was described in Chapter 5. What follows are detailed examples of each type of service as offered by one of the major market research companies.

The Nielsen Retail Index

Nielsen was the first market research organisation to establish continuous retail tracking operations in the UK, and it is still the largest operator in the country. The Nielsen 'Index' is not an index in the statistical sense (that is, a ratio of a current value to a past value expressed as a percentage), but rather refers to a range of continuous sales and distribution measurements derived from retail tracking operations. There are currently 10 separate indexes covering:

- grocery,
- health and beauty,
- confectionery,
- home improvements,
- cash and carry outlets,
- sportswear,
- liquor,

- toys,
- tobacco,
- electrical.

These indexes together measure a large number of sales and distribution variables for over 600 different product categories and over 120,000 brands and associated brand variants. Each index has its own sample of shops selling the products to be included, and with sample sizes varying from about 450 to over 1,300 shops.

All the indexes include shops that are classified into 'multiples', 'co-operatives' and 'independents'. A multiple is a group or organisation with 10 or more outlets. Each shop type is then subdivided by turnover range. Sampling of potential shops for the panel is done on the basis of **disproportionate stratified sampling**. The strata are shop type, turnover range and region. The number of shops selected of each type for each turnover range in each region (a cell) is not directly proportional to the total number of shops in each cell, but is determined by a formula which, while taking that into account, also includes the universe variation in turnover for shops in that cell, plus a factor that measures the cost of auditing that type of shop. The selection of individual shops for recruitment to the panel is done on a judgemental basis that reflects a fair representation of store locations (shopping centre, town centre, out-of-town complex, rural area and so on) and places within the area. For multiples, the number of shops in a named group, like Tesco, is kept proportional to the total number in that area.

Sales data for the major multiples (Asda, Gateway, Sainsbury and Tesco) are collected from their EPOS systems. For other types of shop where EPOS data are not available, it is necessary to undertake a monthly audit of stocks and, using data on deliveries, deduce what the level of sales must have been since the last audit. This is established by taking stocks at the last audit, adding deliveries and subtracting stock at the end of the audit to give sales. A separate calculation is made for each brand and brand variant. Data on stocks are captured by auditors from Nielsen using hand-held terminals to enter quantities in various locations in the shop.

Most clients subscribe on an annual basis into the appropriate index or indexes that contain the product categories they require. For most indexes, they will receive 12 monthly reports in hard copy containing standard tables and charts along with monthly presentations. The tables give sales, deliveries, stock and price data for each brand and brand variant, and this may be broken down by region and shop type. The large multiples give access to their data and to their stores only on the understanding that the data are not presented to clients by named groups. Accordingly, data, for example for grocery, are available only in categories broken down into 'key accounts', 'total multiples', 'co-operatives' (large and small) and 'independents' (large and small) – a typical table is illustrated in Figure 7.1.

Unit Basis Tons Average & R.S.P. – lbs.
£ basis – thousands to 1 D.P.

	Consumer sales £ at R.S.P.	Consumer sales volume	Deliveries	Retailer stocks total	Days supply	Distribution					Averages stocks wt sales	R.S.P. P	Stocks in sales area
						Max shop AC PC	OOS	OSF	Del	Mer			
Product class 2 Total all items	4,115.6 100.0%	1,713.9 100.0%	1,704.5 100.0%	91.9 100.0%	1.7	63 93 99	15 6 2	15 6 3	60 93 100		5.9 54.7 37.1	107.2	88.1 100.0%
Brand A Standard	764.1 18.6%	307.2 17.9%	305.4 17.9%	13.9 15.1%	1.4	16 48 53	6 7 7	6 7 7	17 48 53		3.2 34.9 13.1	111.0	13.1 14.9%
Extra	710.5 17.3%	268.4 15.7%	267.6 15.7%	13.9 15.1%	1.6	12 49 55	4 8 10	4 9 10	12 48 53		4.6 44.7 10.9	118.1	13.5 15.3%
Brand A total	1,474.5 35.8%	575.6 33.6%	573.0 33.6%	27.8 30.3%	1.5	19 53 57	6 8 7	6 8 7	18 51 55	– 2 1	5.9 61.5 22.0	114.3	26.6 30.2%
Brand B Standard	314.6 7.6%	127.7 7.5%	127.1 7.5%	8.0 8.7%	1.9	12 27 29	5 6 5	5 6 5	12 26 28		2.6 20.4 9.1	110.0	7.6 8.6%

Extra	373.3 9.1%	141.0 8.2%	140.1 8.2%	9.0 9.8%	2.0	9 36 41	4 7 6	4 7 7	8 34 40		4.1 32.1 8.0	118.1	8.9 10.1%
Brand B total	687.8 16.7%	268.7 15.7%	267.2 15.7%	17.0 18.5%	2.0	14 41 45	6 7 5	7 7 6	13 40 44	– 1 1	4.9 39.0 13.3	114.3	16.5 18.7%
All other total	1,953.2 47.4%	869.6 50.7%	864.3 50.7%	47.1 51.3%	1.7	46 55 63	11 7 5	12 7 5	43 53 62		4.6 37.7 31.5	100.3	45.0 51.1%

Figure 7.1 A Nielsen table

Source: Nielsen

Total product category Z–GB

Units (000)

BRAND A – SMALL

	Dec	Jan '91	Feb	Dec	Jan '92	Feb
Months supply	1.3	1.3	1.0	1.1	1.1	0.9
Stocks	143.6	137.8	145.0	163.2	149.7	141.8
Yr ago % CH				+26	+35	+14
Unit sales ———	132.4	105.0	147.0	157.8	141.6	162.7
Purch - - - -	114.4	98.5	142.2	144.6	127.9	158.2
£ Deliv. dist.	56	57	59	61	64	64
Price	119.0	118.2	117.1	118.9	118.6	119.5
Wt R.O. sale	3.1	2.7	3.4	3.2	3.3	3.8
£ Hand	71	73	74	80	80	80
£ O-O-S	2	4	6	3	3	4

BRAND A – LARGE

	Dec	Jan '91	Feb	Dec	Jan '92	Feb
Months supply	0.9	1.0	0.9	0.7	0.7	0.8
Stocks	75.2	75.1	70.7	88.7	80.6	88.0
Yr ago % CH				+49	+58	+44
Unit sales ———	81.1	75.0	78.4	120.5	116.5	120.6
Purch - - - -	64.5	73.8	68.6	116.5	107.8	112.7
£ Deliv. dist.	30	33	30	41	43	45
Price	106.3	106.3	106.3	106.8	107.4	107.0
Wt R.O. sale	3.4	3.3	3.1	4.1	4.2	3.9
£ Hand	41	41	38	49	51	53
£ O-O-S	2	6	1	5	4	5

BRAND A – TOTAL

	Dec	Jan '91	Feb	Dec	Jan '92	Feb
Months supply	1.1	1.2	1.0	1.0	0.9	0.8
Stocks	218.8	212.9	215.7	251.9	230.3	229.8
Yr ago % CH				+36	+44	+25
Unit sales ———	196.9	178.8	220.6	274.3	258.1	278.8
Purch - - - -	195.5	173.5	215.6	265.1	235.7	275.4
£ Deliv. dist.	59	61	63	67	68	69
Price	113.7	113.2	113.3	113.4	113.5	114.4
Wt R.O. sale	4.8	4.4	5.3	6.0	5.8	6.2
£ Hand	74	75	74	81	81	81
£ O-O-S	1	4	2	2	1	1

Figure 7.2 A Nielsen chart

Source: Nielsen

This shows a range of measures on sales, deliveries and stocks for brands A and B, which together constitute product class Z (for a detailed explanation of these figures, see Kent 1989). To show trends and changes since the previous period, Nielsen uses charts similar to those in Figure 7.2, which show sales, purchases (deliveries) and stocks for the current month compared with the previous two months and the same months in the previous year. From these, it is possible to understand what has been happening to sales and distribution on a month-by-month basis. Increasingly, clients receive their data electronically on databases, in support of which Nielsen has developed a range of data management and analysis software. A service it calls Inf*Act Workstation offers a powerful yet flexible personal, computer-based, decision-support system.

AGB's Superpanel

Consumer panels have traditionally relied on diaries or home audits to collect data. However, both Nielsen and AGB have recently launched new panels based on in-home scanning. Each panel household is equipped with a hand-held laser-scanner or light pen for reading the bar-codes on the products they buy. This has revolutionised the consumer panels, obviating the need for consumers to fill in diaries. All panellists need do is run the scanner or light pen over the bar-code as they unpack their shopping after each shopping trip. The bar-code instantly records the country of origin, the manufacturer and the product and product variant. Other information can be keyed in at the same time using the number keys attached to the scanner, including price, source of purchase, date of purchase, promotions and who made the purchase.

AGB's Superpanel consists of 8,500 households, covering the purchases of some 28,000 individuals aged 5–79, resident in domestic households in mainland Great Britain and the Isle of Wight, and who live in telephone-owning households. Because the work of the panellist is considerably less than for diary techniques, a wider range of products can be included, so all products previously covered by AGB's Television Consumer Audit (groceries, frozen foods, meat and poultry) are included along with those previously measured by separate panels for toiletries and cosmetics, and for fresh foods and a range of other items. Superpanel has now replaced all these separate services.

Panel recruitment uses a multi-stage procedure. First, a large sample of households is screened to identify households in each sampling point eligible for the service and with known demographics. For this purpose, AGB uses personal home interviews – some 200,000 annually – carried out for its **omnibus** and **market tracking surveys**. These surveys use a master sample for all fieldwork based on 270 parliamentary constituencies selected with probability proportionate to size after **stratification** by television region and population density. In each constituency selected, a **random location sampling** method is used based on allocating to interviewers blocks of addresses within postcode sectors. Within each block, interviewers are given a target number of interviews to achieve plus non-interlocking quotas set by sex and household status – male, housewife, other woman.

In the second stage, a subsample is selected of those households with the relevant target demographics. Targets are based largely on the most recent establishment survey carried out for BARB (see television audience measurement below). Third, the housewife (who may be either sex) is contacted by phone. The Superpanel service is described, together with an outline of the personal tasks involved and the incentives offered. The names of those interested are then passed to recruiters who contact the screened homes by phone to make an appointment for a visit. The scanner equipment is demonstrated to all members of the household and the service is explained in detail. If the household is willing to continue, the necessary equipment is installed and a detailed questionnaire is administered. This collects details of shop usage (for unique store identification) and a full set of household and individual demographics.

Data collection is through a personal data terminal equipped with a laser light pen. The terminal is designed to resemble a digital phone and is kept in a modem linked to the domestic power supply and the telephone socket. Data capture is via overnight polling, that is, the central computer at AGB dials each panel number in turn (ringing is suppressed) and accesses the stored data in the modem. The terminal has a small screen which is used for prompts and messages. When switched on, it asks, 'Shopping trip?' If 'Yes' is entered, then purchaser and shop name are scanned from a code book that identifies each shop with a unique bar-code. The total amount spent is keyed in, each product is then scanned for the bar-code, and price and quantity are keyed in. Details of non-bar-coded products are entered by scanning the code book. The terminal software automatically records days of the week and time of day of data entry, length of time taken for the task, the number of purchase records entered, and the number of product codes keyed in rather than scanned due to poor print quality or difficult pack design. This information is used for quality control purposes.

All the data are **weighted** to population parameters before being **grossed up** to the population. Reporting is both weekly and four-weekly. The former is confined to data for the country as a whole and is intended as early top-line data. The four-weekly reports contain the kinds of analyses described earlier under consumer panel research.

Taylor Nelson's Omnimas

This service, so its management claims, is one of the largest single random omnibus surveys in the world. Some 2,100 adults aged 16 and over are interviewed face to face every week on behalf of industry, commerce and government. Sampling is **random sampling**, using the Electoral Registers from which to draw lists of names and addresses. It is a multi-stage procedure that begins by selecting 233 parliamentary constituencies with probability proportional to size within each of the 10 standard regions of the UK. Within each constituency, all wards are listed and two are chosen at random, giving two **sampling points**. Each sampling point is then used in alternate weeks. This allows a chance to 'top-up' interviewers' lists while they are doing the other ward the following week. It also means that over a two-week period there are twice as many sampling points. Not all 233 points are used every week; some cannot be worked because the interviewer is ill or on holiday. Typically, 180–190 are used. The actual names and addresses are selected from the Electoral Registers at random using a systematic procedure, taking a random starter between 1 and 10 and taking every tenth person thereafter. The average ward is about 5,000, so the procedure gives a list of about 500 names which are forwarded to interviewers in chunks. If the specific person selected is not at home, the Omnimas procedure allows for up to three further callbacks over a period of time, which may be in subsequent measurement periods.

If the household has moved in the previous year, a substitute in the new household is taken, thus giving a sample of new movers who would not otherwise be on the Registers. The Registers do not list 16 and 17 year olds, so when a contact is made with a named person, they are asked if there is a 16 or 17 year old in the household. If so, that person is interviewed in addition to the person on the list. For new homes, 30 interviewers selected at random in any one week are asked to find a new premise or home and interview a person within it.

The interviewer will have a minimum of 13 interviews to do a week. The only quota set is that the interviewer should obtain either six men and seven women or vice versa. So, there is a control on sex, but everything else depends on the randomness of the sample.

The Omnimas questionnaire is divided into three sections: a continuous section that includes questions that are asked on every survey and are inserted on behalf of a particular client; an ad hoc section of questions that are included on a one-off basis; and a classification section that contains all the demographic questions.

Omnimas does not allow questions on some topics, for example, on home security (e.g. 'Do you have a burglar alarm in your home?'). The usual length of the questionnaire is limited to an average of 25 minutes' completion time. It takes an average of 20–30 seconds to administer an average question, so the total number of questions will not be more than 60–70. Occasionally, one client may buy up all the space remaining after the demographic and continuous questions have been accounted for. The usual number of questions clients take is about 6–10 .

Most questions will be set-choice, but some clients require open-ended questions and they will be charged up to double the amount per question. If clients require help in framing questions, then this is included in the price. Clients can have breakdowns of each question inserted by any of the demographics, up to 30 cells (e.g. a 6 × 5 table). The demographics include:

- sex, age and social class,
- marital and working status,
- household size and composition,
- telephone and car ownership,
- region (either Registrar General's or ITV),
- household tenure.

Optional extras include charts, mini-reports, brand mapping, **cluster analysis** or analysis by ACORN. The figures in the tables are grossed-up volume figures, and weights are applied. There is a 72 cell matrix – age within sex within region – that is used to weight responses in each cell. **Standard errors** are not usually provided, but will be offered at no extra cost if asked for.

Question sets from clients are finalised on a Tuesday, fieldwork begins three days later and is completed by the following Tuesday. Basic tabular reports are available eight working days thereafter.

As an adjunct to the main service, Omnimas maintains a **database** of previous respondents who have indicated their willingness to participate in further research. It can be used to reduce greatly the cost and timescale of undertaking ad hoc research amongst particular minority groups in the population.

BMRB's Target Group Index

In 1968 the British Market Research Bureau (BMRB) launched its Target Group Index (the TGI). This is a **regular interval survey** that is also 'single source', that is, it covers both product usage data and data on media exposure. Its purpose is to increase the efficiency of marketing operations by identifying and describing target groups of consumers and their exposure to the media – newspaper and magazine reading, television viewing, and the extent to which they see or hear other media. Being single source means that it is possible to identify on an individual-by-individual basis both what products they use and what media they are exposed to. Respondents are questioned about:

- their use of 400 different products covering 3,500 brands,
- their readership of over 170 magazines and newspapers,

- going to the cinema,
- the ITV channels they watch, and the radio stations they listen to,
- their lifestyles based on nearly 200 attitude questions.

The TGI questionnaire is self-completed, but left personally by an interviewer who collects basic demographic data at the same time. This gives some information on the people who refuse or who do not return the questionnaire. The major product fields covered are foods, household goods, medicaments, toiletries and cosmetics, drink, confectionery, tobacco, motoring, clothing, leisure, holidays, financial services and consumer durables. Respondents are asked about their use, ownership or participation – not about purchases made or prices paid. In the case of branded product fields, questions on frequency or weight of use are asked, along with questions on the brands used most often, plus others used in the last six months. For food and household products, it is the family use of the product that is recorded; otherwise it is personal use.

The press media questions are designed to collect responses similar to those obtained by the National Readership Survey. Television questions ask about day-by-day viewing 'on the average' for that day in 15-minute blocks before 9.30 a.m. and half-hour blocks thereafter. Each channel is covered separately. The lifestyle questions are in the form of Likert-type attitude statements with which people are asked to agree or disagree on a five-point scale from 'definitely agree' to 'definitely disagree'. The statements cover the main areas of food, drink, shopping, diet/health, personal appearance, DIY, holidays, finance, travel, media, luxury/British goods, motivation/self-perception, plus questions on some specific products and attitudes to sponsorship.

The current questionnaire runs to 85 pages and takes an average of four hours to complete. The questionnaire is totally pre-coded and adapted for optical mark reading; respondents indicate their replies by marking appropriate boxes with a pencil. The answers are then read electronically using infra-red sensors. There are three versions of the questionnaire – for men, for housewives and for other women. At the time of placing the questionnaire, a financial incentive is provided by BMRB.

Recruitment for the TGI is on the back of BMRB's weekly omnibus survey (which it calls 'Access'). This samples 2,000 adults every week, selected on the basis of random location sampling. All interviews are face to face. Approximately half of the interviews are selected, on a representative basis, for attempted TGI questionnaire placement. Of these, 12 per cent usually refuse to take the TGI questionnaire, 14 per cent accept but do not return it, and 12 per cent are rejected by the TGI control unit as unusable due to incomplete data. This results in over 25,000 completed questionnaires during the year.

Data from the questionnaires are weighted in two stages:

VODKA

	Population '000	All users A '000	All users B % down	All users C % across	All users D index	Heavy users A '000	Heavy users B % down	Heavy users C % across	Heavy users D index	Medium users A '000	Medium users B % down	Medium users C % across	Medium users D index
All adults	44871	10781	100.0	24.0	100	1631	100.0	3.6	100	3681	100.0	8.2	100
Men	21583	5398	50.1	25.0	104	819	50.2	3.8	104	1828	49.7	8.5	103
Women	23287	5383	49.9	23.1	96	812	49.8	3.5	96	1853	50.3	8.0	97
15–24	8825	3401	31.5	38.5	160	695	42.6	7.9	217	1393	37.9	15.8	192
25–34	7929	2559	23.7	32.3	134	398	24.4	5.0	138	846	23.0	10.7	130
35–44	7612	1948	18.1	25.6	106	254	15.6	3.3	92	541	14.7	7.1	87
45–54	6032	1312	12.2	21.7	91	155	9.5	2.6	71	411	11.2	6.8	83
55–64	5865	826	7.7	14.1	59	84	5.1	1.4	39	247	6.7	4.2	51
65+	8607	735	6.8	8.5	36	45	2.7	0.5	14	243	6.6	2.8	34
AB	7864	1863	17.3	23.7	99	212	13.0	2.7	74	646	17.5	8.2	100
C1	10162	2540	23.6	25.0	104	390	23.9	3.8	106	889	24.1	8.7	107
C2	12453	3233	30.0	26.0	108	488	29.9	3.9	108	1062	28.8	8.5	104
D	8027	1965	18.2	24.5	102	344	21.1	4.3	118	677	18.4	8.4	103
E	6365	1180	10.9	18.5	77	197	12.1	3.1	85	408	11.1	6.4	78
ABC1	18026	4403	40.8	24.4	102	602	36.9	3.3	92	1535	41.7	8.5	104
C2D	20480	5198	48.2	25.4	106	832	51.0	4.1	112	1739	47.2	8.5	103
ABC1 15–34	6541	2297	21.3	35.1	146	410	25.1	6.3	172	907	24.6	13.9	169
35–54	6173	1426	13.2	23.1	96	148	9.1	2.4	66	427	11.6	6.9	84
55+	5313	679	6.3	12.8	53	44	2.7	0.8	23	201	5.5	3.8	46
C2DE 15–34	10214	3663	34.0	35.9	149	683	41.9	6.7	184	1333	36.2	13.0	159
35–54	7472	1834	17.0	24.5	102	261	16.0	3.5	96	525	14.3	7.0	86
55+	9160	882	8.2	9.6	40	85	5.2	0.9	25	289	7.8	3.2	38

Figure 7.3 A product usage table from the Target Group Index

- Demographic cell weighting, taking age within region, and social class within region for men and for women who are not housewives. For housewives, weightings are applied for working status and presence of children, again by region.
- In order to remove the small differences in the estimates of readership levels that would otherwise exist between the TGI and the National Readership Survey, a specially designed, rim-weighting system has been developed.

Combined weights of up to 19.9 are used. The figures are then grossed up to the population.

The tables of product usage (see Figure 7.3) give four measures or indexes of product usage:

- the total number of product users in each demographic category,
- the per cent down, which gives the percentage in each demographic category,
- the per cent across, giving penetration for demographic items and composition for media items,
- an index of selectivity, taking penetration (or composition) in comparison with the universe as a whole.

Each of these indexes is broken down by heavy/medium/light and non-users, and, for product fields and for brands with more than one million claimed users (about 1,400 brands), are crosstabulated against a range of demographic variables including sex, age, social class, area (Standard and ITV region), number of children, plus media usage and other selected variables.

Thus in Figure 7.3 there are 10,781,000 users of vodka (an estimate derived from people in the sample who had indicated 'Yes' when asked if they ever drink it, and grossed up to the population figure), of whom 5,398,000 or 50.1 per cent are men. The users account for 24 per cent of all adults. Users who are male account for 25 per cent of all males, while adults aged 15–24, for example, were 60 per cent above the average for all adult users (i.e. 38.5 per cent compared with 24 per cent).

Besides the product field information, there are brand usage tables, listing users of the product group who use the brand exclusively (solus users); those who prefer it, but another brand is also used (most often users); and those who are more casual in their use, that is, they have used the brand but use another brand more often (minor users). This facilitates some measure of brand loyalty.

Demographic tables use demographic groupings as headings and include breakdowns of respondents by savings and investments, ownership of durable items, leisure items, motoring, drinking, smoking, DIY, entertaining and holidays abroad.

In all, 34 volumes are published annually in July and August following the completion of the fieldwork in March. Rolling annual data are available on tape in August and January each year. An introduction to the TGI volumes gives a number of charts similar to those illustrated in Figure 6.5 so that clients can calculate their own confidence intervals based on standard errors at the 95 per cent level, and incorporating a design factor of 1.2 to allow for the effects of clustering and weighting.

The TGI gives measures of market penetration and weight of use rather than estimates of market size or market share. It allows conclusions to be drawn about the levels of penetration to a target group among different demographic and media audience groups, and it is possible to see how these differ from the population as a whole and how they differ from other groups.

Subscribers have on-line access to datasets for which they have subscribed, or they can analyse the data on their own personal computers where they are provided on CD or cartridge. It is possible to do special analyses that crosstabulate anything by anything or break down the data by geodemographic segmentation (such as ACORN areas) or by any of the lifestyle questions. Cluster analysis is often used on the lifestyle data to group respondents into segments similar in terms of such lifestyles. This facilitates the more creative use of the TGI since these groupings can then be cross-analysed by any of the other variables.

Media owners are constrained to purchase the full set of 34 volumes, but non-media clients can purchase TGI data on a volume-by-volume basis, or they can buy data for a product field, or, indeed, on a brand-by-brand basis.

The use of market measurement data

Market measurement information is required both by top company executives and by marketing and sales managers for one or more of a number of key purposes:

- to reduce the risks in or to maximise the opportunities from taking strategic or operational decisions in respect of marketing mix variables,
- to monitor changes and developments in the marketplace as they occur,
- to build up a marketing database that can be used as a resource for a variety of analyses,
- to use as a common currency in negotiations with suppliers, distributors, retailers, business customers, advertising agencies or media owners,
- to act as an input to market segmentation analyses.

A marketing manager will often want to know, for example, whether or not a strategy of maintaining a full range is maximising the firm's competitive advantage; whether, from past experience, adding new brand variants of a product is likely to cannibalise sales from the other variants or will increase overall total sales; whether a new product is reaching its target for market penetration and repeat purchase rate; whether a price reduction is increasing or decreasing total revenue; or whether the last advertising campaign was successful in raising brand awareness.

A company that knows what is happening in the marketplace as it happens is able to react to these changes immediately. Knowing, for example, that there was a significant increase in the number of shops handling your brand who were out of stock last week or last month will alert the company to distribution problems or lack of production volume, and it can take corrective action before sales are seriously dented.

A marketing database will include all back data from market measurement activities and, very often, a customer database. If, for example, a company is concerned about the level of its prices in the shops in relation to those of its competitors, by using back data it can see what happened to sales or market shares or market penetration when price differentials between its brands and the brands of its main competitors were at varying amounts.

Any manufacturer will want to know its market share and how this has been changing when negotiating with retailers as to whether its brands should be accepted as part of their range, what stocks they should hold, and what shelf space they should give it. By the same token, media owners need market measurement data to make a case for an advertising campaign using their medium. Advertising agencies use such data for clients for media selection, creative input, account planning, and to monitor campaigns.

Market segmentation is the process of dividing up the target market into sub-groups with the idea of aiming at those sub-groups different or modified marketing mixes designed to maximise marketing opportunities in each. Market segmentation is an alternative to mass marketing or product variety marketing, in which the manufacturer offers a range of product variations, but these just offer choice and are not targeted at specific groups.

The role of marketing research in market segmentation is to identify market segments, ascertain their size and structure, and the nature of consumer behaviour and attitudes associated with them. In some cases, this amounts to no more than researching the structure of the total market in a little more detail and separating consumers into those with higher and those with lower probabilities of buying a brand or a product; in others, sophisticated techniques are used to determine those characteristics which, singly or in combination, will result in the optimum or 'best' way of segmenting the market in pursuit of specified marketing objectives.

Sometimes market analyses have as their primary objective this process of segmentation; in other situations, segmentation is a spin-off or secondary objective of research that was designed for other purposes. Thus a client wishing to monitor the marketplace on a continuous basis may subscribe to a consumer panel and receive regular, four-weekly reports of sales broken down by a number of demographics. In looking at the reports, it may become clear that certain groups of customers have systematically different patterns of buying behaviour from others. This may suggest that a policy of segmentation, or further segmentation, may be worth considering. Market analyses that are more strictly directed at segmentation are more likely to use the more complex and sophisticated segmentation techniques.

The data used for segmentation analyses, whether simple or complex, implicit or explicit, are normally derived either from continuous market measurement research, or from ad hoc usage and attitude studies. The latter are described in the next section. The most frequently used bases for segmentation may be grouped into four main categories:

- demographic,
- geographic,
- behavioural,
- attitudinal.

Demographics, whether consumer or business, are collected in almost any piece of market analysis, whether to be used for segmentation purposes or not. These demographics were described in detail earlier in the context of questionnaire design. Segmentation may be on a basis of a single variable like sex or age, or on a more complex combination of several variables interlaced. Some proprietary classification systems, for example SAGACITY, developed by Research Services Ltd (RSL), offer standardised cross-referencing of variables such as disposable income, occupation and life-cycle (see Cornish 1981 for more details).

Analysis of market data by region is also commonplace, but other geographic bases for segmentation may be using some kind of urban/rural distinction, or by neighbourhood types, again perhaps using one of the proprietary geodemographic systems such as ACORN, MOSAIC or PiN (see Leventhal 1990, for a clear account of six major systems).

Behavioural segmentation, at its simplest, could be on the basis of those who buy a given brand and those who do not. More complex segmentations may be based on usage occasions, frequency of purchase, brand loyalty, or all three in some combination.

Attitudes may be general states of mind, for example, 'experimentalists' and 'loyalists', or attitudes towards particular products, types of product or brands. Attitude measurement was explained earlier in the context of questionnaire design.

The bases for segmenting business markets may be a little different, for

example, taking into account different technologies used by client organisations, or their purchasing approaches or policies, or on particular product
applications.

At their simplest, the techniques used in segmentation analyses will
involve crosstabulating a number of variables, typically a behavioural variable by one or more demographics, but one at a time. Thus heavy, medium
and light usage may be crosstabulated against sex, age and social class.
Sometimes data may be 'dredged' to see what demographics, geodemographics or attitudes are most strongly associated with product purchasing
behaviour. More sophisticated techniques used for segmentation can be
divided into those that impose segmentation and those that allow segments
to emerge from the data.

In the latter category are **factor analysis** and **cluster analysis** (explained
in Chapter 6 on data analysis). Factor analysis groups variables that are
interrelated; the latter groups respondents with similar characteristics, and
is of more direct application to segmentation. However, factor analysis may
be used as an input to cluster analysis, that is, respondents are clustered on
the basis of the factors identified in the first phase. One problem that arises
with such analyses, however, is that the clusters generated may be difficult
to locate or contact with the appropriate marketing messages.

Crosstabulation, clearly, imposes the segmentation variables by using a
priori decisions about what variables to crosstabulate. More complex techniques that also impose segmentation variables include discriminant
analysis such as AID (Automatic Interaction Detector – see Sonquist and
Morgan 1965). The technique identifies a dependent variable (e.g. user
versus non-user of a brand) and a series of variables, again chosen a priori,
that might discriminate between users and non-users. The sample of
respondents is then divided into smaller and smaller groups on the basis of
maximising the proportion of brand users in one grouping, and minimising
the proportion in the other at each new split.

At the end of the day, market segments must be measurable, accessible
to marketing messages and propositions, fairly substantial in size to be
worth addressing with a specific marketing mix, and defensible against
competitors. Some companies may address all segments; others may
address only some, or even just one segment – sometimes known as 'niche'
marketing. The ultimate in segmentation, of course, is customisation where
products are designed for each client or customer. While this is common in
business markets, in consumer markets it is more usual to address broader
categories of customer.

Usage and attitude studies

U&A studies, also sometimes referred to as 'market studies', provide the
basic building blocks for marketing activity since they are used largely to

provide an in-depth understanding of the market in which a particular brand is being sold. They describe a market very much from the consumer's point of view and will cover:

- brand or product awareness (including advertising awareness where applicable),
- brand or product choice behaviour, for example, trial, adoption, loyalty and brand repertoires,
- brand or product purchasing – frequency, source, prices paid, and quantities and size/style of pack,
- usage patterns,
- attitudes to or beliefs about the brand(s) or product(s),
- the needs that the brands or products do or do not meet as far as the consumer is concerned.

Many of the variables, for example brand choice behaviour, brand purchasing, and usage patterns, are similar to consumer panel data. However, U&A studies, unlike consumer panels, also collect data on brand and advertising awareness, and on attitudes towards brands or products. Furthermore, a more important distinction is that they are ad hoc, both in the sense that they are not continuous, and in the sense that they are usually custom-designed for individual clients rather than syndicated.

In the 1960s and 1970s it was fairly common for U&A studies to be carried out regularly, perhaps quarterly or six-monthly, but nowadays they tend to be on an occasional basis, perhaps once every two or three years, or even less regularly. There are two main reasons for this. First, they are in-depth 'dip-stick' operations that go into great detail to provide an understanding of the marketplace at one point in time. Typically, there will be between 1,000 and 2,000 face-to-face interviews in a single study, with each interview lasting up to an hour. In consequence, they are expensive, typically £50,000 to £60,000 at today's prices. Second, because of the development of tracking studies and consumer panel data, they are no longer required to monitor changes in the key market variables Changes could not, in any case, easily be measured in the depth to which U&A studies go. In short, they are not required so frequently. They nowadays do not even seek to replicate earlier studies because a lot of things will have changed in the marketplace in the meantime.

Related to the issue of depth is the notion that in-depth work has to be tailor-made for each client. It would be unlikely for several clients to agree on a common format for the purpose of sharing costs. Although there have been examples of syndicated U&As, they are not usual.

The main focus of U&A studies is on the brand, since it is not helpful to look at advertising on a one-off basis. They are usually conducted using face-to-face interviews, often over a four-week period. Postal questionnaires may be used, although they tend to have too low a response rate, while the use of the telephone is limited because it is usually necessary to present visual stimuli to respondents. Interviews typically begin by asking about brand awareness, for example, 'Which brands of product X can you think of/have you seen/bought/used/seen advertised?' Usually some timescale is attached – typically a week, but sometimes 'in the last 24 hours', 'in the last two weeks', or just 'recently'. Such questions are unlikely to be prompted, and will aim for 'top-of-the-mind' reactions. The interviewer may then turn to particular brands – perhaps the brand leader and the brand being researched – to ask about purchasing behaviour.

Attitudes towards brands will usually be measured using five- or seven-point rating scales, so that the ratings of different people and different brands can be compared. Such ratings may well, however, be in batteries of statements that go for across-the-brand comparisons, as illustrated in Figure 7.4. It is important that respondents understand the characteristics they are being asked to rate, and that such characteristics comprehensively cover all the key areas likely to differentiate between products or brands. Where different types of product are the focus of interest, it is, in addition, necessary to ensure that the product typologies or groupings are made in terms familiar to consumers. The development of these attributes is, in consequence, usually undertaken using **qualitative research** – **group discussions** or **depth interviews**. The questions themselves may be tested in an omnibus survey.

Consumer needs may be tapped by asking about their 'ideal' product, using either open-ended questions or with product features as prompts. Respondents are also likely to be asked about what factors are or were important in choosing a particular brand. In many U&A studies, the opportunity is taken to look at other issues like pricing, packaging, reactions to new product concepts, media use, or product ownership.

Here is a list of drinks that you might find in off-licences or supermarkets. I would like to know your impressions of these drinks, even if you've not actually tried them. Which of these brands do you think:
(You can mention as many or as few as you like)

	BRAND			
	A	B	C	D
IS AN 'EVERYDAY' DRINK?	1	1	1	1
IS FOR WEEKEND DRINKING?	2	2	2	2
IS A CUT ABOVE THE AVERAGE DRINK?	3	3	3	3
IS DULL AND UNINTERESTING?	4	4	4	4
IS PARTICULARLY STRONG IN ALCOHOL?	5	5	5	5
IS APPEALING TO OLDER PEOPLE?	6	6	6	6

Figure 7.4 An attitude battery of statements for an alcoholic drink

Standard demographics will normally be collected for both structural and analytic purposes. Increasingly, these will include lifestyle, life-cycle and geodemographic variables.

Samples used in U&A studies will usually be of current users in the product field, and may vary in size from about 500 to 2,000 depending on the need for sub-group analysis, regional breakdowns, or segmentation analysis. Well-known brands purchased by many people may require smaller samples than minority brands. Booster samples of consumers most likely to use less well-known brands may well be used. Most sampling is **quota** since probability samples are likely to be too expensive and take too long to carry out. In some cases, the research may be extended to look at non-users or users of products in related fields.

The standard analysis of U&A data will typically take the form of cross-tabulating all the usage and attitude variables against all the demographics. A lot of useful information about the brand being researched and its competitors can be derived from basic tables of this kind. However, to derive the full value from the research, more sophisticated analyses will often be carried out. Thus batteries of attitude statements may be factor analysed to see which sets of statements inter-correlate. The factors thus generated may then be used as inputs to a cluster analysis to generate market segments by revealing groups of respondents who are similar in respect of a number of variables. Many U&A studies include questions on preferences for product characteristics. Provided these are ranked, they may be used as inputs to **conjoint analysis** that generates a utility score for each characteristic and an overall optimum product formulation. Mapping techniques and sensory evaluation (see Martin 1990) may be used where the U&A is to act as an input to product positioning. Besides their key role in market segmentation and brand positioning, U&A studies may also be used in the longer-term development of promotional strategies and in the targeting of new products or relaunched modified products.

Research International's CONCEPTOR

A problem with many U&A studies is that they are normally carried out in markets which clients have been addressing for some time and with which they are already familiar. If all you do is ask people about their usage and attitude, the data tend to be uninteresting, and the response is, 'Well, we knew all that!' At the same time, markets are becoming increasingly complex, dynamic and segmented into niche markets. The broad-brush approach of the typical U&A study is becoming less relevant. In consequence, some market research companies have developed more refined techniques. Thus Research International has expanded the U&A study to include not just usage, but usage occasions. People tend to have a repertoire of brands that they use on different occasions, so they are asked about the last occasion they used the product – time of day, type of occasion, who was involved, what it was used with, what other products or brands might have been considered on that occasion. They are then asked in similar detail about the previous occasion. In this way, it is often possible to establish particular market niches that brands fill.

This approach Research International has turned into a proprietary technique it calls 'CONCEPTOR'. By looking at needs on particular occasions, and how far they are met by the particular brand or product, CONCEPTOR allows the influence of attitudes and needs on usership to be assessed, and enables gaps or niches in the market to be identified. The interrelationships between aspects of use occasion can then be analysed, for example, both need and substitutes considered may be related to type of occasion, to who was involved, and to attributes of the product. Substitution in particular is sensitive to occasion, for example, a possible substitute for a chocolate bar may on one occasion be another brand of chocolate bar, but on another may be a biscuit, an apple or a yoghurt. Asking about potential occasions for use of new product concepts may be of considerable value for helping to position the new product in the marketplace.

Advertising tracking studies

A key problem with any ad hoc research, even if carried out at regular intervals, is that important features of a trend may be lost. For example, two snapshots or 'dipsticks' of brands A and B taken at time T_1 and time T_2 may well overlook what has been happening to the trend in the meantime, as illustrated in Figure 7.5. Furthermore, such studies will inevitably tend to be timed around the marketing activities of the brand being studied, so it will not give a clear picture of what competitors are up to, since the timings of their activities will be different. It would be easy, but not helpful, inadvertently to bias advertising evaluation research so that one's own advertising appeared in an unrealistically favourable light merely through timing. Furthermore, it would be difficult to know whether any changes out of line with earlier dipsticks were an aberration or part of a new trend, until the next dipstick was taken. In addition, clients are inclined to believe that improved brand measures will remain high rather than slip back to where they started from. A series of dipsticks, provided some are between bursts of advertising, may overcome this to some extent.

Continuous research, by contrast, will reveal trends. Continuous monitoring is particularly important for tracking the impact of advertising over a period of time, and it is largely in the area of advertising that tracking studies have developed. Early campaign evaluations often involved pre-/post-designs that typically took the form of a baseline study carried out before the advertising began, followed up by periodic checks

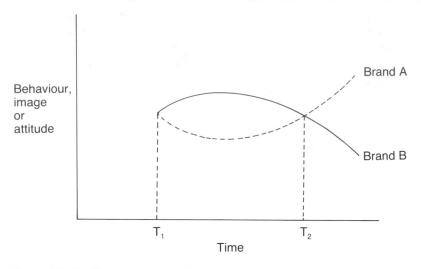

Figure 7.5 Continuous versus ad hoc measurement

once the campaign was under way. A control group, unexposed to the advertising being researched, was often the subject of parallel measurements (Sampson 1987). The effects of the campaign could then be evaluated by comparing the change over time in the test group with changes that may have occurred anyway in the control group (a before-and-after with control experimental design).

These early studies were thus essentially ad hoc, simplistic in design, and geared to measuring how far the advertising met its objectives. The underlying assumption was that successful advertising would change brand measures regardless of whether the strategy sought to do so. In addition, their timing was always a problem since it would be difficult to determine an optimum point at which to take the post-campaign measurements. Pre-/ post-studies are, however, still carried out, for example, because they are cheaper, or because a three-week advertising campaign just before Christmas would be too short for continuous research. The modern tracking study, however, tends to be regarded as synonymous with continuous measurement and planning. It will monitor all the key brands in a product field, usually on a weekly basis, in order to provide the input to improve substantially the understanding of the brand and market being researched. Continuous research overcomes the problem of timing measurements both on the part of the brand being researched and its competitors, and allows trends to be measured both for monitoring purposes and as inputs in making predictions.

What was probably the first modern tracking study in the UK was that carried out by Millward Brown for Cadbury in 1977 (and subsequently continued for 15 years). Cadbury had many advertised brands in the same market and needed to be able to track them all, and to compare their performance with that of their competitors. The tracking study provided an information system for making such comparisons, both across brands and across time. Millward Brown now runs over 120 such studies in the UK alone.

The ultimate goal of any advertising is to influence purchasing behaviour and sales. It is often supposed that advertisers can measure advertising effectiveness simply by seeing how many additional sales are being generated. Unfortunately, many other factors besides advertising influence purchasing behaviour; for example, availability of the products in the shops, their prominence on the shelves, the use of special offers or coupons, the price, variations in all these for competitor brands – the list is endless. All these will affect product trial, brand choice behaviour, and repeat purchasing. For a large established brand, the advertising will probably be a relatively minor influence and only needs to produce a very small percentage increase in sales to pay for itself. There has been a lot of interest in trying to model the sales effects of advertising over the longer term. Only relatively recently has it been possible to do so accurately enough to say that one commercial for a brand is better than another (see Colman and Brown 1983, for a review).

The majority of advertisers have to be content with determining the probable effectiveness of their advertising by asking people questions. These may be questions about the brand or about the advertising. Brand-related questions will include brand recall (prompted, unprompted or both) in the product field, respondent images of these brands, and attitudes towards them. Questions about the advertising will include respondent recall of the ads, the brand they were linked to and the messages conveyed. From the brand questions, it is possible to determine whether and to what extent brand awareness increases and attitudes to the brand improve when advertising takes place; and from the advertising questions it can be determined whether the advertising 'worked' in terms of attracting consumer attention and conveying messages linked memorably to the brand.

Advertising tracking studies always use independent samples rather than panels, since it would be inappropriate to ask a panel about their awareness of advertising on a repeated basis. In a typical tracking study there will be independent weekly quota samples of about 100 respondents in the target market for the product field. Typically, 20 or so respondents will be interviewed every weekday, and the interviews each week will be conducted in different geographical locations on a four-weekly cycle. The results from any consecutive four weeks are thus nationally representative and comparable with any other consecutive four-week period. Data are normally analysed on a rolling four-weekly basis, so that weeks 1–4 will be cumulated and compared with weeks 2–5, 3–6 and so on. Analysis may be carried out over longer periods, so long as they are multiples of four weeks. So, although the number of interviews in any one week is not large enough to enable weekly analyses, grouping them together in this way still allows weekly comparisons to be made. Since interviewing is normally carried out over 50 weeks in a year (a brief period over Chrismas is often left out), over 5,000 interviews are carried out annually. This inevitably makes costs quite high, frequently over £70,000 a year – but actually not a lot more than a single, one-off U&A study.

Most tracking studies are carried out by market research companies on a client-specific basis, although some are syndicated. The advantage of the former is that the client has total control over the study, particularly the questionnaire. The downside is that such research is more expensive than syndicated research, and it is often difficult to build up a database of all the key brands in the marketplace as a key resource. While syndicated research is cheaper, it is, however, difficult to change any of the key dimensions as you go along in order to meet the changing needs of the company. Some agencies offer both syndicated and client-specific tracking research.

The typical tracking study will measure:

- product use in the product field, for example, 'Which of these alcoholic drinks do you drink nowadays?',
- spontaneous awareness of brands, for example, 'What brands of cider can you think of?',
- prompted awareness, for example, 'Which of these brands have you heard of?',
- trial, for example, 'Have you ever tried any of these brands?',
- past purchase, for example, 'Which of these brands have you bought recently?',
- future purchase intent, for example, 'How likely would you say you are to buy brand X in the next three months?',
- brand images, for example, using attitude batteries like those for U&A studies, but shorter,
- advertising recall, for example, 'Which of these brands of cider have you seen advertised in local newspapers or magazines recently?',
- advertising content recall, for example, 'What can you remember about the last TV ad you saw for Red Rock?'

Clearly, there is considerable overlap between tracking studies and usage and attitude studies in terms of the information sought from respondents. The key difference lies in the fact that tracking studies are continuous and tend to be used to monitor the effects of marketing activity, especially advertising, on existing brands or recently launched brands. U&A studies tend to be ad hoc and undertaken in pre-launch situations or before proposed changes to the marketing mix are made. Tracking studies are also far less detailed than U&As – an interview will typically last less than 30 minutes.

A key measure used in all advertising tracking studies is advertising awareness, usually based on recall of advertising. There are, however, many different ways of measuring recall, and what characterises differences between the approaches of different market research companies to advertising tracking is often the question posed to respondents to measure it. One distinction is between verified or proven recall and claimed recall. The former uses the answers to subsequent questions about the content of the advertising to verify that the respondent did actually recall the correct ad and is not confusing it with some other ad or making false claims. Claimed recall, on the other hand, takes the respondents' claims at face value. It is sometimes argued that verified recall is misleading, since some ads are very much easier to describe than others and since it is, in any case, biased in favour of long-running ads or campaigns. In consequence, claimed recall may be used since this may be a better indicator of the extent to which advertising 'got through' to consumers and associated itself with the brand.

Another distinction is between prompted and unprompted recall. In the former, respondents are given a list of brands and asked which of them they have seen advertised, while in the latter they are asked to recall what brands they remember being advertised. Millward Brown, the brand leader in market tracking studies and which tracks for 50 of the 100 top UK advertisers, found that you get very different results on measures of awareness depending on the question asked. Thus you could ask 'Have you seen any advertising for brand X on television recently?' or 'What brands have you seen advertised in the last three months?' or 'Have you ever seen a television commercial in which ...?' Advertising awareness will decay more rapidly between advertising bursts if you ask about advertising seen 'recently', and hardly at all if you ask about advertising 'ever seen'. Millward Brown prefers 'recently' because this relates best to sales effects, and it is possible, if awareness dies away rapidly, to see what happens during the next burst. In addition, advertising awareness accessed through the brand (as in the first question) relates better to other tracking measures than awareness triggered by reference to the advertising. It is important, furthermore, to see how memories or recall of your advertising swings into the brain in association with mention of the brand name.

The proportions mentioning the brand being advertised are usually plotted at four-weekly intervals and compared with the television ratings (TVRs) achieved. TVRs are measured by totalling the percentage of the population watching television each time it goes on air over a week. They are a good measure of exposure to the ad and are a better measure than taking the cost of the ad, which may vary by time of year, the effectiveness of the advertising agency in buying airtime, and by target group. How these ratings are measured is explained in the next section on media audience measurement.

Figure 7.6 shows brand X being advertised using two different

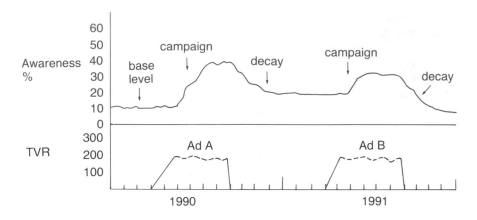

Figure 7.6 Advertising awareness and television exposure

campaigns over a two-year period. The bottom half of the graph shows the TVRs achieved by each. The top half shows the percentage who recall the ad using the Millward Brown question. The timescale points are four weeks apart, so there are 13 in a year. Both ads were screened more or less continuously over a 24-week period, achieving about 200 TVRs. There was a base level of about 10 per cent awareness before advertising began, which will have been influenced by past advertising. The campaign using ad A was, clearly, more effective than the campaign using ad B. The former raised awareness from about 10 per cent up to nearly 40 per cent. When the ad finished, there was a period of decay, but the awareness fell back to only about 20 per cent. Campaign B raised awareness from 20 per cent to 35 per cent, a gain of 15 per cent compared with a gain of 30 per cent for ad A.

To compare these gains in advertising awareness directly, however, is to assume that all other things are equal – which usually they are not. The advertising may, for example, be for different lengths of time, achieving different TVRs over the campaign. Getting a directly comparable measure of advertising effectiveness (in achieving awareness) can be quite complicated.

Millward Brown's Awareness Index

By looking at back data, Millward Brown discovered that, while more advertising results in increased awareness, the amount of the increase associated with a given amount of advertising exposure varies enormously from one advertising campaign to another, depending on how 'good' the ad is, the amount of past advertising, and a number of other factors. However,

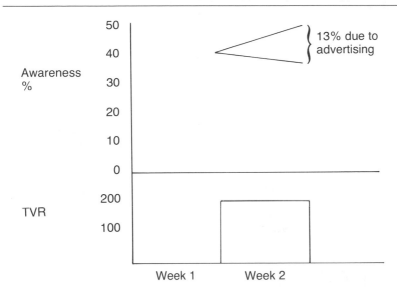

Figure 7.7 Calculating the Awareness Index

At the beginning of week 2, awareness was 40 per cent. At the end of the week it had risen to 50 per cent. However, in the absence of advertising, assuming a base of 10, it would have declined to 37 per cent, that is 40 per cent less 10 per cent of the decayed 30 per cent above the base (40% − 3%). During week 2, 200 TVRs were deployed, so the Awareness Index is:

$$\frac{\text{Increase due to advertising}}{\text{TVR}} \times 100 = \frac{13}{200} \times 100$$

$$= 6.5$$

the interesting point is that *within* an advertising campaign, this relationship tends to be remarkably stable; so much so that Millward Brown call it their 'Awareness Index'.

   Awareness, as measured by level of recall at any one point of time, is a combination of two factors. First, an underlying base level, which is a residual awareness and is a level to which awareness is assumed to return should the brand not be advertised for a long period. This base changes only slowly over time, and is assumed to be constant over an advertising campaign. Second, there is the short-term awareness which is directly a result of the present advertising. It is this element that the Awareness Index measures, and it is defined as the increase in television advertising awareness generated per 100 TVRs. To calculate this figure, it is necessary to know what awareness would have decayed to since the previous week in the absence of the current advertising, and add this to the absolute increase that took place. Awareness, it has been found, decays at a steady rate of 10

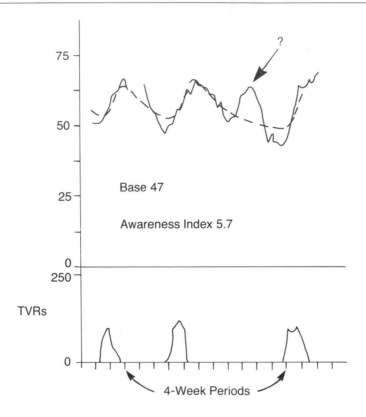

Figure 7.8 Model fitting by eye

Although there are only three bursts of advertising, there are four peaks on the advertising graph. The third happened to correspond with a single burst of advertising for another brand in the same market. Fitting 'by eye' allows this to be ignored in calculating the Awareness Index (from the dotted line).

per cent per week – in other words, the retention factor is 90 per cent. This makes it possible to calculate decay.

The difference between the decayed and actual awareness is how much is due to the present week's advertising (see Figure 7.7). It is this difference which is related to exposure to work out the extra ad awareness per 100 TVRs. The calculation is the equivalent to advertising in some theoretical television area which had never been exposed to the advertising for the brand previously. In other words, a comparison is being made between commercials on how they would perform if put on an equal footing. The Awareness Index is thus a pure measure of the efficiency of a given commercial in generating advertising awareness.

The calculation of the Awareness Index, however, depends on what

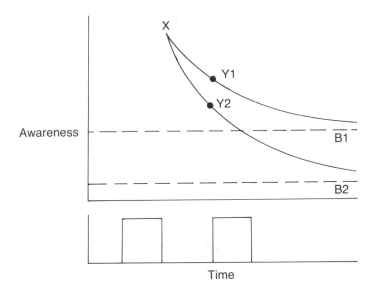

Figure 7.9 Determining the base level from the shape of the decay curve

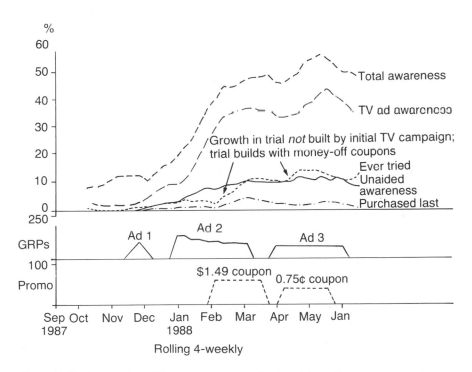

Figure 7.10 Comparing different measures of advertising effectiveness against adverting exposure

assumptions are being made about the base level. The base interacts with the Awareness Index – the higher the base, the lower the AI and vice versa. Accordingly, the existing pattern may be achieved from different combinations of base and Index (given the decay rate). While this has been the basis of criticism of the Awareness Index (see Feldwick *et al.* 1991), Brown (1991a) argues that the choice of solution is limited in a number of ways. First, allowance is made in the model for the fact that it is more difficult to shift awareness from, say, 50 per cent to 60 per cent than from 10 per cent to 20 per cent. Second, the modelled data are fitted to the actual data by eye (see Figure 7.8). This allows Millward Brown to bring to bear their experience in interpreting the data, for example, to ignore misfits for which there is an obvious explanation. A 'best fit' is found by applying a number of rules derived from this experience, for example, not allowing the base to undergo a step change unless the campaign has changed. Third, the base level is indicated by the shape of the decay curve (see Figure 7.9). Finally, for some brands, the pauses between advertising give some indication of what the base might be.

The base, of course, may change slowly over time, responding to changes in the weight of advertising and the memorability of the ad. The Awareness Index, too, may change during a campaign due to an ad 'wearing in' or 'wearing out', but a 'best' fit is one that assumes a degree of stability during the campaign.

Advertising awareness, as explained above, can be measured in a number of different ways, using a variety of different questions so that either claimed or verified recall, prompted or unprompted recall, may be plotted against TVRs, or against any other measures of advertising exposure like press advertising spend or radio advertising spend. Awareness of brands (as opposed to advertising), again prompted or unprompted, may, similarly, be plotted against TVRs or other measures. So might other tracking measures like brand image or brand evaluation. All these in any combination may be plotted in a manner similar to Figure 7.6, or may be combined on to the same graph as in Figure 7.10. Figure 7.10 shows how neither television advertising awareness nor total awareness responded very well to the first of the three ads, but both responded very well to the second. However, trial responded only to the money-off coupon, while unaided awareness built up only very slowly.

Awareness, of course, is only one aspect of advertising communication. What is being communicated by the advertising, and the extent to which it relates to the brand, are also crucial for 'good' advertising. So while, on the whole, it is a good thing to get good advertising recall, that is, all other things being equal – which they usually are not, so an ad with a relatively low Awareness Index may be better than one with a higher Index because it says the right things and is memorably linked to the brand.

Tracking advertising awareness for press advertising is in many respects

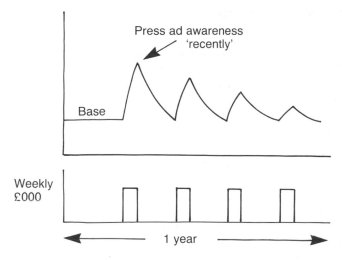

Figure 7.11 Tracking press ad awareness

quite different from advertising on television. People tend to get bored with press ads over time and stop noticing them. A typical pattern may be as in Figure 7.11. Overall awareness for any one ad declines on repeat printing. An Awareness Index for press can measure extra ad awareness per £100,000 spent, and this usually declines sharply after the ad's first couple of appearances. How much time a reader spends looking at a press ad is up to the reader. People may read or glance at the ad two or three times, but will turn the page once they have 'seen it'. For television, this is not the case. A 30-second ad is often watched for 30 seconds every time or most times it is screened. Furthermore, it will be watched whatever the level of interest in the product itself. When people watch television ads repeatedly, they tend to 'home in' on the bits they enjoy watching rather than take in more detail. In short, whereas for press ads it is necessary to grab attention creatively, for television ads attention is assured; but what people remember is what they enjoy, and creativity is needed to link that enjoyment to the brand being advertised.

Advertising tracking is basically diagnostic and retrospective. It cannot be used directly to make a quantified prediction of trial, repeat behaviour, purchase cycles and so on. However, by giving an overall diagnosis of how well an advertising campaign went, the results can feed into the planning of future campaigns. If the advertising has a good Awareness Index and appears to be conveying the right messages, it is doing as well as it can in the circumstances. If a brand is in terminal decline, then no amount of effective advertising will do more than prop it up temporarily. It would be wrong in these circumstances to 'blame' poor advertising for not producing better results.

BJM's Stochastic Reaction Monitors

Some commentators on tracking studies, for example Donius (1985), have emphasised that modern tracking studies are used (or should be used) as strategic planning tools. The distinguishing characteristics of such studies, continues Donius, are, first, the integration of data from a number of sources and, second, a total market perspective which is fully integrated into planning and setting performance goals for the future, rather than being restricted to retrospective monitoring. They allow for the reassessment of strategy by confronting management with the results of their decisions in making changes to the marketing mix.

One system that explicitly integrates diagnosis, evaluation, tracking and the planning of marketing strategy has been developed by BJM Research and Consultancy. Called 'Stochastic Reaction Monitors', its objective is to act as a marketing tool that provides fast, continuous, quantified feedback on the cost-efficiency of all marketing activity related to a brand. It is a system for tracking and evaluating the success of marketing strategies in the marketplace relating to brand positioning, advertising and trade activity. The first step is an evaluation of current strategies for branding, advertising, and below-the-line and trading activity. This is then followed by data collection from weekly independent samples of respondents interviewed in-home, covering:

- communication,
- behaviour,
- attitude,
- image.

The usual brand questions, 'What brands of product X have you seen advertised recently?' or the prompted 'Which of these brands have you seen advertised?', according to BJM, tend to confuse advertising awareness with brand saliency. Advertising awareness has more to do with what messages are being communicated by the advertising than with what brand names can be remembered. Consequently, BJM ask respondents simply to describe in words the advertising they have seen in a particular market sector, for example, 'Describe to me the advertising you have see on ....', and 'What else do you remember?' They are then asked what brands the advertising was for, and what the advertising was trying to tell them apart from getting them to buy or use the product. This process may be repeated two or three times, for example, 'Now tell me about the next advertising you remember.'

The result is that it is possible to disentangle true awareness of the advertising from whether or not the product is adequately branded. The percentage of respondents who recall and articulate various messages divided by the percentage who correctly name the brand gives an index of the adequacy of the branding. This describes the effectiveness of the

1	Those who insist on buying brand X above all others	INSISTORS
2	Those who prefer to buy brand X amongst others	PREFERERS
3	Those who are interested in buying brand X	INTEND
4	Those who would buy brand X under certain circumstances	ACCEPTORS
5	Those who have heard of brand X, but don't know much about it	NO OPINION
6	Those who have never heard of brand X	UNAWARE
7	Those who would never buy brand X	REJECTORS

Figure 7.12 Attitude scaling for BJM's Stochastic Reaction Monitors

communication, which is the extent to which brand-linked messages are being conveyed to target markets. Data on what messages are linked to the brand will reveal how the brand is currently positioned.

On behaviour, the Stochastic Reaction Monitor takes the share of the brand as a proportion of all the brands purchased in the product field on the last occasion. This is a derived measure of market share, not an observed one. However, it does relate reasonably well to data on actual brand shares from consumer panels (where these are available), and does provide a measure of change, even if the absolute level is not totally accurate. Respondents are also asked about the brand itself – whether the last purchase was the first time they had bought it, or had they bought it previously? This gives a measure of trial and repeat purchase. Analysis of these data facilitates answers to questions about market penetration, the effect of marketing activity on trial and brand loyalty, the effects of competitor activity, the impact of advertising on trial, and the impact of attitude change on loyalty.

Attitudes are measured on a six-point scale of disposition to buy, as illustrated in Figure 7.12. This combines both positive and negative dispositions to buy with lack of knowledge or awareness. The objective of marketing activity is to push the brand upwards. For a new brand, the aim will be to push awareness into willingness to try it. The share of positive attitudes (1 and 2) is what BJM call the 'stochastic share', which may be calculated for all key brands. It is, in a way, the share of the consumer's mind which is the result of all marketing activity to date.

Stochastic share is then compared with the actual share to see whether the brand is achieving its potential. If, for example, the short-term share is above the stochastic share, it is a measure of the short-term vulnerability of that brand; it will probably fall or be artificially maintained by marketing activity.

Image is measured with a series of attribute positioning statements supplied by the client or its advertising agency about what the advertising is trying to do and what the communication activity is trying to say about the brand. These are then given to respondents to indicate how important each of these is to them. The analysis will expose discrepancies between actual brand profile and advertising, as well as identifying a brand's strengths and weaknesses, and what the important attributes are.

The essence of the system is to infer relationships, not by using a statistical 'black box', but trying to understand patterns of cause and effect. Problems tend to emerge as the analysis proceeds, and the discussion in the presentation of the findings is frequently about the development of future marketing strategy, as well as about the short-term, tactical brand issues.

Media audience measurement

In deciding which type of medium to use to communicate with consumers in chosen markets, and in selecting which particular channels, stations, newspapers or magazines will be most effective, it is essential to know which media the individuals and households in the target market use, how much they use them, when they use them, and how they use them. The purpose of media measurement is to provide both quantitative and qualitative data on media usage by audiences and readers.

The 'media' include all means of communication with large numbers of people in an impersonal manner. The so-called 'mass' media may reach millions of individuals and households in the process, while specialised media, for example, minority magazines and radio programmes, may have relatively small audiences. The concept of an 'audience' is common to all the media, which include:

- the broadcast media – television and radio,
- the print media – newspapers, magazines and books,
- outdoor media – posters, billboards, on buses, on the underground and so on,
- film and video – cinema and video shops.

Manufacturers and other types of organisation are normally interested, for marketing communication purposes, only in those media that carry advertising, or that allow sponsorship of programmes or printed material.

In the UK, this excludes the outputs of the BBC, but very little else, except perhaps books. UK advertisers spend over £3,000 million on advertising on television, in newspapers and magazines, and on the radio. It is not surprising, therefore, that the advertising industry (which includes the advertisers, the advertising agencies and the media owners) finances carefully designed and expensive research into the viewing, listening and reading habits of the population. Each industry has set up, at some stage, joint industry committees or other bodies that are responsible for commissioning and overseeing the specification of such research.

The main advantages of joint industry research are that it provides a generally acceptable currency for the buying and selling of space and time, and it uses funds in the most economical way by avoiding duplication and fruitless arguments about the technical merits of competing systems. It is also true that many organisations would be unable to afford research whose costs were not shared with other organisations. There are, however, disadvantages: changes are difficult to push through, and the fact that part-time committee members are often not research specialists leaves too much influence in the hands of the research suppliers, according to Cox (1988). The result has tended to be a focus on technical competence rather than on the needs of the users. The original Joint Industry Committee for Television Audience Research (JICTAR) was, for a variety of reasons, replaced in 1981 by the Broadcasters' Audience Research Board (BARB), which, since then, has been responsible for commissioning television research. New joint industry committees have been set up, however, the most recent being the Joint Industry Committee for Regional Press Research (JICREG), which began its operations in 1989 (see Holland and Shepherd-Smith, 1989).

Detailed information about audience size and structure, and about audience use of and attitudes towards the advertising media and their offerings, is required by four main groups of people:

- programme makers, broadcast schedulers, and newspaper and magazine editors who are planning the development of their media,
- media owners selling to manufacturers and other organisations the opportunities to communicate with an audience through advertising and sponsorship,
- buyers of such opportunities – the advertisers, whether in manufacturing, commerce or non-profit-making organisations,
- advertising agencies and market research agencies.

The techniques used for the measurement of particular media audiences is a vast topic which really deserves a book to itself (see Kent (ed.) *Measuring Media Audiences*, forthcoming). However, an overview of current procedures for measuring audiences for the broadcast media will illustrate some of the applications of marketing research in these areas. For the print media, outdoor (poster) advertising and cinema advertising, see Kent (forthcoming).

Television audience measurement

Since it began in 1955, Independent Television has depended on advertising for its revenue. To sell advertising time effectively, audience measurement data were needed, so in 1957 the Joint Industry Committee for Television Advertising Research (JICTAR) was set up to represent the Incorporated Society of British Advertisers (ISBA), the Institute of Practitioners in Advertising (IPA) and the Independent Television Companies' Association (ITCA). The first contract for measuring television audiences was awarded to Television Audience Measurement Ltd (TAM). In 1968, JICTAR appointed Audits of Great Britain (AGB) to provide a research service based on a television panel of UK households, the costs to be borne by the three organisations represented on JICTAR.

At the time, the BBC had its own research system, but a joint system for recording both BBC and ITV audiences was begun in 1981. This set up a company jointly owned by the BBC and the ITCA called the Broadcasters' Audience Research Board (BARB). The company board consisted of directors exclusively from the two organisations. There were, however, management committees on which the IPA and ISBA were represented. AGB continued to supply the quantitative audience measurement service, while the qualitative audience reaction research was carried out by the BBC Audience Research Department. In 1984 BARB reawarded the contract to AGB for a further seven years until August 1991.

In awarding the contract to run from 1991, the board of BARB split the contract between two research contractors. AGB would operate the television panel and produce the data using its enhanced model of the peoplemeter. Panel recruitment and quality control, however, was passed over to a company jointly owned by Research Services Ltd and Millward Brown, called RSMB Television Research. The IPA joined BARB as a shareholder along with the BBC and ITCA.

Panel recruitment and panel control is based on an 'establishment' survey which establishes the reception and viewing characteristics of households in the 15 ITV regions into which the UK is divided (see Figure 7.13). The information is then used to design, monitor and control the composition of the sample panel in each region, and to provide a pre-screened address bank from which homes may be recruited when they are required to meet control targets in their area. Until 1990 the establishment survey was carried out once a year over a four-week period on a random sample of about 20,000 households. It was then increased to over 40,000 households and carried out on a continuous basis. The increase was needed because the new panel from 1991 was itself increased from 3,500 homes to

Figure 7.13 ISBA non-overlap marketing regions

Source: ISBA

about 4,700 homes to take account of audience fragmentation and the vast expansion in viewing possibilities. Accordingly, a bigger file of potential households was required.

Respondents are interviewed in-home by interviewers from Research Services Ltd and Millward Brown. Four different sections cover:

- *television and related equipment owned or rented by the household,* for example, the number of television sets, whether colour, teletext, remote control, video cassette recorder, plus satellite or cable television decoders,
- *reception* – what channels can be received. Which actual ITV transmitters the household can receive is established by where it is located. This is important for defining the geographical areas reached by each transmitter and delimits overlap areas served by more than one,
- *viewing characteristics* – this is crucial for establishing whether household members are heavy, medium or light viewers. It is based on the number of hours the respondent (who is usually the housewife) says each set in the household is used, and whether for BBC or ITV,
- *household demographics* including family size, presence of children, their ages, socio-economic status of head of household, and so on.

Information from the establishment survey is combined with basic population demographics from the Office of Population Censuses and Surveys to produce universe size estimates for panel control purposes and to weight survey results.

Adding up the area panel sizes for the new BARB panel gives 4,435 homes. To this is added 6 per cent to allow for non-response from some households. This gives a total of about 4,700 homes. With an average of 2.56 individuals per household, the sample size of individuals is over 12,000. These individuals aged from 4 upwards are the basis for reporting viewing.

The panel in each area is balanced by size of household, presence of children, age of housewife, presence of working adults, and socio-economic status and educational status of the head of household. These together create a structure that represents stages of the life-cycle, for example, 'pre-family/one-person/ABC1/late terminal education age households', 'pre-family/two person/ABC1/early TEA households', and so on. There are 24 groups in all. Each combination of characteristics is then checked and held in balance for average weight of television viewing.

The development of television set meters was described in Chapter 4 (under electronic recording devices). The current peoplemeter, which is placed in every panel home, is the AGB 4900 model. This records viewing on a second-by-second basis and has the ability to record up to 255 channels as well as the use of the VCR for time-shift viewing. It can track the viewing habits of eight members of any one household, plus up to seven guests. Demographic data on age and sex of the guests are entered via the handset, following prompts on the display screen on the peoplemeter. Viewers are prompted to check that the correct buttons are pressed every 15 minutes while they view in order to maximise the accuracy of the information being recorded.

Access to the audience measurement data is largely electronic, although there is a basic weekly report of the viewing figures. Electronically, there are two databases. Database One contains the original microdata on households; Database Two contains calculated audiences on a 15-minute programme and minute 'spot' basis. Some of the data are available daily (the so-called 'overnight' ratings); others are available only weekly. This is on a rolling basis, nine days after transmission. Data are available in many different forms. Data processing bureaux can provide on-line access or print hard copy following customised client requests. Data may be accessed directly on floppy disc, tape, or CD ROM for companies to analyse the data for themselves.

The new system will give the UK what is probably the most sophisticated and accurate gauge of a nation's viewing habits in the world. Compared with previous systems, the new panel is 50 per cent larger, it is a more efficient sample design, and many more audience groups can be analysed. However, advertising agencies are having to learn new skills in accessing the data in electronic form and in coping with more complicated data. With the rapidly developing use of VCR to time-shift viewing, viewing behaviour is becoming more complex, so there are more ways of measuring ratings. Thus 'consolidated' ratings will consist of ratings achieved at the time of the broadcast plus any ratings accrued to the same programme if it has been recorded on a VCR and played back within a seven-day period. This may sound simple, but the combination and permutation of live and playback ratings with household and guest viewing, adult and child ratings, people viewing only fragments of a playback or zipping chunks of it, or viewing it on several occasions, will facilitate vastly more complex analyses when users require them. However, while advertising agencies have full access to the figures, BARB publishes only the consolidated figures in its press releases. While this attempt to establish the consolidated figures as the main currency for buying commercials gives a bonus to the independent televison companies (since they will be able to charge for the additional playback audiences), the public will no longer know who switches on to see a particular programme.

Qualitative assessment and evaluation of television programmes is undertaken by the BBC's Audience Reaction Service. The data are obtained from a Television Opinion Panel, which is a national panel of individuals with an achieved sample size of about 3,000 respondents per week on which the 13 ITV regions are represented according to size. In addition, there are regional boost panels, making the achieved sample in each region up to 500 respondents. Members of the regional boost panels complete a diary once every four weeks and each region participates on a four-weekly cycle. National panel members, of which there are 4,600, are contacted weekly and, with a response rate of about 65 per cent, give the achieved sample of 3,000. If people do not respond for two or three weeks, they get a letter asking if they wish to continue; otherwise they are dropped. There are 5,400 on the regional boost panels.

Panel controls are similar to those for the BARB panel, but weightings are applied to adjust for biases from over- and under-representation of certain groups amongst those responding. Panellists are given a seven-day booklet running from Monday to Sunday which is in three sections:

- a list of all programmes on a day-by-day basis asking respondents to give a score on a six-point scale for each programme seen (see Figure 7.14),
- more detailed questons are asked about selected programmes. Some of these questions are open-ended; others use Likert-type scales,
- questions about series that have just finished, long-running serials or questions of a more general nature.

From the first section, an Appreciation Index (AI) is calculated. This is done by allocating a score out of 100 in each level of response. The AI is the average of all the responses. Most AIs are between 50 and 90, but they are not absolute numbers; rather they facilitate comparisons. These comparisons are made with programmes of a similar type, for example, 'feature films', 'sport', or 'news and current affairs'. Weekly AI reports list each category separately and are broken down by age, sex and social class.

		ALLOCATE SCORE
6	Extremely interesting and/or enjoyable	100
5	Very interesting and/or enjoyable	80
4	Fairly interesting and/or enjoyable	60
3	Neither one thing nor the other	40
2	Not very interesting and/or enjoyable	20
1	Not at all interesting and/or enjoyable	0

Figure 7.14 The BBC Audience Appreciation Index

The aim is to cover all programmes, but where fewer than 25 responses for a programme have been received, no AI is calculated; if less than 50 responses, separate AIs are not calculated for demographic groups.

It has been found that, overall, there is little correlation between AI scores and audience ratings – bigger audiences do not necessarily mean higher appreciation scores and vice versa. However, Barwise *et al.* (1979) argue that if a distinction is made between information and entertainment programmes, then there is a small positive correlation between audience appreciation and size within these types, but that the correlation between the types is negative. Menneer (1987) argues that there is no reason to expect a relationship, since they measure different things. Audience size for any programme is determined largely by the time of day it is broadcast and what the competing programmes are, irrespective of the quality of the programme. AIs are a crucial and necessary complement to estimates of audience size in evaluating channel and programme performance. AIs also have a useful role in predicting, and later explaining, the audience delivery for a series of programmes.

Radio audience measurement

The UK is unique in Europe, if not in the world, in the extent and scale of radio audience research conducted, at present, separately and independently by the BBC and by Independent Local Radio (ILR). The proportion of gross advertising revenue devoted to audiences for British radio is, in fact, considerably higher than for British television, and higher than elsewhere in Europe. Since there is no commercial advertising on any BBC broadcasts, marketing people are interested mainly in the research conducted for ILR.

Most ILR stations are members of the Association of Independent Radio Contractors (AIRC), a typical trade association which offers its members access to radio audience research, some say in its conduct, and represents the stations on such regulatory matters as performing rights and needle time. The conduct of radio audience research is currently controlled by a Joint Industrial Council – JICRAR. It is an organisation that comprises the Incorporated Society of British Advertisers (ISBA), the Institute of Practitioners in Advertising (IPA), the Association of Media Independents and the AIRC, so the interests of the advertisers, the advertising agencies and the media owners are jointly represented in the specification, supervision and execution of radio audience research. The AIRC, however, plays a dominant role in JICRAR, and the contract for the conduct of the research (currently held by Research Surveys of Great Britain – RSGB) is with the AIRC, not with JICRAR. The research is paid for from the membership subscriptions to the AIRC, which makes no further charge to its members for reports of the research.

EVENING 4.00PM–5.00AM		Radio Clyde 1	Radio Clyde 2	Radio Luxembourg	BBC Radio 1	BBC Radio 2	BBC Radio 3	BBC Radio 4	Local BBC Radio	Any other station	Listened at home	Listened in car	Listened elsewhere.	
Wednesday		07	01	96	91	92	93	94	95	97	X	O	A	
43	4.00– 4.15													43
44	4.15– 4.30	▌									▌			44
45	4.30– 4.45	▌									▌			45
46	4.45– 5.00	▌									▌			46
47	5.00– 5.15	▌									▌			47
48	5.15– 5.30												▌	48
49	5.30– 5.45	▌											▌	49
50	5.45– 6.00				▌								▌	50
51	6.00– 6.15							▌			▌			51
52	6.15– 6.30							▌			▌			52
53	6.30– 6.45							▌			▌			53
54	6.45– 7.00							▌			▌			54
55	7.00– 7.15													55
56	7.15– 7.30													56
57	7.30– 7.45													57
58	7.45– 8.00													58
59	8.00– 8.15													59
60	8.15– 8.30													60
61	8.30– 8.45							▌			▌			61
62	8.45– 9.00													62
63	9.00– 9.15													63
64	9.15– 9.30				▌						▌			64
65	9.30– 9.45			▌										65
66	9.45–10.00			▌										66
67	10.00–10.15			▌										67
68	10.15–10.30			▌							▌			68
69	10.30–10.45			▌									▌	69
70	10.45–11.00			▌									▌	70
71	11.00–11.15			▌									▌	71
72	11.15–11.30			▌									▌	72
73	11.30–11.45													73
74	11.45–12.00													74
75	12.00–12.30													75
76	12.30– 1.00													76
77	1.00– 1.30													77
78	1.30– 2.00													78
79	2.00– 2.30													79
80	2.30– 3.00													80
81	3.00– 3.30													81
82	3.30– 4.00													82
83	4.00– 4.30													83
84	4.30– 5.00													84
		07	01	96	91	92	93	94	95	97	X	O	A	

Have you remembered any listening away from home or in the car?

Figure 7.15 A radio diary page

The allocation of radio frequencies, the licensing of operators, the sale of franchises, and the control of the performance of operators is undertaken by the recently created Radio Authority, a government body that 'owns' the transmission facilities. It took over from the Independent Broadcasting Authority (IBA) in 1991.

For advertising purposes, the radio stations sell listening hours – the number of listeners multiplied by the number of hours per listener. It is to obtain estimates of these figures that the JICRAR survey is undertaken. The survey used to be carried out annually, but in 1987 it went over to continuous fieldwork throughout the year. The problem with this was that the smaller stations had to wait for a year before the accumulated sample size was large enough to make sensible estimates. So in 1989 the system was changed again so that there were four quarterly 'sweeps' of eight weeks each. However, since not every station wanted four lots of research a year, one sweep or 'wave' was to be the universal quarter (undertaken in the spring) in which all members were expected to participate. The other quarters were to be optional, although for the winter quarter the larger stations were expected to take part. The eight-week sweeps, however, it was felt by airtime buyers, were open to abuse since the big stations could still make uncharacteristic promotional efforts during the crucal eight weeks to boost their figures. So, the waves were extended to 12 weeks, making 48 weeks of research in all, but compared with the earlier continuous surveys, the whole thing has to be set up four times a year, with four sets of independent samples and so on. This makes it an expensive operation and there are ongoing debates about the rules of enforced participation.

The population researched for the JICRAR survey is adults aged 15 and over (children are sampled separately) in private households in mainland Britain and the Isle of Wight, plus Northern Ireland, and where these households fall within the broadcasting area (called a Total Survey Area or TSA) for one or more radio stations who are members of the AIRC. This, in fact, covers over 90 per cent of all individuals in private households in the UK and is estimated to comprise about 42.7 million people in all. The boundaries of each TSA are a matter of agreement between the station concerned and the Radio Authority. There are fewer than 50 TSAs in all, but there may be two or more services offered by any one station. Currently, there are over 100 ILR services.

For sampling purposes, each TSA is subdivided into overlap and non-overlap areas and each is separately sampled. The non-overlap area is solus to one station, while there may be several overlap areas each overlapping with different stations. The London TSA, for example, is made up of about 20 such areas.

The minimum sample size for any one TSA is 500 adults if the data are to be published in an AIRC report. This minimum does not apply if the data are to be used only for a station's own purposes. There is no maximum size, which may go up to 2,000 in one TSA. However, a minimum of 800 is required for certain breakdowns. In each overlap and non-overlap area, a number of Electoral Districts (EDs) are selected on the basis of disproportionately sampling those nearer to a centre of population for that TSA, and within each a quota sample is taken. Quotas are based on a six-cell matrix of sex by three employment statuses (full-time, part-time and non-working), but the quota sizes vary depending on the local population structure. The number of EDs is determined by taking the sample requirement for each overlap or non-overlap area (itself done by allocating the contracted sample size for the TSA to these areas on a proportional basis) and dividing by 13 (rounding up to the nearest whole number) to give the number of EDs required as sampling points. The figure of 13 is based on what historically has been needed to give the required number of sampling points, allowing for the normal response rate and the minimum number of sampling points required by the JICRAR specification.

An interviewer is given a listing of all addresses within the ED that he or she is to work, and is asked to select 15 adults aged 15 or over, but meeting the quota requirements for that ED, and persuade them to take a diary for completion. Some 80–90 per cent of the diaries placed are returned. Some people, of course, refuse to take the diary. This procedure is repeated for all stations participating in that quarter. For overlap areas, there may be competing requirements from adjacent stations, but the larger number of sampling points is always drawn.

The diaries placed cover a complete week from Monday to Sunday. The main diary pages feature a double spread per day, pre-printed with a time-grid and column headings listing the stations (see Figure 7.15). The grid runs from 0500 in half-hours to 0600; from 0600 to 1200 midnight in quarter hours, and half hours again to 0500 the next morning. Respondents are asked to indicate their listening to each station by putting a vertical line through all the time slots that relate to the time and station listened to. *Any* listening in a quarter-hour or half-hour period is recorded. The stations printed in the diary are unique to a given non-overlap or overlap area, so there are up to 180 different diary versions. The stations listed cover ILR, BBC network and local stations, and Radio Luxembourg. The listings themselves may be printed in up to four different orders of listing, but complete rotation is not used.

In addition to the stations listened to, respondents are also asked to say where the listening took place ('at home', 'in car' or 'elsewhere'). They are also given space on a last page to write any comments about the content or timing of programmes.

Data from the diaries (which are collected personally by the interviewer), are aggregated, weighted and then grossed up. The weighting and grossing up is done separately for each overlap or non-overlap area using demographic profiles for each. The weights used are the ratios of the population estimates to the achieved samples. These areas are then aggregated to produce estimates at the TSA, region and network levels. In addition to TSA reports, there is a JICRAR requirement to publish data quarterly for the entire ILR network, based on a minimum sample size of 2,000. Regional data, which relate to the aggregation of stations, are published annually.

In the analysis of the results, two key variables are used: reach and average audience. Reach is the number of *different* people listening during a specified time period. It represents the potential group that can be exposed to advertising on a radio station. Average audience is the average number of people listening over a period of time. Thus the total number of different people listening in one or more of the 15-minute time segments in an hour of programme may be greater than the average of the four separate time segments because not everybody will have listened to the whole programme. The data are published in various stages. First the station receives its own figures from the most recent wave; subsequently the sales houses receive them, followed by buyers of airtime.

The BBC, through its Broadcasting Research Department, has since 1939 been taking nationally representative samples of 1,000 people aged 4 and over on a daily basis to ask about their listening 'yesterday'. The Daily Survey, as it is called, uses random location sampling to obtain a fresh sample every day so that 365,000 people are interviewed over the course of the year. There are some 750 interviewers who use aided-recall techniques to take the respondent through their listening in the previous 24 hours. Like the ILR diary, the questionnaire is in 15-minute segments, but unlike the diary, the respondent must have listened at least half of the time (7 minutes) in each segment.

The two systems – JICRAR and the BBC Daily Survey – in fact duplicate each other since they both ask about both ILR and BBC programmes. However, as indicated earlier in the section on diaries, they consistently produce different results. On balance, the diary technique is favoured in those countries where radio research is undertaken with any degree of regularity. Furthermore, although the diary is more expensive than an interview, seven times more information is being collected for a given sample size. Both JICRAR and the BBC currently spend over £1 million annually on their services, so it is not surprising that there are now plans to merge the research operations. From the autumn of 1992 there will be an organisation which is the equivalent of BARB for television called Radio Joint Audience Research (RAJAR), and the research will be based on a weekly diary given to 1,000 respondents. The Daily Survey will be abandoned and JICRAR will vanish. The BBC and the AIRC will be shareholders of RAJAR. The main benefit of the new system is that there will be a common currency in radio audience measurement.

Like BARB, JICRAR – and RAJAR after 1992 – produces figures only on audience measurement, not on audience appreciation of the programmes. The BBC has been obtaining audience reaction to BBC radio networked programmes since 1941 from a listening panel. It does not cover BBC local radio or ILR. The panel consists of 3,000 listeners aged 12 and over who serve for only two years. They are sent a questionnaire each week which lists about 50 programmes and they answer questions only on those programmes they happen to hear – they are not asked to listen specifically. Measurement takes the form of a Reaction Index which is a six-point scale from 'outstanding' to 'poor'. In addition, a number of more detailed issues are explored using Likert-type scales. The panel is balanced according to type of listener, for example, solus Radio 1; Radio 1 plus local/regional ILR. Nine categories are used in all. Names and addresses are supplied by the Daily Survey (and by RAJAR after 1992). Infrequent and light listeners are not recruited to the panel. Radio 4 listeners are oversampled and weighted down in the analysis of the results. Finding Radio 3 listeners is very difficult, so special appeals to join the panel are broadcast from time to time. Since they are unrepresentative, comments made by Radio 3 listeners on the other programmes are not analysed.

In many ways, the measurement of radio audiences is more complex than for television. First, listeners are not always aware of, or correctly identify, the station to which they are listening (for television this is automatically recorded by the peoplemeter). Second, radio listening is often casual and undertaken while other activities are being pursued, or may be just background. Although there are problems over what counts as 'watching' a television, at least presence in the room in which there is a television switched on (and peoplemeter attached) is clearer than 'presence' when a radio can be heard. Third, listeners tend to be mobile – some 20–35 per cent of listening takes place outside the home, often on radios not owned by or tuned in by the listener. This creates problems both for recall and for diary-keeping. Fourth, radio is a highly fragmented and rapidly expanding service. At present there are over 100 programmes. By 1996 there could well be another 30 or so. In addition, there will be up to three Independent National Radio services (which will compete head on with the BBC's networked services). The first of these is due to come on air in the autumn of 1992. Also, by 1996 a block of FM spectrum will become available for ILR, which could, eventually, permit up to 300 more local services. Keeping track of all these developments is rather more complicated than for television channels, even with satellite television. The BBC still has about 60 per cent of all listening, but its share is declining and that of ILR is rising. This will result in further audience fragmentation.

PREDICTIVE TECHNIQUES

Once the problems of an organisation and the circumstances of its competitive environment have been fully diagnosed, managers may wish to generate specific proposals for marketing activity and then predict which ones are likely to be 'best' in terms of fulfilling organisational objectives. They may want to know which ideas for new products are likely to be acceptable to consumers; whether consumers would buy a specific product formulation; whether advertising will convey the right messages linked memorably to the brand; or what sales are likely to result for a new or modified product. There is a panoply of predictive techniques that market research organisations and in-house researchers use, but the remainder of this chapter will focus on just three key techniques:

- testing products and product concepts,
- advertising pre-testing,
- volume and brand share prediction.

Testing products and product concepts

Market research can play a role at many points in the development of new or modified products. Table 7.1 summarises some of the key direct inputs that market research can make at various stages in the process. There will, in addition, be indirect influences from marketing research; for example, marketing and sales personnel may be stimulated to think of new ideas by exposing them to the results of consumer studies; or research and development technicians may be kept aware of consumer needs. Most of the techniques listed in Table 7.1 have already been explained. This section will concentrate on techniques for product concept testing and the testing of the products themselves. Later sections will, in turn, consider advertising pre-testing, and volume and brand share prediction techniques.

Product concept tests

Ideas for product development are evaluated and 'rounded out' using product concept tests. Many companies offer proprietary concept tests, sometimes as part of a wider package which includes product testing and perhaps even with a volume prediction technique bolted on. In product concept testing, ideas about potential new products are exposed to a sample of consumers who are then asked questions about them. The exposure may take a number of forms. These were described earlier in the context of stimulus materials for group discussions and included concept boards, storyboards, animatics, narrative tapes and physical mock-ups.

The sample of respondents from the target market should include anybody likely to have any part in influencing a decision to purchase: it

Table 7.1 Marketing research inputs to product development and testing

Stage	Market research unit
Reviewing company strategy for new product development	Executive interview Business research Usage and attitude studies Corporate image research Market measurement and market segmentation
Idea generation	Qualitative research Market intelligence Usage and attitude studies
Product concept development	Product concept tests Qualitative research Survey research
Product formulation	Product testing Volume and brand share prediction
Marketing strategy	Advertising pre-testing Media audience measurement
Tracking the results	Advertising tracking Market measurement

should not be defined too restrictively. A product developed for a particular market segment, for example, mothers with babies – may be used by other groups (e.g. baby shampoo may be used by adults). The test may be administered in a number of different ways and in different types of location. Thus the test could be:

- in-home by personal call by an interviewer,
- sent by post with a postal questionnaire,
- sent by post with a telephone follow-up,
- in a hall test, van test or test centre.

The concept test may be **monadic** or **comparative**. If there is just one concept to be evaluated, then the test will be monadic. There is a problem here of knowing what counts as a 'good' or a 'bad' result unless comparisons can be made with other concepts similarly tested in the past. Comparative tests may be arranged according to a number of different experimental designs:

- *matched monadic* separate subsamples are given one concept each and the ratings are compared,
- *paired comparisons* getting respondents to compare concepts by expressing a preference in each combination of pairs of concepts,

- *complete ranking* putting all the concepts in order of preference,
- *trade-off or conjoint analysis* respondents are asked to choose between all combinations of product attributes,
- *comparison with existing products* for example, against the current brand leader.

The questions that can be addressed to respondents depend very much on the information needs of the marketing manager. It is usually necessary to ask one or more questions about overall acceptability. This may be by way of simple rating questions, for example, 'Overall, would you describe this product as excellent, good, fairly good, poor or very poor?' or by purchase intention, for example, 'How likely are you to buy this product: very likely, fairly likely or unlikely?' Respondents may be asked if they would actually like to buy the product at a given price. Diagnostic questions may follow up particular aspects, for example:

- understanding the product idea,
- perceptions of its attributes,
- its believability (as a possible new product),
- its perceived advantages and disadvantages,
- its rating on specific product attributes,
- when and how the product might be used,
- how often,
- what products it might replace,
- the sort of people it might appeal to.

Responses to product concept tests may be analysed by counting up the proportion who respond in particular ways, or using some scoring system on the rating scales that enables an average and a measure of dispersion to be calculated. These may then be crosstabulated against demographics, especially age, sex, lifestyle, life-cycle or general attitudes. This may help to pinpoint groups most interested in the concept.

Product tests

The result of the concept test should be to weed out ideas that are non-starters or that compare poorly with other ideas. The ideas remaining may then proceed to product testing, which is the evaluation and development of the products themselves from a marketing point of view. This is different from testing the physical functions of products to ensure that they meet technical and safety standards. Product testing means having a physical product to which a representative sample of target consumers may be exposed under controlled conditions; which they can use under realistic circumstances; and about which they can express their opinion in a structured way.

The designs of product tests vary considerably and the use of any particular procedure by a company is often the result of some historical evolution, habit, or the researcher's or manager's familiarity or comfort with the chosen procedure (Batsell and Wind 1980). Yet different product test designs will give different outputs and different results, so it is necessary to try to establish the most appropriate designs in the circumstances. These circumstances include:

- management information requirements,
- the type of product,
- the type of market,
- cost and time constraints,
- the required comparability across studies.

Management may want a product test to identify the most promising product from a set of candidates under consideration. It may want information that could guide product development to arrive at the best formulation of the product in terms of shape, features, colours, ingredients, materials and so on. It may want to know whether a chosen product idea warrants further investment of time and money. It may want information that would enable it to design a strategy for the introduction of the selected product.

Characteristics of products that are likely to affect the design of testing procedures include:

- the extent to which the product is assessable on the spot,
- the extent to which the product is new to users,
- the extent of information search carried out by consumers in product or brand selection.

Snack-type foods and soft drinks are usually instantly assessable and are suitable candidates for hall tests and van tests. Fragrances (perfumes, eau de toilettes, after-shaves and so on) may also fit into this category. Alcoholic drinks may be too affected by the time of day to be assessable on the spot. Some products either require a longer period of use (for example batteries), or need to be tried out in the home, for example, a cake-mix, a floor polish or a shampoo. Some products cannot be reused (for example, a device for unblocking a sink) or are very complex and require users to familiarise themselves with their operation. Highly innovative products or really new products are not amenable to comparison with other products and this will affect the test design. Low-involvement convenience goods where information search and brand choice behaviour is limited, will require procedures different from high-involvement shopping goods. The former need analysis of the selected circumstances that consumers use in brand choice, while the latter require a close analysis of the importance and evaluation of product features.

Product testing will vary considerably according to type of market. Some markets are highly branded with lots of advertising, in which case the test product may well need to be branded and promoted. If the target market consists of children or elderly people, then their ability to perform certain tasks may need to be taken into account. Product testing in industrial markets or organisational markets will be very different from consumer markets.

Testing procedures vary in terms of the costs involved and how long they take. Some products, like confectionery, do not require extensive testing since they may be tried out in the real market for a period and withdrawn with very little loss if they are not successful. The development of a new model of car, on the other hand, merits considerable expenditure at all stages in the new product development process. Cost and speed may need to be traded off against the reliability or accuracy of the results.

Testing procedures may be affected lastly by the need for comparability across studies. There are advantages to be gained from the standardisation of test procedures across a wide range of products. Researchers will gain more experience of such procedures, the procedures themselves can be refined, performance benchmarks may be established, and the results of different tests are more likely to be comparable.

The key dimensions along which product tests vary and which testers need to decide upon include:

- what kinds of people should act as testers,
- what they are to be asked to do,
- the size of the sample,
- the analysis techniques to be used on the data collected.

The main choices concerning who should act as testers include:

- current users of the brand,
- current users in the product field,
- users in the product field plus potential users,
- a general cross-section of the population.

Decisions about what types of people are most appropriate in the circumstances depend on many factors and it would be difficult to lay down any rules. If a product is completely new, then there can be no current users of the brand; there may even be no comparable product field and the selection may have to be of people who in some way are likely to be favourably disposed to the new product. If the objective of the test is to see if people notice the substitution of cheaper ingredients or components, then only current users of the brand need to be involved in the assessment procedure. If the product has been improved, then users of that type of product currently not using the brand will need to be included in the test to see if they can be persuaded to switch brands or at least to include it in their repertoire. At the same time, sufficient current users of the brand also need to be included to ensure that the changes will not alienate them. For some products, like soap, no amount of improvement will persuade current users to use more, even if they agreed it was a better product, so the focus may be on potential new users. Some products are used by nearly everybody in the population, so a general cross-section may be included in the test. On the other hand, potential users may be a very selected group, for example, a new device to help the blind. If the test is of a product function, like how well it cleans a floor, then it may not matter whether the testers are users or non-users of the brand being researched.

As a general rule, the more restrictions placed on the selection of testers, the more expensive it is to obtain a sample. Thus a sample of the population at large will be cheaper than a sample of users in the product field. The most expensive is usually a sample of users of the brand, since few brands are used by more than 10 per cent of the population.

What testers are asked to do depends on the kind of test. Following Batsell and Wind (1980), we may distinguish four main kinds of test:

- monadic,
- comparative,
- sequential,
- conjoint.

In monadic testing, each person is given just one product to evaluate. This type of testing will tend to be used where the product is completely new, or where the product is a line extension and the client already has backdata on the other products in the range. However, monadic testing may be used to compare several products by dividing a sample of testers into as many groups as there are products to be tested. The scores (whether preference ratings, intention to purchase, degrees of liking, and so on) for the various groups are then compared and subjected to a test of statistical significance. If statistically significant differences emerge, the most promising product (or formulation of a product) is selected for further development.

In comparative testing, testers are given two or more products to compare on the same occasion. It will typically be used where there is a new product formulation. Where there are three or more products or formulations, then evaluation may take the form of paired comparisons, complete ranking, a rating scale for each, or a constant sum of points which is divided between the products by the tester. The advantage of comparative testing is that the comparisons are made directly by individuals rather than by arithmetic comparisons of mean scores. The downside is that comparisons are entirely internal to the set of products being tested, whereas with monadic tests, so it is sometimes argued, comparisons are implicitly being made with all the other brands with which consumers are familiar. Comparisons may be internal to the company's brands, or may be against competitor brands. The former is more likely where there is a formulation change, and the latter if there is a marketing argument to be won, if the client company is losing market share, or if it needs to test the competitors' products anyway.

Sequential testing is comparative, but evaluations are made on different occasions. The tester is asked to try one product, wait a specific period of time, try the second, and then give an opinion. This procedure, so it is argued by its advocates, more closely resembles the way in which consumers actually compare products. However, it does take longer, of course, and is more expensive, particularly where in-home placements are required.

Conjoint analysis focuses on product features and instead of simply identifying the single most promising product, it tries to clarify the relative importance of features, thus providing guidance for the construction of new product formulations.

Other choices facing the researcher in terms of what testers are asked to do include:

- whether the products should be branded or blind,
- whether competitors' brands should be included amongst the products to be tested,
- in comparative tests, in which order the products should be presented,
- whether the test should be on the spot or in use, usually at home,
- which attributes are to be tested,
- the length of time testers are to be given.

The branding of a product is as much part of the total offer as, for example, price, so wherever possible, branded tests will be used. However, they tend to suffer from halo effects, that is, testers tend to respond more favourably to a product they regard as 'their' brand. If the main focus of the test is to obtain reactions to product features or new formulations, then blind tests are probably more appropriate. If, on the other hand, the interest is in likely purchase behaviour or it is a straightforward monadic test, then branded tests should be considered.

The inclusion of competitor brands depends, again, on the objectives of the test. If the focus is on future purchasing behaviour, then they should; otherwise, probably not.

Where products to be compared are very different, then the order in which they are presented makes little difference, but where they are similar, there is a tendency to prefer the product tested first (Day 1969). Some system for rotating the order of presentation will certainly improve the reliability of the tests.

As explained earlier, some products are more amenable to on-the-spot evaluation than others. Where **in-home placement tests** are used, there will usually be a recall interview, either face to face or over the phone, typically using five- or seven-point rating scales. Some clients have their own requirements in terms of scales, wording of scales and show cards that they are used to. Other factors also intervene, for example, the nature of management information requirements, the speed with which results are required, and so on.

Attribute lists are usually managerially derived unless qualitative research has been conducted on consumer perceptions. Managers decide which product features they want evaluated, based on their experience and familiarity with the market or with the results of earlier tests. However, de Chernatony and Knox (1990) argue that product testing is presented predominantly as a mechanistic process with minimal consideration of the underlying assumptions about user behaviour, consumer perceptions or consumer psychology. The authors suggest that consumers interpret products as arrays of cues, and that judgements are based on very limited samples of cues that consumers believe to be indicative of product characteristics (for example, assessing the quality of wrapped bread from the feel of the packaging). In this way, information search is very restricted. If researchers are interested largely in different product formulations, then these cues need to be the focus of the enquiry. For fast-moving consumer goods, particularly, there is limited information search, and researchers should concentrate on the few salient attributes deemed important by the purchaser – this may vary from one purchaser to another. In short, attribute lists should be very short and geared to the product concerned; perhaps even to particular types of consumer. In practice, however, it is unusual to use different attribute lists for different categories of customer. This would have implications for sample size, design and cost.

The length of time testers are to be allowed to use the product is often a problem. The pressures are usually to produce a quick result; at the same time, many products are used infrequently in real life, while opinions do often change after extended use.

In terms of sample size, the cost of a product test increases with the number of testers, but so too do the usefulness and reliability of the results. Below a certain minimum number of testers, the results may be too unreliable to be useful; above a certain number, the addition of more testers will not significantly improve the results. It is difficult to say exactly what these minimum and maximum figures are because a number of factors are involved, for example, the number of products or formulations to be tested, regional variations and so on. However, fewer than 30 testers is likely to be unreliable and more than 1,000 will cease to be cost-effective. Typically, for a straightforward monadic test, a sample size of about 200 would be regarded as adequate. Samples in practice are seldom more than 300 or so.

The procedures used for the analysis of the data from product testing depend in the first instance on the type of test chosen. Product tests designed for absolute evaluation will summarise the data either by counting the proportions who respond in particular ways or by generating scores on the attributes selected for testing and calculating averages. Confidence intervals may be calculated, but are worthwhile only if the selection procedure was random probability from a defined population. Where there are many attributes, then factor analysis on the attribute scores may be carried out. Product tests designed for comparative evaluation will tend to rely on using tests of significance against the null hypothesis (either the t-test for small samples, or the normal distribution for larger ones) on the differences between groups testing different products in monadic tests, or on the differences in mean scores or proportions on product attributes for comparative tests. Because most testers are selected by quota sample, a **design factor** of 1.6–1.7 should be applied, but in practice, this is often not done.

The Taylor Nelson Opti-test

Most market research companies that offer product-testing services customise each test for the client. There are, however, some proprietary techniques. One is Opti-test offered by Taylor Nelson. This offers a structured approach to optimising product formulations for food and drink products and can also be used for home and personal care products. It is based on the idea that while consumers are good at telling you how much they like or dislike a product in general terms, they are not so good at diagnosing why. In fact, any reasons given may bear little relation to actual product ingredient or formulation differences. So, instead of asking consumers about particular product features (for example, 'Do you like the sweetness?'), they are asked simply to say which of two product formulations they prefer. Samples of respondents are given at random a particular combination so that all combinations are tested. Since the manufacturer knows how the products vary, it is possible to work out those combinations of features that maximise preferences. Furthermore, they will know the effect of adding or removing ingredients on preferences in taste and texture terms.

The set-up of the test requires discussion with the client about the different ways in which the product can be made, and what are the key factors that they are able to vary. The result is a matrix of product combinations. An example is illustrated in Figure 7.16. Samples of 30–50 consumers are given each product combination. They are asked to give an overall absolute rating of the products plus an overall preference between the two products. This enables the consumer to say, for example, 'I prefer A to B, but neither is very good.' Testers are, in addition, asked about likes and dislikes, and to rate the product on the more traditional dimensions such as appearance. These are less relevant to the product designers than to creative ad developers, who can see which aspects of the product relate to the brand and the words and phrases used to describe it. **Analysis of**

COLOUR	LIGHT		MEDIUM		DARK	
TEXTURE	FINE	COARSE	FINE	COARSE	FINE	COARSE
SUGAR LEVEL 1	C53 5.24	F48 5.25	R67 5.21	P24 CURRENT PRODUCT 5.00	G29 5.00	A88 4.95
SUGAR LEVEL 2	B37 6.21	M21 6.19	C36 5.28	W55 5.11	H61 5.09	J12 5.10
SUGAR LEVEL 3	Y18 5.75	Q16 5.60	V32 5.46	L45 5.12	N2 5.16	T22 5.00

█ OPTIMUM PRODUCTS

Figure 7.16 Product combinations for Taylor Nelson's Opti-test

variance is used to identify which variables most influence consumer preferences and evaluations, and which product combinations perform best overall. The results can be used to reposition a product, for market segmentation, for cost saving, for new product development, or for fundamental product research to help understand how to improve product formulations.

Burke's COSMOS

A proprietary technique using standard conjoint analysis is that offered by Burke Marketing Research. Called 'COSMOS', it helps in the making of complex marketing decisions in the areas of new product design, optimising existing brands, and managing price strategies. COSMOS I, Concept Designer, looks at the potential for a large number of new product mixes and at each price in order to determine which mix is most likely to attract first-time buyers. COSMOS II, Product Optimiser, is for existing brands, and predicts the likely change in consumer demand for each possible brand modification, and simulates the effect of competitive reactions. COSMOS III, Price Strategist, calculates the change in consumer demand for each possible price scenario and provides the optimal price strategy.

Advertising pre-testing

We have seen how advertising tracking is used to diagnose how well an advertisement has performed and in what ways. Such procedures are sometimes referred to as post-testing. Post-testing provides data on what *has* happened, while pre-testing influences what *will* happen. It is an activity that takes place before resources are fully committed, and provides data on the likely outcomes of marketing initiatives so that a decision can be taken:

- to go or not to go with a particular idea or product,
- to modify the idea or product to improve its likely performance,
- to select the best of a number of ideas or products.

Advertising pre-testing takes place either before an ad is printed or put on air, or just after initial screening. It may be designed to weed out those ads that are unlikely to work, to select the best of the remaining candidates for creative advertising development, to predict the performance of the ads chosen, to provide early feedback, or to make last-minute changes to the ad. Pre-testing of advertising has long been associated with the use of qualitative research, but in recent years there has been a growing demand for quantified predictions of likely future performance in real conditions before the costs of screening or printing ads are incurred.

The precise measures used in quantitative advertising pre-testing are closely related to implicit or explicit theories about the way in which advertising works. The traditional model, of which there are a number of versions (see Crimp 1990: 181–6 for a succinct review), suggests that consumers begin by becoming aware of a product or brand, formulating some attitude towards it or image of it, generating a desire to try it, and finally purchasing it. Figure 7.17 illustrates the process.

The result has been a debate not only over the techniques to be used to measure each of these, but over whether awareness, attitudes, image or desire to try should be the focus of pre-testing measures. One school of thought argues that, clearly, the nearer you take your measurement to the actual act of trial or purchase, the better will be the prediction. However, this sequence of events has been questioned, and it has been suggested, for example by Brown (1991b), that attitudes and images of products and brands are more likely to be formed *after* purchase, so the sequence becomes that illustrated in Figure 7.18.

If this is the case, it is inappropriate to base pre-testing on the measurement of attitudes or images; the best measures must be based on awareness and stated intention to buy or to try. Attitudes towards and images of the products and brands may influence the subsequent repurchase pattern, and this may involve brand switching or inclusion in a brand repertoire, either of which may be with varying numbers of repurchase occasions and lengths of purchase cycle.

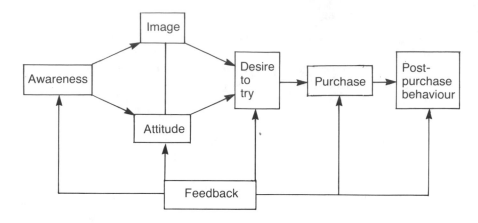

Figure 7.17 A traditional model of consumer behaviour

While, as we have seen, it is perfectly possible to measure advertising awareness in tracking studies by asking people to recall the brands and the advertising they have seen, in pre-testing, once you have shown people an ad in a hall or in a van, you cannot within a few minutes start asking them about ad and brand awareness and whether they recall which brand the ad was for. The traditional solution has been to substitute the 'stand out' value of an ad as a predictor of future recall or awareness. In a reel test, a sample of maybe 50–100 respondents are shown a mock-up of an ad in a reel of six or ten ads (which may be in printed form or on a video). The test ad has to compete for attention with ads for similar or related product fields. These ads may be for competing products or they

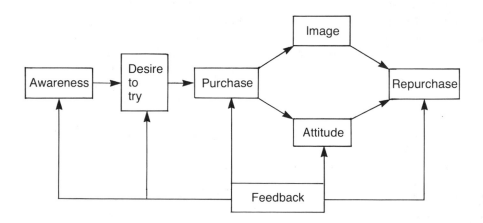

Figure 7.18 An alternative model of consumer behaviour

may be other versions of an ad for the same product. Respondents are then asked which ads they noticed or recalled, both unprompted, then prompted. Respondents may be asked which ads they liked most and least, and their attention is then gradually focused on to the test ad and recall of its content or theme. Generally, either the test ad will be in a fixed position in the reel, for example, sixth in a reel of 10, or the order may be rotated.

The results of such reel tests, however, have been shown (for example, by Brown 1991a) not to tie in well with subsequent measures of awareness in tracking studies. The development of more sophisticated ways of pre-testing advertisements by market research agencies have taken one of two directions: making measures of pre-test recall more sophisticated, or abandoning the idea of recall altogether. Both Research International and Burke Marketing Research have taken the former route.

Research International's Publitest

Research International has combined quantitative measurements from reel tests with qualitative diagnostics in a technique it calls Publitest. Advertising increasingly needs to appeal to the more non-rational and emotional reactions to brands and their advertising. This means considering advertising taking place amongst consumers with established ideas and expectations. The procedure begins with the standard reel or folder test with a sample of about 100 respondents in a hall. They are shown a video containing the test ad, and impact is measured by seeing what they can recall. They are then shown the test ad again and asked a series of open-ended diagnostic questions concerning respondent first impressions of the ad, the messages conveyed, the understanding of what is happening, its commercial appeal, the image that respondents have of the brand, what they liked and disliked, and their intention to buy. Usually there is a control sample who are shown simply the brand logo, or just a picture of the pack. The difference between the test and the control group shows what the ad can do beyond simply showing people the brand – otherwise there is little point in spending a lot of money on a commercial. In addition, Publitest provides the option of further depth interviews among separately recruited target group respondents to look at branding, advertising claims and emotional involvement. These factors are analysed in the context of the brand's advertising heritage, the competitive context, and its position in the product life cycle.

Burke's Ad-Visor

Burke Marketing Research offers a refinement of the pre-test recall technique and adds two further measures it calls 'persuasion' and 'diagnostics' into the prediction equation. Burke had already developed a recall

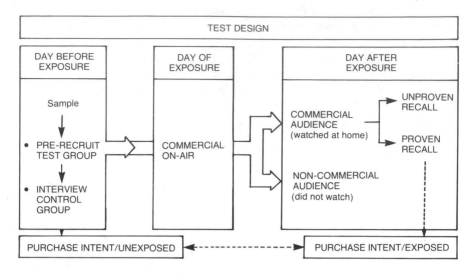

Figure 7.19 Burke Ad-Visor test design

technique for on-air advertising by measuring day-after recall (DAR) rather than using a reel test. In a new proprietary advertising pre-testing technique called 'Ad-Visor', Burke invites a representative sample of consumers who have already indicated that they would watch a particular programme to view a particular slice of an evening's television schedule at home. Viewing is thus in a natural viewing situation. No particular reference is made to the advertising. The test commercial is screened within this specified period. Recall interviews are conducted the next day by telephone.

In addition, responses from a control group sample are collected the day before screening – so they cannot possibly have seen the ad. Both those unexposed to the commercial and those who demonstrate proven recall of the ad are asked their purchase intent in relation to the test brand. The difference between these two measures gives an indication of the persuasive value of a commercial. The test design is shown in Figure 7.19.

Using data from Burke's BASES (see next section), the raw consumer responses are modelled into realistic purchase probabilities. The difference in purchase probabilities between consumers exposed and unexposed to the commercial gives what Burke call its Persuasion Index. This is expressed as a percentile position against all other commercials, so it is not just giving a score, but is related to all the other commercials that have been tested. A persuasion model takes account of the impact of environmental influences, such as cultural differences, the structure of the market, brand age and distribution. More than 100 experiments in five different European markets were conducted to parametise the model. Together, recall and persuasion give an effective evaluation of advertising. They are independent parameters and are not necessarily correlated – both could be high or low for the same commercial, so both are required.

Further diagnostic information from those exposed to the ad is added to help explain the recall and persuasion measures achieved. A series of eight open-ended questions probe details of content recall, messages communicated, and specific likes and dislikes. A battery of attitude statements measures perceptions of relevance, involvement, interest, conviction, originality, clarity and appeal.

Ad-Visor thus tests after the first on-air screening, but before all the campaign is put behind it, and before all the media time is booked. Strictly speaking, Ad-Visor is not a 'pre-test'; neither is it a 'post-test' in the sense of market tracking, but lies somewhere between the two. While Ad-Visor entails having a finished ad, it does accurately measure impact – the number of consumers being reached with the commercial. This cannot be done with the standard reel test – the commercial needs to be actively going on air with people sitting there watching it in their own homes. It also means that it is possible to measure, in addition to impact, how much people are being persuaded by the ad, what messages the commercial is communicating, and whether or not the brand name is being accurately related to the advertisement.

Millward Brown's Link

While Research International and Burke Marketing Research have relied on refining the pre-test recall technique, Millward Brown, having found that the correlation between reel tests and its own Awareness Index was less than 0.5 on over 300 tests, decided to try a different approach. By looking at a large number of ads that worked and those that did not in terms of tracking measures, four key factors of a successful advertisement were identified:

- it draws attention to the ad,
- people enjoy watching it,
- it is easy to follow,
- there is a strong link between the advertising and the brand.

These factors form the basis of a new advertising pre-testing procedure called 'Link'. A sample of 150 respondents is shown the test ad along with four other commercials to provide a context. They are then asked to rate the ad of one of the other four commercials as a warm-up and to act as a benchmark. The four factors are measured on four- or five-point rating scales. Thus attention-getting is measured on a four-point scale in response to the question 'How much will this ad make you pay attention each time you see it?' The responses go from 'It will definitely make me pay attention' through 'probably', 'probably not', to 'definitely not' pay attention. Enjoyment is on a five-point scale from 'I'll enjoy watching it a lot' to 'I won't enjoy watching it at all'. Ease of following is on a four-point scale from 'very easy' to 'very hard' to follow, and the link on a five-point scale from 'Nearly everyone will notice the ad is for (brand X)' to 'People will probably not realise what it is advertising at all.'

Respondents are then asked to rate the test ad using the same scales. The results are then corrected for the halo effect, that is, the more enjoyable ads tend to be rated too highly on the other three scales, so these are corrected using responses to the enjoyability rating. The results of these key ratings are then used in a empirically derived model which makes a prediction of the likely Awareness Index. Comparison with subsequent tracking results shows that this prediction is at least as good as the earlier reel test. This prediction, however, is further refined in two ways. First, a subset of 100 of those who have undertaken the first stage is questioned about the content of the ad, their comprehension of it, and their likes and dislikes. This facilitates a qualitative evaluation of whether the main focus of the ad is successfully linked to the brand, and whether it has been understood in the way the advertisers intended. If, for example, the ad has been misunderstood, a subjective down-rating to the predicted Awareness Index can be made.

Second, another sub-group of 75 respondents (who may be a subset of those from the first stage, but not the second) are shown a video tape of the ad, and they record their own subjective level of interest while the ad is being shown by moving a lever on a machine which captures electronically the level of interest on a second-by-second basis. The responses of respondents are aggregated and plotted out on hard copy. Ideally, interest should be high when the brand is being mentioned. If it falls away every time this happens, the key features of the ad are not being successfully linked to the brand. The video is stopped at various points and respondents are asked to point to the place on the screen where they were looking. The point is electronically captured as crosses that are overlaid on the still. This may show, for example, that most people are not looking at the point on the screen where the brand is being shown.

By adding in judgement from these qualitative elements, Millward Brown has improved the correlation between the pre-tests and subsequent Awareness Index to 0.9. Furthermore, such qualitative elements provide a diagnosis about *why* an ad is likely or unlikely to generate the required awareness. Thus it could well be that the main thing that stands out in an ad is unlinked to the brand. Each element of the ad may then be separately diagnosed and the likely messages that will be communicated may be predicted. Link essentially is taking the ad to bits to understand the structure of it, to see whether the parts that are supposed to be linking it with the brand and getting the message over are, in practice, going to work.

While advertising pre-testing procedures such as those described above give an evaluation of ads in terms of impact and communication, they cannot be used as a basis for making any prediction of sales that will eventuate. To do that, special techniques have been developed, and it is to these that we now turn.

Volume and brand share prediction

The track record of market research in predicting new product successes or failures has not, until recently, been good. Various empirical studies have shown that between 60 per cent and 97 per cent of new products, whether innovative, line extensions or relaunches of modified products, fail to achieve company objectives. A lot depends, however, on the particular industry. For UK food manufacturers, Ramsay (1982) estimated that only 3–4 per cent of new food brands are successful.

It may be argued that this situation is largely a result of lack of research (or lack of attention to the results of research) rather than of inadequate research, but a lot of market research *has* been carried out on behalf of new products, yet the identification of product failure has still been limited. Traditionally, two main approaches to the prediction of the share of market and sales volume that would be achieved by new products have been used:

* the screening and evaluation of attitudes to new products in product and product concept tests,
* test marketing.

Attitude measurements in product tests that produce a rating on a five- or seven-point scale have, on the basis of past experience, been insufficient to allow accurate predictions to be made about future sales. Just because a high percentage of a sample of respondents say they like a product, or say they will buy it, or say it is good value for money (or all three), does not mean that people in general will necessarily try it; or if they do try it, that they will buy it again. There are many other factors that need to be taken into account before such predictions are possible.

As was explained in Chapter 5 in the section on exploratory research, test marketing has, over the years, fallen out of favour. Even attempts to offer mini-test markets, such as that run by Research International, and which proved a unique success for over 20 years, were finally abandoned.

A number of market research agencies began looking at the possibility of laboratory test markets that would simulate a shop as part of a hall test. Others developed the use of concept tests and product tests in which samples of respondents were given statements about the proposed new products on a concept board or, at a later stage, given a mock-up or actual product to try, either on the spot or to take home. Such tests have been used for a long time, but they only gave a score on one or more rating

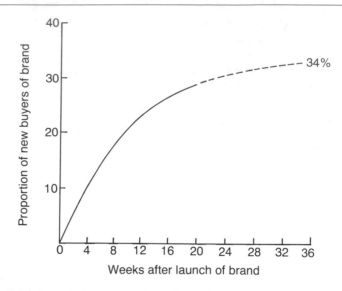

Figure 7.20 Cumulative penetration of brand

Source: Adapted from Parfitt and Collins, 1968

scales, and could not be used to make specific predictions about sales. However, mathematical modelling techniques began to be applied to 'interpret' the answers given in such tests. The idea was to build up a prediction of sales based on the number of people who would try the new products, and the number who would subsequently repurchase. Trial and repeat purchase became the two ingredients that were common to all subsequent attempts at simulated test marketing.

The Parfitt and Collins model

One of the earliest models to use these concepts was developed by Parfitt and Collins (1968). It was not, strictly speaking, a simulated test marketing model, but a market performance evaluation model that used existing consumer panel data from the early weeks of a product launch to predict the eventual market share that would be achieved. Their model was based on estimates of three key variables:

- cumulative penetration,
- repeat purchase rate,
- buying rate index.

Cumulative penetration is a measure of trial and is based on the cumulative growth over time in the number of individuals (or households, as appropriate for the product) who have purchased the brand (irrespective of

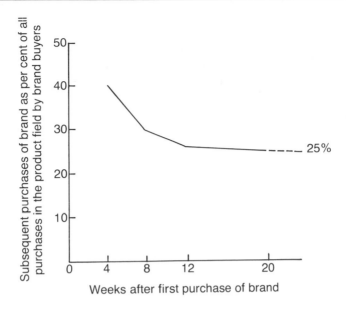

Figure 7.21 Repeat purchasing rate for brand

Source: Adapted from Parfitt and Collins, 1968

the frequency or quantity of such purchases), expressed as a proportion of the total number of buyers in the product field. This proportion will tend to level out after a number of weeks when there are no new buyers. Once the shape of the curve is determined, it is possible to make an estimate of the ultimate likely market penetration. Thus from Figure 7.20 it is estimated that 34 per cent of individuals will eventually have made a purchase after 36 weeks, based on the pattern of purchasing in the first 20 weeks.

The repeat purchase rate is a measure which combines adoption and frequency of purchase and is the extent to which buyers purchase a new brand again. It is expressed as a proportion of the number of all purchases for the product field represented by repeat buyers of the brand being studied. The repeat purchase rate will normally decline and level off. Again, this can be estimated in advance. From Figure 7.21, for example, it is estimated that, eventually, 25 per cent of all purchases in the product field will be by repeat buyers of the brand.

The buying rate index is the rate of total product field purchases of the buyers of a brand compared with the average of all buyers in the product field. Thus if buyers of the brand under investigation have an average propensity to buy the product at a particular rate, the buying rate index will be unity.

Predicted brand shares are obtained by multiplying these components together. Thus if a newly launched brand of toilet soap reaches a cumulative penetration estimated to be 34 per cent of all buyers of toilet soap, and the proportion of total purchases of toilet soap bought by repeat buyers of the brand in successive weekly intervals levels out at 25 per cent, then the predicted brand share will be 25 per cent of 34 per cent, or 8.5 per cent, provided that new purchasers have an average buying rate.

There are three key problems with the original Parfitt and Collins model. First, purchase data from consumer panels over several weeks are required before a prediction can be made. In other words, brand shares can be estimated only after market entry and the decision to launch the product has been taken. Second, the prediction is of brand shares rather than sales volume. The problem with brand shares, particularly in ill-defined markets, is that it all depends on how a 'product field' is defined. Thus does 'toilet soap' include liquid soap, hand cleansers, facial scrubs and so on? In short, brand share of what? Third, there were no built-in parameters that could be used as weightings to simulate different estimates based on different inputs or different assumptions.

The models that followed developed in different directions. Some continued to use data collected after market entry and were concerned primarily with evaluating test market results. Others tried to tackle the problem of establishing likely sales before launch, and either developed simulated store techniques or based results on product and product concept tests. Some stuck to predicting market shares, others developed prediction of sales volumes. Most models added in inputs from management on their assumptions or proposals about distribution, advertising, promotional activity and brand awareness, plus inputs that relate to marketplace variables like number of competitor brands, seasonality, or geographical differences.

Research International's SENSOR

An example of an early simulated store technique is that developed by Research International which it calls SENSOR. In this, a sample of individuals is recruited to be representative of users in the product field that the new product is entering. In a hall test, respondents are shown advertising of the test product (placed in the middle of a reel of other products in the field) in order to generate awareness. The respondent is taken to a simulated shop containing the test product along with other brands. The respondent is given coupons, typically covering the prices of all the items in the display, and is asked to make a purchase.

If respondents buy the test brand, they can then take it home to try for a specified time period before being reinterviewed and given the opportunity to purchase the test brand with their own money. They will normally be asked to allocate preference points between the test brand and other brands in their repertoire, and they may be asked about the frequency and quantities of their purchasing in the product field.

Trial is estimated from purchasing observed in the simulated shop (downweighted using projected awareness and distribution figures supplied by the client). The numbers repurchasing with their own money and the preference scores in the reinterviews are used to provide estimates of the likely levels of repeat purchase. Purchase frequency and quantities purchased will be derived from answers to questions about the product field as a whole.

Burke's BASES

The problem with the simulated store approach is that the research needs to be conducted using finished products, packaging and advertising, which involves considerable time and cost. An alternative is to dispense with the simulated point-of-sale element and establish estimates of trial and repeat purchase from survey questions in a consumer survey or in a hall test. These questions might cover:

- intention to purchase,
- product evaluation,
- perceived value for money,
- claimed purchase frequency,
- average number of units purchased,
- competitive/substitute product usage.

Answers to these questions are then entered into a mathematical model containing experimentally derived weighting factors to arrive at estimates of trial, repeat purchase, sales volumes and market shares.

The most long-lived and commercially successful of these models was that developed by Burke Marketing Research. Called BASES, it was launched in the UK in the mid-1970s. The model was from the outset a volume prediction model and based on a monadic test. Respondents are not asked to compare the test product with other brands in the test itself. It is argued by supporters of this model that it is better for the respondents to evaluate products within their own frames of reference, particularly their own competitive set of brands. In evaluating the test product, respondents are, in any case, implicitly comparing it with the products they normally use and in situations in which they normally use them. Comparative tests, by contrast, tend to impose a comparison set. Furthermore, in some markets it may be difficult to put together a comparative set: for example, it is diffi-cult to know what competes with Perrier – soft drinks, milk, fruit juice, or tap water? It may, in addition, be argued that monadic tests allow you to *ask* the respondent which brands the test product would be competing against, enabling some calculation to be made of source of volume.

The model was originally set up by taking about 80 different new products, interviewing people before the product was launched, and then tracking their subsequent purchasing behaviour using consumer panels. This enabled answers concerning purchase intention and so on to be 'interpreted' and corrected for overclaiming and underclaiming. The result was a series of weighting factors that were built into a mathematical model that has subsequently been refined and improved as the results of more studies have become available. Burke Marketing Research now has about 8,000 cases on its database.

The two key measures in the BASES model are trial rate and repeat rate. The trial rate is measured by market penetration – the proportion of the total market who buy the brand being researched at least once. The repeat rate is the proportion of trialists who repeat buy. The trial rate is estimated in a standard concept or product test in which consumers are asked both before trial and after trial if they:

- definitely would buy,
- probably would buy,
- might or might not buy,
- probably would not buy,
- definitely would not buy.

For the trial rate, the *pre-trial* intention to buy is used. However, this statement of purchase intent always produces a degree of overclaiming, that is, not all consumers who say they will buy the brand will actually do so in a given period of time. The proportion who, from the historical database of previous predictions, actually did make a purchase in each of the response categories is then used as a weighting for each response in the actual test. Thus if 40 per cent of respondents who answer 'probably would buy' are found subsequently to make a purchase, then for the product being tested, if 10 per cent give this response, then 40 per cent of 10 per cent (4 per cent) of those in that response category will, it is predicted, actually buy. Estimates for each response can then be added together.

The calibration from intention to actual purchase is strongly affected by many factors, for example, type of product, the cultural (particularly national) background, the unit price, and the age of the consumer. Thus teenagers generally overclaim more than adults; Italians and Spaniards are more likely to overstate than Germans. Using this statistical calibration, the correlation between statement of purchase intent and subsequent actual purchase has been improved to over 0.9. The trial rate estimate is based on this adjusted probability of trial, taking account of clients' estimates of weighted distribution build, advertising plan or brand awareness estimates (which may be from an earlier usage and attitude study), promotional activity and seasonality.

Besides intention to purchase, consumers in both the pre- and post-trial tests are asked about:

- intended frequency of purchase,
- purchase quantities,
- degree of liking,
- product evaluation,
- perceived value for money,
- substitute/competitive usage.

Degree of liking is on a six-point scale: four of the points are positive, one neutral and one negative. Perceived value for money is on a five-point scale from very good value down to very poor value.

Repeat rate is estimated from the number who are still favourably disposed towards the brand after the trial. Favourability is estimated by using multiple non-linear regression techniques based on a combination of intention to purchase *post-trial* (again suitably downweighted for over-claiming), degree of liking score, and perceived value-for-money score. The conversion rates post-trial tend to be more stable than pre-trial ones. Purchase cycle is based on after-use intended purchase frequency among after-use favourable respondents, adjusted for overstatement and the build of the trial curve.

To obtain estimates of future sales volume (S_t) at time t (the number of weeks since retail availability) the BASES model adds a predicted trial volume (T_t) to a predicted repeat volume (R_t), that is:

$$S_t = T_t + R_t$$

Trial volume, T_t is estimated by taking the cumulative trial rate over the period between now and time t, multiplying by the target market size (the number of households in the target market area) and the purchase quantity (the average amounts purchased at trial). An adjustment is made for trial rate build-up over the year. Repeat volume is estimated from first repeat volume plus second repeat volume plus third repeat volume ... nth repeat volume. The first repeat volume is derived by multiplying the number of triers by the first repeat rate (the number of consumers repeating at least once) and the average quantity. The second repeat volume takes the number of first repeaters and multiplies by the second repeat rate (the number of consumers repeating at least twice) and the average quantity. Subsequent repeat volumes are calculated in a similar manner. The model also builds in a decay rate for people who stop buying after a number of repeats.

The result of applying the BASES procedure, then, is to produce separate estimates of:

- sales volume,

Table 7.2 Example of output from Burke's BASES

	Plan 1	Plan 2	Plan 3	Plan 4
Awareness (%)				
Year 1	33	35	35	35
Year 2	40	40	35	35
Distribution (%)				
Year 1	50	45	40	35
Year 2	60	55	50	45
Cumulative trial (%)				
Year 1	20	18	15	13
Year 2	27	24	22	19
Sales (000 units)				
Year 1	245	217	210	163
Year 2	565	370	330	270

- trial rate,
- repeat purchase rate,
- purchase cycle.

The output might look like Table 7.2, which shows different estimates of year 1 and year 2 trial and sales volume, depending on the assumptions that are made about awareness and distribution. This shows that getting a 60 per cent distribution by year 2 is crucial for lifting sales. Such tables also enable clients to ask varying 'What if ... ?' questions. Estimates of repeat purchase rates can also be particularly helpful in gauging the overall likely success of the product, since in practice these are related (see Figure 7.22).

BASES, like other similar models that were developed at the time, reconstructs the data that would be provided by a consumer panel, but from a two-stage, before-and-after trial data collection exercise, within a short space of time and before the product is launched – it may be a new product, a line extension or a relaunch. Models like BASES were originally used to make go/no-go decisions, but nowadays are increasingly used to determine optimum launch policies. Thus if there is a good trial rate, then the focus needs to be on getting repeat.

Burke Marketing Research has developed a family of BASES procedures. BASES I is just the front-end concept test which provides an estimate of year 1 trial based on samples of 200–300 respondents. BASES II is the full model as described above and incorporates BASES I to provide estimates of repeat purchase and volume sales in addition to trial. Year 2 and year 3 estimates can also be made, but BASES II requires a product mock-up for respondents to try. BASES IV is essentially a tracking operation for a product in test market or national launch in its early stages.

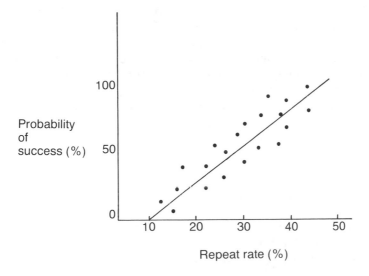

Figure 7.22 Repeat rate and probability of success

Standard tracking data are collected on awareness, purchase behaviour and intention to buy. This enables longer-term predictions to be made.

BASES LX is for product line extensions. These are more difficult types of launch to test because it is necessary to take account of brand heritage dilution and cannibalisation. Experience and data from the Burke database show that line extensions give higher levels of awareness and have better conversion rates from awareness to trial and from trial to repeat. BASES LX first divides the line extension into one of five types:

*   adding new flavour or variety,
*   adding a new size or pack format,
*   moving the brand name into a new sub-category,
*   moving the brand name into a new category,
*   moving the company name into a new category.

Each of these has different implications for awareness and ghost purchasing intent, and each needs a different test design. A source of volume analysis shows the likely extent of cannibalisation – the sales that are likely to be taken from the parent brand.

Novaction's forecasting systems

While the BASES models are monadic, predict volume, and are dependent on normative data from consumer panel operations or past databases in parallel markets in order to parametise models, a completely different approach is taken by Novaction, which uses comparative testing, predicts market shares as well as sales volumes, and does not require normative data. Products are tested in comparison with existing brands, so information is collected on the competing brands as well as on the test brand. This means that data are built up for each market to provide a large experience database so that tests can be customised for each market.

Like all simulated test market models, the key focus is on trial and repeat purchase. However, while the BASES systems take awareness as an assumption based on client input, the Novaction system models awareness and makes a prediction based on:

- the support which is to be offered to the brand in terms of advertising spend (or television ratings),
- the distribution levels likely to be achieved,
- the level of proposed promotional activity,
- the type of branding (new brand or line extensions of various types),
- the likely advertising and packaging impact,
- the concept quality and uniqueness,
- the purchase cycle.

Data on support and brand type come from the client, while the rest are derived from diagnostic questions addressed to samples of the target market, for example, on advertising recall, beliefs about the brand, understanding, likeability, relevance, differentiation and intent to buy. The effect of each of these factors is weighted in an awareness model using parameters derived from the experience database. The projections may then be compared with client forecasts or assumptions about awareness to see if they are reasonable.

Novaction argues that four factors are critical to marketing success:

- impact,
- differentiation,
- total quality,
- value.

Impact, which is measured from total brand recall and shelf visibility, is the brand's capacity to create strong identification with the target consumer. It derives from advertising, packaging and the branding environment. To what extent, for example, does advertising create interest in the brand and brand identity? How far does packaging have impact, shelf stand-out and distinctiveness? Is it a new brand name or a line extension? Other things being equal, there will be a *lower* awareness and impact for a line extension than for a new brand – a finding contrary to that of Burke Marketing Research, but Novaction's awareness is discounted for 'ghost' awareness, that is, people claiming awareness of products that do not exist. However, it is also true that other elements to a line extension's marketing mix can offer an enhancement by the halo effect of the parent brand.

Table 7.3 Importance of critical success factors

Critical success factor	Score	Per cent of brands that meet company objectives
Impact	High	65
	Medium	39
	Low	23
Differentiation	Radically different	67
	Very different	55
	Similar	26
Total quality	High	78
	Medium	28
	Low	15
Value	Superior	88
	Medium	43
	Inferior	11

Differentiation is the uniqueness of the brand compared with the competition as seen by the consumer. Key factors here are the proposition or claim in the advertising, brand image or personality being projected, positioning and product performance.

Total quality is the brand's image and performance to the consumers and includes the quality of concept relevance to the consumer and the perceived performance of the product. The first of these affects trial and the second affects repeat. Value is the total quality that is delivered at the price. The evaluation of a brand's performance on the four marketing factors are part of what Novaction calls its IDQV system.

Each of the four factors has been shown from the experience database to be critical to success (see Table 7.3, which shows success outcomes on average for those brands achieving high, medium and low scores on the success factors). All brands are evaluated on the four factors to diagnose performance, and for the purpose of running simulations to show, for example, what will happen if you take the brand to a higher level of impact or differentiation. A brand may not do exceptionally well on all four factors yet may still succeed, but if it is mediocre on all four or doing badly on a couple, the chances of success are remote.

The importance of these factors for any one brand depends on the state of the development of the market, the quality of existing offers, and existing price levels. Thus in a relatively underdeveloped market, the most important factor will be impact, because the relative quality and value are less important. In a developed market, it is necessary to evaluate the strength and performance of existing brands on the market. This is what one of the Novaction systems – DETECTOR – does: it scans markets to assess what the opportunities are. It evaluates sales potential for a given entry strategy or marketing mix. Clients fill in a questionnaire on their market. It asks them about the proposed branding strategy and how it is going to be supported in the market. Sometimes the information in the questionnaire is sufficient to see how much room there is in the market and what the marketing action standards need to be. Sometimes it is necessary to do full consumer tests.

DETECTOR uses a sales model based on assessments of penetration and long-term repeat. Penetration is a product of awareness, distribution and initial trial. The penetration model is outlined in Figure 7.23. This shows that the probability of a consumer being aware of a brand and the probability of finding it on the shelves is a function of brand support, branding strategy and market status. Market status, in turn, is judged from the degree of market development, the purchase cycle, the status of the current offer, and the degree of market fragmentation – how many brands account for 80 per cent of total volume, how big the brand leader is, and how big is the number two brand. The probability of buying the new brand, when a person is aware of it and has found it, is affected also by the brand

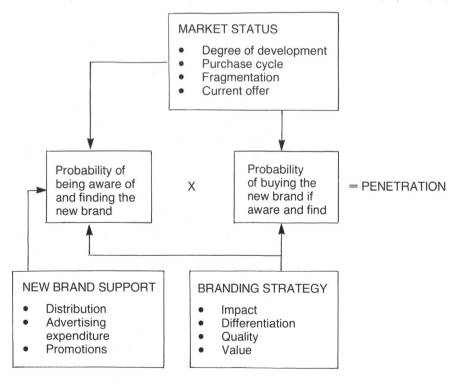

Figure 7.23 Novaction's Penetration Model

strategy and market status. Long-term repeat is a combination of the number of people who will repeat, the repeating interval, and what the usage rate will be. These are determined from the branding strategy and market status. In short, the sales potential for any entry strategy is, for a given market, determined by the support given to a brand, the market status and the branding strategy. All have an impact on market penetration and repeat purchase. Precisely what that impact is can be determined from the analysis of the market status and the weightings in the model, which are market specific.

Besides the DETECTOR system, Novaction also offers three other models called DESIGNOR, PERCEPTOR and ALLOCATOR. DESIGNOR gives consumers actual shopping opportunities in a simulated store and incorporates a higher level of modelling, including preference modelling, which gives greater precision and robustness. The system also allows a separation between triers and non-triers, the repeaters and non-repeaters. This facilitates digging further into understanding why people do or do not try a product. Its use is more for fine-tuning a mix than for understanding what targets should or should not be.

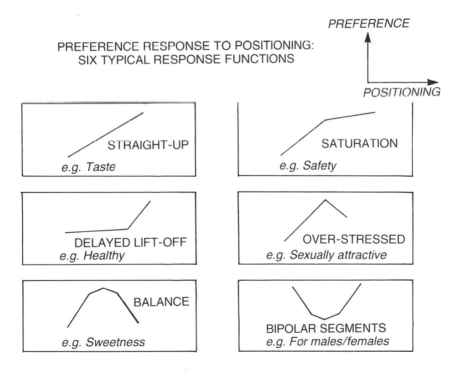

Figure 7.24 Novaction's Preference Analysis

PERCEPTOR collects preference data as well as ratings on image attributes. It determines the broad perceptual discriminants or dimensions consumers use to distinguish between brands, and the relative importance of these discriminants. Its focus is on product development and generating the right branding and positioning policies based on consumer perceptions and viewpoints. Preferences can be plotted against positioning to show how preferences change according to each dimension (see Figure 7.24). Thus, for taste, the stronger your position, the more preferences will be accorded to the product, while on safety, there are diminishing returns. It is also possible to calculate how much preference is explained by each dimension.

ALLOCATOR is designed to improve brand profitability by optimising the use of allocated marketing resources for both new and established brands by using an analysis of the critical success factors to isolate and measure the effects on sales of each major component of the marketing mix.

The Novaction systems thus combine models of consumer behaviour with an experience database and marketing principles to engage in what it calls 'brand engineering' – making a brand work harder in its market. It is one thing to predict what will happen given certain input variables, it is another to take the present plans or scenarios and to improve them by finding a better marketing mix. In other words, it is engineering a better performance both from new brands and from existing brands. It is a system that diagnoses what is wrong with a brand and how best to rectify it. For a new brand, it may be a question of how to maximise trial, and then how to maximise repeat purchase. The evaluation of an entry strategy will depend on the stage reached by the client is in the process of new product development, for example:

- pre-evaluation,
- concept evaluation,
- product evaluation,
- advertising evaluation,
- final mix evaluation.

The predictions made by Novaction systems are of both market share and sales volume. However, it is share of usage occasions rather than of sales in a product category (as was the case with the original model, ASSESSOR) on which the Novaction systems were originally based. Novaction establishes what the brand is going to be used for, how often these usage occasions occur, and how the market segments by levels of usage. The model provides share of occasions when something is needed to solve a particular problem, so it may not necessarily be of branded goods but may, for example, be of tap water. What needs to be established is with what a product may be competing and how well it will do in that context – that is, in what environment it will be operating.

Research International's MicroTest

Most of the volume and brand share models are 'macro' models in the sense that they aggregate answers of respondents on a question-by-question basis, and analyses are performed on the totals. An alternative, however, is 'micromodelling', which makes a prediction on an individual-by-individual basis by looking at the pattern of responses to a number of questions, putting them into a computer algorithm, and coming up with a probability that that person will try and subsequently adopt the product or brand under investigation.

Research International has developed a micromodelling technique it calls MicroTest, launched in 1987. This uses a simple product concept test amongst a sample of the target population to predict trial. Respondents then take the product home, try it, and are subsequently reinterviewed and questioned about product acceptability. MicroTest is a volume prediction model based on predicting, individual by individual, the probabilities of trial, adoption, frequency of purchase, and quantity per occasion. Trial and adoption are modelled separately. The trial model includes three key factors:

- the predisposition on the part of the consumer to experiment with new products,
- the acceptability of the new product concept to the respondent,
- the visibility of the brand being studied.

It is clear from behavioural and attitudinal data that the probability of trial depends crucially on the level of an individual's experimentalism – the predisposition to experiment with new products. This is measured on a behavioural scale by asking respondents about the new brands they have ever tried. Some people are highly experimental by nature, and if all you do is appeal to them, your sales go up rather nicely – and then come crashing down again.

The acceptability of the new product concept is measured by asking respondents about their attitudes to the proposed price and their propensity to buy. The concept may be presented in a variety of degrees of sophistication from a simple verbal description through to a finished television commercial.

The visibility of the brand measures the opportunity an individual has to try it. This is affected by distribution, advertising spend, and how well known the brand name is (or heritage). Information on the first two of these is provided by the client. Heritage is included in the consumer interviews. The combined effect of these environmental factors is then predicted using a sophisticated visibility model. A diffusion submodel predicts the build-up of trial (cumulative penetration) over a period of time.

The adoption model includes two key factors:

- product acceptability,
- brand fidelity.

Product acceptability is measured by enquiring into purchase intentions and the extent to which the new product meets expectations. This gives a measure of the relationship between pre-trial and post-trial response for each individual.

Brand fidelity is measured by asking respondents which of the new brands they have ever tried they are still using. There are some experimentalists who do show fidelity to brands, while others are just inveterate experimentalists.

Once the probabilities of trial and adoption have been estimated, then volume can be predicted after frequency of purchasing and quantity per purchase occasion have been established. Frequency of purchase for each individual is predicted by asking respondents to project future purchasing of the test product; and 'weight of purchasing' is predicted by asking about projected stocks of the product.

The full model is shown in Figure 7.25. The result is a probability for each individual. These are then aggregated and grossed up to the population, whatever that happens to be, for example, mothers with young children. Forecasts are made of sales in years 1 and 2, and the ongoing level thereafter, while sales breakdowns are given between trial and adoption along with estimates for cumulative levels of trial and adoption.

Research International uses Micro Test to advise clients on 'launch manage-

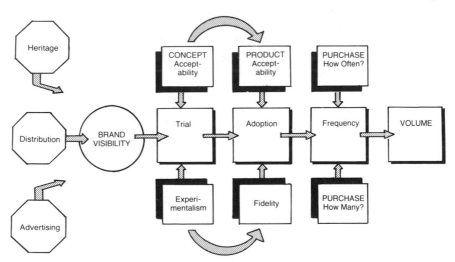

Figure 7.25 Research International's MicroTest Model

Source Research International

ment', for example, what sorts of advertising support they should give. MicroTest is performed on samples of respondents in the target population of 200–300. The cost (1991) is approximately £15,000 per test. Over 500 MicroTests have been carried out, so it is possible to begin applying market validation studies.

MicroTest has subsequently been developed into a family of products. There is MicroTest Concept, which is just the front-end product concept test which can be used at an even earlier stage to predict trial potential. There is MicroTest Laboratory, which is MicroTest with a shop display built on to it. This may be used for more developed products and can represent more real-world influences, such as on-shelf impact, advertising in a competitive context, and actual response from the consumer. Micro-Test Market recruits a tailor-made, short-term panel (for about 12 weeks), and the agency does all the shopping for that type of product, for example, toilet soaps. Panellists are called upon once a week and the results provide more accurate measures since adoption and frequency of purchase are observed from natural purchasing behaviour rather then being estimated from responses to a questionnaire or from simulated behaviour.

Nielsen's Quartz

While Burke's BASES, Novaction's DETECTOR and Research International's MicroTest are currently the three main STM systems being used, Nielsen has recently developed its own model, called Quartz, which makes full use of its access to real-market consumer panel and retail panel data on a worldwide basis, and of its accumulated experience and expertise in retailing and distribution. Like other STM models, Quartz works on the back of a standard product concept test, which will usually involve an in-home placement and subsequent recall, and makes estimates of trial and repeat purchase. However, there are important differences. First, Quartz is based on a nationally representative sample of the adult population. Second, since the model is thereby not restricted to users in the product category, it is possible to distinguish between switchers and new buyers. Respondents are asked, both before and after trial (or home placement), 'If you were to use/consume this product in your household, which products would "X" totally or in part replace?' Those who give an answer to this question in terms of defined product categories are termed switchers and are asked to make comparative judgements. Those who do not answer are defined as new buyers and asked to make monadic judgements. In this way any volume which is likely to come from new buyers is picked up and added into the prediction of sales volume. By using the database from Nielsen's own Homescan consumer panel, which collects data on every product, it is possible to re-create the competitive market of each individual respondent. Calibration of the model for overclaiming can thus be adjusted to individual competitive sets of products.

Respondents selected as part of the sample (usually of about 410 respondents, which provides a minimum of about 350 at the recall stage) are shown concept boards of the new product and asked key questions about likes/dislikes, product image, the question above about the competitive set of products, likelihood of purchase, anticipated frequency and weight of purchase, and pricing. For likelihood of purchase, respondents are asked 'Which of the following sentences apply most to what you will do when the product will be on sale in your usual shops?' Responses range from 'Certainly buy it' down to 'Certainly not buy it'. The product is then placed with everybody who will take it home to try. They are then reinterviewed and asked the same questions. Changes between the pre-trial concept interview and the post-trial interview become key variables in the Quartz model.

Estimates of trial and repeat purchase are then made separately for the switchers and the new buyers, so the ratio of switchers to new buyers becomes an important element of the analysis. For switchers, a trial model for each individual estimates the probability of buying a product derived from four key elements:

1   the probability of being aware of the product,
2   the probability of finding the product on the shelf,
3   the probability of buying a product in the product category to which the new product belongs,
4   the probability of choosing the new product, given 100 per cent awareness and 100 per cent availability.

The first two probabilities are based on external inputs from the manufacturer and from media research. The probability of being aware of the product depends on whether or not there is advertising. If there is, then

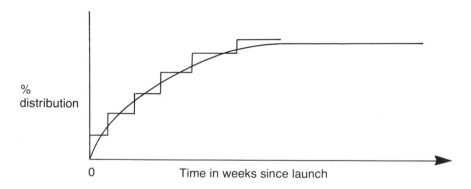

Figure 7.26 Distribution over time

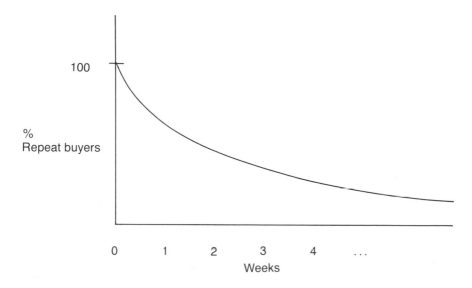

100

%
Repeat buyers

0   1   2   3   4   . . .

Weeks

Figure 7.27 Repeat-buying decay function

cumulative ratings are used as a basis for the calculations; without advertising, awareness is considered largely as a function of distribution. The probability of finding the new product on the shelf is a function of the distribution build over a period of time, as illustrated in Figure 7.26.

The third and fourth elements are internal inputs. The probability of buying a product in the product category is derived from a special distribution to estimate the number of purchase acts using the Nielsen consumer panel database. The probability of choosing a new product comes from the pre-trial and post-trial responses in the survey and is a function of the number of brands included in the respondent's competitive universe, the product's rank order in the preference ranking versus competitors, and a general parameter that reflects product class behaviour and is constant for all consumers.

For repeat purchase for switchers, a repeat buying decay function is built on, showing how the number of repeat purchases for individuals decays, but eventually stabilises at a fixed percentage of buyers who repeat continuously, as illustrated in Figure 7.27. This repeat decay function is itself a function of two elements: a 'true' preference, leading to substitution, plus an 'inertia effect', which generates a few repeat acts after trial, but does not result in final loyalty.

For new buyers, a separate but parallel calculation is made which substitutes a general probability of buying the new product under the assumptions of 100 per cent availability and 100 per cent awareness for the two internal inputs. Adding together the results for switchers and for the new buyers gives a range of predictions for:

- sales volume,
- brand share,
- penetration after a period of time,
- repeat buying rates,
- average number of buying rates,
- weight of purchase,
- source of business,
- price sensitivity,
- competitive universe.

With additional information on the quantity bought (information determined from the Homescan panel), it is possible also to derive sales volume during the period under consideration.

The Quartz analysis is particularly useful when the new product is a line extension because it facilitates a source of volume analysis from the switchers and the extent to which cannibalisation is likely to take place. The new buyers analysis tells the manufacturer how much incremental volume to expect. Furthermore, the actual sales volumes (and all the components of the prediction model) can be tracked using Nielsen panel data, so the model will be continuously validated and recalibrated where necessary. Predictions are made not just for one- or two-year periods, but in terms of four-weekly intervals up to two years ahead, so a picture of ongoing change enables the model to be dynamic in the sense that predictions can be re-adjusted in the light of actual four-weekly figures from panel data. Clients' own estimates about distribution build and advertising spend are evaluated by Nielsen Retail Index division, using their experience of distribution.

Quartz is normally sold to Nielsen clients who have subscribed to one or more of the Nielsen Retail Indexes and who receive monthly panel data. If a product is launched following a Quartz test, its progress will be monitored and the results bolted on to the presentations that are part of the Retail Index service. If the product begins to depart from predictions, then an early warning may be given so that corrective action may be taken if necessary. Predictions may be made on the basis of a variety of different assumptions about advertising, distribution build, awareness build, product design and price.

Conclusion

The models used for volume and brand share prediction have, over the years, been given different names such as 'sales decomposition/recomposition models', 'pre-test market models' and 'market-mix testing', but the term now generally recognised is 'simulated test marketing models', or just

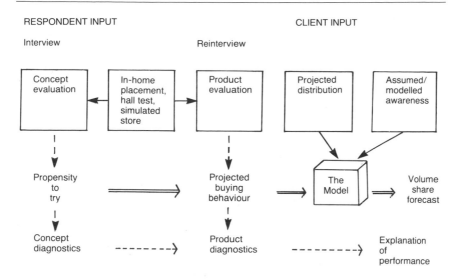

RESPONDENT INPUT   CLIENT INPUT

Figure 7.28 Simulated test marketing – a summary

STM models. Sampson (1987), however, argues that they are not so much 'models' as 'systems', since they have been developed into strategic tools within the mainstream of marketing decision-making.

All STM models use the concepts of trial and repeat purchase, and substitute for simulated or real purchasing behaviour in the marketplace a standard or fairly standard concept test or product test in which a sample of respondents are asked questions about the new product (or existing product being tested) and about their purchasing behaviour. These responses are then used in statistical models of various kinds that weight the replies and produce predictions of a number of variables. The process is summarised in Figure 7.28.

There are, however, significant differences between the models in terms of general methodology, the variables included, the approach to parametisation, and the kinds of predicted output. Any manufacturer wishing to compare the advantages and limitations of the various STM models available would have a hard time. The advocates of each particular model will argue persuasively that their approach is best. A start can be made, however, by recognising the various choices or dimensions along which models vary. In terms of general methodology, the main choices are between:

- comparative or monadic testing, or some combination,
- macromodelling or micromodelling, or some combination,
- whether client inputs, for example concerning distribution, advertising or brand awareness, are modelled or assumed,

- whether various elements that make up the final prediction are modelled separately, thus trial and adoption may be modelled separately, as might switchers and new buyers,
- whether the respondents selected tend to be either product category users, or a general cross-section of the adult population.

It must also be remembered that sample sizes used for STM models vary from a minimum of about 200 per test to about 500. It is important to remember that an STM is a test, not a survey, so although sampling is important, no attempt is usually made to obtain a large representative sample. It is, however, necessary to get a regional spread of fieldwork. In terms of the variables included in the model, while all take trial and repeat purchase as the key variables, the main variations include:

- the number and depth of questions used as inputs to predict trial and repeat purchase. Some models rely on responses to just one question, for example, on intention to buy, while others include competitive sets, degree of experimentalism, brand visibility and so on,
- the number and depth of questions used as diagnostics to explain the predicted outcomes. These may include the standard demographics and, in addition, questions on corporate or brand image, likes and dislikes and so on.

The parametisation of models may use:

- normative or real-market data,
- a variety of statistical techniques, including regression and Bayesian techniques.

Outputs from the models vary in terms of:

- the number of variables being predicted, which may be limited to predicted volume, predicted shares, estimated trial and repeat purchase, or may include, for example, frequency and weight of purchase, source of volume or price sensitivity,
- the time periods for which the predictions are made. These may be for a year, two or more years, and may or may not include intervening monthly projections.

A key advantage of STM modelling is that the risks of launching products that turn out to be unsuccessful are reduced considerably, but without the costs of full test marketing, or even the cost of mini-test marketing. Manufacturers, furthermore, get very precise indicators of the likely performance of the new product. This enables them to generate strategies appropriate to the results. Thus if management have high expectations for a product and the forecast is for increasing volume, then they may decide to go straight for a national launch. If the new product begins from a low base, but will need time to build sales volume, then a test market and tracking operation to test different tactical approaches to boosting sales may be required. If the product begins with a high base, but is not expected to grow, then a national launch with minimum support to maximise profitability may be advisable. Products not expected to move up from a low base, or expected to decline from a higher one, may not be launched at all.

Other advantages of STM modelling are as follows:

- They can be used at a relatively early stage in new product development.
- They may be used to isolate problems before too much cost and effort have been expended.
- Tests which do not use shop displays can be used for products that do not fit into any well-defined market category or product field.
- A wide range of alternative marketing scenarios can be examined by making changes in parameter values: for example, producing estimates on the basis of different assumptions regarding distribution and awareness, launching at different prices, or using different promotional expenditures.
- Parameters and weights can be validated when historical data on the effectiveness of predictions become available.
- Products can be tested without revealing details of the composition or manufacture to competitors.
- They are relatively quick; 8–12 weeks would be a normal timespan for a full STM prediction.
- It is possible to exercise total control over the testing process
- On the whole, STM systems have proved to be extremely accurate. Sampson (1987), for example, reports that over 8,000 tests have been carried out using BASES in 34 countries and across many product categories. By comparing the estimates with what actually happened, typically the estimate is within plus or minus 10 per cent of the actual in 70 per cent of the cases, and plus or minus 15 per cent in 90 per cent of the cases.

One major disadvantage of STMs is that they are complex, and as the sophistication of the modelling grows, it becomes more difficult for clients to understand the analysis, which in turn makes it difficult for clients to judge the advantages and limitations of the various models on offer and makes them more reliant on the market research company to provide interpretation of the results. Another disadvantage is that it is difficult to give clients access to the data to make their own 'What if . . . ?' simulations because the formulae used for model calculations would be revealed or at least deducible, so agencies normally insist on processing simulations themselves.

The overall trend seems to be away from using STM models to make go/no-go decisions and towards launch management that will determine not only optimum launch strategies, but also ways of manipulating these strategies to generate extra trial or extra repeat purchase. A further trend is for agencies, having developed a successful basic model, to generate a variety of options from using only the front-end trial prediction, to enhanced models with additional facilities and measures bolted on. These may include, for example, an optional simulated store test, a brand tracking operation, or models specifically designed to examine line extensions. A third trend is towards the increased use of diagnostic questions that will help to explain why a prediction is poor (or good). Diagnostics may also be used to evaluate an existing brand or brand strategy. These may take into account not only the characteristics of the products and the internal support given to them, but also the circumstances of the external market-place.

SUMMARY

Instruments of data capture, data collection methods, and data analysis techniques are combined in a variety of ways to produce research techniques and applications that enable companies to diagnose the situations they face, to make predictions about the likely consequences of their marketing decisions, and to monitor the progress being made by, or the success of, past marketing activity. Key diagnostic and monitoring techniques include market measurement, usage and attitude studies, advertising tracking, and media audience measurement. Instead of looking at the more traditional forecasting methods like time series analysis, which are well covered in books on marketing research, statistics and social research, the focus here is on three currently widely used predictive techniques and applications for the testing of new products and product concepts, advertising pre-testing, and volume and brand share prediction using simulated test market modelling.

EXERCISES AND POINTS FOR FURTHER DISCUSSION

■   The ex-factory shipments of jams and preserves from a UK-based company have been declining steadily over six months, having previously been stable for many years. The managing director wants a detailed market analysis to discover exactly what is happening in the marketplace. Suggest key market measurements that will need to be taken to facilitate such an analysis. Recommend sources for obtaining the data, giving your reasons.

■   To what extent is a market segmentation analysis simply an extension of the use of market measurement data?

- An airline wants an in-depth understanding of domestic customer usage and attitudes towards the company's services. Suggest the key questions that will need to be included in a usage and attitude study.

- Review the key measures taken by market research companies of the success of advertising when they engage in advertising pre-testing and advertising tracking and suggest what advertisers need to do to create successful advertisements.

- The size of a television audience is measured using a representative panel whose presence in the room with a television switched on is monitored. Suggest some of the problems in using such a measure. Can you explain why, in the light of these problems, advertisers and advertising agencies nevertheless continue to pay a lot of money to obtain television audience ratings?

- It has been suggested that the measurement of radio audiences is more complex than that for television. Do you think measurement of the levels or readership for advertisements in newspapers is simpler or more complex than either? Give your reasons.

- If simulated test market models are so good at predicting volume sales and the market shares that will be achieved by new or modified products, why are there so many new product failures?

- Review the details of STM models described and generate a list of factors that manufacturers need to attend to in order to ensure, for a new or modified product, a good trial rate and a good repeat purchase rate.

Chapter 8

Research design

Chapters 2–7 have examined the considerable range of tools that are available for the marketing researcher to use. It is now time to see how these tools are assembled in the design of research that is intended to address specific marketing problems. The nature of these 'problems', however, can be put into two very broad but distinct categories. These were hinted at in Chapter 1 on perspectives in marketing research, and they result in two very different approaches to the design of research. We need to distinguish between:

- research that is designed to further organisational objectives,
- research that is designed to further academic objectives.

Most commissioned research, whether ad hoc or continuous, is designed to further organisational objectives, and so is most research that is conducted in-house by a company or non-profit-making organisation. Research to further academic objectives will include scholarly research carried out for career purposes by students and academics, and not undertaken on behalf of any particular client (although it may be funded by one of a range of organisations that support research), and also some research which is undertaken by individuals in market research companies which is not specifically commissioned, but is intended for publication. Sometimes the distinction between these two kinds of research is not very clear-cut, for example, an academic who uses research that he or she has been commissioned to do, but feeds into research for publication. However, the objectives and design of the two kinds of research are very distinct, and the researcher wishing to use commissioned research for academic purposes will have to be very careful not to reveal confidential information about a company.

RESEARCH FOR ORGANISATIONS

Research designed to achieve organisational objectives is not neutral research – it is research that takes sides: the side of the organisation for which the research is being conducted. Its purpose is not restricted to scientific study of the ways in which marketing variables relate or function; the focus is rather on producing solutions to problems. It is predisposed towards making recommendations for action, and is likely to take the activist perspective that was described in Chapter 1. This is interventionist and partisan. If the researcher is not part of the solution, then he or she is part of the problem: the point is not to study the world but to change it. The design of research to achieve organisational objectives will include the following activities:

1 diagnosing organisational problems or issues,
2 assessing organisational strengths and weaknesses,
3 clarifying the decisions that need to be taken,
4 specifying the information that will be required,
5 formulating the objectives of the research,
6 producing a research brief,
7 presenting a research proposal,
8 undertaking exploratory research,
9 collecting the data,
10 analysing and interpreting the results,
11 reporting the findings,
12 making recommendations.

The researcher – whether in-house or in a market research agency – is not necessarily involved in all of these stages. The first six stages are often undertaken by the organisation itself, although, as indicated in Chapter 1, there is a tendency for research companies to involve themselves increasingly in the earlier stages, perhaps as part of a consultancy commission, or perhaps just by taking part in discussions at the problem diagnosis stage. The market research agency will commonly undertake steps 7–11, although the organisation may retake control over step 12. Sometimes steps 9 and 10 alone are commissioned to a 'field and tab' agency.

Diagnosing the problem

It is sometimes said that a problem properly defined is a problem half solved. This could be put a little differently: a problem inadequately diagnosed will result in wasted research. Problem diagnosis is, unfortunately, often given insufficient attention before research is designed. One reason for this is that it is often the most difficult (and in some cases, depressing) part of the process. Sometimes the person requesting the research has no clear idea about what the key problems of an organisation are that the research can tackle, or what decisions depend on the results of the research. What is perceived as 'the problem' may well differ from one person to another. One person's 'problem' may be another's opportunity.

Furthermore, what individuals may be describing are the symptoms rather than the underlying causes.

It may be helpful to think about a number of related issues when diagnosing problems:

- the nature of the discrepancies between actual and desired performance,
- the relationship between problems, and between problems and symptoms,
- the seriousness of the problems,
- the factors that affect or might be affecting the problem.

Problems arise where there is some discrepancy between the actual, current or anticipated future performance of the organisation, and the desired performance or outcome. The discrepancy may be:

- *historical*, for example, the organisation is not performing as well as it has in the past; profits are declining or sales stagnating,
- *environmental*, for example, the organisation is not performing as well as competitors or other similar organisations. Which organisations are taken as a standard, and which measures of performance are used, may be crucial in making such comparisons,
- *planned or budgeted*, for example, there may be variances between budgeted costs of materials and the actual costs, or between planned growth and actual growth,
- *theoretical or analytical*, for example, the organisation may be less marketing oriented than the theory of marketing suggests should be the case, or the organisation's planning procedures may not match the principles of marketing planning.

It will be helpful to understand what comparisons are being made when the nature of the marketing problems facing an organisation were being considered. Making historical comparisons may lead management to view the problem rather differently than if comparisons are being made with selected competitors.

There is seldom just one problem facing an organisation at any given point of time; problems are often interrelated and form clusters of related issues, for example, problems in terms of sales, profits and market shares. There is frequently a hierarchy of problems and symptoms; each symptom is the result of a more basic problem. The 'problem' may be declining sales; but this may be a symptom of other aspects of an organisation. Such deeper problems, like rising costs, may themselves be symptoms of still more fundamental issues, like work practices. Sometimes the relationship between problems is reciprocal rather than hierarchical. For example, advertising expenditure affects sales which, in turn, affect future expenditures on advertising. Sometimes several causes combine to produce a single effect; sometimes a single cause may produce several effects.

Whenever a problem is being described, it is often a good idea to ask 'Why?': Why are sales declining? Why are costs rising? Why are work practices inefficient? There is no ultimate cause, but such probing may help us to dig deeper into the structure and processes of an organisation.

Some problems are more serious than others: some are urgent, but not important; others may be important, but not urgent: some may be both. Some are easier or quicker to solve; some are more central. Such a diagnosis may be necessary for deciding in which order to tackle problems. Information may be needed to measure exactly how serious a problem is. Some of this information may already be available, some may require market research. In any event, it is helpful to spell out exactly what information is required for this purpose.

Factors that may affect the problem may be internal or external to the organisation. Internal factors may relate to such things as payment or incentive systems, industrial relations, changing technology, depreciation of plant and equipment. External factors will include the immediate micro environment of trends in market size, changes in market structure or in buyer behaviour and attitudes, competitor activity, supplier power, and the role of intermediaries like retailers and wholesalers. The wider macro environment will include changes in demographics, the economy, technology, politics, the legal environment, and the social and cultural environment. We have seen the role that marketing research plays in market measurement and market analysis, and a lot of this activity assists in problem diagnosis.

Strengths and weaknesses of the company

Any marketing action will need to build upon company strengths or particular capabilities. What these are is not always obvious or easy to diagnose, and may require further analysis or research. It is likely that many of the weaknesses will have surfaced as 'problems' at the problem diagnosis stage. However, there may well be other weaknesses that are not connected with or obviously related to the problems being diagnosed. Assessment of strengths and weaknesses is often undertaken as part of a 'SWOT' analysis that also looks at the opportunities and threats in the marketplace. Such analyses assume that information is readily available and that accurate assessments can be made of each element. Marketing research often has a key role to play in the more systematic marketing auditing process which is usually comprehensive, periodic, and undertaken by a group that is independent of those being audited. The audit will normally have both an internal and an external element. The internal audit will seek to identify:

- those factors that give any company in a market sector or in an industry a strategic advantage,

- the capabilities and incompetences of the company,
- those capabilities that link with the strategic advantage factors.

Marketing research can help assess each of these elements. Where a capability matches a strategic advantage factor, then it is a company strength; where it does not, it may be a weakness. The external audit will take a systematic look at the environment, particularly the immediate environment, and will, for example, seek to discover:

- who are the major competitors,
- what are their objectives and strategies,
- what are their strengths and weaknesses,
- what are their typical reaction patterns.

From this it should be possible to identify the extent of any threat from competitors, the power possessed by customers and suppliers, and the threat of substitute goods and services emerging. Environmental analysis may include gathering market intelligence, perhaps from documents of various kinds; scanning reports, newspapers and journals; speaking to the salesforce, consultants and academics; or attending meetings or conferences. The marketing researcher may be involved in all, some or none of these activities.

The decisions to be taken

It is one thing to feel that you now fully understand the situation facing the company; it is another to be clear about the decision or decisions that need to be taken. Decisions are needed at two different levels:

- marketing objectives,
- marketing strategies.

Marketing objectives are, or should be, derived from the strategies determined at the corporate level for fulfilling corporate objectives. Thus besides marketing objectives, there will be objectives for production, finance, personnel, research and development, and so on. Marketing objectives specify what products are to be addressed to what markets; in particular, such objectives may include:

- expanding the total market demand or penetration for the product class as a whole,
- increasing or protecting market penetration or market share of current company brands in existing markets,
- developing new brands or line extensions for existing markets,
- developing new markets for existing brands,
- developing new brands for new markets,

Table 8.1 Elements of marketing strategy

Market analysis

   Market measurement
   Market forecasting
   Market segmentation
   Market positioning

Product specification

   Design and materials
   Features
   Branding
   Packaging
   Labelling
   Pricing

Customer service

   Pre-sale, for example, display, demonstration
   Installation
   Maintenance
   Trial, for example, test drive
   Hire services
   Guarantee/warantee
   Trade-in
   Credit
   Discounts

Communication

   Advertising
   Personal selling
   Sales promotions
   Publicity
   Direct mail

Distribution

   Channels
   Warehousing
   Transportation
   Stocks

- eliminating brands or brand variants that do not fulfil company objectives,
- demarketing – moving out of some market segments to focus on selected segments or niches,
- concentration – eliminating brands and demarketing at the same time.

Which of these objectives is appropriate depends to a large extent on whether the company is already a market leader, a market challenger, a market follower or a market nicher. Furthermore, such objectives need to be realistic, consistent with one another, and stated in quantitative terms – for example, taking an analysis of the current market penetration for company brands and generating quantitative targets that are achievable over a given period of time. In this context, market research can play a crucial role in determining the current situation, reviewing trends and projecting the parameters for what might be accomplished in the next two to five years.

Marketing strategies define how these objectives are to be achieved through policies for market analysis, product specification, customer service, marketing communications, and distribution. Some of the elements that make up these strategies are detailed in Table 8.1. Ideally, the company should consider *all* the major options and alternatives available to it before making a selection. Marketing research can help in this process by providing information on the basis of which the 'best' marketing objectives and marketing strategies may be selected. Inputs from marketing research may be required to facilitate the use of various decision-making techniques, for example, portfolio analysis, using the growth-share matrix developed by the Boston Consulting Group, or the market attractiveness–business strength matrix developed by the General Electric Company. Various procedures for ranking, rating, using quantitative decision analysis, linear programming or optimisation techniques all require data from marketing research.

Any course of action thus involves taking a whole series of subdecisions. A decision to expand the range of products offered entails subdecisions about how many new products to develop, over what period of time, what kinds of products they are to be, and their specification, promotion and distribution. Furthermore, it needs to be clear when these decisions need to be taken by. This may, of course, mean reflecting back on the urgency of the problem, but may need to take into account other factors such as seasonality of the demand for the products concerned, the pace of changing technology, or actual or likely competitor behaviour.

At this point, serious consideration needs to be given to which of these decisions requires further research. This means evaluating exactly what information is needed for each decision.

The information required

Once the decisions have been clarified, it is necessary to consider:

- what decisions require further information from marketing research before they can be reasonably taken,

- exactly what information is required,
- how the results of research will relate to the decisions.

It is only too easy to argue that marketing research is needed before any decision can be taken without first clarifying which decisions depend on further information. Sometimes sufficient information already exists, but is overlooked. The result is that, when the research is completed, managers will say, 'It cost us a lot of money, but it only told us what we knew anyway.' Arguments at this stage can easily get clouded by internal politics. The marketing manager may simply wish to delay making a decision so that he or she can consolidate his or her power base; so the research becomes a delaying tactic. The manager may, in fact, already have taken the decision, but wants supportive evidence to back arguments and reinforce positions.

Knowing what information is needed for making a particular decision is often a matter of experience or gut feeling. However, if the decisions to be taken have been clarified, then if, for example, one decision is what size of pack to use for a new product, it should be clear that information is required on the sales of existing pack sizes both for the company and for competitors, on how consumers react to existing packs, and how they would react to new sizes or types of pack. In short, it should be possible to list the key concepts that need to be addressed, and perhaps begin to suggest the key variables that need to be measured.

It may also be necessary to consider at this stage:

- the quality of information required,
- when it is required by.

The quality of information will include accuracy, detail and comprehensiveness as well as sample quality. Thus random samples will produce higher-quality data than quota samples. Bigger samples will produce higher quality than smaller ones (but by a declining amount). At the same time, getting high-quality data will be more costly, so a degree of trade-off may be required.

The date information is required by will, of course, be governed largely by when the decision needs to be taken; however, other considerations, like the time needed to analyse and digest the information, may need to be kept in mind. If the decision has to be taken before any worthwhile research can be carried out, it may be necessary to consider whether you:

- take the decision without any research,
- delay taking the decision,
- do a 'quick and dirty' study.

Each of these has its problems, and in making the choice, very careful consideration has to be taken of the cost (in financial and customer relationship terms) of getting the decision wrong, or making a sub-optimal decision. If there *is* time to do the research, then how much time is available will place constraints on the commissioning, phasing and completion of the research.

When it has been concluded that there is a genuine information gap, it may still, however, be unclear what the research results would imply unless action standards have been defined. These standards specify in advance which research results attach to which alternatives. A decision about whether to launch, modify or drop a new product idea may depend on prespecified scores in a product or product concept test. A decision about whether to lower the price of an existing brand may depend on whether a price sensitivity analysis from a consumer survey reached a prespecified level. If these standards are not set in advance, it is only too easy to make an argument for almost any position, whatever the result.

The objectives of the research

These spell out what the research is designed to explore, measure or explain. Exploratory, descriptive and causal research were indicated as three key objectives in Chapter 1. For exploratory and descriptive research, the objective may simply be to collect the information that has been specified at the earlier stage. Explanatory or causal research may, however, need to go beyond the simple collection of information to spell out what has to be discovered or tested from the data collected. Thus the information required may concern a range of customer demographic characteristics and measures of the degree of price awareness. The research objectives may be to find out which characteristics are most strongly associated with price awareness.

The objectives may be spelled out in terms of generating hypotheses that link variables together, or in terms of testing univariate, bivariate or multivariate hypotheses spelled out in advance of data collection. It is sometimes helpful to formulate research objectives as questions that the research is designed to answer, for example:

- What is the relationship between advertising and sales for brands A, B and C over the last five years?
- What is the likely market share for brand Z in three and five months' time?
- How do consumers go about making a purchase of an automatic washing machine?

Notice that the responses to these questions will not, in themselves, provide precise answers to specific tactical decisions that may need to be taken, for example:

- How much should be spent on advertising next year?

- Should we invest in new machinery to make product Z?
- How should we promote our washing machines?

The research provides the information; the manager takes the decision. However, if the research objectives are phrased as a question, then at least it is clear what question or questions the research has to answer – and, when the results are obtained, whether or not it has answered them. Specifying the information required and the objectives of the research should, together, ensure that the right kinds of data are collected and that the appropriate kinds of data analysis can be supported by them.

The research brief

The research brief is a formal document that is, or should be, sufficiently detailed to enable the researcher to formulate a proposal for marketing research that will produce results that can be used effectively for marketing diagnosis, planning and control. Sometimes the company prepares its own brief; sometimes it is prepared with the assistance of a market research company or business consultant.

The brief will contain the results or summary of the elements considered so far: a diagnosis of the problem, an assessment of company capabilities, a clarification of the decisions that need to be taken, a specification of the information required, and a statement of the objectives of the research. The brief will also typically contain further details of background information on the company and how the present situation or problem arose, suggestions about the kind and scope of the research envisaged, some indication of the likely budget for the research, a timescale for when a proposal is required and when the research results will be needed, and whether or not the brief is competitive. There may need to be considerable discussion both within the client organisation and between client and agency over details of the brief unless the research is very straightforward or it is repeat business. Very often a company's analysis of its own problems may relate more to symptoms than to underlying causes, so the research executive may need to probe by continually asking 'Why?' as symptoms or stated problems are described. Such discussions may take place over the telephone, but for unusual or complex briefs, they will probably be face to face. An example of a research brief, which is derived from the case described in Chapter 1, is illustrated below.

RESEARCH SPECIFICATION

Attitudes to the Use of Specialised Flour in the Home

John Ambrose wishes to commission a survey to investigate housewives' attitudes towards the use of specialised flour for home baking.

Background

John Ambrose is a medium-sized, family-owned, flour-milling business which has been in existence for over 100 years. It supplies a complete range of flours to the bakery trade to cover every specialised need. Its customers are mostly small to medium-sized family bakers who have been customers for decades. It does not supply anything to the general public; it has no advertising and only limited sales representation.

Sales have been falling steadily in the last few years to a point where the company will need to take corrective action to stay in business. Among the alternatives being considered is to supply the general public the same highly-specialised flours currently supplied to the trade. These would be more expensive than standard flours.

Research objectives

In order to investigate the feasibility of offering specialised flour for domestic use, John Ambrose needs to know:

- what proportion of households keep flour of any description in stock,
- what kinds of flour are usuallly kept,
- what other kinds of flour housewives may be aware of,
- what flour is currently used for,
- what are the main kinds of home baking,
- which groups of people are most likely to make use of specialised flour,
- what quantities they are likely to buy,
- would they be prepared to pay a slightly higher price?

Methods

The research should consist of a qualitative preliminary to establish the main dimensions of flour usage in the home, attitudes to home baking, and the possibilities for use of specialised flour.

The main study should be a quantitative survey of about 1,200 house-wives to establish the extent of various usages and attitudes.

Qualitative research

Please include a proposal for depth interviews and/or group discussions with housewives of all ages and social classes, and including those who do no or little home baking. The qualitative stage should take place in at least two regions. Costing for the qualitative work should be separate from that of the main stage.

Quantitative research

A nationally representative sample of housewives who usually do home baking is required. Would you please quote separately for the alternatives of random or a quota sample design, discussing their relative advantages and disadvantages and giving details of how the design would ensure a representative sample.

The qualitative stage will further inform decisions on the content of the questionnaire. At this stage we envisage covering the following areas:

- whether the household currently has flour in stock and what kinds/brands/pack sizes/quantities,
- how long the flour is usually kept in the house,
- what types/brands of flour they can recall,
- how often they buy and the price paid,
- what kinds of baking they do, on what occasions, how often, and what flour they use,
- what they view as their successes and failures in home baking,
- whether they feel that specialised flour could help with the 'failures'.

Timetable

We would like to commission the work at the end of July and to receive an interim report on the qualitative stage in time for execution of the main field-work stage in November. A full written report is required as soon as is reasonably possible after that.

Submission of tenders

Please submit two copies of tenders to John Ambrose no later than 15 June. Meetings to discuss the shortlisted tenders will take place on 26 June. If you wish to discuss the research prior to submission of a tender, please contact John Ambrose.

Evaluation of tenders

The tenders will be evaluated on the following criteria:

- understanding of John Ambrose's requirements,
- ideas and methodology proposed,
- suitability of staff (please identify experience),
- cost,
- ability to deliver promptly.

The research proposal

Like the research brief, the research proposal is a formal document, but it is drafted by whoever is conducting the research. Any organisation seeking research from a market research company will base its commission on such a document. From the perspective of the market research executive, the key objective of the proposal will be to obtain the commission from the client, perhaps in the face of stiff competition. The proposal in practice often has to be drafted on the basis of a less than adequate brief from the client. The research executive may seek further discussion and clarification from the client before submitting a proposal.

The proposal is a formal statement of the methods and techniques that the researcher feels are required in the circumstances, and should contain:

- a statement of the background of the research. This should indicate that the researcher has fully grasped the brief and any subsequent discussions about it. It should demonstrate that the researcher fully understands the problem which is the focus of the research, the decisions that have to be taken, and the information required,
- a statement of the objectives of the research,
- definitions of the main concepts, their operationalisation into variables, any hypotheses to be tested or models to be used,
- details of the actual research techniques proposed. These should include a definition of the population of cases to be studied, the size of the sample, the techniques for selecting cases, the data capture instruments, the data collection methods, and the specific applications to be used,
- the personnel who will be involved in the research, including some indication of their qualifications, experience and background,
- a time schedule, outlining the dates or periods of time between each phase of the research, (typically, this is done on a month-by-month basis),
- details of the data analysis procedures – for survey research, this will outline the procedures for editing, coding, processing and tabulating data,
- the costs of the research – this would normally be a global sum, but occasionally clients ask for a breakdown of costs.

In planning the methods and techniques to be used, the basic considerations are whether the research should be ad hoc or continuous, and if ad hoc whether it should be qualitative or quantitative. In selecting from the range of market research techniques available, the research executive will need to bear in mind the resources and the time that will be needed for each technique, along with the appropriateness of each for minimising the risks among the decisions identified as needing to be taken. A checklist of useful questions here could be:

- Will depth interviews with key informants, experts, technicians, colleagues, or suppliers provide sufficient information to take the decision?
- Will group discussions be needed with consumers to explore issues more thoroughly, and if so, what kinds of groups, how many groups, and how are they to be selected?
- Will some form of experimental research be appropriate? If so, should it be laboratory-type experiments or field experiments?
- Will some form of survey be required? This is the most expensive,

resource-heavy, time-consuming form of research and should be resorted to only when information from other sources is clearly going to be inadequate. Careful thought will need to be given to the size of the sample required, the type of sampling, and the mode of delivery of the questions, for example, face to face, by telephone or in the post.

A company considering commissioning research will normally ask up to three agencies to submit proposals for research in response to a research brief. These would then be evaluated and compared. For large-scale undertakings, the agency may be invited to present these proposals in person so that they can be questioned about them. Alternatively, where a client is coming back for repeat business, there may not even be a research proposal – an understanding of what the research is to cover and the cost may be all that needs to be clarified.

It would be unreasonable for the client to expect that the agency has done a great deal of work on the problem before the research is commissioned. In particular, it is unlikely that the agency will include a questionnaire even in draft format this stage. An example of a response to the brief in the above box (pp. 321–3) is illustrated in Appendix 1.

Exploratory research

For research into consumer markets using standard ad hoc or continuous techniques, exploratory research may not be needed. For most business research or for consumer research in unfamiliar markets, an exploratory phase will probably be essential. Exploratory research includes all work that is preliminary to the main stage of data collection and which is used in shaping the direction, design and operation of the main study, or to check that earlier designs will work satisfactorily.

One of the problems in seeing the conduct of ad hoc research as a series of stages is that the stages are often not carried out in exact sequence. Thus exploratory research may be undertaken, indeed in many cases should be undertaken, before the research is designed at all. In fact, exploratory research may well be used at the outset to help diagnose and analyse the nature of the problems facing an organisation.

It is possible to identify five key purposes of exploratory research:

- Diagnosing, analysing and evaluating the real nature, seriousness and urgency of the problem or problems facing an organisation.
- Increasing the researcher's familiarity with a topic, with a company, or with a market. Very often the researcher at the outset does not know enough about the situation to be able to design the research or submit a worthwhile research proposal.
- Establishing priorities and objectives of the research. Exploratory work may be needed before it is possible to decide which particular issues

require further investigation, and before being able to decide exactly what the research is expected to achieve.

- Providing information on practical problems. It may be necessary, for example, to find out whether certain organisations are willing to co-operate before embarking on a particular style of enquiry. We may need to know certain things about the population before being able to design our sample.
- Generating ideas, gaining insights or suggesting hypotheses that could be tested.

Any of the available instruments of data capture, data collection methods, or techniques and applications may be used for exploratory purposes. A formal, quantitative survey could, for example, be undertaken and used as a preliminary stage for a larger, more comprehensive investigation. By the same token, we could carry out a few informal enquiries with informants or experts in the field and decide that sufficient information had been acquired to make a decision.

The distinction between 'exploratory' and other forms of research may be unclear, and could change as the researcher or the marketing manager reconsiders the role or conduct of the research. Thus a study that began as a 'final' piece of research may be continued so that the results are used as preliminary inputs to further investigation. An enquiry that began as an exploratory study may not be continued, so it becomes 'final'.

Whatever its purpose, most exploratory research is characterised by:

- flexibility,
- lack of formality,
- personal intervention.

The researcher, in the exploratory phase, is likely to follow his or her own hunches; to allow personality, judgement, feelings and insight to enter into the conduct of the enquiry. Plans may be changed as new evidence or data come to light. Certainly, talking in an unstructured way to experts, consultants, other researchers, colleagues and informants will often play a key role in the early stages of most research.

Data collection, analysis and interpretation

The various methods of data collection were described in detail in Chapter 5, and the processes of data analysis in Chapter 6. The selection of appropriate methods of data collection and data analysis, and of the more specific application techniques to be used, will have been made at least by the research proposal stage, if not earlier by a client in the brief presented to the agency. The analysis of the results should be guided by the specification of the information required, and the interpretation of the findings should be guided by the objectives of the research.

It is becoming increasingly accepted (in spite of some strongly expressed views to the contrary) that it is the responsibility of the researchers to interpret the findings rather than confining themselves to presenting just the factual results of the analysis. The client is not always in the best position to work out the implications of the findings for his or her own organisation, and, so it is sometimes argued, the researcher should not shrink from offering opinions and recommendations. Where action standards have been set, the implications of the findings are manifest. Even where such standards have not been clarified, the researcher is increasingly, both through the growing sophistication of market research activity and because research executives often specialise in certain market areas and become expert in them, able to make a valid contribution to marketing strategy. Research executives in market research companies are nowadays often seen as part of the marketing team in the client organisation. This said, it is still sometimes the case that the brief from the client makes it clear that only a statistical report is required. The client may feel that the company has sufficient competence to be able to interpret the research for itself and may, furthermore, wish to keep its marketing strategies confidential. This is likely to happen, however, only when the client has been very specific about the research required.

Reporting the findings

While the research, as explained above, is not neutral, it is or should be objective in the sense that 'correct' procedures have been followed rigorously and systematically, and that bias, as far as possible, has been eliminated. But however valid and insightful the research, the findings will be of little value unless they are communicated effectively to those who commissioned the research and to those responsible for incorporating the findings into tactical or strategic decisions. Reports of research may take either or both of two main forms:

- a face-to-face presentation,
- a formal written report.

The manner in which findings are reported will be affected by the complexity of the problems being researched, the audience to whom the presentation or report is to be addressed, and the degree of importance attached by the client to the form of the report. Not every client wishes a face-to-face presentation, but where one is required, it is usually an opportunity for the research executive to give preliminary results and conclusions, and for the client to ask about the research before the final report is written. The presentation is usually given by the research executive who was involved in the initial discussions with the client and who has been responsible for the design and execution of the research. The presentation

Table 8.2 Key components of a management report for marketing research

Title page

This should state:

- title of report,
- who commissioned it (name plus agency),
- who prepared it,
- date submitted.

Contents page

This should:

- systematically number sections and subsections,
- list tables and figures.

Executive summary

This is a one-page abstract of the entire report, and may be all that a busy business executive reads. It should:

- explain the terms of reference, the purpose and scope of the report,
- state the key methods and approach used,
- list the main conclusions,
- list the key recommendations (where asked for).

Main text of the report

This consists of a series of sections arranged under headings and subheadings that typically would include:

1 Background – often a detailed analysis of the current situation or problem.
2 Research methodology – this should include:
    2.1 objectives of the research and the operationalisation of the key variables
    2.2 the population of case studies and the sampling procedures for selecting cases
    2.3 data capture instruments used
    2.4 data collection methods
    2.5 specific research techniques and applications
    2.6 data analysis procedures
3 Market analysis
4 Findings on research objectives
5 Conclusions
6 Recommendations

Appendices

This may include:

- any explanatory notes that would clutter up the main report,
- tabulations and calculations not included in the text,
- references,
- copies of questionnaires or visual materials used.

will normally take place in the client organisation, and nowadays the visual aids used can get quite sophisticated with the increasing availability of desk-top publishing packages for use with laser printers, some of which can produce coloured overheads for overhead projectors. However, it is all too easy to attempt a picture-/slide-show that dwells too much on the methodology of the research. What the audience wants to know are the key findings and the practical implications. The language used needs to be kept free of jargon, and diagrams need to be clear and simple. There are many excellent books on the skills required for giving good presentations, for example, Scott (1986) and Vardaman (1981).

The formal report, like the face-to-face presentation, is above all a method of communication, so the author should bear in mind the kinds of people who are likely to read it and what their needs are. Reports will normally be written in management report style. This means clear, concise, grammatical English, free of jargon or complex sentences, and organised in a way that allows the reader quickly to assemble and digest the content of the report. A fairly standard approach is to use plenty of headings and subheadings, and arranged into a format similar to that suggested in Table 8.2. Wherever possible, graphs, tables, charts and diagrams should be used to illustrate and clarify arguments. Ideally, these should be incorporated into the text, each numbered according to the appropriate section, for example, 'Table 4.1.2', and referred to in the text, which gives an interpretation or extracts the key points or lessons to be derived from it. Guidelines on table layout and presentation were given in Chapter 6. A good report is persuasive and convinces the reader that the conclusions and recommendations make good sense.

The number of copies of the report to be made available to the client is usually specified in the research proposal. Sometimes reports may be available and distributed before the face-to-face presentation; more often the formal report will be submitted afterwards so that the points raised in the discussion of the research can be addressed and included.

Making recommendations

The researcher may, at the request of the client, stop short of making recommendations, alternatively, such recommendations may be specifically asked for. The research itself may, of course, be only one input among others that is taken into account when deciding upon some course of action. The client may, for example, have to review the company's financial situation if implementation will require considerable expenditure. Making recommendations, however, is one thing; implementing them is another. It is not usually up to the market research company to suggest how its recommendations should be put into practice, but if some of the recommendations are carried out, it may be called upon to provide information that will be used to monitor or track the results. Thus advertising tracking studies and various market tracking and market measurement research may be used for this purpose. Sometimes, of course, perhaps too frequently, the research gets ignored. This may be for one or more of the following reasons:

- No action standards have been defined, so the implications of the research findings are open to a range of differing, probably competing, interpretations.
- The results of the research are inconclusive, for example, a product concept test reveals only a moderate acceptance of a new product idea.
- The research was commissioned by individuals in the client organisation who have objectives that do not depend on the research results.
- The resources are not available for implementation.

Using research for planning research

The design of research for organisations thus involves a large number of elements. The twelve activities detailed on p. 313 should not be taken as a series of 'steps' in research design. Certainly, the first five elements may be completed in a different order or even in parallel. There may be iterations between one element and the next. Exploratory research may be undertaken separately or jointly for many of the activities, for example, diagnosing the problem, or assessing organisational strengths and weaknesses. Previous market research may play a role in providing evidence at any of the stages, while primary research conducted for just one of the elements will probably be only for exploratory purposes.

The research company perspective

The major objective of the research executive in a market research organisation in designing research and in offering a formal research proposal will be to obtain the commission from the client. He or she will need to bear in mind the strengths and weaknesses of the market research company in terms of styles of research, and its loading of resources already committed to other projects currently underway. If it is a large company, it will be able to offer the full range of research so that if, for example, it looks as though qualitative research is appropriate to the client's problem, then the client can be passed on to the division or subsidiary company in the organisation that specialises in that type of research. In smaller specialised agencies, the research executive will, of course, try to show why its particular expertise is just what is needed to help the client.

In reviewing briefs received by potential clients, the agency will need to bear in mind:

- the nature of the brief,

- its understanding of the brief,
- its acceptance or rejection.

Briefs may be formally written down and extensive, they may be short notes, or they may be communicated informally over the telephone. The client may be a new client or a client who is coming back for repeat business. The client may be from a commercial or from a non-profit-making organisation.

In understanding the brief, the agency will need to consider:

- the purpose of the research,
- how the data are to be used (and by whom, when and how),
- any limitations in terms of time and money,
- the scope of the research in terms of geographical area, size of sample, the information required, the input to research design needed from the research executive, and the end-product – restricted to data analysis, or to include interpretations and recommendations,
- the kind of report required,
- the competition – how many other agencies are quoting?

In considering acceptance or rejection of the brief, it may need to be decided whether it is to be kept in the division approached by the client, passed on to another division, or declined. Before the final decision can be taken, there may need to be further contact with the organisation submitting the brief. If accepted, then the agency will proceed to the preparation of a research proposal.

In drawing up the proposal, the agency will need to consider all those aspects that will affect the design and cost, for example:

- the availability of past research or published data,
- the size, spread and contactability of the sample,
- the data collection method,
- the need for exploratory research,
- the need for a pilot survey,
- the need for personal briefings,
- the length of the questionnaire,
- the number of open-ended questions,
- the need for evening, weekend or holiday time interviewing,
- the scale and complexity of the data analysis required,
- the type and scale of reporting.

Any design, at the end of the day, needs to meet four key criteria:

- It is relevant to the client's problem or situation.
- It offers adequate quality of research.
- It uses cost-effective methods.
- It is practical.

The client perspective

From the perspective of the manufacturer or other type of organisation wishing to purchase research services, the objective will, of course, be to buy good research, that is, research that is good value and which addresses effectively the problems, issues or opportunities that the company faces. Before approaching any market research company, however, the client first of all needs to consider:

- whether research is needed at all,
- whether a research brief is needed and, if so, whether it is able to produce one in-house,
- whether it can do what research is needed entirely in-house,
- whether it wants to commission a 'full' study or just part of the activities required, for example, employing only field and computer tabulation assistance, or putting a number of questions into an omnibus survey,
- what companies or agencies to approach for a proposal.

The client company may decide against doing any research if:

- the data or information needed already exist or can be purchased, for example, from business publishing houses, from market research organisations, or by subscribing to continuous research services,
- there is not enough time to conduct research before a decision has to be taken,
- the cost of getting the decision wrong is relatively low, so the cost of any worthwhile research would be greater than the likely payoff,
- the situation is too complex with too many factors and variables for research to have a significant impact on the decision that needs to be taken.

In choosing what market research companies to approach for a proposal, some clients will have a 'pool' of tried and tested companies that they have a habit of using. Others rely on listings, for example, by the Market Research Society handbook, or on recommendations from contacts in other organisations. It would be normal to obtain up to three proposals and to advise the market research organisations that it is a competitive proposal, indicating how many have been or will be approached.

The final selection will be based on some combination of:

- evidence that the research executive has fully understood the brief and the problem to be researched,
- the overall approach suggested, including a clear statement of the research objectives, a definition of the population to be studied, the sampling techniques, the fieldwork methods to be used, and the data handling and analysis procedures,

- the experience of the researchers assigned to the project,
- the quality of communications with the agency so far,
- the cost, usually a global sum, but it should be clear what that sum includes, for example, a written report and a face-to-face presentation.

The client may need to bear in mind that the 'cost' of the research includes not only paying the market research company, but the opportunity cost of what is *not* being done as a result of devoting resources to the research, and the indirect costs of managerial time spent on further contact. However, the client may also need to consider whether the research, besides being used as a basis for taking a decision, may also be a useful input to a marketing or management information system, or may be used as 'currency' in negotiating with advertisers, advertising agencies, distributors, retailers and so on.   Findings on brand loyalty, interpurchasing and frequency of purchase may, for example, be used to persuade a retailer to allocate more shelf space to the client's brand.

A commissioning letter will be sent to the chosen market research company accepting the proposal as a formal contract. Thereafter, the client will wish to monitor progress to ensure that deadlines are met, and that the questionnaire, when drafted, meets with its approval. The client may wish for some degree of participation in the research – for example, attending one or two group discussions – and may request that it be consulted over the final coding of answers when the questionnaires are received.

Finally, it would be wise to evaluate the market researchers in a systematic manner by giving a series of ratings against a number of selected criteria, for example:

- response to the brief,
- quality of the research,
- client service,
- verbal presentation,
- written report.

Such ratings can then form the basis for making future research commissions.

ACADEMIC RESEARCH

In contrast to research for organisations, academic research pursues scholarly objectives, the end-product of which is to add to the stock of publicly available knowledge about the ways in which marketing variables relate, and to further our understanding of why marketing phenomena happen in the way they do. It attempts not only to be objective but also to be neutral. It does not take sides, although, of course, the findings may be very useful to one or more organisations. A key feature of academic research is that the findings are generally accessible, usually in published form, for example, in an article in a journal or in a book. Such research may be undertaken from either the positivist or interpretive perspectives outlined in Chapter 1, and this will have implications for the design of the research. However, academic research from either perspective does possess common features that differentiate it from organisational research:

- There is no client and not necessarily (in fact not usually) one single organisation whose problems are being diagnosed as a preliminary to writing a research brief, nor are there strengths and weaknesses to be considered, nor decisions and action standards that need to be clarified.
- The findings are reported to an academic audience, which will have different expectations and apply different criteria on which to judge the 'worth', 'value' or 'excellence' of the research.
- There may be no specific recommendations for action, but there will probably be more general implications that organisations may take on board in their decision making.

Because there is no client, it is usually up to the researcher to decide on the key issues to be addressed, and on the direction and methods of the research. Research may, however, be constrained by the need to apply for research funding and there may be a degree of 'grantsmanship' in picking the size and scope of a project that will appeal to the fund-giving body. For the student, there will be a supervisor who approves or suggests modifications to proposals made, while the research is more an exercise that demonstrates to the examiner an ability to design, conduct and analyse the results of original research. It will be judged by scholarly standards that relate to the thoroughness of the review of the literature; the development or testing of theory, concepts or models; the originality of the ideas; and the sophistication and appropriateness of the techniques deployed to the stated objectives of the research.

The cost implications of student research are very different from organisational research. Thus students will not be charging themselves for the time spent interviewing, but they will have to pay for travel or postage used in a mail survey. Some forms of research (for example, telephone research) may be just too expensive for students to undertake. At the same time, there are seldom any cost implications for the use of computer time or advice from supervisors. All these factors affect the design of the research.

Key elements in the design of academic research include:

- a clear statement of the nature, purpose and objectives of the research,
- a justification of why the research is important and to whom it is important,
- a review of the literature relevant to the research objectives, including the general theory, principles and concepts of marketing that are important,

- a selection and justification of an appropriate methodology, including the operationalisation and measurement of variables, the selection of cases, and the methods of data capture, data collection and data analysis,
- the presentation of the results in such a way that they have a demonstrable validity, but at the same time acknowledging the limitations of scope and methodology,
- a conclusion that relates the findings to the literature and to the research objectives, demonstrates how knowledge and understanding have been advanced, speculates on the wider implications of the research, and outlines what further research may be needed to continue and to deepen understanding of the issues.

The nature, purpose and objectives of the research are decided by the researcher, not by a client. The objectives are more likely to be stated in the form of questions that refer to variables that apply to a range of organisations or marketing situations, for example, 'What diagnostic routines do companies follow for detecting weak products in their range?' or 'What factors affect consumer price awareness for fast-moving consumer goods?'

Since there is no client, the academic is always open to the accusation that what he or she is doing is 'trivial', 'lacks practicality' or is 'irrelevant'. While there are proponents of 'pure' research – research for its own sake – it is at least arguable that in marketing there should be practical outcomes or implications. This is not to undermine the value of theory: on the contrary, there is nothing as practical as a good theory – one that can be applied with successful results in a number of different contexts. The development and testing of theory is, then, a key activity for academic researchers. Pointing to the practical implications of, or who might use, a new concept, a new way of measuring a variable, a new theory, a new hypothesis or a new mathematically specified model is a way of justifying why the research is important.

While organisational research may utilise what data or statistics are already available, academic research will also consider what concepts and theories, variables and hypotheses, principles and models form the background to current thinking on the topic. The researcher may see gaps in the literature, shortcomings of approach or methodology, or the potential to apply an idea in a new context. All this literature will be carefully documented with a commentary on how it has developed and with full references to sources in a bibliography. A client commissioning organisational research is seldom interested in such literature.

The research methodology for academic research is just as constrained by cost as is commissioned research – but the cost implications, as indicated earlier, may be very different. Where an academic is applying for research funds, it is difficult to justify 'pile-it-high-and-sell-it-cheap' research. Research councils and other official and semi-official funding bodies are likely to favour random probability sampling over quota sampling, even if it is more expensive. Most government-funded research does tend to use this more expensive sampling procedure. Its justification is that if the results, and perhaps the data, are to be available to other users, then the sample needs to be a microcosm of the population of cases from which the sample was drawn and representative in all respects, not just in respect of the variables used for quotas.

The results and conclusions of academic research are likely to be presented in person by the researcher at a staff seminar or academic conference. Some conferences publish all or a selection of papers presented. Researchers may seek further outlets in academic journals, contributions to edited books, or as research monographs. In all these situations, the research is subject to peer review, and weaknesses of methodology and research design will, or should be, exposed.

A word of caution is perhaps necessary at this stage on the notion of 'hypothesis-testing'. If you look up the topic 'hypothesis-testing' in books on statistics or market research, you will find that they are talking about testing the null hypothesis in the context of statistical inference and significance testing. If you look up a book on the logic of social enquiry, you will find references to the debate about whether hypotheses can in principle ever be finally proven or disproven, and whether the processes of induction or deduction are the ones that produce our 'knowledge' about the world. In consequence, it is helpful to distinguish between:

- testing the statistical significance of a hypothesis, perhaps more appropriately called testing against the null hypothesis (these procedures were considered in Chapter 6 on data analysis),
- comparing univariate, bivariate or multivariate statements against data derived from the research process and coming to some conclusion about whether or not, or the extent to which, the data support or undermine those hypotheses.

Remember that the former process is appropriate only when some form of random sampling has been used and indicates only that there is a known probability that the data did or did not come from a population of cases in which the null hypothesis is true; in other words, was our result a sampling fluctuation? Null hypotheses relate only to the calculation of proportions, averages and measures of association or correlation. They have no impact on conclusions that may be drawn about the kind or nature of relationships between variables. For that, the criteria needed to establish causal relationships or just degrees of influence need to be kept in mind. These criteria were outlined in Chapter 6.

If the results of quantitative research have been shown not to be a sampling fluctuation, it is still down to the researcher to demonstrate that the estimates obtained of quantities, or the degree of association or correlation between variables, do confirm or undermine the original statement. If the original hypothesis is that 'A is a major influence on B', then an achieved coefficient of association of, say, 0.5, which will probably be statistically significant, does not on its own justify the conclusion that the hypothesis is 'proven'. Too often researchers take the achievement of a statistically significant result as 'proof' of a statement, rather than an indication that further analysis is worthwhile. Other variables that may 'explain' the relationship between A and B need to be measured and tested in three-way crosstabulations or other form of multivariate analysis. The search for spurious relationships needs, ideally, to be thorough.

Some philosophers make a distinction between hypotheses and empirical statements. The former are deduced from general theory and are the guesses or predictions set up in advance of the research about what may confidently be expected or discovered in reality if the theory is true. If research contradicts the prediction, then doubt is cast upon the theory. If the research discovers what is predicted, then credence is given to the theory, but probably not 'proof'. This is because any one finding may be consistent with a number of different theories. Some philosophers argue that theories can be disproven through contrary evidence, but can never be conclusively proven.

Empirical statements, on the other hand, are induced from the findings. We discover some pattern, for example, that variable A is correlated with variable B. Since it is inappropriate to 'test' the statement on the same data that suggested it in the first place, it is useful to bear in mind that such statements will require further tests on other data. Furthermore, since they have not been deduced from theory, there is no theory that the empirical statement can either contradict or support.

Sometimes students ask if it is necessary to have a hypothesis for their research. On the whole, if the research is quantitative and is aimed at measuring or testing concepts or ideas, then it is a good idea that the hypotheses are spelled out clearly in advance so that subsequently they can be compared with the data collected. If the research is exploratory or just qualitative in nature, then one of the objectives of the research will be to generate hypotheses that could be tested in subsequent research. In this situation, it is clearly not possible or necessary to spell out hypotheses in advance.

SUMMARY

Designing research to achieve organisational objectives is rather different from research designed for academic purposes. With the former, there is a client on whose behalf the researcher is working. While such research is, or should be, objective, it is seldom neutral. There will always be the client's particular situation to be diagnosed before a brief for the research can be produced and a proposal written. It is also necessary to bear in mind the differing perspectives of the research company and of the client. One is a seller of research services and the other a buyer. The ultimate test is client satisfaction with the service offered.

Academic research, by contrast, will be judged by scientific criteria that have to do with establishing clearly the validity of the findings, usually through appeal to the 'correctness' of the methods and techniques used.

CASE STUDY

James McKelty and Co. Ltd

James McKelty and Co. Ltd has been well established in the preserves industry for more than 50 years. It is a large supplier of marmalade in the UK with almost 30 per cent of the total market; in jams the company has just over 12 per cent. Recently, its jam market has been threatened by the development of a new jam made by a different process which, it is claimed by a competitor, retains more of the flavour and vitamin contents of the original fruit. This new jam is being marketed by one of McKelty's oldest competitors and threatens to make considerable inroads into McKelty's jam sales.

The new process is more expensive than the traditional one, so the competitor has a price per jar that is similar to McKelty's, but the jar is only 12oz against the 16oz, which is usual in this trade. The new jam has been actively promoted and advertising has been extensively aimed at both the distributor and the customer. The total sales of jam from all suppliers has declined steadily since the mid-1950s, and to counter both this general decline in sales and the new threat, McKelty has increased its advertising considerably in the last few months.

After discussion amongst senior executives, it is felt that there are three main courses of action open to the company:

- Expand the range of jams currently offered, for example, bringing out new flavours, offering variety packs, low calorie or sugar-free jam, high-grade conservation quality jam, and so on.
- Make the new jam itself.
- Move over to 12oz jars and reduce price to use its price advantage.

EXERCISE BASED ON CASE STUDY

- Briefly diagnose the problems faced by McKelty.
- Outline what appear to be the organisation's strengths and weaknesses.

- Clarify the decisions that need to be taken.

- Specify the information that will be required.

- You have been asked by Mr McKelty to present a research proposal for marketing research that will enable him to evaluate these three courses of action. Draft a proposal along the lines of Appendix 1.

Glossary

Ad hoc research A once-off piece of research that has a beginning point and ends with a final report of the results.

Advertising pre-testing A form of advertising research in which an advertisement is tested before it is printed or put on air.

Advertising tracking The continuous measurement of advertising or brand recall and related measures for all the brands in a product field in order to measure the success of past advertising or branding activity.

Analysis of variance A technique for testing the statistical significance of a relationship between a metric dependent variable and a non-metric independent variable. It is based on the ratio of the variance between groups to the variance within groups of the non-metric categories.

Arithmetic mean See Mean.

Attitude questions Questions that ask respondents about their likes and dislikes, preferences or positive/negative evaluations of objects, persons, organisations, events or situations.

Attitude scaling Several questions, each relating to a slightly different aspect of the attitude object, are asked and a scoring system is used to add up responses into a total score.

Average A measure of central tendency for a set of values. The three main measures are the median value, the arithmetic mean, and the mode.

Behaviour questions Questions that are essentially factual and relate to what people actually did in the recent past, are currently doing, or may do in the near future.

Bias The over- or under-representation of types of case in a sample as a result of procedures that always produce error in the same direction.

Bivariate analysis Looks at the patterns of relationships between variables two at a time.

Brainstorming A method of stimulating group creativity. The group is given a specific problem and ideas for solutions are just listed without evaluation. Freewheeling and re-combinations of ideas are encouraged.

Brand share The proportion of total sales in a product category either by volume or by value accounted for by a brand over a period of time.

Business research Takes organisations that use a client's products or services in the provision of a further product or service as the point of data collection.

Case The type of object, person, group of people, organisation, situation or event whose characteristics are being measured and recorded in the process of data capture.

Causal research Establishes cause-and-effect relationships in an attempt to explain why things happen.

Cell The combination of a row and a column in a data matrix.

Census A study involving the total set of cases that are the focus of the research.

Chi-square A measure of departure of observed from expected frequencies. Expected frequencies may be derived either from a theoretical distribution or from the null hypothesis of independence between two variables.

Classification questions Questions that are usually factual and refer to demographic characteristics.

Clustering A grouping together of face-to-face interviews into limited geographical areas, usually called 'sampling points' by market researchers.

Cluster analysis A range of multivariate techniques for grouping cases that have characteristics in common.

Commissioned research Research that is paid for on a fee basis by a client and is designed to serve the interests of the client.

Comparative test A laboratory-type experiment in which respondents are presented with two or more products or versions of products in order to make comparative evaluations.

Concepts Abstract ideas that we use to order, classify and think about our impressions and experiences of the world.

Confidence interval A range of values derived from sample results between which it is possible to be certain with a predetermined probability that the real population quantity, proportion or average lies.

Conjoint analysis A multivariate technique that looks at the ways respondents trade off combinations of product characteristics when attempting to maximise their overall satisfaction, and calculates the degree of importance or 'utility' that respondents place on each characteristic.

Consultancy research Research that includes, in addition to data collection and analysis, research that may assist in the diagnosis of organisational problems, help draft a research brief, make recommendations and monitor implementation

Consumer panel A representative sample of individuals or households whose purchase and use of a defined group of products is recorded either continuously or at regular intervals, usually over a considerable period of time.

Consumer research Takes the end user – private individuals or households – as the point of data collection.

Continuous metric scales A result of calibrations that give a measure of the distance between one measurement and the next.

Continuous research Taking measurements on a regular basis in order to monitor changes that are taking place in the market.

Contract research Research that is limited to data collection and data analysis according to client specification.

Correlation An estimation of the direction and strength of a linear relationship that exist between two variables.

Correlation matrix A table whose cells contain correlation coefficients between every variable and every other variable in a set being analysed.

Crosstabulation A table that presents the results of two or more variables whose values are interlaced.

Customised research Research that is tailor-made for a particular client to meet the needs of that client.

Data The product of systematic record-keeping.

Database The accumulation of several or many datasets into a combined system of data storage and retrieval.

Data matrix A particular format for a dataset that interlaces each case with each variable to produce a cell containing the appropriate value.

Dataset All the values for all the variables for all the cases in a piece of ad hoc research or data collection phase or period in continuous research.

Demographic A variable regarded as relatively unchanging for the purpose of a piece of research or measurement period.

Dependent variable A characteristic that the research is trying to predict or explain.

Depth interview An informal discussion between an interviewer and a respondent (or small group of respondents in which the main lines of communication are between interviewer and respondents) concerning an agreed topic that is the focus of the research.

Descriptive research Measures or estimates the frequencies with which things happen, plus the degree of correlation or association between variables.

Design factor A factor greater than one by which calculations of samping error need to be multiplied to take account of departures from simple random sampling.

Desk research The proactive seeking out of data that already exist and which may be useful for the analysis, planning or control of marketing activity.

Diary A document used as an instrument of data capture in which the respondent records behaviour which is repeated at frequent intervals over a specified period of time.

Dichotomy A scale of values containing only two values: one for cases that possess a characteristic and one for those that do not.

Discrete metric scales Arise from counting up the number of times an event occurs as a measure of size.

Disproportionate stratified sampling A form of random stratified sample in which the number chosen in each stratum is not proportional to the size of that stratum in the population.

Estimation The process by which sample values are used as a basis for generating statements about population values with a calculable probability of error.

Experimental research A data collection method in which the market researcher tries out some marketing action on a small scale, carefully observing and measuring the results and controlling, as far as possible, for the effects of factors other than the marketing actions being taken.

Exploratory research Whatever style of research is seen by the researcher to be a preliminary phase before the main research is set in motion.

Factor analysis A multivariate technique that systematically reviews the correlations between each variable forming part of the analysis and all the other variables, and groups together those that are highly inter-correlated.

Factorial design An experimental design in which two or more independent variables are manipulated simultaneously.

Field experiment A study conducted in a natural setting in which products are exposed to the open marketplace and tested in situations where they will be bought, used or consumed in circumstances similar to those where these activities will normally happen.

Frequency The number of times a scale value occurs in a given analysis.

Frequency table A table which contains either the actual number of times each scale value occurs or the percentage in each of two or more categories, ranges of values, or in each cell.

Geodemographics The classification of individuals or households according to the demographic composition or structure of a small local area.

Grossing up Multiplying sample values by a factor that reflects the proportion a sample represents of the population in order to scale up the results from the sample to the whole population or market.

Group discussion A small number of respondents (typically eight) who have been gathered together as a group to discuss products, purchasing behaviour or advertising copy in the presence of a moderator, and where the verbal and social interaction between respondents assumes a key role.

Hall test A form of laboratory experiment in which respondents are recruited off the street or shopping precinct in the vicinity of a hall or room hired by the market research company and shown products, packages or advertisements to measure their reaction.

Independent variable A characteristic which is taken to be a cause or influence on what the research is attempting to predict or explain.

In-home placement test A form of field experiment in which respondents are given products to try at home and report back.

Interpretive perspective An approach to research that takes into account the subjective dimension of human behaviour.

Interviewer-completed questionnaire A questionnaire completed by an interviewer on behalf of the respondent.

Laboratory experiment A study conducted in an artificial environment in which the experimenter has direct control over most of the factors that might affect the experimental outcome apart from the independent variables.

Latin square An experimental design that allows for two extraneous sources of variation without having to test every combination.

Lambda A measure of statistical association based on the notion of the extent to which errors in predicting categories of a dependent variable can be reduced by using knowledge of categories of an independent variable for each case.

Life-cycle A variable, often used as a demographic, that defines a respondent in terms of the stage of family development he or she is currently at.

Lifestyle A variable that classifies respondents according to groupings of characteristics that take account of activities, interests, attitudes and opinions.

Likert scale An attitude-scaling technique that uses five-point rating scales that have been item-analysed to generate a total score from a set of attitude statements.

Market analysis The process of researching markets, which includes measuring the size and structure of a market, analysing purchasing behaviour, product usage and attitudes, segmenting markets, market tracking, volume and brand share prediction, and forecasting trends.

Market measurement The recording or estimation of market characteristics on a regular or continuing basis using either panel research or regular interval surveys.

Market penetration The number or proportion of individuals or households in specified categories who are considered to be potential buyers who have actually made a purchase of the brand over a period of time in a geographical area irrespective of the quantities involved.

Market research The activities of those people involved in the market research industry who buy and sell data or research services.

Market segmentation The process of dividing up a target market into subgroups with the idea of aiming at these subgroups different or modified marketing mixes designed to maximise the marketing opportunities in each.

Market tracking survey A form of regular interval survey in which the market research company designs the whole questionnaire and collects the data which are then sold to as many clients as possible.

Marketing The matching of organisational characteristics with the environment in which the organisation exists, and doing so in ways that will achieve the organisation's planned objectives.

Marketing research The collection, analysis, interpretation and use of data both on the company and on its environment, so that information can be provided that is relevant to the diagnosis, planning and control of marketing activity.

Mean A measure of central tendency for a set of metric values derived from adding up all the values and dividing by the number of values in the set.

Median value A measure of central tendency in a set of metric values derived from ascertaining that value above which and below which half of the observations lie when arranged in ascending or descending order.

Metric table A table that contains the values of metric measurements.

Micromodelling A multivariate technique that analyses the patterns of response in a single individual in order to make a prediction, for that individual, of his or her likelihood of trying a new product and subsequent repurchase. The predictions of a sample of individuals are then aggregated so that forecasts can be made of future sales.

Mini-test marketing A form of field experiment designed to simulate test marketing conditions, but without exposing the product to the open market and without incurring the cost of a full test market.

Mode A measure of central tendency for non-metric or grouped metric data which specifies the most commonly occurring value.

Monadic tests A type of laboratory experiment in which respondents are presented with only one version of a product.

Multi-answer questions These allow respondents to pick more than one response from a list of alternatives.

Multi-dimensional scaling A multivariate technique that infers underlying dimensions from a series of similarity or preference judgements provided by respondents.

Multiple regression An extension of bivariate regression so that a single dependent variable may be predicted from two or more independent variables.

Multivariate analysis Allows the analysis of three or more variables simultaneously.

Nominal scale A set of categories that are exhaustive and mutually exclusive, but in no particular order.

Non-random sample A sample in which the selection of cases is made on a basis that is not independent of human judgement.

Non-sampling error Error that is unconnected with the procedures for selecting cases and may arise even when a complete census is taken.

Null hypothesis A statement about a population value or a relationship between values that is made before being tested on sample data.

Omnibus survey A survey run by a market research company with a stated frequency and with a predetermined method; clients buy space in the questionnaire by adding and paying for questions of their own.

Open-ended question A question in a questionnaire that leaves respondents free to formulate replies in their own words.

Operational definition Any description on a concept in terms of how it is to be measured.

Ordinal scale. A set of categories that are exhaustive and mutually exclusive and in which there is an implied order from high to low or big to small.

Panel research A form of continuous research in which the same data are collected repeatedly from a representative sample of the defined survey population.

Pearson's r See Correlation.

Percentage A proportion multiplied by 100.

Phi-square A measure of statistical association based on Chi-square and used in crosstabulated data where either rows or columns have only two categories.

Population The total set of cases from which the researcher wishes to draw a sample.

Positivist perspective An approach to research based on the methods used in the natural sciences.

Post-coding The classification of responses to open-ended questions once the questionnaire is completed and sent back to the office of the researcher.

Pre-coding The numbering of all response categories on the printed questionnaire so that all responses receive a number as they are given.

Primary research The collection of data specifically for the problem or research at hand.

Product concept tests Ideas about potential new products are evaluated and rounded out by exposing the ideas to a sample of consumers who are then asked questions about them.

Product tests The evaluation and development of products from a marketing point of view, usually by showing them to a sample of respondents and obtaining their reactions.

Projective techniques The use of ambiguous stimulus material in qualitative research which is designed to reveal unconscious, repressed or projected feelings and emotions.

Proportion A relative frequency calculated by dividing the number of cases in a category by the total number of cases.

Purposive sample The selection of cases is made by the researcher using his or her own judgement.

Qualitative data Arise as words, statements or commentary and may be spoken or written down.

Qualitative research Based primarily on the collection of qualitative data, largely in the form of narrative and based on open-ended interview methods.

Quantitative data Arise as numbers and are a result of the process of measurement.

Quantitative research Based primarily on the collection of quantitative data.

Questionnaire A document used as an instrument of data capture which lists all the questions the researcher wishes to address to each respondent and provides some mechanism for recording the responses.

Quota A predetermined proportion of respondents to be sampled from different sub-groups.

Quota sample A selection of respondents by interviewers according to quotas.

Random error Over- or under-representations of types of cases in a random sample and may be in either direction.

Random location sampling Within a sampling point, the sample is chosen in such a way as to reflect that particular area and not quota controls on social class. This is achieved by removing quotas on social class and selecting streets at random with probability proportionate to size and confining the interviewer to those streets.

Random route sampling Within a sampling point, the sample is chosen in such a way as to reflect that particular area and not quota controls on social class. This is achieved by giving the interviewer a random starting point together with instructions about how to proceed along streets and at road junctions.

Random sample A selection of cases from a sampling frame made on the basis that it is independent of human judgement, giving each case in the population a known probability of being selected.

Randomised block An experimental design in which cases to be tested are 'blocked' and selected at random according to key independent variables and each group is given a test.

Ranking scale An ordinal scale where there are as many rankings as cases.

Regular interval survey A form of continuous research in which surveys of respondents are carried out at regular intervals using independent samples in each measurement period.

Reliability The extent to which repeat measures produce similar or consistent results.

Representative sample A sample that is chosen in such a way that it reproduces the structure and features of the population of cases from which the sample was drawn.

Retail audit The physical counting of stock in shops that are members of a retail panel at the beginning and end of an audit period in order to calculate the sales that have taken place on a product-by-product, brand-by-brand basis.

Retail panel A representative sample (or the complete universe) of retail outlets whose acquisition, pricing, stocking and display of a defined group of products are recorded either continuously or at regular intervals.

Routing Guiding the respondent or interviewer in a questionnaire to the next relevant question depending on the answer given.

Sample A sub-set of cases selected by the researcher to study in detail for the purpose of being able to draw conclusions about the entire population of cases.

Sampling distribution A curve that arises from plotting the frequency with which values of a particular statistic arise from every conceivable sample of a given sample size that could be taken from a population.

Sampling error Error that arises from the sampling process and reflects the difference between a sample result and the result that would have been achieved by taking a complete census.

Sampling frame A complete list of the population to be sampled.

Sampling point A geographical area within which an interviewer is to operate for the purpose of face-to-face interviewing.

Scale A set of values that at a minimum are exhaustive and mutually exclusive and refer to a single dimension.

Scholarly research Research that is non-interventionist and non-partisan.

Its aim is to add to a growing body of knowledge and understanding rather than meet the needs of a specific client.

Secondary analysis The further analysis of existing data in a statistical manner that goes beyond simply gathering and re-presenting them in their original or condensed form.

Secondary research Based on data that have been previously collected for purposes other than the research at hand.

Self-completed questionnaire A questionnaire filled in by the respondent. Usually sent through the post.

Semantic differential An attitude scaling technique that generates a profile of images from bipolar adjectival descriptions of the attitude object.

Set-choice question A question that gives respondents a list of possible answers from which to choose.

Simulated test market (STM) modelling A form of experiment that uses sophisticated mathematical modelling techniques to provide estimates of trial and repeat purchase for new or modified products based on responses to product concept test or product tests.

Single-answer questions Allow the respondent to pick only one response from a list of alternatives.

Simple random sample A sample that uses either randomised or systematic selection techniques from a sampling frame, giving all cases an equal chance of being selected.

Spearman's rho A measure of statistical association where there are two variables, both rank ordered. It is based on the differences in ranking for each case on the two variables.

Standard error The standard deviation of a sampling distribution.

Standard deviation A measure of dispersion for a set of metric values derived by adding up squared differences between the mean and each value, dividing by the total number of values in the set, and taking the square root.

Store tests A form of field experiment in which packaging or point-of-sales promotion is tried out in selected retail outlets, ideally with matched control stores.

Stratification A sampling procedure that uses information contained in sampling frames to construct a sample in which random selections are made within strata (sets of cases that are similar in respect of the variable being used for stratification purposes).

Structured questionnaire A questionnaire that lists all the questions to be asked, puts them in logical sequence, specifies the precise wording to be used, and provides predefined categories for recording replies.

Survey research The collection of data based on addressing questions to respondents in a formal manner and taking a systematic record of their responses.

Synectics A technique for stimulating group creativity. The problem is not defined except in very general terms to begin with. The focus is on approaches and perspectives, for example, towards 'closure'. The problem is then refined or defined more specifically, for example, ways of closing a waterproof suit.

Syndicated research Either the research process or the research data are shared between a number of clients.

Systematic error See bias.

Table Any layout of two or more pieces of information into rows and columns.

Television rating A measure of the extent to which audiences watch a programme or specific slot based on totalling the percentages of the population watching television each time it goes on air over a week.

Test centre A form of laboratory experiment in which respondents are invited to a centre to test products that are too large or expensive to use for hall tests or van tests.

Test marketing A form of field experiment in which one or more elements of the marketing mix are tried out in one or more limited, but carefully selected parts of a market area.

Unit of analysis The set of cases that form the basis for any particular calculation, display or interpretation.

Univariate analysis The analysis of variables one at a time.

Universe data Data that cover the complete set of cases that the researcher wishes to investigate.

Unstructured questionnaire A questionnaire that consists of open-ended questions.

Usage and attitude studies These provide in-depth understanding from the consumers' point of view of the market in which a particular brand is being sold.

Validity Evidence that the instrument technique or process used to measure a concept does indeed give a true reflection of the intended concept.

Value What is actually recorded in the process of record-keeping.

Van test A form of laboratory experiment in which respondents are recruited off the street or shopping precinct to a mobile van so that they can be shown products, packages or advertisements to measure their reactions.

Variance The average of squared deviations of values about the mean.

Variable A characteristic, feature or property of the case which is being measured or classified.

Weighting A multiplying factor applied to some or all of the responses given in a sample survey in order to reduce the impact of bias caused by imbalances in the demographic profile of the sample.

References

Alt, M. (1990) *Exploring Hyperspace. A Non-Mathematical Explanation of Multi-variate Analysis*, London: McGraw-Hill.

Assael, H. and Keon, J. (1982) 'Nonsampling versus sampling errors in survey research', *Journal of Marketing* 46, spring: 114–23.

Baker, K. and Fletcher, R. (1989) 'OUTLOOK – a generalised lifestyle system', *ADMAP*, March: 23–8.

Batsell, R. and Wind, Y. (1980) 'Product testing: current methods and needed developments', *Journal of the Market Research Society* 22 (2): 115–39.

Barwise, T.P., Ehrenberg, A.S.C. and Goodhardt, G.J. (1979) 'Audience appreciation and audience size', *Journal of the Market Research Society* 21 (4): 269–84.

Belsen, W.A. (1986) *Validity in Survey Research*, London: Gower Press.

Birn, R., Hague, P. and Vangelder, P.A. (1990) *A Handbook of Market Research Techniques*, London: Kogan Page.

Blalock, H.M. (1972) *Social Statistics*, New York: McGraw-Hill.

Bohrnstedt, G.W. and Knoke, D. (1982) *Statistics for Social Data Analysis*, Itasca, Illinois: F.E. Peacock.

Brown, G. (1991a) 'Response: Modelling advertising awareness', *Journal of the Market Research Society* 33 (3): 197–204.

—— (1991b) 'Big stable brands and advertising effects', *ADMAP*, May: 307.

Bryson, J., Keeble, D. and Wood, P. (1990) 'Survey of small market research companies: some preliminary findings', Market Research Society Newsletter, December: 36–7.

Chisnall, P. (1992) *Marketing Research* (4th edn), London: McGraw-Hill.

Churchill, G.A. (1987) *Marketing Research, Methodological Foundations* (4th edn), Chicago: The Dryden Press.

Colman, S. and Brown, G. (1983) 'Advertising tracking studies and sales effects', *Journal of the Market Research Society* 25 (2).

Converse, J.M. and Presser, S. (1986) *Survey Questions*, Beverly Hills, CA: Sage.

Cornish, P. (1981) 'Lifecycle and income segmentation: SAGACITY', *ADMAP*, Oct.: 522–6.

Cox, T. (1988) 'Media research: do JICs help or hinder?', *ADMAP*, July/August: 50–2.

Crimp, M. (1990) *The Marketing Research Process* (3rd edn), Hemel Hempstead: Prentice-Hall.

de Chernatony, L. and Knox, S. (1990) 'How an appreciation of consumer behaviour can help in product testing', *Journal of the Market Research Society* 32 (3).

Day, R.L. (1969) 'Position bias in paired product tests', *Journal of Marketing Research* 6 (1): 98–100.

Davies, V. (1991) 'What have we done to BARB?' *Campaign*, 10 May: 16.

Donius, J.F. (1985) 'Market tracking: a strategic reassessment and planning tool', *Journal of Advertising Research* 25 (1).

Feldwick, P., Carter, S. and Cook, L. (1991) 'How valuable is the Awareness Index?', *Journal of the Market Research Society* 33 (3): 179–95.

Goodyear, M.J. (1990) 'Qualitative research', in R. Birn, *et al. A Handbook of Market Research Techniques*, London: Kogan Page.

Gordon, W. and Langmaid, R. (1988) *Qualitative Market Research, A Practitioner's and Buyer's Guide*, London: Gower Press.

Griggs, S. (1987), 'Analysing qualitative data', *Journal of the Market Research Society* 29 (12): 15–34.

Holland, R. and Shepherd-Smith, N. (1989) 'The JICREG project: a schedule-planning breakthrough for the regional press', *ADMAP*, July/August: 15–17.

Irvine, J., Miles, I. and Evans, J. (eds) (1979) *Demystifying Social Statistics*, London: Pluto Press.

Kent, R.A. (1981) *A History of British Empirical Sociology*, London: Gower Press.

—— (1986) 'Towards a theory of product range policy', *European Journal of Marketing* 20 (10): 5–17.

—— (1989) *Continuous Consumer Market Measurement*, London: Edward Arnold.

—— (ed.) (forthcoming) *Measuring Media Audiences*, London, Routledge.

Kish, L. (1965) *Survey Sampling*, New York: John Wiley.

Leventhal, B. (1990) 'Geodemographics' in R. Birn *et al. A Handbook of Market Research Techniques*, London: Kogan Page.

Martin D. (1990) 'Sensory evaluation', in R. Birn *et al. A Handbook of Market Research Techniques*, London: Kogan Page.

Menneer, P. (1987) 'Audience appreciation – a different story from audience numbers', *Journal of the Market Research Society* 29 (3).

—— (1989) 'Towards a radio "BARB" – some issues of measurement', *ADMAP*, February: 42–5.

Mosteller, F. (1968), 'Nonsampling errors', in *Encyclopedia of the Social Sciences*, New York: Macmillan.

O'Brien, S. and Ford, R. (1989) 'Can we at last say goodbye to social class?', *Journal of the Market Research Society* 46 (3): 289–332.

Parfitt, J. and Collins, B.J.K. (1968) 'Use of consumer panels for brand share prediction', *Journal of Market Research* 5.

Payne, S.L. (1951) *The Art of Asking Questions*, New Jersey: Princeton University Press.

Piercy, N. and Evans, M. (1983) *Managing Marketing Information*, London: Croom Helm.

Ramsay, W. (1982) 'The new product dilemma', *Marketing Trends*, 1, A.C. Nielsen.

Rothman, J. (1989) 'Different measures of social grade', *Journal of the Market Research Society* 31 (1): 139.

Sampson, P. (1987) 'The tracking study in market research', in U. Bradley (ed.) *Applied Marketing and Social Research*, Chichester: John Wiley.

Sargent, M. (1989) 'Uses and abuses of qualitative research from a marketing viewpoint' in S. Robson and A. Foster (eds) *Qualitative Research in Action*, London: Edward Arnold.

Scott, B. (1986) *The Skills of Communicating*, London: Gower Press.

Sharot, T. (1986) 'Weighting survey results', *Journal of the Market Research Society* 28 (3): 269–84.

Sonquist, J.A. and Morgan, J.N. (1965) 'The detection of interaction effects', *Monograph No. 35*, Survey Research Centre, Institute of Social Research, Michigan: University of Michigan.

Sudman, S. and Bradburn, N.M. (1982) *Asking Questions. A Practical Guide to Questionnaire Design*, San Francisco: Jossey Bass.

Sudman, S. and Ferber, R. (1979) *Consumer Panels*, American Marketing Association.

Sykes, W. (1990) 'Taking stock: issues from the literature on validity and reliability in qualitative research', *Journal of the Market Research Society* 33 (1): 1–12.

Tuckman, B.W. (1965) 'Developmental sequence in small groups', *Psychological Bulletin* 63 (6): 384–99.

Twyman, T. (1989) 'Measuring the total radio audience: a rejoinder to Peter Menneer', *ADMAP*, March: 30–3.

Vardaman, G.T. (1981) *Making Successful Presentations*, New York: AMACOM.

Ward, J. (1987) 'Lifestyles and geodemographics: why advertising agencies shun a single-source approach', *ADMAP*, June: 53–6.

Willis, K. (1990) 'In-depth interviews', in R. Birn, *et al. A Handbook of Market Research Techniques*, London: Kogan Page.

Wimbush, A. (1990) 'Clinics', in R. Birn, *et al. A Handbook of Market Research Techniques*, London: Kogan Page.

Wind, Y., Mahajon, V. and Cardozo, R.N. (1981) *New Product Forecasting. Models and Applications*, Mass. USA: D.C. Heath and Co.

Wolfe, A.R. (1982) 'Sampling error and significance tables for research executives', IMRA occasional paper, London.

——— (ed.) (1984) *Standardised Questions. A Review for Market Research Executives*, Market Research Society.

Appendix 1

A response to the brief from John Ambrose

ATTITUDES TO THE USE OF SPECIALISED FLOUR IN THE HOME

June 1993

Prepared for:
John Ambrose and Co. Ltd

Prepared by:
Marketing Research in Action
The Research Centre
East Gate
London

Contact:
R.A. Kent

CONTENTS

1 INTRODUCTION

John Ambrose and Co. Ltd is considering the possibility of offering to the general public the same highly specialised flours that it currently supplies to the trade. The company now wishes to commission research to examine attitudes to the use of specialised flours in the home.

Marketing Research in Action has been invited to present proposals for this piece of research. These have been prepared by our Consumer Research Division. They are based on a written brief received in May of this year and subsequent telephone conversations with Mr John Ambrose.

2 OBJECTIVES

A combination of qualitative and quantitative research is required to examine:

- what proportion of households keep flour of any description in stock,
- what kinds of flour are usually kept,
- what other kinds of flour housewives may be aware of,
- what flour is currently used for,
- what are the main kinds of home baking,
- which groups of people are most likely to make use of specialised flour,
- what quantities they are likely to buy,
- would they be prepared to pay a slightly higher price?

The research will comprise two elements. The first stage of qualitative research will provide in-depth information on the main dimensions of flour usage in the home, attitudes to home baking, and the possibilities for the use of specialised flour. This will provide the basis for designing the questionnaire to be used in the second stage among 1,200 respondents.

3 PRELIMINARY QUALITATIVE RESEARCH

3.1 Discussion

We propose to conduct a mixture of group discussions and individual interviews. Group discussions are most appropriate for a proportion of housewives because:

- groups often produce a more relaxed and discursive review of a topic, and encourage spontaneous comments and comparisons,
- groups are less expensive 'per head',
- differences between consumers are highlighted.

However, depth interviews are often very useful as a 'control' for, or supplement to, groups since they enable individual histories and attitudes to be probed more fully. Furthermore, it is sometimes difficult to get a group of older people together. They often need more reassurance and there are frequently mobility and hearing problems. The majority of such interviews will be with a single respondent; however, we will also seek to include a small number of interviews with married couples.

3.2 Sample summary

We suggest six standard groups of eight housewives aged 18 or more, resident in the UK for at least three years. 'Housewives' are defined as those persons most directly concerned with shopping and cooking for the household. In some cases such a person may be male. Groups will be mixed in terms of age but separated by social class. However, there will be quotas on these two variables in order to ensure that they are represented in the same proportions as in the UK population. Social class will be measured according to the occupation of the head of the household.

Forty depth interviews are proposed, weighted towards the elderly or immobile.

The sample structure will be as follows:

6 groups

Social class: 3 × BC1 + 3 × C2D
Location: 3 × South + 3 × North or Midlands

20 depth interviews

Sex: all female
Social class: 10 × B or C1 + 10 × C2 or D
Location: 10 × South + 10 × North or Midlands

20 depth interviews

Sex: all female
Age: 65+
Location: 10 × South + 10 × North or Midlands

3.3 Recruiting and moderating procedures

Marketing Research in Action uses interviewers specially trained for qualitative recruiting. We are members of IQCS. We will rely mainly on random street or house recruiting, boosted by recruitment in carefully selected public locations appropriate to the particular subgroups or respondents being contacted.

The interviews will be conducted in a domestic setting (a recruiter's home). It may, however, be necessary to hold some interviews in respondents' own homes.

All the groups and interviews will be moderated by a member of the Marketing Research in Action research team. All discussions will be tape recorded, and the transcripts of the groups can be made available if required.

3.4 Interview topics and stimulus materials

A detailed discussion and interview guide will be prepared on commission. Currently we envisage focusing on perceptions of the current range of flours available, attitudes to home baking, and the possibilities for the use of specialised flour. Particular attention will be paid to vocabulary, common assumptions, and areas of possible confusion likely to affect the qualitative study.

3.5 Timing

Following commission, a period of three weeks will be required for group and individual interview recruitment. Further recruitment will take place concurrently with the fieldwork. We envisage a period of about eight weeks will be required for the qualitative phase.

All interim reports should be available by the end of September, assuming commission in July. A full written report could then be produced within four weeks and integrated with the quantitative stage once this is complete.

4 QUANTITATIVE RESEARCH DISCUSSION

4.1 Sampling

Option 1 Random sampling

We suggest a three-stage sampling procedure. First, a set of 100 electoral constituencies will be selected with probability of selection proportional to the size of the electorate. Second, an individual elector will be chosen at random from each constituency. The sampling point will then comprise the electoral ward of which that elector was part. Third, every fiftieth name will be selected from the Electoral Register referring to that ward and these will be given to interviewers. Interviewers will determine who is the 'housewife' in the household of the selected elector and asked if they have baked any cakes, scones, biscuits or pastries on the last four weeks. Those who have not are screened out. The interviewer continues until a quota of 12 completed interviews with housewives who do home baking is filled.

Option 2 Quota sampling

Stages 1 and 2 will be similar to Option 1. However, for stage 3, the interviewer will be free to work wherever he or she likes in the defined areas to achieve a quota of interviews. Quotas will vary by region to reproduce the regional profile of females by age and social class, with non-bakers screened out as for Option 1.

There is the danger that this method will over-represent the 'at-home' population and under-represent working housewives. However, quotas could be applied additionally to working status.

For both Option 1 and Option 2 the achieved sample results will be weighted to the population profile in terms of age, social class and working status.

4.2 Sample size

There is an estimated 23.3 million housewives in Great Britain (excluding Northern Ireland), of which 15.5 per cent (or 3.6 million) are male. It would be unwise to exclude these, so about 180 of the sample of 1,200 will be male. Results will be grossed up to this population.

4.3 Screening respondents

Both options will involve a screening procedure based on any baking activity over the last four weeks. Similar research we have conducted recently leads us to suggest that approximately 6 per cent of identified housewives cannot remember whether or not they have done any home baking in that period. We suggest that these, too, should be screened out on the basis that they are unlikely to be frequent home bakers.

5 QUANTITATIVE RESEARCH METHOD

5.1 Contact procedure

For Option 1, the interviewer will continue to call at selected addresses up to a maximum of four times, varying the time of day and day of the week at each call.

In the case of Option 2, interviewers will be asked to record details of all contacts made and whether there was immediate refusal, a non-eligible respondent who refused interview, who was extra to quota, or whether a full interview was achieved.

5.2 Questionnaire design

The questionnaire will be developed in consultation with John Ambrose and Co. Our costings have allowed for a questionnaire that will take on average 40 minutes to administer. Wherever possible we hope to be able to pre-code questions, drawing on the answers obtained previously in the qualitative research. We have allowed for up to six open-ended questions within each questionnaire. Section 6 describes the procedures for piloting.

5.3 Quality control

All interviewers will be supervised by our regional field directors. Ten per cent of interviews will be subjected to checkbacks. All interviews meet not only the standards of IQCS, but our own additional training ensures a quality of interviewing that few of our competitors can match.

5.4 Coding

We will prepare codeframes for the open-ended questions based on extractions from 100 questionnaires. These will be submitted to John Ambrose for approval before coding begins.

5.5 Manual editing

The objective is to ensure that information is in the correct format for data entry. It includes checks on the presence of leading zeros in quantity fields and full details of sample points. Our policy is to return any questionnaire that lacks key information to the interviewer concerned.

5.6 Data entry

The computer edit is a comprehensive data validation exercise that ensures the logical consistency of information as well as completeness. Any discrepancies it reveals are checked by a research executive against the original questionnaire.

5.7 Analysis

We have developed costings on the basis that 500 pages of computer tabulations will be required. The specification for the analysis will be discussed with John Ambrose before the analysis is run, including requirements for tests of statistical significance. We will supply two bound copies of laser-printed tabulations.

We will need to discuss with John Ambrose the issue of weighting the data. Using the quota approach, it will be necessary to weight the data to take account of undersampling of working housewives. Weights will also be applied to take account of differential response rates.

5.8 Reporting

In addition to the computer tabulations, we have allowed for the preparation of a detailed technical report and an interpretive report. The latter will be structured to meet the needs of John Ambrose. It will be illustrated with charts and diagrams drawn from the computer tabulations. Both reports will be submitted in draft and after approval we will supply four copies of each.

We have not allowed for a presentation of the quantitative research findings, but would be happy to discuss this should one be required.

6 PILOT RESEARCH

We have indicated the additional cost of pilot research in our section on fees. While it is always desirable to pilot questionnaires, we feel that a pilot survey could be dispensed with in this project, given our familiarity with the market. However, should one be required, we would recommend that the pilot be conducted in three sample points with 12 interviews in each. The procedure for the pilot would be exactly the same as for the main stage quota option, given that the main purpose is to test the questionnaire rather than the sampling method.

Interviewers would attend a personal briefing at Marketing Research in Action at our head office. We would produce a brief report on the pilot, suggesting amendments to the questionnaire or survey design for the main stage. The report would also comment on the implications of any changes for the fee for the main stage.

7 INTERVIEWER SELECTION

Interviewers will receive personal briefings at one of six centres nearest to their home. Our regional managers will attend so that they are completely familiar with the survey. The sessions will be conducted by Marketing Research in Action executives responsible for the survey and will last about two hours. Attendance by relevant personnel from John Ambrose will be warmly encouraged.

The main purpose of the briefing will be to ensure that interviewers and managers are totally familiar with:

- the administration of the questionnaire and any question areas of particular difficulty or complexity,
- the type of respondent they will be likely to interview,
- the type of information that needs to be collected.

There will also be a mock interview to highlight the points made during the session.

Interviewers will, in addition, be given a set of written instructions which reiterate in more detail the points made at the briefing session.

Marketing Research in Action has a national panel of about 950 interviewers. Mostly they are self-employed, but they work to standards and administrative procedures laid down by our operating manual. They are organised under a team of twelve Regional Managers, all of whom are full-time employees of Marketing Research in Action.

We are members of the Interviewer Quality Control Scheme, whose professional standards we either meet or exceed. Normal backchecking and accompaniment procedures would be applied to this survey. This, in summary, requires that:

* interviewers should be accompanied at least once in each six-month period,
* 10 per cent of the work will be subject to backcheck procedures,
* the backchecking will comprise 10 per cent postal checks; the remainder will be face to face or telephone checks.

8 TIMING

Our best estimate of how the timing could proceed is as follows:

Weeks 1–7	Qualitative research
Week 8	Qualitative presentation
Week 11	Qualitative report available
Weeks 8–11	Quantitative questionnaire development
Week 12	Pilot briefing
Week 13	Pilot debriefing
Weeks 14–15	Questionnaire alterations and printing
Week 16	Main stage briefings
Weeks 17–19	Main stage fieldwork
Weeks 18–21	Codings and data preparation
Week 22	Analysis produced
Week 25	Draft report available

This follows the timetable suggested in the brief and we believe it to be realistic, but it could be amended in the light of further discussions with John Ambrose. Thus if there is no pilot survey, the project can be shortened by two weeks.

9 PROJECT STAFFING

The project will be carried out by the Consumer Research Division of Marketing Research in Action, under its Director, Kay Brent, who has had many years' experience of consumer survey work. She has specialised in the application of research techniques to the food industry and, before joining the company in 1982, had spent five years as consultant to the Ministry of Food and Agriculture.

Responsibility for the project would be given to Ken Bray, an Associate Director of the Division. He joined the company in 1983 and since then has managed a variety of ad hoc projects, several of them in the food sector.

10 FEES

The fees quoted below are exclusive of VAT, and are subject to Marketing Research in Action's standard terms and conditions of contract. The fees are subject to the assumptions contained in these proposals and may have to be amended should any assumptions prove to be incorrect.

	£
Qualitative research	20,750
Quantitative pilot research	2,500
Main stage – random sampling	73,900
Main stage – quota sampling	53,200

Index